A Social Reading
of the Old Testament

FORTRESS PRESS BOOKS
BY WALTER BRUEGGEMANN

The Land: Place as Gift, Promise, and Challenge
in the Biblical Faith (1977)

The Prophetic Imagination (1978)

The Creative Word: Canon as a Model
for Biblical Education (1982)

David's Truth in Israel's Imagination and Memory (1985)

Hopeful Imagination: Prophetic Voices in Exile (1986)

Israel's Praise: Doxology against Idolatry and Ideology (1988)

Finally Comes the Poet: Daring Speech for Proclamation (1989)

Interpretation and Obedience:
From Faithful Reading to Faithful Living (1991)

Old Testament Theology:
Essays on Structure, Theme, and Text (1992)

Texts under Negotiation:
The Bible and Postmodern Imagination (1993)

A Social Reading of the Old Testament:
Prophetic Approaches to Israel's Communal Life (1994)

The Psalms and the Life of Faith (1995)

The Threat of Life:
Sermons on Pain, Power, and Weakness (1996)

A Social Reading of the Old Testament

Prophetic Approaches to Israel's Communal Life

Walter Brueggemann

Edited by Patrick D. Miller

FORTRESS PRESS   MINNEAPOLIS

A SOCIAL READING OF THE OLD TESTAMENT
Prophetic Approaches to Israel's Communal Life

Cover design: Peggy Lauritsen Design Group

Library of Congress Cataloging-in-Publication Data

Brueggemann, Walter.
    A social reading of the Old Testament : prophetic approaches to
Israel's communal life / Walter Brueggemann : edited by Patrick D.
Miller.
      p.   cm.
    Includes bibliographical references and index.
    ISBN 0-8006-2734-2
    1. Bible. O.T.—Criticism, interpretation, etc. I. Miller,
Patrick D. II. Title.
BS1192.B75   1994
221.6–dc20   93-34115
                                                    CIP

Manufactured in the U.S.A.   AF 1-2734
03   02   01   00   99   3   4   5   6   7   8   9   10   11   12

Contents

Part Three
A Social Reading of Particular Issues

Abbreviations

AB	Anchor Bible
AnBib	Analecta biblica
ANQ	*Andover Newton Quarterly*
ATANT	Abhandlungen zur Theologie des Alten und Neuen Testaments
BA	*Biblical Archaeologist*
BASOR	*Bulletin of the American Schools of Oriental Research*
BBB	Bonner biblische Beiträge
BJS	Brown Judaic Studies
BT	*The Bible Translator*
BTB	*Biblical Theology Bulletin*
BZAW	Beihefte zur *ZAW*
CBQ	*Catholic Biblical Quarterly*
CurTM	*Currents in Theology and Mission*
FRLANT	Forschungen zur Religion und Literatur des Alten und Neuen Testaments
HBT	*Horizons in Biblical Theology*
HSM	Harvard Semitic Monographs
HTR	*Harvard Theological Review*
HUCA	*Hebrew Union College Annual*
ICC	International Critical Commentary
IDB	*Interpreter's Dictionary of the Bible* (G. A. Buttrick, ed.)
IDBSup	Supplementary volume to *IDB*

Int	*Interpretation*
IRT	Issues in Religion and Theology
JAAR	*Journal of the American Academy of Religion*
JBL	*Journal of Biblical Literature*
JNES	*Journal of Near Eastern Studies*
JRT	*Journal of Religious Thought*
JSOT	*Journal for the Study of the Old Testament*
JSOTSup	Journal for the Study of the Old Testament—Supplement Series
JTS	*Journal of Theological Studies*
LXX	Septuagint
MT	Masoretic Text
NRSV	New Revised Standard Version
OBT	Overtures to Biblical Theology
OTL	Old Testament Library
RevExp	*Review and Expositor*
RSR	*Recherches de science religieuse*
RSV	Revised Standard Version
SBLDS	SBL Dissertation Series
SBLMS	SBL Monograph Series
SBLSP	SBL Seminar Papers
SBT	Studies in Biblical Theology
TBü	*Theologische Bücherei*
TLZ	*Theologische Literaturzeitung*
TWAT	G. J. Botterweck and H. Ringgren (eds.), *Theologisches Wörterbuch zum Alten Testament*
USQR	*Union Seminary Quarterly Review*
VT	*Vetus Testamentum*
VTSup	Vetus Testamentum, Supplements
WMANT	Wissenschaftliche Monographien zum Alten und Neuen Testament
WW	*Word and World*
ZAW	*Zeitschrift für die alttestamentliche Wissenschaft*
ZTK	*Zeitschrift für Theologie und Kirche*

Introduction

Patrick D. Miller

KNOWN PRIMARILY as an Old Testament theologian, and deservedly so,[1] Walter Brueggemann has brought his theological pursuits together with a long-standing interest in social analysis in his interpretation of biblical texts. The two concerns—theological and sociological—are so thoroughly linked in his thinking and writing that chapters in this volume might well have been located in the earlier collection on Old Testament theology and vice versa.

The essays in this volume are grouped under the rubric "A Social Reading of the Old Testament." The phrase "social reading" does not mean in Brueggemann's case simply an application of the categories, methods, and analyses of sociology to biblical texts. He is much too sophisticated sociologically for that. (Unlike most Old Testament scholars, Brueggemann has studied sociology academically. In fact he began there—it was his college major—before turning to theology.) He is also much too theological to be content with or even interested in a sociology of the religion of Israel or a sociological analysis of the origins of early Israel—though he knows and uses the results of others' work in this area (see chap. 1).

The social character of our theology, more specifically, of our notion of God, is underscored in these essays. This does not mean that God is simply a social projection, although that idea does not seem

1. See the collection *Old Testament Theology: Essays in Structure, Theme, and Text,* ed. Patrick D. Miller (Minneapolis: Fortress, 1992).

to bother Brueggemann very much. But our reading of the presentation, or "rendering"—to use a favorite term Brueggemann borrows from Dale Patrick—of God in the Bible is very much shaped by our social situation, and one of Brueggemann's aims is to shatter our *picture* of the biblical God by the *reality* of the biblical God. This is a crucial matter. "Everything is at stake because how we judge it to be in heaven is the way we imagine it to be on earth.... There will be no new community on earth until there is a fresh articulation of who God is" ("Covenant as a Subversive Paradigm"). This notion points to Brueggemann's implicit conviction that the Bible may be the one thing—despite its own social character (see below)—that can break through and criticize our socially shaped view of God.

It is no accident that "subversive" is a favorite word of Brueggemann's. (He has a number of such words. They are often helpful clues to his concerns and intentions.) He is committed to showing the way the Bible subverts our personal and social systems and ideologies. If the Bible is ideological, it also seems to be a tool for subverting ideologies, even those of interpreters. Indeed the branch of sociology with which he seems especially to resonate is the sociology of knowledge and its critique of ideology. The effort to uncover the hidden agendas, the unidentified programs that underlie the making and reading of Scripture, is a constant dimension of his biblical interpretation.

At its simplest and most important level, Brueggemann's social reading is a constant awareness of the social dimensions of every aspect of the text, its transmission, and its interpretation, that all of these realia take place within worlds—albeit often very different ones—and those worlds must be in view to hear the text with any hope of authentic contact with that about which it speaks or any hope of connecting it with a present listening community. Vested interests have been and remain at work in all aspects of the communication of the text (and so the richly dangerous task of the interpreter, whether scholar, preacher, teacher, who is a part of a social nexus, shaped by it, and given a slanted view of reality by that nexus). Much social reading of the Bible is primarily interested in the sociology of the world of the text. And many of the essays that follow reflect that interest, particularly as Brueggemann tries to lay bare the effects of monarchy on Israel's life and their reflections in the texts. But he is more concerned than many for the sociology of the world of the interpreter, the world of those who hear and read the text now (see chap. 12). He does not engage in social analysis of contemporary society in any formal sense, but he has his ear to the ground—always with an intensity that is characteristic of both his person and his work. This reading of the contemporary social world takes place in a variety of ways, from wide contact with individuals and groups in one of the heaviest speaking and lecture schedules of any scholar in the field, to his detailed perusal of the *New York Times* and other newspapers (whose articles, editorials, and cartoons he is always clipping, not only for his own files but to send to family, friends, and colleagues), to a voracious reading schedule that blends culture analysis and criticism with contemporary theology and psychology as well as significant fiction (he does not seem to be caught by mystery and detective fiction, as are a number of his scholarly colleagues), to viewing the latest movies (he is a movie addict though too non- [if not anti-]technological to bother with a VCR; his colleagues and peers are amazed to discover that his prolific writing is all done with a pen as he refuses to bother with a computer, questioning implicitly and explicitly whether technology really enhances scholarly productivity). All of this talking, reading, and seeing keeps Brueggemann "in touch." If that mode of social analysis seems impressionistic rather than precise, well and good. It is just those impressions of this world—culled from a church member, Anthony Lewis, Karl Marx, Stephen Toulmin, Karl Barth, Flannery O'Connor, or *Baghdad Cafe*—that give him clues about the way we are and how the Bible confronts (I use that conflictual word advisedly) our way and ways.

This attention to the world of *his* text means that his essays are definitely time-bound. They interact with the latest literature at the time of writing—and in various fields—as well as with immediate issues and currents. Precisely because they are up-to-date at the time of their original writing or publication, there is a significant datedness to some of these essays but not an outdatedness. They do not depend upon the latest election or political controversy at the time of writing; rather, they engage deeper issues that are present in the literature. Thus, Brueggemann was one of the earliest scholars to take up the work of George Mendenhall and Norman Gottwald in their different but related efforts to look at the sociology of early Israel. Some of the essays that follow, therefore, were written prior to the publication of Gottwald's magnum opus, *The Tribes of Yahweh*, but already attentive to the issues he was raising. Others respond to and draw upon that work quite heavily. There has been no attempt to update bibliography, nor is there any need to do so, in most instances, as far as the substance of Brueggemann's argument is concerned.

One of the features of Brueggemann's mode of thinking is to work with dualities and tensions, and he has responded positively to those such as Paul Hanson, Claus Westermann, and Samuel Terrien who work in a similar fashion.[2] The result is a highly dialectical way of doing theology and of analyzing biblical texts. In these essays, there are two particularly pervasive dualities or tensions. One represents a conflictual tension in ancient Israel. It is found in Brueggemann's discernment of *royal* and *liberation* trajectories as fundamental to the course of Israel's life and thought, an analysis worked out in the first, programmatic chapter, "Trajectories in Old Testament Literature and the Sociology of Ancient Israel." These are to be related rather directly to the equally programmatic categories around which he has oriented his approach to Old Testament theology, "structure legitimation" and "embrace of pain."[3] Brueggemann also risks a connection to contemporary theological movements, seeing process hermeneutics as a continuation of the stabilizing, socially conservative *royal* trajectory and liberation theology as a continuation of the historically specific, socially revolutionary *liberation* trajectory. Brueggemann's own theological affinity for the liberation trajectory is evident in his writing, as is his suspicion of the structure-legitimating royal trajectory.

The other dialectic that is prominent in these pages is suggested in the titles of the first two essays and specifically in the phrases "subversive paradigm" and "social possibility." The tension in mind in this instance is one that can exist within a single framework, for example, the covenant or prophecy. What he points to in these phrases and the articles in whose titles they appear has been elaborated in one of his most widely read books, *The Prophetic Imagination.* In the present volume, one may turn to his essays "Social Criticism and Social Vision in the Deuteronomic Formula of the Judges" (chap. 4) and " 'Vine and Fig Tree': A Case Study in Imagination and Criticism" (chap. 5) to see the same dialectic developed in different contexts. What Brueggemann uncovers is the way in which both covenant and prophecy are able to function as critical tools,

---

2. See Brueggemann, "Futures in Old Testament Theology," in *Old Testament Theology,* 111–17.

3. See Brueggemann, "A Shape for Old Testament Theology, I: Structure Legitimation," and idem, "A Shape for Old Testament Theology, II: Embrace of Pain," in *Old Testament Theology,* 1–44.

undercutting prevailing ideologies and practices while at the same time—or at another time in some instances—also identifying possibilities not yet dreamed of for a new society directed by God's word, faithful to God, and effecting righteousness and peace in the human community. The subversive dimension of prophecy and covenant is the critical tool; the new possibilities are found in an exercise of imagination that points to a new future. This dual function in the prophetic role enables Brueggemann to hold judgment-prophecy and salvation-prophecy together against the common tendency to regard them as separate activities belonging to different phases of a prophetic career or different times in Israel's history.

Chapter 5, "Vine and Fig Tree," is a prime example of Brueggemann's approach. It is textual and exegetical,[4] giving attention to important literary features in the text—in this case, irony—for their interpretative significance. He uncovers the social criticism explicit and implicit in the text and effects a bold and sometimes risky juxtaposition of seemingly unrelated texts, a hermeneutically heuristic example of intertextuality. This particular study also demonstrates what I would call Brueggemann's imaginative hermeneutics, the ability and willingness to see and envision possibilities within a text for the way it connects with our world. Such connections and models, which others may not discern, are often provided not so much by a hermeneutical method as by a powerful intuition and imagination fertilized by a detailed knowledge of Scripture together with wide and diverse reading. In Brueggemann's work, interpretation is both disciplined exegetical work and artistic craft. Perhaps that is what it should be always. If so, such interpretation can be taught only so far. The rest is practice and, whether we like it or not, gift. Brueggemann's own way of viewing the matter is to see the connection between the rhetoric and shape of a text and the present social reality as not effected by a hermeneutical move, an "application of the text," but by a reading of the text where we are.

The application of the criticism-imagination duality to the literature about the period of the Judges in chapter 4, "Social Criticism and Social Vision in the Deuteronomic Formula of the Judges," involves an effort to look at "the sociology of the deed-consequence teaching" as well as of the cry-save formula. In the latter case, Brueggemann takes up one of the most fundamental themes in all of

---

4. On Brueggemann's consistent focus on particular texts, see my introduction to *Old Testament Theology.*

Scripture, the cry to God of the oppressed or suffering victim and God's delivering response.[5] He shows how this cry-save structure breaks with the well-ordered, managed, and manageable world in which deeds have their inherent consequences, "the one [namely, deed-consequence] marked by a presumption of control, the other [cry-save] by risking trust."

The focus on *covenant* is not to be missed in these essays. It should be noted that some of them were written before the heavy scholarly criticism of the emphasis on covenant and, more particularly, the presumed connection of covenant to ancient Near Eastern treaties. But Brueggemann would probably still persist—and rightly so—in claiming that covenant is "a pervasive biblical notion" and not confined to the presence of the term *běrît,* "covenant." What particularly interests him, however, is not the origin or history of the notion of covenant, much less its Near Eastern analogues, real or imagined, but its "important socioeconomic, political counterparts" as well as its theological assumptions and implications. Somewhat surprisingly, he does not see covenant as a paradigm of power. Less surprisingly, he does see it as having to do finally with faithfulness—human and divine. A "different mode of God" and a "different notion of social life and practice" are mediated by the metaphor of covenant, for example, attention to marginality. One of the aims of these essays is to demonstrate in large strokes and in more detailed exegesis how and in what ways both "differences" are to be seen.

A particular example of this is his treatment of the *sexuality of Israel's God,* which not only relates that to the primary image of covenant but once more develops the topic in dialectical fashion, vis-à-vis "a contrast between a *promissory* and a *conserving* notion of God" (chap. 8, "Israel's Social Criticism and Yahweh's Sexuality"). His discussion of property in the Bible also places great weight on the covenant as well as assuming the royal/urban and covenantal/liberation trajectories presented in the first essay as the framework in which the whole matter is to be discussed. Thus, the intentional plural in the title of chapter 14, "Reflections on Biblical *Understandings* of Property." While many would interpret such a plural as a reference to the variety of perspectives that everyone now acknowledges is present in biblical literature, Brueggemann regards such a pluralistic approach as too idealistic and neutral. The plurality in which he

---

5. Cf. Richard N. Boyce, *The Cry to God in the Old Testament,* SBLDS 103 (Atlanta: Scholars Press, 1988).

is interested is more rooted in the social situation and begs for some stance and commitment from the interpreter.

The concentration on social analysis in these essays includes also a political dimension. In chapter 6, "At the Mercy of Babylon," for example, Brueggemann turns explicitly to the politics of Israel and the nations and what they have to tell us about the politics of God. Here also he shows other philosophical influences at work in his thinking—from J. L. Austin to Terry Eagleton to François Lyotard— as he reflects on speech as a political act and texts as major acts of power. This essay and others (for example, chap. 7, "A Poem of Summons [Isaiah 55:1-3] and a Narrative of Resistance [Daniel 1]," and chap. 13, "Rethinking Church Models through Scripture") show a considerable interest in the sociopolitical aspects of texts arising from exile. Once again Brueggemann's work is on the forefront of the field where a renewed focus on the exile is leading many to find there the most formative period for biblical literature. The work of Daniel Smith, *The Religion of the Landless*, appearing after most of these essays were first published, takes up some of the concerns for the postexilic period that Brueggemann has placed to the fore.

The essay on Isaiah 55 and Daniel 1 referred to in the preceding paragraph poses as forthrightly as any the methodological issues arising from the kind of intertextuality and imaginative hermeneutics that Brueggemann carries out. Indeed he presents it explicitly as an example of "new methods," that is, intertextual and sociopolitical readings. Here inner-biblical interpretation wins out over historical-critical interpretation, which has focused on the historical setting of Daniel and fixed it firmly in the second century B.C.E. The large historical separation of Isaiah 55 (exilic or early postexilic) and Daniel 1 is set aside in favor of relating the two texts on the basis of the typological issues of resistance and alternative. He calls Daniel 1 a "midrashic commentary" on Isaiah 55 but is ambiguous as to how much he understands that as an intentional dependence of the one text upon the other. Such intentional connection seems not to be a matter of large concern to him. He himself says that such an approach as he takes in this juxtaposition of texts "may be more impressionistic, reflecting enormous interpretative freedom and imagination." Such an admission invites the reader to see if freedom has become license and imagination fantasy. Brueggemann gives every indication of welcoming such "close reading" of his free interpretation, as long as it is accompanied by a close reading of the texts to see if such free interpretation cannot also turn out to make sense.

The challenge to assumed modes of reading and interpreting is present in a similar fashion in his treatment of Solomon as patron of wisdom (chap. 12, "The Social Significance of Solomon as a Patron of Wisdom"). He brings to the treatment of the Solomonic period, and especially its cultural and intellectual character—what von Rad called "enlightenment"—a *social analysis* that has not been as much a part of the discussion. As such, he sides more with von Rad than with his critics, to wit, that a broad social transformation took place involving new forms of power and new modes of knowledge. Here his social analysis comes in conflict with literary-critical analysis vis-à-vis Solomon's connection to wisdom, a literary analysis that he accepts. Brueggemann argues, however, that literary evidence is not sufficient for historical conclusions without social analysis also being brought into the picture. Here is his methodological axe. As he puts it, the historical question about Solomon as a wisdom teacher may and has ignored the "larger question of the rationality and intellectual commitments of the world of which Solomon is both sponsor and benefactor." The argument with James Crenshaw and R. B. Y. Scott in this essay is a prime example of Brueggemann's social reading of the texts and the differences with other legitimate and necessary methods. The connection between "economics and epistemology," as he puts it in this essay, needs to be explored, an enterprise Brueggemann pursues in this volume with great energy.

Brueggemann's critique of much discussion of the question of *theodicy* is that it has consistently refused to think about how this problem as a justice issue—that is, justifying the ways of God to human beings—is also a *social* issue (chap. 9, "Theodicy in a Social Dimension"). He hints rather strongly that the social location of most scholars and theologians has led to their treatment of this issue in highly idealistic terms and offers this essay as an explicit corrective. The challenge in this case is laid before theology and ethics as much as biblical interpretation.

Violence in Scripture (see chap. 15) has received a new focus in the light of the work of René Girard. Brueggemann takes up that difficult topic in a substantial but quite different manner than one finds in Girard. Once again, sociological and literary methods are joined in a focus on the theme of "horses and chariots" to take up the difficult question of how texts of violence are to be understood as revelation. In so doing, both the violence of Scripture and its revelatory character are given a fresh reading that does not diminish the disturbing and abrasive character of the texts of Joshua (and elsewhere) but refocuses it in relation to the royal and liberation trajectories set forth in the first essay. This essay provides a powerful testimony to the validity of trajectories Brueggemann discerns in the sweep of the Old Testament and the fruitfulness of such a framework for dealing with difficult texts and difficult topics.[6]

---

6. The essays in this volume, all of which have been published previously, have been reedited only slightly, and in some instances the NRSV translation has been substituted for the RSV of the original publication.

Part One

Guidelines and
Approaches

1

Trajectories in Old Testament Literature and the Sociology of Ancient Israel

IT HAS LONG BEEN RECOGNIZED that there are two circles of tradition in Israel's literature concerning covenant, one derived from Moses and the other Davidic in its formulation.[1] The biblical tradition itself wishes to suggest that the two are continuous, so that the Davidic is a natural derivation from that of Moses and fully faithful to it. Undoubtedly, the circles around David urged this perception of the matter. Recent critical scholarship, however, has now made it reasonable to assume that these two articulations of covenant are not only distinct but also came from very different centers of power and very different processes of tradition building.[2]

---

1. On the extensive literature, see Leonhard Rost, "Sinaibund und Davidsbund," *TLZ* 72 (1947): 129–34; and idem, "Erwägungen zu Hosea 4:14f.," in *Festschrift Alfred Bertholet*, ed. W. Baumgartner et al. (Tübingen: Mohr, 1950), 459–60; Masao Sekine, "Davidsbund und Sinaibund bei Jeremia," *VT* 9 (1959): 47–57; Antonius H. J. Gunneweg, "Sinaibund und Davidsbund," *VT* 10 (1960): 335–41; Murray Newman, *The People of the Covenant* (New York: Abingdon, 1962); David N. Freedman, "Divine Commitment and Human Obligation," *Int* 18 (1964): 419–31; Delbert Hillers, *Covenant: The History of a Biblical Idea* (Baltimore: Johns Hopkins Univ. Press, 1969); Tomoo Ishida, *The Royal Dynasties in Ancient Israel*, BZAW 142 (Berlin: de Gruyter, 1977), 99–117; Ronald Clements, *Abraham and David*, SBT 2/5 (London: SCM, 1967); and the general comments of Dennis McCarthy, *Old Testament Covenant* (Richmond: John Knox, 1972), especially chaps. 2 and 5.

2. Newman (*People of the Covenant*) had already argued that the Abraham-David tradition is derived from the south and the Mosaic tradition from the north. The difference, of course, is more cultural and sociological than geographical. Bernhard W. Anderson (*Creation versus Chaos* [Philadelphia: Fortress, 1987]) has shown the cre-

Tension and, in some ways, conflict between the traditions can be sensed even when one is not attempting to be precise about the points of origin or settings for the two circles of tradition. Recent traditio-historical analyses confirm such a judgment.[3] Two additional observations need to be made in order to provide a better understanding of these circles of tradition. First, we may speak of trajectories running through the tradition. To my knowledge, the categories of James M. Robinson and Helmut Koester[4] have not been applied to Old Testament studies. They urge that pieces of literature and tradition should not be studied in isolation nor in terms of mechanical dependence and relationship through a literary process, but that special attention should be paid to the continuities that flow between various pieces of literature. As a result of social value, use, and transmission, continuities both in terms of cultural context and in terms of theological perspective become decisive for interpretation.[5] Applied to the two covenantal traditions in the Old Testament, "trajectories" suggest that we might be able to trace continuities in the literature shaped and energized by the Mosaic and Davidic covenants. Specifically, as will be evident in what follows, the Mosaic tradition tends to be a movement of protest that is situated among the disinherited and that articulates its theological vision in terms of a God who decisively intrudes, even against seemingly impenetrable institutions and orderings. On the other hand, the Davidic tradition tends to be a movement of consolidation that is situated among the established and secure and that articulates its theological vision in terms of a God who faithfully abides and sustains on behalf of the present ordering.[6] As is clear from the work of Robinson and

---

ative power of the Jerusalem establishment as expressed in the various creation and royal traditions.

3. See the summary of Douglas Knight, *The Traditions of Israel*, SBLDS 9 (Missoula, Mont.: Scholars Press, 1973).

4. James M. Robinson and Helmut Koester, *Trajectories through Early Christianity* (Philadelphia: Fortress, 1971).

5. On the issue of continuity and discontinuity, see especially the discussions of Peter Ackroyd, *Continuity: A Contribution to the Study of the Old Testament Religious Tradition* (Oxford: Blackwell, 1962); and idem, "Continuity and Discontinuity: Rehabilitation and Authentication," in *Tradition and Theology in the Old Testament*, ed. Douglas Knight (Philadelphia: Fortress, 1977), 215–34.

6. See the summary of Claus Westermann, "Creation and History in the Old Testament," in *The Gospel and Human Destiny*, ed. Vilma Vajta (Minneapolis: Augsburg, 1971), 11–38. Westermann has observed how the different traditions yield very different presentations of God. He has not pursued the sociological dimension of the argument, but it is clear that the theological *Tendenz* of a trajectory serves specific interests.

Koester, attention to trajectories is at best imprecise and does not permit a rigid schematization. It does, however, provide a way to see a coherent and persistent *Tendenz* in each stream.

Second, the presence and meaning of two alternative covenant traditions are richly illuminated by attention to sociological factors. While we still do not have a comprehensive overview of this data, the work of George Mendenhall, Norman Gottwald, and Paul Hanson provides some beginnings. Such work makes clear that the literature that stands within the various trajectories is never sociologically disinterested nor singularly concerned with matters theological. Each text and each trajectory reflects important socioeconomic and political concerns.

The following discussion will consider the two covenant traditions in terms of literary trajectories and sociological considerations that may be related to them. Thus far, scholarly presentations have been concerned only with smaller historical periods and not with a comprehensive pattern for the whole. This essay suggests the provisional discernment of a comprehensive pattern that may significantly alter our understanding of the theological import of the texts and the literary-historical questions relating to them.

I

It will be useful to consider relevant scholarly literature in terms of various periods of Israel's history that have been subjected to study. Our presentation will reflect a certain periodization of Israel's history; however, that periodization is used simply as a way of reporting various scholarly studies. None of the scholars mentioned has urged a pattern of periodization, so that it may be regarded simply as an organization of convenience. For the present discussion, the stress is on the continuity of the trajectory rather than the periodization.

As early as 1962, Mendenhall proposed a fresh way of understanding the conquest and the premonarchal period of Israel (1250–1000 B.C.E.).[7] In contrast to the dominant views of conquest, either by invasion or infiltration, Mendenhall urged that Israel was formed by an intentional "bond between persons in an intolerable situa-

---

7. George Mendenhall, "The Hebrew Conquest of Palestine," *BA* 25 (1962): 66–87. His alternative hypothesis has been given a positive treatment by John Bright, *A History of Israel*, 2d ed. (Philadelphia: Westminster, 1972), 133 n. 69, and John L. McKenzie, *The World of the Judges* (New York: Prentice-Hall, 1966), 95–98.

tion."[8] Oppressed people with an alternative vision of social order were able to "reject the religious, economic and political obligations to the existing network of political organizations."[9] The *habiru* mounted a revolution against tyrannical Canaanite city-kings, rejecting the given social order. Bound to a nonhuman overlord by covenant and the solidarity of the newly formed community, they set about fashioning a deliberate alternative social ordering that became Israel. Thus, Mendenhall has interpreted the "conquest" in the categories of oppressed people revolting for liberation versus tyrannical city-kings. In what follows, it will be suggested that these categories provide entry into the two dominant trajectories of Israelite literature.

Related to this hypothesis, several observations emerge from sociological considerations. First, the dominant view of early Israel as nomadic has been sharply placed in question. The sociological data, summarized by Mendenhall[10] and Gottwald and Frank S. Frick,[11] require a fresh sociological realism about Israel as an alternative to the city-state. What is different is not mobility or a lack of a place but a social ordering that is characterized by political decentralization and social egalitarianism in contrast to urban centralization and social stratification with the power in the hands of an elite. In his preliminary paper, Gottwald contrasts the city and the countryside as available alternative models,[12] whereas Mendenhall presents Is-

---

8. Mendenhall, "The Hebrew Conquest," 119.

9. Ibid., 109.

10. George Mendenhall, "The Conflict between Value Systems and Social Control," *Unity and Diversity*, ed. Hans Goedicke and J. J. M. Roberts (Baltimore: Johns Hopkins Univ. Press, 1975), 169–80; idem, "The Monarchy," *Int* 29 (1975): 155–70; idem, "Samuel's Broken Rib: Deuteronomy 32," in *No Famine in the Land*, ed. James W. Flanagan and Anita Weisbrod Robinson (Missoula, Mont.: Scholars Press, 1975), 63–74; and Mendenhall's synthesis in *The Tenth Generation* (Baltimore: Johns Hopkins Univ. Press, 1973), especially chaps. 1, 7, and 8. These studies are derivative from his early work on covenant in 1954; since then he has explored the sociological aspects of that study.

11. Norman Gottwald, "Biblical Theology or Biblical Sociology?" *Radical Religion* 2 (1975): 46–57; idem, "Domain Assumptions and Societal Models in the Study of Premonarchic Israel," *VTSup* 28 (1974): 89–100; and idem, "Were the Early Israelites Pastoral Nomads?" in *Rhetorical Criticism*, ed. Jared J. Jackson and Martin Kessler (Pittsburgh: Pickwick, 1974), 223–55; Norman Gottwald and Frank S. Frick, "The Social World of Ancient Israel," *SBLSP* (1975): 165–78.

12. For our argument and its implications, it is important to note that both Gottwald and Mendenhall are engaged in the construction of alternative models. Obviously, increased data can still be adapted to the regnant models, but the importance of their work is precisely in the proposal of a new comprehensive model for interpretation.

rael's egalitarian movement as a more radical step. Thus, Israel is not to be understood as a group of geographical outsiders but as sociopolitical outsiders who were geographically present but not permitted to share in the shaping of their own destiny. Their marginality is not geographical in character but rather social, economic, and political. Thus, instead of nomad, the suggested sociological identity is that of peasant, a term that means the politically and economically marginal element of society from whose produce the elite draw their life. The peasant is characterized as one whose labor yields produce enjoyed by others.[13]

Second, Mendenhall has urged a rethinking of the notion of "tribe" in characterizations of early Israel.[14] The tribe, he urges, is not to be understood as a natural ethnic grouping but as an intentional community deliberately committed to a different ideology and a different social organization.[15] Such a notion suggests that the central social unit in early Israel is not to be confused either with conventional notions of nomadism or with anthropological ideas of kinship groups.

These groups are historical and not natural. In Israel they did not originate because of necessity or nature but through historical decision making. The tribe in Israel is to be contrasted with the state, a distinction that has received various presentations in the history of sociology. It is especially to be noted that the historical decision making from whence comes such a tribe is an intentional action that is the first step away from historical marginality.

Third, such an understanding of the social unit provides a way by which greater stress may be placed on covenant as an ideology and form of social organization. The hypothesis of covenant (anticipated by Martin Buber and articulated especially by Klaus Baltzer and Mendenhall)[16] of course provides a major conceptual category

---

13. Ernest Wolf (*Peasants* [Englewood Cliffs, N.J.: Prentice-Hall, 1966]) has provided a basic study of this social factor. Cf. John H. Halligan, "The Role of the Peasant in the Amarna Period," SBLSP (1976): 155–70. Concerning what is perhaps a contemporary parallel to this crisis in Israel, Hugo Blanco (*Land or Death* [New York: Pathfinder, 1972], 110) asserts, "We must always keep in mind that the historic problem of the peasant around which all others revolve is the problem of *land.*"

14. Mendenhall, *Tenth Generation*, chap. 7, and more recently, idem, "Social Organization in Early Israel," in *Magnalia Dei: The Mighty Acts of God*, ed. Frank M. Cross, Werner Lemke, and Patrick D. Miller Jr. (Garden City, N.Y.: Doubleday, 1976), 132–51.

15. Mendenhall, *Tenth Generation*, 19–31.

16. Martin Buber, *The Kingship of God*, 3d ed. (New York: Harper and Row, 1966), especially chap. 7. It is remarkable that Buber had seen this long before the work

for understanding Israel. But that conceptualization has in scholarly discussion stayed largely in the sphere of theological interpretation. Indeed, Baltzer's excellent study is confined to literary and form-critical concerns. Only relatively recently has the notion of covenant been handled sociologically to suggest that it provided ground for a "systematic, ethically and religiously based, conscious rejection of many cultural traits of the late Bronze Age urban and imperial cultures."[17] The covenant, then, is more politically radical and historically pertinent to early Israel than has often been recognized, for it permitted a political *novum* in history and a radical break with urban culture. Mendenhall has in schematic fashion contrasted the regnant social organization and the alternative made possible by covenant.[18]

While Mendenhall in 1954[19] did turn scholarship in a new direction, his major sociological intent has been neglected. Mendenhall's crucial presentation had two parts. The first dealt with the "treaty-form" and ancient Near Eastern parallels discovered in Hittite and Assyrian texts. The second was concerned with the innovative social vision and social organization derived from a covenant-treaty. Scholarship has largely embraced the former and has busily identified elements of the treaty-form in many places, although some identifications are exceedingly doubtful.[20]

For a number of years, Mendenhall's major concern for social vision and social organization was not recognized or pursued by scholars. It was Mendenhall's own more recent work that indicated that covenanted Israel embodied not only a theological novelty but also a social experiment as well.[21] The theological factor has required a quite new discernment of God as a faithful covenanter who

---

of Mendenhall and Baltzer. See Klaus Baltzer, *The Covenant Formulary* (Philadelphia: Fortress, 1971). George Mendenhall, *Law and Covenant in Israel and the Ancient Near East* (Pittsburgh: Biblical Colloquium, 1955).

17. Mendenhall, *Tenth Generation*, 12.

18. Mendenhall, "The Conflict between Value Systems and Social Control." In tabulating the contrasts between social theories based on "covenant" and "law," it is likely that he uses "law" in the same sense as does Paul in his radical critique of the theological function of the law.

19. Mendenhall, *Law and Covenant in Israel.*

20. See the summary of McCarthy, *Old Testament Covenant.*

21. The earlier scholarly consideration of Mendenhall's work focused on the radical theological break with the religion of the day. Only more recently has the social counterpart of that radical theology been more widely considered. The links between the theological and sociological are evident in *Tenth Generation*. See also Gottwald, "Biblical Theology or Biblical Sociology?" and especially M. Douglas Meeks, "God's Suffering Power and Liberation," *JRT* 33 (1977): 44–54.

engaged in the history of Israel and who was impacted by Israel's history, its acts and praises, but who nonetheless has independent purpose and authority not derived from the covenanted partner. Conversely, the theological self-understanding of Israel permitted a new people that had no other identity—linguistic, racial, ethnic, or territorial—except exclusive allegiance to its God. That much has been widely observed.[22]

What has not been sufficiently appreciated are the social implications of this theological novelty. Covenantal commitment to this God, unknown by name and without credential in the empire, carried with it a rejection of loyalty to the gods of the empire and a rejection of the ways of ordering that society.[23] Thus, the theological vision, either as impetus or as justification,[24] made possible a radical discontinuity in the social organization of Israel. Israel was no longer bound to the religion of the empire that had now been effectively delegitimated, and Israel could no longer and need no longer rely upon the self-securing technology of the empire.

This way of interpreting the data presumes a close link between

---

22. A model articulation of that insight is offered by G. Ernest Wright, *The Old Testament against Its Environment*, SBT 2 (London: SCM, 1950).

23. Gottwald ("Biblical Theology or Biblical Sociology?") is especially attentive to the social use and function of religion, an insight surely Marxist in its awareness. His summary of the break in sociology asserted by Yahwism is this: "In brief the chief articles of Yahwistic faith may be socio-economically 'de-mythologized' as follows: 'Yahweh' is the historically centralized primordial power to establish and sustain social equality in the face of oppression from without and simultaneously provincialism and non-egalitarian tendencies from within the society.... Yahweh is unlike the other gods of the ancient Near East as Israel's egalitarian inter-tribal order is unlike the other ancient Near Eastern social system.... The social-organization principle in Israel finds its counterpart in a symbolic ideological exclusionary principle in the image of the deity" (p. 52).

24. Acknowledgment must of course be made of Feuerbach's criticism that every religious statement is indeed a projection of social reality. Gottwald ("Biblical Theology or Biblical Sociology?" 48) appears to move in this direction: "It seems that it is primarily from the historico-social struggle of a sovereign inter-tribal community that the major analogies for conceiving Yahweh are drawn." Mendenhall more readily appeals to the category of revelation and exercises a kind of theological positivism. Thus, there is a difference between them on this point. Mendenhall (*Tenth Generation,* 16) alludes to the problem: "Do the people create a religion, or does the religion create a people? Historically, when we are dealing with the formative period of Moses and Judges, there can be no doubt that the latter is correct, for the historical, linguistic, and archaeological evidence is too powerful to deny. Religion furnished the foundation for a unity far beyond anything that had existed before, and the covenant appears to have been the only conceivable instrument through which the unity was brought about and expressed." In any case, their critical approaches disclose in fresh ways the fact that not only the dominant theology but the dominant scholarly methodology is not disinterested.

theological vision and sociological organization. A totalitarian, hierarchical social order has its counterpart and justification in the static religion of the empire in which the gods have no independent existence but are only an integral part of the social system.[25] Most obviously, the pharaoh, manager of the social process, is at the same time the embodiment of the gods. There is an identity of social process and theological vision, an arrangement that assured changelessness and that denied any standing ground for theological criticism of social reality.[26]

When the "new" God of freedom and justice is accepted as covenant partner, the totalitarian, hierarchical social order is no longer necessary or viable. Thus, the Israelite order from Moses until the time of David, 1250–1000 B.C.E., represents a sociological experiment to determine if a society is possible when not sanctioned and protected by the imperial gods. It is admittedly a precarious social experiment based on a precarious theological vision. That experimentation stands in sharp discontinuity with its political context as well as its theological milieu and is justified only by the bold theological novelty of Yahwism, a novelty focused on justice and freedom.[27]

So far as I am aware, Mendenhall at no point appeals to a Marxist criticism of society. Gottwald, however, does allow for it.[28] The discernment of the new situation is in keeping with the insight of

---

25. Meeks ("God's Suffering Power and Liberation") has discerned how a notion of God who is passionless serves well a psychology and a sociology that are compassionless. This observation appears to be especially important to the liberation movements as they address the theological and sociological paradigms of dominance. Cf. Jane Marie Luecke, "The Dominance Syndrome," *Christian Century* 94 (1977): 405–7, for a summary of the matter.

26. Mendenhall has seen that to the extent that God is continuous with the socioeconomic system, outsiders have no court of transcendent appeal against the dominant ordering. That linkage of sociology and theology is especially evident in Egyptian religion, which, on the one hand, is committed to order and, on the other hand, regards pharaoh as an embodiment of that ordering divinity. On both sociological and theological grounds, revolution is unthinkable. See Henri Frankfort, *Kingship and the Gods* (Chicago: Univ. of Chicago Press, 1948). The subtitle is telling: "A Study of Ancient Near Eastern Religion as the Integration of Society and Nature." Such integration brings with it social conservatism.

27. The Mosaic tradition is premised on the affirmation of a God who has freedom from the regime. On the freedom of God in this tradition, see Walther Zimmerli, "Prophetic Proclamation and Reinterpretation," in *Tradition and Theology in the Old Testament*, 69–100. Zimmerli sees the tradition as being concerned with the fact that "Yahweh in his freedom can utter his word anew."

28. In addition to the various articles in *The Bible and Liberation*, ed. Norman Gottwald (Maryknoll, N.Y.: Orbis, 1983), which make primary use of Marxist critical

Marx that the ultimate criticism is the criticism of heaven, which then radically criticizes all earthly, historical institutions.[29]

This insight, only recently reasserted by Mendenhall in a discussion of the covenant hypothesis, presents a quite shifted paradigm for biblical study, one that will need carefully to be studied, tested, and considered. In both the "peasant revolt" theory of "conquest" and the "covenant law" theme, Mendenhall has understood Israel in sharp discontinuity with its context. It may be argued that this is simply a class-conflict reading of the text, or perhaps the emergence of an alternative consciousness.[30] In any case, it provides a way to hold together (1) a sense of religious radicalness that either is unexplained or appeals to "revelation" and (2) the awareness of urgency about social reality evident in the text. For the moment, setting aside literary-critical judgments, such a view permits us to understand the militancy of Deuteronomy[31] as it urges an alternative understanding of reality and the high-risk venture Israel's faith is shown to be in the book of Judges. Much more is now seen to be at stake in the pressure of syncretism, for it is not just a choosing among gods or a matter of loyalty to this especially jealous one, but the shape and character of human community are in question along with the God-question. Human society, as ordered by Moses, is covenantal because the cov-

---

tools, see especially Gottwald, "Early Israel and the Asiatic Mode of Production," SBLSP (1976): 145–54.

29. Marx's programmatic statement in his "Critique of Hegel's Philosophy of Right" is: "Thus the criticism of heaven is transformed into the criticism of earth, the criticism of religion into the criticism of law, and the criticism of theology into the criticism of politics" (see *The Marx-Engels Reader*, ed. R. C. Tucker [New York: W. W. Norton, 1972], 13). My criticism of Gottwald, from whom I have learned so much, is that he has not given sufficient attention to a critique of heaven.

30. In Israel, poetry may be understood as the rhetoric of the alternative community that refuses to abide by the prose of the empire. On the act of poetry as an assertion of liberation, see David N. Freedman, "Pottery, Poetry and Prophecy: An Essay on Biblical Poetry," *JBL* 96 (1977): 5–26, and less directly, idem, "Divine Names and Titles in Early Hebrew Poetry," in *Magnalia Dei*, 55–107. In the latter essay, the discernment of "militant," "revival," and "syncretism" in poetry (pp. 56–57) is worth noting because the categories suggest the social use of the poems. On rhetoric as a tool for an alternative community, see Rubem Alves, *Tomorrow's Child* (New York: Harper and Row, 1972).

31. See Norbert Lohfink, "Culture Shock and Theology," *BTB* 7 (1977): 12–21, on culture crisis and the constructive function of Deuteronomy. For an alternative understanding of the social function of Deuteronomy, see Joseph Gutmann, *The Image and the Word* (Missoula, Mont.: Scholars Press, 1977), 5–25. Gutmann appeals especially to the hypothesis of W. E. Claburn, "The Fiscal Basis of Josiah's Reform," *JBL* 92 (1973): 11–22.

enant God both sanctions and expects it. And Israel must resist every
religion and every politics that would dismantle the covenant.

These discussions of peasants, tribe, and covenant prepare the
way for Gottwald's major study of early Israel as a community of
radical liberation. His book[32] argues that conventional historical interpretations do not appropriate the sociopolitical radicalness of a
movement that is profoundly religious in its commitment to the God
of the exodus and dangerously political in its rejection of the status
quo with its oppressive consciousness and practice.

We do not have (nor are we likely to have) a parallel consideration of the religion of the tyrannical city-kings of Canaan. Obviously,
that lies outside the scope of Israel's normative faith and is treated
by the Old Testament texts only in reaction and with contempt and
hostility. The social organization of the period, however, provides a
clue to the religious ideology that undoubtedly legitimated it. We
may presume that this religion concerned a god of order who surely
served to legitimate the way things already were. While one cannot
be very precise, clearly the structure of liberation faith vis-à-vis a religion of legitimated order is already evident. That trajectory of a
religion of God's freedom and a politics of justice will be important
for the subsequent periods.

II

The second period we shall consider is that of the united monarchy. Obviously, something decisive happened to Israel in this period.
The tensions revealed in 1 Samuel reflect a battle for Israel as to
whether it will be "like the other nations" (1 Sam. 8:5, 20) or whether
it shall be *'am qādôš,* a people holy to the Lord. While that issue has
long been perceived, it is now possible to conclude that this was not
only a battle over gods and theological identity but also a battle concerning social values and social organization. The innovations and
inventiveness of David and Solomon (expressed, for instance, in temple, bureaucracy, harem, standing army, taxation system, utilization
of wisdom) embody an imitation of urban imperial consciousness of
Israel's more impressive neighbors and a radical rejection of the liberation consciousness of the Mosaic tradition. While the texts shaped
under the aegis (note the word) of the monarchy in their present

---

32. The book is entitled *The Tribes of Yahweh* (Maryknoll, N.Y.: Orbis, 1979).

form stress continuity with and propose fidelity to the tradition of Moses, the discontinuities can scarcely be overstated. Mendenhall has described this as the "paganization of Israel."[33] It is clear from his work that the social innovation of Moses and its corresponding theological novelty of a God aligned with the marginal ones were abandoned in monarchal Israel. Social innovation and theological novelty sustained the community for 250 years, but only as a marginal, minority community preoccupied with survival. That now is given up when the community has the resources and breathing space not only to survive but also to dominate its context, as Solomon was able to do.[34] The radical experiment of Moses is given up and there is in Israel an embrace of the very imperial notions rejected from Egypt.[35] This imperial consciousness combines a religion of a static, guaranteed God together with a politics of injustice and social domination, precisely antithetical to the religion of the freedom of God and the politics of justice introduced by Moses and kept alive in the community of premonarchal Israel.

The change can be observed in a variety of ways. First, the organizational and institutional changes are well known: from traditional to bureaucratic leadership, from tribal ordering to governmental districts, from "holy war" ideology to hired mercenaries, and the introduction of a harem as an appropriate royal accoutrement. Thus, the presuppositions of public life were drastically altered, indicating an abandonment of the vision that powered the "peasant revolt."

Second, the discernment of God's relation to the community is reshaped. That change may be presented in terms of tent and house. The old tradition of "tent" asserts a claim of mobility and freedom for God. The "house" tradition is surely royal in its orientation and stresses the abiding presence of Yahweh to Israel. Thus, the tension of the freedom of God and the accessibility of God to Israel is now tilted in a new direction.[36] The older Mosaic tradition stressed the

---

33. Mendenhall, *Tenth Generation*, 16, 182, 195–96; idem, "The Monarchy," 157–66; idem, "Samuel's Broken Rib," 67.

34. It is evident that the critical perversion came not with David but with Solomon. See Frank M. Cross, *Canaanite Myth and Hebrew Epic* (Cambridge, Mass.: Harvard Univ. Press, 1973), 237–41, and Walter Brueggemann, *In Man We Trust* (Richmond: John Knox, 1972), 64–77.

35. On the Solomonic fascination with Egypt, see T. N. D. Mettinger, *Solomonic State Officials* (Lund: Gleerup, 1971), and G. Ernest Wright, *Biblical Archaeology* (Philadelphia: Westminster, 1957), 120–63.

36. On this tension, see Walter Brueggemann, "Presence of God, Cultic," in *IDBSup* (New York: Abingdon, 1976), 680–83.

freedom of God, and the notion of presence was precarious. Now the notion of presence is primary and God's freedom is severely constricted, for the royal regime must depend on a patron and legitimator who is unreservedly committed to the shrine and its social arrangement.

Third, in the context of social transformation and theological revision, Frank M. Cross has offered a persuasive construction of the history of priesthood in Israel.[37] Clearly, the priestly narratives must be read with attention to the conflicted and political interest that seems always to have been at stake. It is clear that David was able to achieve a remarkable balance in having two priests, Abiathar and Zadok, and it is equally clear that Solomon brashly dissolved the balance with the enhancement of Zadok and the elimination of Abiathar (1 Kings 2:26-27).

By carefully piecing together the fragmentary evidence, Cross concludes that David held together the priestly rivalry to serve his dominant interest of political unification. According to Cross, one priestly interest, represented by Abiathar, is the Mushite house with old links to Shiloh and Nob; the other is the house of Aaron, represented by Zadok, with roots in Hebron and, ultimately, in Jerusalem.[38] Further, after the period of the united monarchy, Jeroboam I, in setting up his two shrines, balanced a Mushite shrine in Dan with the Aaronid shrine of Bethel.[39] Thus, the narrative, as Albrecht Alt has recognized, shows David holding together the imperial and covenantal constituencies. In terms of social vision and organization, it is plausible that David managed the process so that he did not finally force the issue that was so clearly and ruthlessly forced by Solomon.

The Davidic-Solomonic tradition with its roots in Abrahamic memory provides an important alternative theological trajectory.[40]

---

37. Cross, *Canaanite Myth*, 195–215.

38. Cross's location of Zadok clearly is an advance beyond the position of Harold H. Rowley (see Cross, *Canaanite Myth*, 209). Nonetheless, Rowley ("Zadok and Nehustan," *JBL* 58 [1939]: 113–41; idem, "Melchizedeq and Zadok [Gen 14 and Ps 110]," in *Festschrift Alfred Bertholet* [Tübingen: Mohr, 1950], 461–72) already had seen that Zadok represents a cultic tradition essentially alien to the Mosaic tradition.

39. Cross, *Canaanite Myth*, 211.

40. Here we are concerned with the traditioning process and not with consideration of historically objective issues. But note must be taken of the radical position of John Van Seters, *Abraham in History and Tradition* (New Haven: Yale Univ. Press, 1975), and Thomas L. Thompson, *The Historicity of the Patriarchal Narratives*, BZAW 133 (Berlin: de Gruyter, 1974).

We may identify two theological elements that are surely linked to this movement and that are important to the subsequent faith and literature of the Bible. First, it is generally agreed that the emergence of creation faith in Israel has its setting in Jerusalem and its context in the royal consciousness.[41] The shift of social vision is accompanied with a shifted theological method that embraces more of the imperial myths of the ancient Near East and breaks with the scandalous historical particularity of the Moses tradition. The result is a universal and comprehensive worldview that is more inclined toward social stability than toward social transformation and liberation. Thus, creation theology, like every theological effort, is politically interested and serves to legitimate the regime that in turn sponsors and vouches for this theological perspective.

Second, clearly from this tradition comes messianism, the notion of God's promise being borne in history by an identifiable historical institution. Thus, the Davidic house now becomes not only historically important but theologically decisive for the future of Israel, and all promises and futures are now under the dominance of this institution. It will be clear that in both ways, creation and messianism, the royal perspective is in tension with the Mosaic tradition. In the Mosaic tradition, narratives of concrete liberation are much preferred to comprehensive myths of world order. In the Mosaic world, precarious covenant premised on loyalty is in deep tension with the unconditional affirmation of a historical institution. In these major ways, the Davidic-Solomonic period witnesses the emergence of an alternative both in theology and politics that is in radical tension with Mosaic tradition and congenial to the non-Mosaic and pre-Mosaic royal traditions.[42]

For purposes of tracing literary-theological trajectories, it is important to recognize that the Mushite priesthood was heir to the liberation faith rooted in Moses and preserved among the northern tribes, likely at the shrines of the confederation. Conversely, the Zadokite rootage, from what can be reconstructed, belonged to a royal consciousness based in an urban context. The priestly conflict is not just an in-house power struggle of priestly interests, but it is again a battle for the life of Israel between a liberation faith and a

---

41. See Anderson, *Creation versus Chaos.*

42. On Ezekiel's resolution of the role of the messiah in the Mosaic tradition, see Jon D. Levenson, *Theology of the Program of Restoration of Ezekiel 40–48,* HSM 10 (Missoula, Mont.: Scholars Press, 1976), chap. 2. On the reassertion of the older, pre-Mosaic traditions, see Cross, *Canaanite Myth,* 343–46.

religion of legitimated order. The issue of the earlier period (to use
the construct of Mendenhall) between "peasants" and "city-kings"
appears to apply here.

On the basis of such a reading of the evidence, the Hebron/
Shiloh, Aaronid/Mushite, Aaron/Moses pattern and the vindication
of the former in each case show that the consciousness of the united
monarchy was finally shaped decisively by a tradition rooted in very
old pre-Israelite royal traditions. Specifically, it provided a shrine
that legitimated order at the expense of justice, that presented the
king as the principle of order and not as a child of the torah, and
that placed stress on dynastic continuity at the expense of critical
transcendence in history.

The tradition of the Canaanite city-kings to whom Mendenhall
has applied the term "tyrannical" found its continuation in the royal
theology focused on creation and messiah. The Mosaic tradition
found its muted continuation in the priestly house of Abiathar, in
occasional prophetic criticism, in the symbolic but revolutionary rejection of the Davidic house (2 Sam. 20:1; 1 Kings 12:16), and in
protests against the institution of monarchy (1 Samuel 8; 12) and its
"sacred space" (1 Kings 8:27).

III

The two trajectories can be discerned in development throughout
the period of the divided monarchies, 922–587 B.C.E. For this period
there has not been the enormous scholarly activity of a sociological character as for the other periods. The tensions revealed here
are also better understood when placed in the frame of the earliest
confrontation of peasants and city-kings.

The political institutions of the northern and southern kingdoms are likely vehicles for these two traditions of religion and
social vision. Thus, the split of 1 Kings 12 represents a departure
of the community of historical liberation from the ordering regime
of David. It is important that the split did not happen over a theological dispute; nor was it simply a gradual growing apart; rather, it
was triggered by a concrete issue of political oppression and social
liberation. There is no doubt that the royal consciousness was committed to the maintenance of order at the cost of justice. This is not,
of course, to claim that the northern kingdom did not practice similar oppression as under Ahab, but the northern kingdom appears

to have been peculiarly open to and vulnerable to the transforming impact of the Moses tradition. This entire phase of Israel's history is easily understood as a confrontation of kings and prophets, thus continuing the claims of the Davidic-Solomonic commitment to order and continuity and the Mosaic affirmation of freedom even at the cost of discontinuity. We may mention four occasions of the traditions in conflict, in which these trajectories are at work.

1. The confrontation of Elijah/Ahab (Jezebel) in 1 Kings 21 is nearly a pure paradigm of the issue. Elijah stands in the old tradition of "inheritance" (*naḥalāh*), whereas the royal figures are committed to the right of royal confiscation that overrides older inheritance rights (*yāraš*).[43] The prophet appeals to the unfettered work of Yahweh that calls kings to accountability and dismantles kingdoms (vv. 17-19), whereas the king utilizes mechanizations of the torah for the sake of royal interest. Elijah believes that covenant curses follow violations of torah, even against the royal person, whereas Ahab believes the torah is only a tool of royal policy.

2. The confrontation between Amos and Amaziah (Amos 7:10-17) is of the same character. Amos speaks against any who violate torah[44] or who try to stop the free word of Yahweh, even if it touches the king. By contrast, Amaziah does not doubt the authority of torah but believes the royal reality has immunity. Thus, the king's world has created a situation in which there is no transcendence outside royal management to which appeal can be made. It follows that there is no free God who can evoke or sanction radical social change, precisely the situation pharaoh wished for in the Egypt of the thirteenth century.

3. The confrontation of Isaiah and Ahaz (Isa. 7:1—9:7) is somewhat different because Isaiah is not so unambiguously placed in the Mosaic trajectory[45] though of course he does affirm a transcendence beyond royal perception in his use of the key words "glory" (*kabôd*)

---

43. Questions of literary history and unity in the narrative are difficult. See Odil H. Steck, *Überlieferung und Zeitgeschichte im der Elia-Erzählungen,* WMANT 26 (Neukirchen-Vluyn: Neukirchener Verlag, 1968), 40–53; and Georg Fohrer, *Elia,* ATANT 53 (Zurich: Zwingli, 1968), 24–29.

44. On Amos and the torah, see Robert Bach, "Gottesrecht und weltliches Recht in der Verkündigung des Propheten Amos," in *Festschrift Gunther Dehn* (Neukirchen-Vluyn: Neukirchener Verlag, 1957), 23–34.

45. That the Isaiah traditions will not fit any neat scheme is evidenced by the decision of Gerhard von Rad (*Old Testament Theology* [London: Oliver and Boyd, 1965] 2:147–75) to place him in the Jerusalem tradition. For a more refined judgment,

and "holy" (*qadôš*). Thus, it is not quite so clear that his position in the face of the king is so unambiguously critical. Nonetheless, he calls the king to radical faith (7:8) and urges the king to a wholly new perception of reality that calls the king out from his self-securing posture.

The resolution of the unit on the Syro-Ephraimite War (Isa. 9:2-7) demonstrates the delicate balance worked by the prophet. The future is indeed Davidic, with appeal to the royal promissory tradition rooted in 2 Samuel 7. The promise indicates enormous confidence in the royal tradition and royal institution, for it makes reference to Yahweh's unreserved commitment to this institution. Thus, the expectation of the prophet (if it is in fact his poetry) is very different from the radicalness of Amos. Amos, in extraordinary boldness (now placed after the Amaziah encounter), had finally said "end" (*qēṣ*).[46] There had never been a pronouncement more radical than this. In a different way, Isaiah in his appeal to the Davidic promise concludes "no end" (*'ên qēṣ*) (v. 6).[47] (If, as some argue, Amos is committed to the Davidic reality, then his word is against the north and not in conflict with Isaiah; but that seems unlikely, even if Amos's words refer to the north.)

4. A final example we cite of the tension of traditions in this period is in the poem of Jer. 22:13-19 in which Jeremiah contrasts two kings, Jehoiakim and Josiah. Jehoiakim, so quickly dismissed by the Deuteronomist (2 Kings 24:1-7), is presented as an embodiment of royal self-serving, dominated by injustice and unrighteousness. The son practiced oppression and violence; the father cared for the poor and needy—that is, he understood covenantal knowing. The poetry of Jeremiah (passing over the death of Josiah) presents him as "well," that is, faithful in covenant, and Jehoiakim as destined to an ignoble death (which did not happen). The poem is not a report on which happened but a projection of what may be anticipated from the tradition.

---

see Odil H. Steck, "Theological Streams of Tradition," in *Tradition and Theology in the Old Testament*, 193–94.

46. Ronald Clements (*Prophecy and Covenant*, SBT 43 [London: SCM, 1965], 39–43) has observed that the drastic announcement of an end represents a new radical announcement in Israel.

47. It may, of course, be too subtle to relate the "end" of Amos to the "no end" of Isaiah, for Isaiah clearly refers to Davidic Israel, while Amos presumably refers to the northern kingdom. See also Frank Crüsemann, "Kritik an Amos in Deuteronomistischen Geschichtswerk," in *Probleme Biblischer Theologie*, ed. Hans Walter Wolff (Munich: Kaiser, 1971), 57–63.

Special note should be taken of Josiah, who occupied a crucial place in this period near its end and who also holds an enigmatic position between the traditions. On the one hand, he is clearly a Davidic figure. His credentials are unquestioned, and his conduct of office shows he did not flinch from that role. On the other hand, it is equally clear that unlike almost every other David, he subordinated his Davidic role to the claims of torah. In terms of traditions that concern us, the Davidic claims are subordinated to Mosaic claims.[48]

The contrast of Jehoiakim (*lō'-ṣedeq, lō'-mišpāṭ*) and Josiah (*mišpāṭ, ṣedeq*) articulates well the trajectories of the older period. Jehoiakim is obviously a practitioner of the same oppression as the city-kings and no doubt had a theology of order to legitimate it. Josiah, from a religion of torah, engages in political practice quite in keeping with the liberation movement of Moses.

It is possible that the trajectories in this period can be discerned in the variant expressions of the normative tradition designated J and E. There is little doubt that J is an attempt at unitive and comprehensive theologizing, concerned both to secure the place of the Davidic house in normative theology and to make cosmic claims in terms of linking Jerusalem's centrality and creation theology.[49] Conversely, the E tradition, to the extent it is a distinct and identifiable piece, is a separatist statement concerned for the purity of the community and aware of the threat of syncretism.[50] Clearly, purity is no concern of J, and unitive issues are remote to E. Thus, the old trajectories of marginal people with a primary concern for freedom and established people with a large concern for stability are reflected in the shape of the J and E traditions. The main issue, in terms of community identity (south and north), communal function and office

---

48. It is clear that the Davidic promises do not function in the poetry of Jeremiah. Indeed it is precisely his opponents who continue to rely on them. And in the Deuteronomistic Historian, surely closely related to Jeremiah, the balance between Mosaic and Davidic factors is in dispute, but there is little doubt that the Mosaic tradition is decisive. The situation is quite different in Ezekiel, as Levenson has shown.

49. See Walter Brueggemann, "David and His Theologian," *CBQ* 30 (1968): 156–81; idem, "From Dust to Kingship," *ZAW* 84 (1972): 1–18; and Walter Wifall, "Gen 6:1-4: A Royal Davidic Myth?" *BT* 5 (1975): 294–301; idem, "The Breath of His Nostrils," *CBQ* 36 (1974): 237–40.

50. See Hans Walter Wolff, "The Elohistic Fragments in the Pentateuch," in *The Vitality of Old Testament Traditions*, by Walter Brueggemann and Hans Walter Wolff (Atlanta: John Knox, 1975), 67–82; and Alan Jenks, *The Elohist and North Israelite Traditions*, SBLMS 22 (Missoula, Mont.: Scholars Press, 1977).

(king and prophet), and tradition (J and E), stayed alive until the loss of Jerusalem.[51]

IV

The next period we may identify is that of the exile, for which the conventional dates are 587–537 B.C.E. Even if those dates are somewhat problematic, this period presents an identifiable crisis and a responding literature that permits disciplined consideration.

It is clear that with the crisis of 587, the faith trajectories we have presented are thrown into disarray. This is the case particularly with the Mosaic-prophetic covenantal trajectory that seems now to have failed. From the perspective of the normative literature of the Old Testament, the preexilic period is dominated by the Mosaic trajectory, with the royal alternative subordinated (though undoubtedly flourishing in practice). With the exile, we may in broad outline speak of an inversion of the traditions so that the Mosaic theme is in crisis and is apparently less germane, while the promissory royal tradition now becomes the dominant theological mode for Israel.

In recent scholarly discussion, the following are relevant to our theme:

1. The Deuteronomic corpus, either shaped or revised in the exile, represents an insistence upon the Mosaic way of discerning reality and its insistence on radical obedience.[52] It is a call for radical obedience to torah, an embrace of Yahweh's will for justice with appropriate sanctions (positive and negative) for obedience. Thus, it continues the urgent call for purity (2 Kings 17:7-41) with its militant, uncompromising social vision.

Following Gerhard von Rad, it has been argued that Davidic themes of assurance are also present in the corpus.[53] These may perhaps be found in the conclusion of 2 Kings 25:27-30, or in the three

---

51. See J. A. von Soggin, "Ancient Israelite Poetry and Ancient 'Codes' of Law, and the Sources of 'J' and 'E' of the Pentateuch," VTSup 28 (1974): 193–95.

52. The most recent discussion is that of Werner E. Lemke, "The Way of Obedience: I Kings 13 and the Structure of the Deuteronomistic History," in *Magnalia Dei*, 301–26, unambiguously placing the Deuteronomistic Historian in the tradition of Moses and the prophetic demand for obedience. Lemke further develops the direction of Wolff's important essay.

53. Gerhard von Rad, *Old Testament Theology* (New York: Harper and Brothers, 1962), 1:334–47. See my derivative discussion, "The Kerygma of the Deuteronomistic Historian," *Int* 22 (1968): 387–402.

texts now generally regarded as later additions (Deut. 4:29-31; 30:1-10; 1 Kings 8:46-53).[54] It is possible that these somewhat tone down the uncompromising rigor of the literature, but it is equally clear that they do not measurably affect the main theme of the piece, namely, Yahweh's will for a community of obedience and justice.

There can be no doubt that this primal liberation word of Moses has now hardened into an ideology. It serves as a critique of comfortable, culture-accommodating religion, whether toward Babylonian imperialism or Canaanite city-kings. Thus the call for repentance and disengagement from culture-religion persists.

2. In sharp contention with that trajectory, two pieces of literature growing out of the promissory tradition are rooted in another view of reality. First, Bertil Albrektson has argued that Lamentations is a response to the harshness of Deuteronomy.[55] In the poetry of Lamentations, appeal is made to the claims of Jerusalem. Thus, Lamentations casts itself much more willingly upon the graciousness and freedom of Yahweh, the abiding faithfulness of Yahweh that is unconditional and unreserved. That modest affirmation (3:22-24) cannot be derived from the abrasion and urgency of the Mosaic tradition but appeals to an alternative theological model more likely rooted in the confidence of the Jerusalem traditions and institutions. Thus both the assurance of 3:22-24 and the confidence of 3:31-33 appear to be echoes of the promise of *ḥesed* in 2 Sam. 7:11-16. The allusions to the royal psalms, which Albrektson has noted, strengthen the likelihood of such an appeal.

In a similar though more frontal way, the poem of Job may be understood as a protest against the crisp certitude of the Deuteronomistic Historian. If indeed the Deuteronomistic Historian can in moralistic simplicity reduce everything to discernible moral causes, Job counters with an awareness that life will not be so easily explained, that mystery moves in ambiguity and lack of clarity, and that God in freedom has other concerns than exact response to human behavior.[56] Thus the God of Job is not inordinately preoccupied with

---

54. See Hans Walter Wolff, "The Kerygma of the Deuteronomistic Historical Work," in *The Vitality of Old Testament Traditions*, 91–97.

55. Bertil Albrektson, *Studies in the Text and Theology of the Book of Lamentations* (Lund: Gleerup, 1963), 214–39.

56. The fact that both Job and the Deuteronomistic Historian have important connections with Jeremiah make it quite plausible that Job is grappling with the issues forced by the Deuteronomist. Cf. James A. Sanders, "Hermeneutics in True and False Prophecy," in *Canon and Authority*, ed. George Coats and Burke Long (Philadelphia: Fortress, 1977), 28: "Job was surely written in part to record a resounding

"the human condition." There is no doubt that Job protests the moral singularity of his friends, who speak out of a perspective not unlike that of the Deuteronomistic Historian. The speech of Yahweh completely rejects those categories.

The rootage of the alternative perspective of the poet is not so easy to identify. We may note two attempts pertinent to our investigation. Samuel Terrien has located the poem of Job in the new year festival in the Babylonian exile as a paracultic drama of one for whom history no longer holds any promise.[57] The innocent sufferer "has lost all, and for all practical purposes of historical realism, he has died, but will live again by faith."[58] Terrien sees that an appeal to the creation myths (older than Israel's historical memories) makes possible "a poetic discussion of the theology of grace." Indeed the poet presents himself as "theologian of pure grace, over against the fallacies of proto-Pelagianism."[59] Thus the basic themes of the religion of the city-state, a royal person and a creation myth, surface here as resources for Israel when the historicizing morality of the Deuteronomistic Historian has failed. Such a difference of trajectory is apparent, even if linkage of the poem of Job to a historical crisis cannot be sustained.

From a quite different perspective, Cross has reached conclusions similar to those of Terrien.[60] "Yahweh the Lord of history has failed to act. El or Baal, the transcendent creator spoke."[61] In Job, opines Cross, the ancient myths regained their meaning. Cross draws the radical conclusion that Job brought the ancient religion of Israel to an end and evoked the resurgence of the oldest pre-Israelite myths, precisely those myths to which the creation faith of Israel made appeal.

We should not neglect the sociological implication of the embrace of older myth at the expense of historical self-awareness in a time of crisis. Needful though that choice was in exile, such a deci-

---

No to such inversions of the Deuteronomic ethic of election." There is, to be sure, a counteropinion among scholars that it is not possible to link the poem of Job to any specific historical situation. See especially J. J. M. Roberts, "Job and the Israelite Religious Tradition," *ZAW* 89 (1977): 107–14. Even if that be granted, the religious tendency of the poem is surely in a direction other than that of Deuteronomy.

57. Samuel Terrien, "The Yahweh Speeches and Job's Responses," *RevExp* 68 (1971): 497–509.

58. Ibid., 508.

59. Ibid., 498.

60. Cross, *Canaanite Myth*, 343–46.

61. Ibid., 344.

sion is inherently socially conservative. There is not within the return to myth the nerve or energy to take the actions that would transform historical circumstance. Indeed, it was the rejection of those very myths that permitted the Israelite *novum* in history and religion.[62] Conversely, such a "theology of grace" contains within it the acceptance of things as they are, and there is here no call to repentance in terms of historical engagement. Thus, from one perspective, Job reacts against the passionate stridency of the Deuteronomistic Historian that knows too much and asks too much. On the other hand, Job's position reduces historical nerve and asks an embrace of helplessness in the face of the terror of history and the hiddenness of God. Thus, John A. Miles Jr., in a socially conservative position albeit faithful to Job, sees that "there was truth in what had been excluded, and in the book of Job that truth returns."[63] The poet is challenged to retain the old knowledge against the new; and the old knowledge is that God is not always victorious and "Job's comforting is a play about the return of the truth that God and natural reality are inextricably one."[64]

The trajectories are clear in the apparent tension between Job and the Deuteronomistic Historian. Job does indeed represent the "old truth" that oppressive life must be accepted as ordained, surely a comfort in exile, while the Deuteronomistic Historian bears the "new truth."[65] Exile brings these truths to sharp conflict, the one offering assurance of grace, the other the urgency of repentance. Exile may be read, then, either as a destiny to be embraced or as a historical situation to be transformed.

3. Second Isaiah, it is commonly agreed, is the poetic matrix in which the crisis of the trajectories receives a new articulation.[66] In

---

62. The break and the discontinuity caused by the emergence of Israel have been stressed by Mendenhall. See *Tenth Generation*, 1–19, and "Migration Theories vs. Culture Change as an Explanation for Early Israel," SBLSP (1976): 135–43. The problem with a history-of-religions approach to these issues is that it is ideologically and methodologically committed to continuity as the primary agenda.

63. John A. Miles Jr., "Gagging on Job, or the Comedy of Religious Exhaustion," *Semeia* 7 (1977): 110.

64. Ibid., 110–13.

65. The "new truth" of the Mosaic revolution contrasts with the "old truth" of which Miles writes. When the old imperial gods are embraced, social stability is assured. Freedman ("Divine Names and Titles") identifies Judges 5 as among the poems of "militant Mosaic Yahwism." It is the coming of the new God, unknown in the empire, that causes a new social possibility.

66. Deutero-Isaiah has the capacity to utilize all the various traditions. See von Rad, *Old Testament Theology*, 2:238–43.

an earlier essay,[67] Bernhard Anderson showed the extent to which
Deutero-Isaiah utilized the exodus traditions to announce that his
own time was a time like that of Moses, in which Israel as a newness
in history had been willed by God. Thus Second Isaiah is a statement about historical redemption, making ready use of the Mosaic
tradition.

More recently and with more precise focus on covenant, Anderson has concluded that it is the Abrahamic/Davidic covenant that
dominates Second Isaiah.[68] Moreover, "the Mosaic covenant is appropriately absent from Second Isaiah's prophecy, for obedience to
commandments is not regarded as a prerequisite for blessing and
welfare."[69] "The ground for hope, therefore, is not a change on the
side of man but, so to speak, on the side of God."[70]

Second Isaiah is the primary locus in Scripture where the trajectories do come together in a remarkably synthetic way. Both the
history-transcending God of Job and the militant historicality of the
Deuteronomistic Historian come to positive expression. But on balance, Anderson has rightly discerned that the promises of God are
the ultimate word of the poet. Thus, Second Isaiah shows how it was
necessary in the exile to make a major reorientation in traditions
and move the normative faith of Israel from the one trajectory to
the other.

In Second Isaiah, as in Job, creation themes reshape Israel's
memory and hope according to the Jerusalem trajectory. It is the
royal theme of Abraham/Noah/David that gives the poetry of Second Isaiah its energizing power.[71]

Anderson's stress makes it unmistakable that in exile the Abrahamic tradition has gained a new centrality that tilts the religion of
Israel essentially toward promise. In that context, we should note
the bold proposal of Van Seters that the Abraham materials were

---

67. Bernhard W. Anderson, "Exodus Typology in Second Isaiah," in *Israel's Prophetic Heritage*, ed. Bernhard W. Anderson and Walter Harrelson (New York: Harper
and Brothers, 1962), 177–95.

68. Bernhard W. Anderson, "Exodus and Covenant in Second Isaiah and
Prophetic Tradition," in *Magnalia Dei*, 339–60.

69. Ibid., 356.

70. Ibid., 355.

71. It is the faithfulness of God to which appeal must be made in exile. In the
categories of Freedman, now Israel must speak of "divine commitment" and not of
"human obligation." On the abiding *ḥesed* of Yahweh to his people, see Otto Eissfeldt, "The Promises of Grace to David in Isaiah 55:1-5," in *Israel's Prophetic Heritage*,
177–95. While the point of the connection is unclear, the oracle of 55:3 is not
unrelated to the anticipation of Lam. 3:22-24.

formulated in this period to meet the situation of dislocation.[72] That perhaps claims too much. We can observe that the theological inventiveness of the period shows a tendency to return to the royal-creation-promise tradition with its social conservatism, the very tradition that the "new truth" of Moses challenged.

4. Finally for this period, we should note the way in which Hans Walter Wolff[73] has juxtaposed the traditions of D and P in the exile. He begins with the two-sided covenant formula: "I will be your God and you shall be my people," and argues that P and D, reflecting their two trajectories, each stress one part of the formula. P gives emphasis to "I will be your God," and D stresses "You shall be my people." That is a fair summary of the issue in the exile. Obviously, both statements bear a truth and both are essential in exile. The alternative stress indicates not only a different theological reading of the promise and of the resources but also a very different sociological analysis of what is required and what is possible.

V

The final period we shall consider, the postexilic period, may be briefly mentioned by reference to the work of Paul Hanson.[74] Hanson has presented a major proposal, admittedly too schematic, for organizing the postexilic literature of the canon. He proposes that the beginning point for understanding this literature is the dialectic Deutero-Isaiah articulated between vision and reality.

In the period after Deutero-Isaiah, various social groups in Israel each embraced a part of the dialectic and made that part its standing ground for faith and literature. Thus, Second Isaiah provides poetic and theological rationale for both the "pragmatists" and the "visionaries." For Hanson, the pragmatists are identified as the group in power, centering around the accommodating priesthood in Jerusalem. The visionaries are those groups now shut out of power and driven to hope in a new act of God that would invert histori-

---

72. Van Seters, *Abraham in History and Tradition.* Aside from the specific critical judgments he makes, Van Seters has made a strong case that a situation of exile and a theology of promise are precisely appropriate to each other.

73. Hans Walter Wolff, *The Old Testament: A Guide to Its Writings* (Philadelphia: Fortress, 1973), 32–44.

74. Paul Hanson, *The Dawn of Apocalyptic* (Philadelphia: Fortress, 1975).

cal reality and bring them to power. This latter group, pressed by its "world-weariness" to apocalyptic, may be identified with the circles of the Levites who were previously influential and now had become increasingly marginal.

Hanson's work utilizes the sociological paradigm of Karl Mannheim with its definition of ideology as a self-serving justification for the status quo and utopia as the passionate hoping for an alternative future. In presenting such a paradigm, Hanson limits his attention to rootage in Second Isaiah and does not go behind this literature for his purposes. But for our purposes, it is important to observe that Second Isaiah is not the first articulator nor the inventor of this dialectic. It lies deep and old in the tradition of Israel. Thus the "visionaries" and "pragmatists" of the postexilic period continue, in a way appropriate to their time and place, the same stances already discerned in the hopeful liberation movement of Moses and the accommodating, embracing creation-royal faith of the Davidic circles. The visionaries continue the hope and passion of the liberation tradition that believes that the present order is sharply called into question by God's promises. The pragmatists continue the confident affirmation of the present as the proper ordering willed by God, perhaps to be gradually changed but on the whole to be preserved. It is the substantive connections between the work of Gottwald and Mendenhall in the early period, Cross in the history of the priesthood, and especially Hanson in the later period that permit us to speak of trajectories.

VI

We may then suggest a schematic way in which the trajectories can be understood. A trajectory, of course, is not a straitjacket into which every piece of data must be made to fit, but it helps us to see the tendencies that continue to occur and to observe the influences that flow from one period to another. Over the five periods we have considered, generally following the periodization used by recent scholars in delimiting their work, the continuities may be outlined in the form of a table (see table 1).

Up to this point, scholars have focused on the tension in various periods. Mendenhall and Gottwald have concentrated on the early period, Cross on the monarchal period, and Hanson on postexilic developments. The point argued here is that continuities may

Table 1
CONTINUITIES OVER THE FIVE PERIODS

I. Mosaic period (emergence of liberation)	II. The united monarchy ("paganization")	III. Divided monarchy (the clash of traditions)	IV. Exile (traditions in crisis)	V. Postexilic period
A. imperial power and city-kings	Zadok: the Aaronite priesthood, royal theology, and creation faith	royal history	P: "I will be your God"	Zadokite priesthood: pragmatists, urban "haves," scribes, comfortable syncretists (Ezekiel 44)
		in tension 1 Kg 21: Ahab/Elijah Amos 7:10-17: Amaziah/ Amos	2 Isaiah "Look to the Rock from which you were hewn" (51:1)	
		Isa. 7:1—9:7: Ahaz/Isaiah Jer. 22:13-19: Jehoiakim/ Josiah	"Behold, I am doing a new thing" (43:18)	
B. revolt of peasants	Abiathar: the Mushite priesthood	prophetic alternatives	D: "You will be my people"	Levitical priesthood: visionaries, peasant "have-nots," apocalypticists, waiting purists (Isaiah 60–62)

be traced through the various periods in each of the strands, thus permitting us to term them "trajectories."[75]

75. Steck ("Theological Streams of Tradition") has pursued a parallel investigation utilizing the word "stream." However, Steck's presentation tends to identify so many diverse streams that the concept is diffused. Here I suggest that several of Steck's streams might be considered together as belonging to the same general context.

Table 2
COMMON ELEMENTS IN THE TRAJECTORIES

A. *The Royal Trajectory*	B. *The Liberation Trajectory*
(1) prefers to speak in myths of unity	(1) prefers to tell concrete stories of liberation
(2) speaks a language of fertility (creation) and continuity (royal institutions)	(2) speaks a language of war and discontinuity
(3) preferred mode of perception is that of universal comprehensiveness	(3) preferred mode of perception is that of historical specificity
(4) appears to be fostered by and valued among urban "haves"	(4) appears to be fostered by and valued among peasant "have-nots"
(5) tends to be socially conserving with a primary valuing of stability	(5) tends to be socially revolutionary with a primary valuing of transformation
(6) focuses on the glory and holiness of God's person and institutions geared to that holiness	(6) focuses on the justice and righteousness of God's will

Moreover, we may suggest, again in quite schematic fashion, common elements that appear continuously in each of the trajectories. (Some of these are presented in table 2.)

To the extent that this schematic presentation is correct, it means that these tendencies will be found at every period in the appropriate trajectory. A history-of-traditions approach must include a sociological analysis so that we are aware of the social function of each of the traditions, the authority assigned to it, the claims made for it, and power and social vision deriving from it.[76]

---

76. An important resource for further investigation is the book edited by Douglas Knight, *Tradition and Theology in the Old Testament.* Knight's own essay, "Revelation through Tradition," suggests the decisive way in which the traditioning community is engaged in the process of trajectory development.

VII

It is perhaps premature to speak of the emergence of a new paradigm for scholarship, but there are hints in that direction.[77] It is
clear that the older syntheses are now generally perceived as inadequate. This applies not only to the evolutionary scheme of Julius
Wellhausen but in a less incisive way also to the credo-tradition hypothesis of von Rad.[78] Evidences of the emerging consensus around
this provisional paradigm are as varied as Claus Westermann's proposal of a contrast of blessing and salvation[79] and the suggestive title
of Cross's statement, *Canaanite Myth and Hebrew Epic*. Westermann,
in a programmatic way, has shown that blessing and salvation represent quite different theological worlds. He has not gone on to draw
sociological conclusions or to suggest that Old Testament interpretation may be largely organized this way. Cross has finely shown the
dialectic of epic that seeks to be concretely historical and myth that
moves in the direction of syncretism. Cross means to move beyond
both the historical emphasis of the American and German schools
and the mythic inclination of the Scandinavians to show that the
perspectives of the two are mutually corrective.

　1. It can be argued that such a reading of Israel's faith and history is possible only by an appeal to a particular theory of history.
And there is no doubt that a Marxist class-reading of the Bible is

---

　77. It is, of course, presumptuous to speak of an emerging paradigm. The definitional statement of Thomas Kuhn (*The Structure of Scientific Revolutions* [Chicago:
Univ. of Chicago Press, 1970]) has created a new awareness of the ways in which
scholarship changes and/or advances. Gottwald ("Biblical Theology or Biblical Sociology?" 52, 55) both critiques the paradigm of "biblical theology," by which he
means a quite identifiable approach, and hints at the alternative informed by sociology. From quite another scholarly perspective, John Dominic Crossan (*Raid on the
Articulate* [New York: Harper and Row, 1976], xiv) suggests he is raising the question
of "a shift of the master paradigms of our research." He quotes Kuhn in referring
to "a reconstruction that changes some of the field's most elementary theoretical
generalizations as well as many of its paradigm methods and applications." Such
reasoning is not far removed from the issue raised by Gottwald in "Domain Assumptions and Societal Models in the Study of Pre-monarchic Israel." While both Crossan
and Gottwald may speak of a shift of paradigms, the substance of their urging is in
quite divergent directions.
　78. It is likely that Gottwald's critique of the paradigm of "biblical theology" refers
especially to the method and synthesis achieved by von Rad. Brevard Childs (*Biblical Theology in Crisis* [Philadelphia: Westminster, 1970]) has presented a formidable
critique of that synthesis.
　79. Westermann has developed this dialectic in various writings, but his major
presentation is in the Sprunt lectures, in which he contrasts the saving and blessing
of God. Most telling is his assertion that the God who blesses cannot fail or suffer.
Such a conclusion has enormous sociological implications.

not unrelated to this paradigm. Concerning the early period, Gottwald acknowledges this influence and makes a deliberate use of
such a frame of reference.[80] Concerning the later period, Hanson
is decisively guided by the conceptualization of Karl Mannheim.[81]

Having acknowledged the influence (explicit or not) of this
theory of society, several comments are in order:

a. There has been some critical objection to the use of such a
model for interpretation. Alan Hauser[82] has objected to the decisive
role played by a Marxist model. More judiciously, Brian Kovacs[83] observed that by the use of Mannheim's model, Hanson has been led to
and permitted certain conclusions that would have been very different given a different sociological model. Undoubtedly, much more
testing remains to be done, and a clear consensus in this direction
is far from established.

b. It will, of course, be tempting to dismiss the entire approach
by a rejection of Marxist presuppositions.[84] In response to such a
criticism, Robert McAfee Brown has rightly said that the real issue
is not if Marxist categories may be used but if the presentation and
discernment are correct in terms of the data and if the categories
serve responsible interpretation.[85] When that question is answered,
the issue of Marxist presuppositions becomes largely irrelevant.

c. Most importantly, it will need to be recognized again that there
is no "presuppositionless" exegesis. It is not a matter of using Marxist categories or continuing "objective" interpretation. The paradigm
suggested here requires that the critical guild become aware of its
own categories and, indeed, of its own "embourgeoisement."[86] For
example, Hauser seems quite unaware of his own presuppositions

---

80. Most evident in his utilization of the "Asiatic mode of production."

81. Hanson, *Dawn of Apocalyptic,* 213–20.

82. Alan Hauser, "Israel's Conquest of Palestine: A Peasants' Rebellion," *JSOT* 7
(1978): 2–19.

83. Brian Kovacs, "Contributions of Sociology to the Study of the Development of
Apocalyptic," paper read at the 1976 meeting of the Society of Biblical Literature.

84. See, for example, the review by John L. McKenzie of the book of José
Miranda, *JBL* 94 (1975): 280–81.

85. Robert McAfee Brown, "A Preface and a Conclusion," in *Theology in the Amer-
icas,* ed. Sergio Torres and John Eagleson (Maryknoll, N.Y.: Orbis, 1976), xvii: "But
the important question is not, 'Is liberation theology's analysis tinged with a Marxist
hue?' The important question is, 'Is the analysis true? Does it make sense of what it
is describing? Do we understand the world better when we look at it in that way?'"

86. The term is from Helmut Gollwitzer, "Kingdom of God and Socialism in the
Theology of Karl Barth," in *Karl Barth and Radical Politics,* ed. George Hunsinger
(Philadelphia: Westminster, 1976), 105.

and seems to imagine that his own critical approach is socially disinterested. In this view, John McKenzie seems also to misunderstand and to deliver a polemic against Marxist categories without discerning what the argument is about. There is no doubt that every paradigm, that of Wellhausen, von Rad, or any other, including this one, contains presuppositions that govern interpretation. Thus, the present sociological discussion presses hermeneutical considerations even upon our more "objective" work in literature and history.[87]

2. The trajectories suggested here may illuminate the various alternatives in current theological discussion. Most broadly, the alternatives may be grouped in terms of process hermeneutics and liberation hermeneutics.[88] In terms of our previous discussion, process theologies may be generally placed in the trajectory of royal theology, which is concerned with large comprehensive issues, which regards the concreteness of historical memory as a matter of little interest, and which is concerned with the continuities of the process. Current scholarly investigation within this trajectory (*a*) is likely seeking meaningful interface with current cultural forms; (*b*) is most likely to be lodged in university contexts and their epistemological commitments and not primarily interested in the forming of the synagogue/church as an alternative and distinct community of faith; and (*c*) is likely to have an inherent bias toward social conservatism. Of course, persons engaged in this scholarship may indeed be found elsewhere, but the reference group is likely to be the same. It is equally clear that persons in this scholarly tradition may themselves be concerned for an ethical radicalness, but it is not likely to be rooted in this epistemological tradition.

We may cite one example, the judgment of Miles about the "old truth" that "God and the harshness of nature, though they may not be One, are not separable."[89] Such an affirmation clearly inclines to seeing God simply as part of the process and runs the ready danger of giving sanction to the way things are because they cannot in any case be changed. Of course, Miles does not even hint at such an extrapolation. The slide from nature that is not separable from God

---

87. For a persuasive critique of ideological objectivism, see Alvin Gouldner, *The Coming Crisis of Western Sociology* (New York: Basic Books, 1970).

88. On an attempt to engage the two perspectives, see Burton Cooper, "How Does God Act in America? An Invitation to a Dialogue between Process and Liberation Theologies," *USQR* 32 (1976): 25–35. See also Robert T. Osborn, "The Rise and Fall of the Bible in Recent American Theology," *Duke Divinity School Review* 41 (1976): 57–72.

89. Miles, "Gagging on Job," 110.

and cannot be changed to history understood the same way, however, is not a difficult one. Such an understanding of the trajectory does not, of course, imply a criticism of the persons who work in the trajectory, for they themselves may be passionate in other directions. The *Tendenz* itself inclines toward uninterrupted development. Moreover, that *Tendenz* has a remarkable capacity to co-opt and contain the specific angularities of the other tradition, as, for example, Solomon containing the ark in the temple.

3. Conversely, the various liberation theologies in their epistemological abrasiveness likely may be located on the trajectory rooted in Moses. They are inclined to focus on the concreteness of historical memory and regard more sweeping, unitive statements as less important and compelling. Current scholarly work in this trajectory (*a*) is likely not so directly concerned with contact with cultural forms and values but is addressed to a particular faith community living in uneasy tension with the dominant cultural forms and values; (*b*) is most likely to be lodged in a confessing community or a school of it (it is inclined to be concerned primarily with the faithful effectiveness of the confessing community and to believe that the dominant rationality will permit no ready point of contact without co-opting; and, if the scholar is lodged in a university context, it is still likely the case that the main referent is a confessing group); and (*c*) is likely to have an intrinsic bias toward social, ethical radicalness; this does not mean, of course, that in every case the person involved is socially radical, for he or she may in fact be conservative; but the practice of this scholarship will predictably lead to the surfacing of such issues, even without the person intentionally doing so.

The pursuit of this paradigm of trajectories from early Israel until current scholarship, informed as it is by sociological considerations, is important in two ways, both affirming that there is no disinterestedness in the text or in the interpreter. Such a paradigm will permit texts to be understood more effectively in terms of their placement in Israel's faith and life and in the traditioning process. Such a paradigm will regularly force more attention to the interest and hermeneutical presuppositions of the interpreter and his and her community of reference. The pursuit of these trajectories may be a major service biblical study can offer to colleagues in other disciplines, for it may provide ground from which to do serious criticism. This discernment might lead one to expect a very different kind of scholarship, each faithful to a stream of tradition, depending on the context of the interpreter.

2

Covenant as a Subversive Paradigm

I{T IS A BIT} IRONIC that increased attention is being paid to the biblical theme of covenant just at a time when biblical scholarship is moving on to other constructs for interpretation. Clearly, "covenant" is not the single overarching theme of the Bible as previously claimed. Nonetheless, it has important potential for the church in our situation. The central affirmations of covenant stand against and subvert the dominant forms, patterns, and presuppositions of our culture and of cultural Christianity. The subversion (which means undermining and exposure to dismantling) is directed against a theology that knows too much, a God who is too strong, a church that is too allied with triumphalist culture, and a ministry that moves too much from strength.

Against all of these, the covenant theme offers an alternative perception of how things are in heaven and how they could be on earth. Covenant as a recharacterization of God, church, and world is not simply a restatement of conventional Western assumptions; it requires drastically new affirmations. Attention to the theme exposes the failure of a remote God who has not triumphed, a church that has not known so much, and a culture that has not kept its promises.

A God Who Embraces

Everything depends on our confession of God. The covenanting God of the Bible is not to be understood according to the general category "god." Making a theoretical case that this God is unique is not necessary; it is enough to note that in the Bible this God makes a break with all cultural definitions and expectations and stands distant from the other gods who are preoccupied with their rule, their majesty, their well-being in the plush silence of heaven. This is nowhere more vividly stated than in Psalm 82, in which the general self-serving notion of godhood is harshly rejected. The temptation of the church is to force this God back into conventional modes. But the stories of Israel and the church's memories will not have it so. That deep resistance to general categories is most important to those who care for the stories and memories of the church.

In the tradition of Moses, and from then on, this God breaks with the other gods, finding their company boring and their preoccupations inane. The heaven occupied by the other gods is no place for covenanting. Those gods offer no model for faithful interrelatedness, for steadfast solidarity, but only for occasional self-serving alliances. The primal disclosure of the Bible is that this God in heaven makes a move toward earth to identify a faithful covenant partner, responding to the groans of oppressed people (Exod. 2:24-25). We say it is an irreversible move. And the partner now embraced is identified as the "rabble" of slaves that no other god thought "worthy" (Exod. 12:38; Num. 11:4; cf. Luke 7:22-23; 1 Pet. 2:9-10).

This move is decisive not only for earth but for heaven; not only for the slaves embraced but for the God who embraces. It is central to covenant that this One cannot embrace without being transformed by the ones who are embraced. There is no immunity for God here; embracing a partner is not an afterthought but is definitional for God. And the evidence of Scripture is that Israel and the church continued to battle for this discernment of God, always against the temptation to drive God back to heaven, to squeeze God back into the safety, serenity, and irrelevance of the other gods. And that is still the decisive battle in the church.

A New Beginning

The break that God makes is to leave the self-sufficient world of the gods for the sake of groaning humanity. It is the key disclosure to Moses, without which there would be no exodus. Israel is invited to break with pharaoh's "sacred canopy" of oppression precisely because this God has made a break with the boredom of the canopy of heaven. And while that disclosure moves through the long memory of Israel and the church, none has understood it in greater depth than Hosea. It is he who penetrates to the heart of God, who understands that God struggles against conventional godhood (Hos. 11:8), and who finally decides not to operate by conventions, either of heaven or of earth (11:9).

These verses show Hosea in deep conflict with the model of a God who strikes back when offended for the sake of God's own majestic self-definition. But this God does not and will not do that. And the upshot of the anguish of this God in Hosea is that covenant is possible, not because of a suitable partner but because this God has broken with conventions to new kinds of solidarity:

> I will allure her to the wilderness [and begin again];
> I will speak to her heart [and start over]; . . .
> I will betroth you to me in righteousness,
> > in justice,
> > in loyalty,
> > in mercy,
> > in faithfulness,
> and you shall know me. (Hos. 2:14, 19-20)

This anguished poet affirms that there is a new beginning possible on earth. It is possible because God in heaven has committed all godhood to the wayward partner. God has no other claim to make, no special exemptions, but stays with the sorry partner; in the process, both are changed. Hosea has understood as well as anyone that God's committed grief for the partner is the only ground for newness on earth. That is the ground now to be confessed, proclaimed, and practiced among us.

What a God!

> He was despised and rejected by men and women,
> > acquainted with grief,
> > as one from whom they hide their faces.
> He was despised and we esteemed him not. (Isa. 53:3)

This God bears none of the marks of a god. This God has given up power in the certainty that real saving power is found in uncompromising faithfulness, the very posture the other gods in heaven could not countenance.

Everything Is at Stake

Perhaps that is too familiar to us, so familiar we miss how subversive it is. To test its subversive impact, one need only teach it and preach it. For it represents a break with conventional theology. It calls into question the self-sufficiency of God, the entire catechetical tradition of a God without solidarity with earthly partners whom this God values and makes valuable. The conventional God of the catechisms makes all the caring moves *after* everything is settled and there is nothing at stake for the Strong One. But here it is affirmed that not everything is settled in advance. Very much is at stake for God—godhood itself is recharacterized and redecided in company with and in the presence of the mixed multitude.

That is the deep issue in covenant. Does one (God or human) come to the covenantal relationship with everything settled? Or does one come with everything to be redecided? Both postures are offered in the Bible, but it is this radical posture of Moses and Hosea that has the possibility of subverting the death systems around us.

Everything is at stake in this question. Covenant requires a radical break not only with uncritical, scholastic notions of God but also with contemporary views that vote for detachment. Our current consumer culture has need of an irrelevant God for whom nothing is at issue, a kind of indifferent, immune guarantor. Such a God is challenged and destroyed in the claim of covenant. The alternative God of the Bible is impinged upon and exposed. There is no immune quarter, no answer in the back of the book, no safe conduct.

Everything is at stake because how we judge it to be in heaven is the way we imagine it to be on earth. If our mistaken notion leads us to an impassive, self-sufficient God in heaven, then the model for humanity, for Western culture, for ourselves, is that we should also be self-sufficient, impassive, beyond need, not to be imposed on. Willy-nilly, we will be made in the image of some God. The one for whose image we have settled is a sure, triumphant God who runs no risks, makes no commitments, embraces no pain that is definitional. Against that, the covenanting God of the Bible protests and invites us to protest.

Let none among us imagine that the right discernment of God does not matter. On that point, everything is at issue in a culture now in deep failure. The question is whether there is an alternative affirmation to make that can let us recharacterize how it is in heaven and how it might be on earth. Hosea stands as an assertion that only in this alternative God is there ground for hope, possibility for passion, and energy to keep on. It is no different in the New Testament: "This man receives sinners and eats with them"—that is, makes covenant with them (Luke 15:2). This God prefers covenant partners with whom things are yet to be decided, rejecting a situation—in heaven or on earth—where nothing is in question. In such contexts, it is impossible to be genuinely human—or faithfully divine.

A Community on Earth

Along the way we can redecide our notion of church. The covenant construct permits us and requires us to think afresh about the character and business of the church. That is, the move God has made in heaven opens up for us a new agenda: What is possible on earth? God's move to solidarity is a hint that solidarity on earth is possible. And that covenantal theme permits a new ecclesiology. The church is the community attentive to the dangers and possibilities of solidarity in a culture that thrives on and celebrates our divisions and isolations.

Said another way, there will be no new community on earth until there is a fresh articulation of who God is. What the church can be depends on that. There will be no community on earth so long as we rally round old God-claims of self-sufficiency and omnipotence. And the reason is that self-sufficient, omnipotent, isolated, impassive people (reflective of such false gods) are incapable of being in community or embracing any solidarity.

The promise of the new community on earth is made especially by Jeremiah: "Behold, the days are coming, says the Lord, when I will make a new covenant with the house of Israel and the house of Judah" (31:31). It is important that Jeremiah, most anguished of the prophets, speaks this hope, for only one in anguish could hope so deeply. It is equally important that he speaks this anticipation precisely at a time of historical brokenness when there seems no ground for hope. The new community he anticipates is not to be derived from the old shattered one. It depends only and singularly on a new move from God, a response to groans. It is this move that makes possible what was not possible before the groans were received and embraced.

That, of course, is not very realistic sociology. But new community is proclaimed in the Bible on the basis of the new move from God, just at the time when the best possibilities of sociology are exhausted. We are in such a time now, when there is no sociological possibility about which to speak. So we are pressed to speak to each other about this most unlikely thing, a move of solidarity made by God, a move that makes all things new on earth—even human covenanting.

Large Human Questions

The new community now to be proclaimed and called into being bears at least three marks, according to Jeremiah.

1. It is *a community of God's torah:* "I will put my torah in their midst" (31:33; the translation "within them" is excessive personalizing). The new covenant anticipated here is one whose content is torah (to which we do a disservice if we render it "law"). Torah that marks the new community is not a practice of law to clobber people, not a censure to expel and scold people, not a picky legalism. It is rather a release from small moralisms to see things through the eyes of God's passion and anguish. The torah is a reminder that God's will focuses on large human questions and that we also may focus on weighty matters of justice, mercy, and righteousness.

There are seeds here for genuine reform within the community, a reform of communities of *indifference* that do not care much about anything except their own well-being. Torah turns the community from self to the neighbor. And there is a call here away from communities of *triviality* that imagine too much is at stake too soon and too often in every question that comes up. The torah of the biblical God is not written in fine print or with footnotes. It is there in its rich, broad claims for holiness and justice. Foundational torah calls this community away from its self-serving fascinations.

2. The new community of covenant is in *solidarity about the knowledge of God:* "They shall all know me, from the least of these to the greatest" (Jer. 31:34). "Knowing God" is crucial for covenanting. Since this God has made a move to earth, there is no knowledge of God that can focus on the things of heaven to the disregard of the affairs of earth. And, conversely, there is no preoccupation with the things of earth without awareness that disruptive covenanting has caused a break in heaven.

Knowledge of God calls this community away from its many other knowledges that betray and divide. José Miranda has made clear that "knowledge of God" is attentiveness to the needs of brothers and sisters (Jer. 22:13-17).[1] He does not mean that this derives from or comes after knowledge of God; rather, the two are synonymous. One could scarcely imagine a more radical and subversive theological claim. And the matter is the same in the new community of the New Testament. Love of God is intimately and inextricably linked to loving brother and sister (1 John 4:20-21).

The new "knowledge of God" envisioned here does two things. First, it minimizes the importance of much of our knowledge, our expertise and professional skills (1 Cor. 13:2). A different kind of knowing is what is needed. Second, the new knowledge now entrusted to this community (the very antithesis of gnostic secrets) is radically democratized. The least as well as the greatest shall know. The strong and the weak know together (see Rom. 14:1-23). The credentialed and the uncredentialed share the gift. The word to the strong in the community is that the weak ones know some very important dimensions of the news, to which we must all attend. The word to us all is that within the church there are no monopolies on this knowledge, not by wealth or longevity or gender or anything else. Democratizing knowledge in the community is a threat to all of us who preside over the establishment, for we have long known that knowledge, even in the church, is power.

But the knowledge now broadly entrusted is not just "personal experience," not a subjective inclination about this or that. It is a discernment of the "news," of the gospel, of the move God has made to earth where the torah is given. In New Testament categories, the knowledge commonly entrusted to us is knowledge of the *cross,* a sense about how the empty cross bestows life. That is a knowledge that is deeply subversive and now definitional for covenant.

3. The third mark of the community envisioned is that *it knows about, experiences, and practices forgiveness:* "I will forgive their iniquity and I will remember their sin no more" (Jer. 31:34). It is not Lutheran reductionism to say that the single crucial sign of the church is the practice of forgiveness. And that means at least two things. First, the past should be past. Our posture toward each other should not be a grudging, careful management of old hurts but rather a genuine yielding of the past for a hope.

Second, forgiveness is not simply a "spiritual" notion but includes a genuine redistribution of power. Our communities are often organized by bad memories, configurations of mistakes, and seasoned

---

1. José Miranda, *Marx and the Bible* (Maryknoll, N.Y.: Orbis, 1974).

fears. The community of forgiveness means a redress of power in which the weak and the strong, the least and the greatest, really derive their life from each other (see Mark 10:42-44).

Of course, these marks of the covenant community are not new among us. But they characterize a subversive ecclesiology in deep conflict with our conventions. It is important to see how extensively our usual notions of community are refuted here—notions either of communities of *fate* (into which we are locked without choice) or of *convenience* (in which we have no serious or abiding stake). Against both of those, we are to have a *called* community—not a voluntary association but a people addressed and bound in a concrete and abiding loyalty.

Covenant for the World

Finally, we may rearticulate our covenantal hope for the world. So long as this subversive paradigm is kept to God and church, we are safe enough. Its character of surprise and threat becomes clear when the covenant is related to the world beyond the believing community. The covenantal paradigm affirms that the world we serve and for which we care is a world yet to be liberated. A theology of covenanting is not worth the effort unless it leads to energy and courage for mission.

So we are pressed to ask: What might be expected yet for the world? The response is that the world is intended by God to be a community that covenants, that distributes its produce equally, that values all its members, and that brings the strong and the weak together in common work and common joy. Though it is not yet that kind of community, we are assured that soon or late it will be (see Rev. 11:15). And the mission of the believing community is to articulate, anticipate, and practice the transformation that is sure to come.

In the tradition of Hosea and Jeremiah, here we may appeal especially to Isaiah of the exile. One might have expected a poet to exiles to be preoccupied with that little community dealing with its own identity and survival. But this poet has a large vision indeed. And so his words serve to extend and urge the vision of Israel away from itself to the world in which it is placed. The word spoken here begins with a statement about God's move, "I am the Lord," and goes on to call to Israel, who is given for others. But finally, as Israel looks beyond itself, the covenant passes to the world of need, darkness, and prison (Isa. 42:6-7; 49:6).

The poet will not permit Israel to think too long about itself. And so he uses the word "covenant" precisely to speak about mission to others. The crucial phrase is enigmatic, "a covenant to the people." How is this people to be linked to the other people? In covenant? As covenant? It suggests, perhaps, that Israel is a *mediator* toward the others, so that through Israel the other peoples receive the blessings of God. Or perhaps the call is to act as the *partner*, to be in solidarity with those others who are still alienated.

To Know, to Hope, to Expect

What is in any case clear is that covenanting becomes a way to think about the nations and kingdoms of the earth, a way requiring risk, emotion, and solidarity. Covenanting, it is believed and affirmed in this poetry, is the way all of society is intended to be with its markings of justice, freedom, abundance, and compassion. And the people addressed by the poet are to work toward that transformation and not give up on the world.

That is, the faithful community knows something about the world, hopes something for the world, and expects something of the world. What it knows and hopes and expects is that the world is to be transformed. That is in itself no mean ministry: to know, to hope, and to expect. And that, perhaps, is the most important and most subversive thing the church can now do: to refuse to give up on the world and its promised transformation. Those who are victimized by the world in its present order need most of all voices of assurance that what now exists is not the way of the future. Such a voice is always subversive because it goes against our usual presuppositions and against the way the present order wants us to think. We have grown so accustomed to the disorders and inequalities that beset us that we do not expect it to be otherwise. And that is because we believe the world to be autonomous, set on its own course, with no possibility of transformation or intervention. We act as though the world gets to vote on its long-term future.

We have grown accustomed to the ways in which institutions are self-serving, in which every institution serves primarily its functionaries in order to preserve jobs and enhance personal well-being. This is true of government, court, school, hospital, and church. Because the forms of public life are so complex, we despair of change. We expect ourselves and certainly others to be exploited. And we do not imagine that it can be otherwise.

But against all that, this poet of the exile, who knew about the pathos of Hosea and the promise of Jeremiah, flings his dangerous words. He conjures life alternatively as a genuine homecoming. He asserts that a condition of alienation and displacement is not our final destiny; there will be a homecoming of transformation. And the company and followers of this poet (which means us) keep the dream alive. Surely he had to speak of things he did not understand. But he clearly believes (1) that the world is not closed, fixed, or settled; (2) that institutions can be changed and transformed; and (3) that communities of people can be practitioners of other ways of living.

The entire poetry of Isaiah of the exile has a tilt toward freedom and liberation and justice. Those are the ingredients of a covenanted homecoming. His lyrical envisioning of a new possibility is given in the presence of and in argument against the Babylonian gods, Babylonian kings, and Babylonian definitions of reality (see chaps. 46 and 47). This subversive poetry has an unavoidable political realism. It knows that the yearned-for liberation will not happen until there is a dismantling of imperial definitions of reality. That is where the missional activity of Israel is called to be—defiantly and buoyantly against every imperial definition of reality. And so he speaks with nerve and authority, believing that his speech is not idle or futile but that it plays a part in the dismantling.

We live in a time of domesticated hopes, weary voices, and co-opted imaginations. Now is not a good time to join issue with the enslaving structures of the day (see Amos 5:13). And those who have worked at such a calling lately have good reason to stop in futility. But the poet knows better. The poet knows that, even in a world like ours, songs must be sung, dreams must be kept, visions must be practiced. And none of it yields to the despairing cynicism that the Babylonians want so much to encourage.

There is in this poetry no large or sustained strategy. We may note two simple features that likely are decisive. First, in the familiar words of 52:13—53:12, the world is to be *transformed* precisely by one who is *deformed* (53:2-3). And his deforming is for the "many" who lie beyond the immediate community (see 53:11-12). Thus, we must be asking about deformity. Second, in the derivative song of 61:1-4 (cf. Luke 4:18-19), it is by *the action of the spirit* that the dream is mounted and practiced. And where the spirit is quenched, there the mission is domesticated.

The New Covenant

The three belong closely together: a *God* who makes covenant by making a move toward the partner (Hos. 2:14, 18-20); a *community* that practices covenant by the new forms of torah, knowledge, and forgiveness (Jer. 31:31-34); and a *world* yet to be transformed to covenanting, by the dismantling of imperial reality (Isa. 42:6-7; 49:6).

That is how the battle is joined. These alternatives given us in the prophets are subversive. They mean to controvert conventional, non-covenantal loyalties. These three elements belong together and are inseparable. And they are entrusted to our ministry. These affirmations were a fragile minority report in ancient Israel by this line of prophets, who had so little power in their time. The likes of Hosea, Jeremiah, and Isaiah in exile mattered little. These affirmations are a fragile minority report when they come to embodiment in Jesus of Nazareth, who had so little power. And they also are no less a minority report in the fragility of our common ministry.

What we have claimed for these three poets is not new. But that makes it no less urgent. And the question presents itself: How do we stay at it? How do we not yield these radical convictions? I submit that it is in this: these subversive alternatives of God/church/world must be kept close to the eucharistic table where we eat and drink in covenant. The cup poured out for you is the *new covenant* in my blood (Luke 22:20); this cup is the *new covenant* in my blood (1 Cor. 11:25). Whenever we eat this bread and drink this wine, we engage in a subversive minority report. Precisely because of being broken and poured out, this bread and wine will never be fully accommodated to the interests of the old age. The world wants the bread unbroken and the wine still filling the cup. The world yearns for unrisking gods and transformed humanity. But in our eating and drinking at this table we know better. We will not have these subversive alternatives rendered void.

Undoubtedly covenantal discernments will become more dangerous in time to come as resources shrink, as we grow more fearful, as our public world continues to disintegrate. And therefore it is very important that we do not lose heart. Everything is at stake.

3

Covenant and Social Possibility

THE LAST GENERATION of Old Testament studies, largely through the work of George Mendenhall[1] and Klaus Baltzer,[2] has established not only that covenant is a pervasive biblical notion but also that this "religious theme" carries with it important socio-economic, political counterparts. To the extent that covenant asserts what is distinctive in the Bible, it requires different thinking about God and different acting in the world.

I

The Bible is a dispute about the identity and character of the true God. Israel's life is initiated and sustained by Yahweh, the giver of life. But Israel is always tempted and seduced by alternative gods and loyalties (see Hos. 2:8). The polemical question is always, "To whom will you compare me? Who is like Yahweh?" (Exod. 15:11; Isa. 40:18; 44:7).[3] The answer of course is that there is no God like Yahweh,

1. George Mendenhall, *Law and Covenant in Israel and the Ancient Near East* (Pittsburgh: Biblical Colloquium, 1955); idem, "The Conflict between Value Systems and Social Control," in *Unity and Diversity*, ed. Hans Goedicke and J. J. M. Roberts (Baltimore: Johns Hopkins Univ. Press, 1975), 169–80; and idem, *The Tenth Generation* (Baltimore: Johns Hopkins Univ. Press, 1973), chaps. 1, 7, 8.

2. Klaus Baltzer, *The Covenant Formula* (Philadelphia: Fortress, 1971).

3. See C. J. Labuschagne, *The Incomparability of Yahweh in the Old Testament* (Leiden: Brill, 1966).

who is the God who intervenes powerfully on behalf of the poor and the marginal in the face of oppressive power. Such a claim is at the center and heart of the biblical assertion. This God is not known in any speculative or theoretical way but always through acts of social intervention and inversion that create possibilities of human life in contexts where the human spirit has been crushed (see Isa. 57:15) and human possibility choked off.

Three examples of this strange solidarity that Yahweh shows for the weak against the strong:

1. *The Song of Moses (Exod. 15:1-18)* is commonly regarded as a very early liberation song that narrates the entire early memory of Israel.[4] The concrete claim is that Yahweh has triumphed over horse and rider (v. 1), who are in fact the imperial masters of the Egyptian empire (v. 4). The outcome of the triumph is that the imperial slaves are given a homeland (v. 17). Between the triumph and the settlement is the doxology of verses 11-12, which celebrates the distinctiveness of Yahweh, the only one who enacts such a transformational possibility in the face of imperial power.

2. In *Isaiah 46* the same contrast of the gods is offered. The gods of Babylon are named only to be ridiculed as powerless. They cannot save (v. 2). The contrast is made with Yahweh who can "carry, bear, carry, save" (v. 4). Indeed it is this God who has summoned Cyrus ("bird of prey" [v. 11]) to put an end to the Babylonian empire and who creates new life for the exiles. The indignant, polemical question of comparison occurs again in verse 5. The contrast is clear and sharp. The gods of the empire are too enmeshed in silver and gold (that is, surplus value [v. 6]) and so have no power to save. By contrast, Yahweh has no involvement with such surplus value but has power to save. As the gods of Babylon are allied with the oppressive *Egypt* state that guards the surplus value, so Yahweh is allied with the liberated possibility of homecoming. The absence of silver and gold is related to the power to save (on which see Acts 3:6) and the power of the church to heal.

3. The dispute among the gods is most clearly articulated in *Psalm*

---

4. On the primal character of this song and its liberation tendency, see David N. Freedman, "Divine Names and Titles in Early Hebrew Poetry," in *Magnalia Dei: The Mighty Acts of God,* ed. Frank M. Cross, Werner E. Lemke, and Patrick D. Miller Jr. (Garden City, N.Y.: Doubleday, 1976), 57–60, 85–98; and Patrick D. Miller Jr., *The Divine Warrior in Early Israel* (Cambridge, Mass.: Harvard Univ. Press, 1973), 113–17. On the liberation trajectory of the Song of Miriam, see Gail R. O'Day, "Singing Woman's Song: A Hermeneutic of Liberation," *CurTM* 12 (1985): 203–10.

82, a more formal encounter. The high God (Yahweh) puts the other gods on trial for their refusal to act like real gods. In verses 3-4, a proposal is offered for what constitutes "godness":

> Give justice to the weak and the fatherless;
>   maintain the right of the destitute and the afflicted.
> Rescue the weak and the needy,
>   deliver them from the hand of the wicked.

Then the psalm goes on to judge and condemn those gods who will not engage in this action of solidarity.

These three texts (Exod. 15:1-18; Isaiah 46; Psalm 82) summarize the biblical polemic that contrasts Yahweh with the other gods. To be sure, the term "covenant" does not occur in these texts, but our theme of covenant does not admit of a simple lexical analysis.[5] What we notice in all of these texts is that Yahweh is a God who forcefully, decisively, and willingly enters into solidarity with a group of helpless people. That solidarity is for the benefit of people who cannot act for themselves. That solidarity is an act of risk for Yahweh, for it puts Yahweh in conflict with other gods and with the awesome power of the empire. It is this act of enduring, risky solidarity that most decisively characterizes the God of the Bible. In all parts of the Bible, this solidarity marks God's person and shapes history. Even if it is not lexically explicit, that capacity and willingness of God to enter into enduring, risky solidarity are what we mean by covenant. The God of the Bible is a God who makes covenant. The object of that solidarity is characteristically the weak, poor, and marginal, who without such a partner have no voice or visibility in history as it is ordered by the empire. Thus, it is in the very character of this God to be engaged for and available to those without social power or social possibility.[6] It is this mark of God that gives revolutionary impetus to the witness of biblical faith.

To characterize God as the one who makes and keeps covenants has immediate theological implications: (1) It means that issues of human justice and human dignity are always primary and never derivative or optional. (2) It means that this God is best char-

---

5. James Barr, "Some Semantic Notes on the Covenant," in *Beiträge zur Alttestamentlichen Theologie: Festschrift für Walter Zimmerli zum 70. Geburtstag* (Göttingen: Vandenhoeck und Ruprecht, 1977), 23–38.

6. For a fine summary of this data, see Thomas Hanks, *God So Loved the Third World: The Biblical Vocabulary of Oppression* (Maryknoll, N.Y.: Orbis, 1983).

acterized in relational, political categories and not in the conventional theological categories of self-sufficiency, such as omnipotence, omnipresence, and omniscience, or in private categories of psychological-spiritual inclination. Neither set of such categories expresses the radical historical, relational character of Yahweh. (3) It means that this God is characteristically in profound tension with the other gods, each of which tends to be a legitimator of imperial power of one kind or another. In challenging the gods, Yahweh also enters into tension with oppressive power in the world.

This characterization of God is central and decisive for the Bible. Though the categories have shifted, I submit that this characterization of God becomes decisive for the identification of Jesus in the Gospel tradition. In Luke 7:18-22, John the Baptist asks for evidence that Jesus is "the one who is to come." Jesus provides no data for such classical categories but affirms that "the blind receive their sight, the lame walk, lepers are cleansed, and the deaf hear, the dead are raised up, the poor have good news preached to them" (v. 22). This line of reasoning is congruent with the Old Testament we have cited. Where there is intervention on behalf of the powerless, the holy, covenanting power of God is at work. This radical liberation tendency belongs to and is derived from the central covenant texts of the Bible. Covenanting is an assertion that vulnerable relationships of solidarity constitute an alternative way to organize the world. It is evident that not all parts of the Bible share in this perspective. In the Old Testament, the traditions of creation, monarchy, and wisdom present a very different sense of God. They do not fit easily in the paradigm of covenant. I suggest this is important evidence that even in the Bible itself, the radical subversive notion of God as a covenanter is in dispute. To give the covenant theme emphasis is faithful to a main part of the Bible, but the emphasis reflects at the same time a quite important interpretative decision. It is to decide that of all the things the Bible has to say about God, this one is judged to be normative. This is a perfectly legitimate decision, but it is not the only possible one.

II

The idea of covenant is not simply a discussion and clarification about the character of God. Israel understands that every notion of God carries with it a proposal for the organization of society. Thus the theological revolution articulated in Psalm 82, where Yahweh asserts a new mode of "godness," carries with it revolutionary ideas of society when the community is organized around the metaphor of covenant.

The social radicalness of covenant had already been recognized by Martin Buber, who presented the covenant making at Mount Sinai as the enactment of the kingship of Yahweh, which implied the delegitimation of every other political authority.[7] The covenantal notion that Yahweh is king (and Israel is Yahweh's kingdom) is a peculiar juxtaposition of a religious term, "God," and a political category, "kingdom," so that the rule of Yahweh is given political, social concreteness. Israel's public life in political and economic relations is to embody the covenantal solidarity Yahweh practices toward Israel in the exodus, in answering its cry of helplessness and hopelessness (Exod. 2:23-25).

It has been Norman Gottwald more than any other scholar who has seen the far-reaching implications of covenant in relation to social theory.[8] Gottwald's controversial (but I believe compelling) proposal is that early Israel introduced covenant practice and covenant theory as an alternative to the statism known both in the Egyptian empire and in the Canaanite city-states. That statism was a system of administering land and people for the sake of a socioeconomic monopoly, so that some (peasants) worked for the production of surplus value to be enjoyed and controlled by others who did not work.[9] In presenting this hypothesis, Gottwald rejects the evolutionary hypothesis that the covenant community "developed" into an empire and asserts the counterproposal that Israel as a covenanted community represents a radical, intentional, abrupt break in social organization. Israel is "a social experiment" in the world of the ancient Near East to see if a community can be organized in egalitarian (covenantal) patterns, in resistance to the hierarchal, bureaucratic modes of the world of the city-states. The alternative model of social organization seeks to distribute power so that all members are

---

7. Martin Buber, *Kingship of God* (New York: Harper and Row, 1967).

8. Norman Gottwald, *The Tribes of Yahweh* (Maryknoll, N.Y.: Orbis, 1979).

9. On the futility curses, see Delbert R. Hillers, *Treaty-curses and the Old Testament Prophets* (Rome: Pontifical Biblical Institute, 1964), 28–29. It is necessary not only to recognize the form of the futility curses but also to note their social function. The curses themselves anticipate a social system that makes life difficult because of usurpation and confiscation. Conversely, the nullification of such curses (Amos 9:14; Isa. 65:21-22) concerns a new social system that does not practice such usurpation.

treated with dignity, so that all members have access to social goods and social power.

We may identify three blocks of texts that illuminate the thesis that covenantal social theory intends a just, egalitarian social order and process.

1. The narrative justification for such a social possibility is laid down in strident terms in *Exodus 1–15*. To be sure, covenant is not explicitly mentioned here. But it is the dramatic move of Israel, generation after generation, to assert the possibility of such a community. The drama begins in the oppression of Israel (chap. 1) and ends with the celebration of freedom from bondage (15:1-18, 21). The narrative moves from oppression to freedom by way of the summons to Moses (chaps. 3–4), the announcement of Yahweh's intentionality (3:1-14), and the contest between Yahweh and the empire (chaps. 5–11), until it is asserted that Yahweh makes a distinction in behalf of Israel (11:7) and that Yahweh fights for Israel against Egypt (14:14, 25). Gottwald's analysis asserts that the Israel of this narrative is not an ethnic community but a social conglomerate of "tribes," that is, bonded communities that have withdrawn from the claims of the empire or the city-state in order to organize life differently.

Two observations may be made about this narrative foundation. First, Yahweh is a key and decisive actor in the narrative. There is no doubt that this is a theological report in which Yahweh evokes and legitimates the alternative community of justice. But it is equally clear that this is not simply a religious account, for it has to do with the decisive delegitimation of an oppressive, noncovenanting regime. Second, while this narrative is rooted in concrete memory, its shape and function are to serve liturgic reiteration and reenactment so that each new generation is inducted into the rage and resentment against totalitarianism, and into hope and buoyancy toward an alternative social possibility. Each new generation in Israel is taught to read social reality so that the justice questions, that the issues of social power, social goods, and social access, are made major community issues and major concerns of the God of Israel. Israel thus makes the justice issues central in its narrative of God. The issues are not extrinsic or optional but belong to the very core of the narrative.

2. The narrative of *Gen. 47:13-26* appears to be simply a telling of a land-organizing program. But in fact it is a sharp, partisan, and militant piece of social analysis and social criticism. It is placed as a

preface to the exodus narrative to explain how free Israel got into its situation of economic bondage. The process of enslavement consists of the way land is monopolized through a totalitarian regime that finally owns all the means of production (land, cattle). Those without means of production are reduced to helpless subjects of the empire.[10]

It is worth noting that this narrative (in contrast to the exodus narrative) is pure economic social analysis without mention of God. What Israel studies here is the way in which political power, not committed to covenantal norms and values, can reduce people to servitude and helplessness.

3. One task that Israel practices in its texts is the retelling of the foundational narrative. The other major task portrayed is the building of social structures and institutions that will order, sustain, and guarantee the covenant community. All the "torah-law" of the Old Testament, in one way or another, is an attempt to organize concrete social relations around this radical theological vision. This is of course a long, complicated process with successes and failures. But in the end, I suggest, we should mostly be amazed at the achievement. To be sure, Israel drew on legal, political traditions of the Near East. But in its main enterprise, Israel sought to do something without precedent, that is, to order public life around the vision of Yahweh's freedom and justice.

It is peculiarly the tradition of Deuteronomy in which Israel applies the notion of covenant to social relations as a warrant for justice. The legal tradition of *Deuteronomy 12–25* is not a neatly ordered statement, but it consistently bears witness to Israel's radical social vision.

a. The tradition of Deuteronomy opposes images and idols because it knows that such religious equipment reflects surplus value and characteristically reflects monopolies of goods, land, and wealth.

b. Deuteronomy has a peculiar and persistent propensity for the poor and marginal and continually urges generosity and attentiveness toward widows, orphans, and sojourners, those who are legally and economically disinherited.[11]

---

10. Richard Rubenstein (*The Age of Triage: Fear and Hope in an Overcrowded World* [Boston: Beacon, 1983], 34–97) has made a powerful argument that certain kinds of land management, even if legitimated by law, serve as interests of social control and finally of triage.

11. On this emphasis in the tradition of Deuteronomy, see Moshe Weinfeld, *Deuteronomy and the Deuteronomic School* (Oxford: Clarendon, 1972), 282–97. We-

c. Deuteronomy takes special care to maintain the value, dignity, and respect for persons subject to abuse, including runaway slaves (Deut. 23:15-16), day laborers (24:14-15), the poor who are indebted (24:10-13), and those subjected to public punishment (25:1-3).

d. Perhaps most interesting, Deuteronomy is concerned to establish institutions that will order life in covenantal ways, for example, kingship (17:14-20), prophecy (18:9-22), courts (17:8-13), and cities of refuge (19:1-10).[12] Here the covenantal tradition is at its most imaginative because it believed that public power can and should be administered in just ways.

In commenting on this ethic, we should mention the remarkable analysis of Fernando Belo,[13] who has seen that the legal-covenantal tradition of debt cancellation stands in deep tension with the tradition of purity, which is characteristically a conservative social practice designed to maintain the status quo. We do not pay primary attention to that legal tradition here because it appears to be in serious tension with the central covenantal enterprise.

III

The metaphor of covenant mediates to us *a very different mode of God,* one that has broken with the scholastic categories of absoluteness for the sake of marginality. That same metaphor mediates to us *a very different notion of social life and social practice.* It repudiates conventional modes of social organizations that are exploitative and hierarchical in favor of equity, justice, and compassion. The two mediations (of a different mode of God and a different notion of social life and social practice) go together. The absoluteness of God is appropriate for a society that is structured in unequal ways and does not intend to change. The attentiveness of God to the marginal, on the other hand, is a warrant for a social vision strongly attentive to marginality. But the metaphor of covenant offers not only a general model for God and for society. It impinges upon concrete situations, two of which we here consider.

infeld provides a most helpful summary, even if one does not follow his critical assumptions.

12. Norbert Lohfink (*Great Themes of the Old Testament* [Edinburgh: T. and T. Clark, 1982], 55–75) has argued that Deuteronomy offers a constitution for ordering public life in an intentional way.

13. Fernando Belo, *A Materialist Reading of the Gospel of Mark* (Maryknoll, N.Y.: Orbis, 1981).

1. In *Jer. 34:8-22*, a crisis is reported in Jerusalem in the last days before the Babylonian invasion. The narrative account is presented in three parts:

a. Verses 8-10 report that Zedekiah made a covenant and all the leading citizens joined in that covenant. The substance of that covenant is that all slaves should be set free of their bondage. We are not told why this radical decision is made at this critical point. But it is important that the *vow of a covenant* has the *substance of liberation.* To make a social commitment that is beyond conventional social expectation in this way moves in the direction of valuing human life in new and daring ways. Thus the vow itself is an important act of covenantal imagination. Indeed the action in the context of covenant went so far as genuinely setting the slaves free. When it is recognized that such slaves in ancient Judah were likely people in bondage because they were poor and could not pay their bills, it is clear that this act of liberation implies cancellation of specific debts. The action is a decisive one concerning radical economic reorganization.

b. In verses 11-16, the citizens who had taken an oath and the initial act of emancipation reneged on their promise and their act. We are not told how or why. The "why" was probably that the economic risk proved either unthinkable or unnecessary. So they cancelled the emancipation, voided the liberation, and brought people back to debt bondage. Clearly the covenant has been violated.

What is most interesting about this account is that the report of the renege is divided into two related parts. In verses 13-14, in this social crisis, the prophet alludes to the paradigmatic covenant at Sinai, which is understood in relation to the liberation of exodus. The juxtaposition of exodus and Sinai-torah made explicit here indicates how the *event of liberation* and the *social practice of covenant* are fully teamed together. Israel will not have one without the other. Liberation is not an event without ongoing social implications. Covenant is a relationship not of control but of liberation. This memory explicitly quotes the torah provision that debt slaves, no matter how large the debt, cannot be held in bondage over six years. There are limits to the costs the "have-nots" can be held to pay to the "haves." The seventh-year liberation is an act of equalization in which the balance owed is simply cancelled. The text adds tersely, "They did not do it." Israel has found its covenantal social vision too expensive and too dangerous for the status quo.

The contemporary situation of the sixth century is juxtaposed to the exodus and Sinai memory in verses 14-16. What is fundamental to Israel's identity, namely liberation into covenant, is now an immediate issue. Verse 15 describes the positive action taken:

> You have repented,
> you did what was right in my eyes,
> you proclaimed liberty,
> you made covenant.

This fourfold list is worth noting. The repentance means to break with the conventional social practice that causes some to subjugate others for economic reasons. Judah in this very particular case makes a theological move that is at the same time an economic, neighborly act. It is a God-focused act of obedience, "right in my eyes." Specifically, it is an act of liberation, an act of covenant. The specific obedience to the torah provision of Deut. 16:1-8 is thus presented as a reenactment of the old claim of exodus and Sinai. In specific, the community has decided to be Israel. There is only one way to be Israel: to undertake covenant that requires liberation.

The negative counterpart of verse 16 is an indictment. God's name has been profaned by retaking the slaves (cf. Prov. 17:5; 14:31). The honor of God's name is established through the specific practice of neighbor love.

The third element, in verses 17-22, begins with the characteristically awesome prophetic "therefore." Then follows an extended judicial sentence dominated by God's first-person speech of negative intervention. Patrick D. Miller Jr. has shown how strict retribution is enacted so that the violation of covenant is matched precisely by punishment:[14]

> You did not proclaim liberty....I proclaim liberty of sword and famine.
> You broke covenant....You will be like the covenant calf, cut in two.

In verses 20-23, Yahweh has declared war against Judah. The violation of justice precludes peace either among the citizens or between Yahweh and the citizens. The failure to keep covenant is made more poignant by the contrasting narrative of chapter 35, which shows what covenant obedience is in fact like. This counternarrative asserts that covenant is not an impossible religious demand but a serious social possibility Israel can in fact perform (cf. Deut. 30:11-14).

---

14. Patrick D. Miller Jr., *Sin and Judgment in the Prophets* (Chico, Calif.: Scholars Press, 1982); idem, "Sin and Judgment in Jeremiah 34:17-22," *JBL* 103 (1984): 611–13.

The covenant is embodied in the act of liberating slaves. Violation of covenant consists in reclaiming slaves and undoing liberation. This leads to war declared by Yahweh against the covenant violators. The only way to peace with Yahweh (and we may believe in the community) is the practice of liberating covenant in human transactions. And that requires dealing justly in the midst of social inequality.

2. The second concrete example of covenant impinging on the public practice of the community is in *Neh. 5:1-13*. Nehemiah is engaged in rebuilding the city of Jerusalem, whose walls and institutions have long been in shambles. While the popular stereotype of Nehemiah (along with Ezra) among Christians is that he is engaged in a legalistic reconstruction, this text shows him adamant about serious economic reform. The movement of the passage is relatively simple:

a. The economic analysis of 5:1-5 exposes the trouble in the form of a lament. The situation of famine created an agricultural crisis that led to land mortgages (v. 3). Money needs to be borrowed to pay the imperial tax to the Persians (v. 4). The mortgages and taxes together caused debt slavery. (It is worth noticing how recurrent the theme of debt slavery is at the root of covenantal crisis, from the narrative of the exodus to Jeremiah 34 to this text.) The Jews had forfeited their "means of production" and so were hopelessly in debt.

b. Nehemiah, as the voice of the tradition, appeals to it and identifies the key problem as interest payments (vv. 6-8). The problem is not the taxes per se but the money that must be borrowed to pay taxes; and the interest rates then cause foreclosure and loss of property. That practice of mortgage and foreclosure is carried on between Jews, members of the covenanted community, and is not an exploitation by outsiders. In his harsh judgment, Nehemiah speaks of Jews as "brothers," a clear reference to covenantal solidarity. Nehemiah surely appeals to the old torah provision of Deut. 23:19-20, which prohibits interest within the community and explicitly uses the term "brothers." Covenanted people practice a different pattern of economic relationships.

c. In verses 9-13, Nehemiah leads an economic reform. The proposal is to cease charging interest, to return the confiscated land so that the disadvantaged may again take their place in the economic life of the community (vv. 10-11). In verses 12-13, the nobles and officials agree and take an oath to reorder economic life. The covenant clearly has immediate implications for the practice of public life. The power of the narrative is found in the consensus about fundamentals, in which the demands of torah and the claims of covenant override the immediate gains of unjust economic advantage.

From our study of Jeremiah 34 and Nehemiah 5, it becomes clear that covenant has direct and inescapable implications for economic relationships. Moreover, these texts suggest that matters of *economic justice* are prior to matters of *political peace.* That is, economic justice is a precondition to secure, viable, humane order in society. Such humane order as one might term peace is not possible until there is redress of economic disadvantage. In the two cases cited, such redress of inequity clearly requires some to forgo gains they have made, under the mandate of the torah, for the sake of communal well-being.

IV

To be sure, these small episodes in Jeremiah 34 and Nehemiah 5 do not amount to very much in terms of significant social change. They seem to be isolated events that stand against the general tendency of exploitation. The Bible is realistic and lacking in romanticism about society in covenantal modes. The Bible is not optimistic about reformist gains. On the other hand, the Bible clings passionately to the vision that eventually, in God's good time, this alternative covenantal model of social reality will indeed prevail. As covenant is a *memory rooted in the old traditions,* and as it is an *impetus for present practice* in concrete ways, so it is also a *resilient vision* in the Bible that God's covenantal ordering of public life will prevail over all exploitative, oppressive, inequitable systems. The concreteness of the covenantal vision in ancient Israel has its counterpart in the New Testament in the nonnegotiable conviction about God's coming kingdom. God's coming kingdom is the ordering of creation and the historical process around covenantal modes of power and relationship. Two texts of such determined hope may be cited.

1. First and best known is the promise of *Jer. 31:31-34.* Set in the midst of poetic oracles of promise, this familiar assertion anticipates a time to come in which God will initiate a new relationship with God's people. It will not be a covenant marked by disobedience, alienation, and hostility as in the past. It will be a quite different relationship marked in the following ways:

a. The new covenant will be grounded in forgiveness. That is the only antidote to disobedience. Perhaps it is not too much to suggest that as the relation with God is marked by forgiveness, so social, human relationships in this newly covenanted community are to be of the same kind. Such forgiveness may also mean the forgiveness of debts (Matt. 16:12), the end of bondage, the overcoming of social inequity.

   b. The new covenant concerns a community utterly committed to torah obedience. The new covenant does not mean an end to the law but a readiness and capability of obedience to torah (cf. Matt. 5:17-20). A community so committed to the torah would be one in which justice, mercy, compassion, and righteousness characterize all relationships, in contrast to the present pursuit of knowledge, power, and wealth at the expense of the neighbor (cf. Jer. 9:23-24).

   c. The new community will be marked by "knowledge of Yahweh." It is possible that such a phrase denotes a religious relationship, but elsewhere in the tradition of Jeremiah (22:15-16) we are given a different, quite radical reading of the phrase. There, it is asserted that knowledge of Yahweh means attentiveness to poor, needy people, the transformation of social relations and public institutions for the sake of justice.[15] That is the mark of a new covenant community that is here anticipated.

   d. The new community will be egalitarian, for the knowledge of God will be available from the least to the greatest. That is, social rank and distinction will disappear, and every advantage and monopoly will be dissolved.

   The oracle does not imagine that such a community is now available. But the promise invites active hope toward such a gift from God that is as sure as God's self.[16]

   2. The second text that looks to a future covenant community is *Isa. 65:17-25*. The poem does not use the word "covenant," but it clearly envisions a social order in which God's rule is fully established. Here the anticipation is on much larger scope, as large as heaven, earth, and Jerusalem, all of which will be utterly new. In this extraordinarily rich passage, we may mention only the following motifs:

---

   15. See José Miranda, *Marx and the Bible* (Maryknoll, N.Y.: Orbis, 1974), 44–53.
   16. On the problematic of this important passage for the interaction of Jews and Christians, see the suggestive discussions of Emil L. Fackenheim, "New Hearts and the Old Covenant: On Some Possibilities of Fraternal Jewish-Christian Reading of the Jewish Bible Today," in *The Divine Helmsman*, ed. James L. Crenshaw and Samuel Sandmel (New York: KTAV, 1980), 191–205, and Hans Walter Wolff, *Confrontations with Prophets* (Philadelphia: Fortress, 1983), 49–62.

a. In verses 21-22, the "futility curse" (cf. Amos 5:11; Zeph. 1:13) is reversed. In the new world here envisioned, people will enjoy the security of their home and the produce of their vineyard. This means an end to invading armies that occupy and seize and an end to rapacious governments that devastate by imposing oppressive taxation on vulnerable peasants. This confiscating process is terminated not by some magic from heaven but by transformed social practice.

b. There will be a new availability from God (v. 24). There will be no barriers to ready communication between heaven and earth. In this new world of well-being, God will be fully present in immediate ways. The end of mediation is promised. That is a promise with social significance because every such authorized mediation leads to social advantage. The end to mediation is not yet, but it is promised and hoped for in this community of covenant.

c. There will be an end to destructive hostility, both in the enmity of creation (which looks back to Genesis 3) and in the hostility of nations. This hope does not believe that the world must be divided forever into hostile competing forces. It is quite concrete about the new social practices congruent with this hope.

In both Jer. 31:31-34 and Isa. 65:17-25, the Bible maintains an active conviction that God's peaceable kingdom is the intent of God that will not fail.

V

On the twin themes of peace and justice, the alternative realities embodied by covenant, we have dealt largely with justice and the overcoming of unjust and exploitative relationships. That focus (rather than a focus on peace) is due first of all to the fact that this is the main emphasis of the Bible. The Bible seems to worry more about injustice than about the problem of peace. When one looks at the texts, this is where the preponderance of them cluster. Second, the emphasis is on justice because from a biblical perspective, peace follows from justice. Where just social relations and just public institutions are authorized and enacted, hostilities end. The Bible seems to affirm that there can be no peace as long as there are monopolies of unbridled power or as long as there are monopolies of inordinate economic wealth. Peace comes only when such inappropriate concentrations of political power and economic wealth have been overcome. We will examine first an important text that at first glance contradicts this thesis, and then move from there to three texts that support our opinion that covenantal wisdom counters monopolies.

The reign of Solomon is a period of remarkable prosperity and power for Israel. In *1 Kings 4:20-28,* Solomon's situation of affluence is characterized. That achievement is quite clearly based on a productive tax system and on a sturdy arms program. In the midst of the portrayal of success for the regime, it is asserted that there was peace (v. 24) and that all dwelt in safety (v. 25). However, we must approach that royal claim cautiously.[17] First, the caution is required because the peace that is claimed is based on arms. One senses that it is a peace imposed and dominating, which is not and cannot be real peace. Second, one must be cautious because it is clear from 1 Kings 11–12 that Solomon's long reign ended in alienation, rebellion, and disarray. This suggests the reign was a tyrannical one that simultaneously generated and stifled enormous unrest. While Solomon may have been able to repress unrest enough to maintain a semblance of order and keep the lid on, quite clearly he was unable to administer a genuine peace. Thus, I judge this portrayal of peace in chapter 4 to be an act of ideology and a statement of propaganda.[18]

A very different kind of peace is suggested in the three other texts to which we turn. First, in *Ezek. 34:25-31,* the prophet announces a covenant of peace. This newly envisioned social possibility comes at the end of the chapter when the "wicked shepherds," that is, the exploitative rulers, have been expelled. Apparently these rapacious governors are the Israelite kings themselves (perhaps going all the way back to Solomon). These rulers created injustice by their selfish, self-serving governance that is now ended.

In place of such unjust rule is the rule of God that is gracious and compassionate, looks after the lost, strayed, and crippled (vv. 11-16), and is to be embodied in the David who is to come (vv. 23-24). That new peaceful order will permit creation to function productively (vv. 26-27), will end oppression (v. 27), will cause an end of terror and fear (v. 28), and will lead to well-being among the nations.

17. On this passage and its images in relation to the poetic images of Mic. 4:1-5, see chap. 5, below.

18. Barbara Tuchman (*The March of Folly* [New York: Knopf, 1984], 8–11) has cited the kingship of Rehoboam as an early example of folly. But surely the folly is well grounded already in the policy and theory of Solomon, out of which his son Rehoboam continued to act. When one recognizes that Solomon does indeed practice folly as a high political art, then the text will surely be read with suspicion.

The new possibility arises because the false government organized against covenant has now been overcome and dismissed.

Second, in *Ezek. 37:24-28,* the covenant of peace is promised again. This announcement occurs again in the exile, after the old noncovenantal order has been dismantled and a new David is established. The new covenant is a community of obedience to torah (v. 24), a community in which God will be present (v. 27).

A third promise of a covenant of peace is given in *Isa. 54:9-17.* This poetic anticipation is also set in exile. The promise is not only that the old failed structures of Israel have been terminated, as in Ezek. 34:25-31; 37:24-28, but also that the oppressive government of the Babylonian empire is also overcome. This moment of peace is linked to the promise made by Noah (see Gen. 9:8-17), which also envisions a new covenant after the flood. Peace is given because God's faithful promise continues to be at work in the real world. That powerful promise is the source of new social possibility. Specifically, the destroyed, recalcitrant city will start over again. There will be prosperity (v. 13). There will be an end to oppression (v. 14). There will be an end to destructive weapons of war (vv. 15-17).

Israel's poetry is relentless in its critique of imperial, tyrannic rule, whether it occurs in Israel or in any other kingdom. Clearly, peace will never emerge from such social concentrations of power. But Israel is equally resilient in its passionate conviction that the end of such empires is assured. Life will be available in ways that make genuine human community possible. That is why the text maintains an unending critique of every imperial power and every economic monopoly and why it continually offers an alternative vision for the organization of social power. From its inception, the Bible believed that the world could and would be organized in just, righteous, human ways. We dare to say that in Jesus we have received powerful signs and hints of such actualization. The central hint we find is the offer of Jesus' own person, which is given as a covenantal sign of new possibility (1 Cor. 12:24-26) that is not retained in liturgy or sacrament and is not reduced to religious act but evokes new social practice in the world. Jesus' death is finally a delegitimating of all destructive ordering in human life because the best effort at blocking the alternative vision and possibility has miserably failed in the face of the reality of Easter. Finally, the rulers of this age cannot block the vision of justice or the promise of peace. But that vision and promise are mediated to us at an enormous cost, a cost in which we are invited to participate.

Part Two

A Social Reading of Particular Texts

4

Social Criticism and Social Vision in the Deuteronomic Formula of the Judges

THE FOURFOLD FORMULA of the book of Judges is easily identified.[1] It has long been regarded as an identifiable mark of Deuteronomic theology. Walter Beyerlin has reviewed the data.[2] He has subjected the materials to a careful literary analysis, indicating a possible way in which the materials have developed. It is clear from his study (1) that the formula is old and to be dated before the Deuteronomist;[3] (2) that the material of the formula is not a unity and may be treated in its constituent parts;[4] and (3) that the formulation has peculiar connections with Deuteronomy 32,[5] which (following G. Ernest Wright and Otto Eissfeldt)[6] may be dated early.

---

1. This essay assumes Hans Walter Wolff's "The Kerygma of the Deuteronomic Historical Work," in *The Vitality of Old Testament Traditions*, by Hans Walter Wolff and Walter Brueggemann (Atlanta: John Knox, 1975), 82–100. It seeks to advance one element of our interpretation of that theological tradition. The fullest treatments of the fourfold formula of the book of Judges are those of Wolfgang Richter, *Traditionsgeschichtliche Untersuchungen zum Richterbuch*, BBB 18 (Bonn: Hanstein, 1963), and idem, *Die Bearbeitungen des "Retterbuches" in der deuteronomischen Epoche*, BBB 21 (Bonn: Hanstein, 1964).

2. Walter Beyerlin, "Gattung und Herkunft des Rahmens im Richterbuch," in *Tradition und Situation: Studien zur alttestamentlichen Prophetie; Artur Weiser zum 70 Geburtstag*, ed. Ernst Würthwein and Otto Kaiser (Göttingen: Vandenhoeck und Ruprecht, 1963), 1–29.

3. Ibid., 15. Beyerlin has observed that some parts of the familiar, stylized language do not have close parallels in Deuteronomy (cf. Deuteronomy 10).

4. Ibid., 2–7.

5. Ibid., 17–23.

6. G. Ernest Wright, "The Lawsuit of God: A Form-critical Study of Deuteronomy

Two reasons make it possible to reconsider the materials of the formula in light of Beyerlin's careful analysis. First (and most important), Beyerlin's analysis is confined to issues of literary analysis and relations. Since its publication in 1963, much greater attention has been given to sociological analysis of texts.[7] That is, forms as well as substance of the texts reflect cultural interests, power arrangements, and epistemological commitments corresponding to social circumstance. It is the suggestion of this essay that a sociological analysis of the formula in the book of Judges may supplement the results of literary analysis.

Second (and less important), Beyerlin's analysis is a contribution at a time when scholarship generally was particularly preoccupied with the constructs of amphictyony, covenant renewal, and covenant lawsuit. Each of these figures in the judgments of Beyerlin.[8] This is not to suggest that subsequent scholarship has vitiated his analysis, for the formulations of 6:8b-10 and 10:11b-14 apparently do reflect such an intention, which Beyerlin sees as oral proclamations of lawsuit.[9] But it does suggest that some greater distance from those scholarly constructs may permit other discernments as well.[10]

I

Our discussion seeks to build upon the judgment of Beyerlin that the fourfold formula of the book of Judges is not a unity but has two

---

32," in *Israel's Prophetic Heritage: Essays in Honor of J. Muilenburg*, ed. Bernard W. Anderson and Walter Harrelson (New York: Harper and Row, 1962), 36–41, 58–62; Otto Eissfeldt, *Das Lied Moses Deuteronomium 32,1-43 und das Lehrgedicht Asaphs Psalm 78 samt einer Analyse der Umgebung des Moseliedes* (Berlin: Akademie, 1958).

7. See the summary treatment of the important work of George Mendenhall and Norman Gottwald in the *JSOT* 7 (1978) and the summary of the literature in chap. 1 of this volume. Of special importance is the synthesis of Norman Gottwald, *The Tribes of Yahweh* (Maryknoll, N.Y.: Orbis, 1979).

8. Beyerlin, "Gattung," 27–29. It is clear that the formula in Judges is a narrative and not a lawsuit presentation, though it may derive from that form. It is now used for instruction, Beyerlin argues.

9. Ibid., 27.

10. It is clear that alternatives to a lawsuit form in Deuteronomy 32 are possible. Wright's analysis ("The Lawsuit of God," 52–58) perhaps does not fully explain the remarkable shift at v. 39. It may be, as he suggests, that the speaker shifts modes. But what historical, political, or sociological realities relate to that shift? Gerhard von Rad (*Wisdom in Israel* [Nashville: Abingdon, 1972], 295 n. 9) suggests an alternative placement and dating of Deuteronomy 32 that merits consideration. On the danger of patternism in the lawsuit form, see the comment of Aubrey R. Johnson, *The Cultic Prophet and Israel's Psalmody* (Cardiff: Univ. of Wales Press, 1979), 151 n. 2.

distinct parts.[11] Certainly by the time of the Deuteronomistic History, they have been built into a conventional unity.[12] But in order to understand the usage, we may consider the social reality that lies beyond the two parts.

The first part of the formula ("do evil/anger Yahweh") consists in the elements of sin and punishment, or more specifically, apostasy and oppression.[13]

1. The formulary of "sin/apostasy" has variations. But the most common statement is a generalized phrase without specificity: "Israel did evil in the eyes of Yahweh" (2:11; 3:7, 12; 4:1; 6:1; 10:6). In three of these cases (3:7; 4:1; 6:1), this formula stands alone and is immediately followed by the responding action of Yahweh.

In the other cases, the formula is expanded in a number of variations. The fullest statement is that of 2:11-13, which appears to have later development.[14] It includes seven supplementary verbs: "serve" (Baalism), "abandon," "walk" (after other gods), "bow down," "vex," "abandon," "serve" (Baal and Ashtarot). In its present form the series of seven provides an envelope of "serve" (*a*), "abandon" (*b*), followed by three verbs with the closure, "abandon" (*b'*), "serve" (*a'*). The other fuller formula is in 10:6-7, which has the sequence "serve, abandon, not serve." In 3:6-7,[15] in addition to the two uses of "serve," the term "forget" is used, and in 6:10, "not listen."[16]

---

11. Beyerlin, "Gattung," 3–5. See the important comment of Paul D. Hanson, *Dynamic of Transcendence* (Philadelphia: Fortress, 1978), 54–56.

12. That it has become conventional is indicated in the use made of the same reasoning by Job's friends (see Job 5:6-16; 8:4-7; 11:6, 13-20). Cf. von Rad, *Wisdom in Israel*, 211–12. Though the points are not laid out as clearly because of the poetic idiom, the same sequence is apparent.

13. This, of course, is the ground for the lawsuit hypothesis applied here. The formula can be characterized in theological language (sin-punishment) or in a political idiom (apostasy-oppression).

14. See Beyerlin, "Gattung," 2–7, and the judgment of Rudolf Smend ("Das Gesetz und die Völker," in *Probleme Biblischer Theologie: Festschrift G. von Rad*, ed. Hans Walter Wolff [Munich: Kaiser, 1971], 504–6), who discerns late "nomistic" development in v. 17 and who concludes that vv. 20-22 contain late elements. Cf. Walter Dietrich, *Prophetie und Geschichte*, FRLANT 108 (Göttingen: Vandenhoeck und Ruprecht, 1972), 68 n. 6. Neither the work of Dietrich nor that of Timo Veijola (*Die Ewige Dynastie* [Helsinki: Suomalainen Tiedeakatemia, 1975]) bears upon our study in any decisive way.

15. There follows an extended catalogue of the gods that departs from the characteristically lean formula.

16. The statement of 8:33-35 includes a different triad ("play the harlot, . . . establish [Baalberith as god], . . . not do *ḥesed* . . .") so that it has only secondary connections to the main formula. The only other use of *znh*, "play the harlot," is in 2:17, on which see Smend, "Das Gesetz und die Völker."

While there is surely a difference of nuance among these various terms, we can make two general observations. First, they function to interpret and give substance to the larger formula, "do evil." Second, they interpret in an intensely theological, covenantal direction. Their concern is the exclusive and intense loyalty demanded by Yahweh.

The basic formula "do evil in the eyes of Yahweh," is, of course, widely used by the Deuteronomistic History. But taken by itself, that is, without the other elements of the formula, it is older. While it surely has theological overtones, it is equally clear that it is used to maintain social order and at times social control. That is, it is not a disinterested theological formula. For the Yahweh that is displeased is always the Yahweh championed by someone. And not unexpectedly, the one who champions Yahweh (or a certain aspect of Yahweh) is a person in authority, whose authority is closely linked to Yahweh. Thus the formula is not ever without its political implication. This would not seem to be evident in Gen. 38:7, 10. There is no evident ploy here for social power. But it surely is used for the defense and maintenance of social practice (Levirate marriage). The issue of social power and control is more evident in Lev. 10:19;[17] Num. 23:27; 24:1;[18] and Num. 32:13.[19]

We may also mention four uses that seem to be crucially placed concerning the matter of social control and political power. The first of these, in 1 Sam. 12:17, concerns asking for a king as evil "in the eyes of Yahweh." On critical grounds, it is not clear how this text relates to the Deuteronomistic History, and so it may not be an independent witness to the formula. The other three are clearer. In 1 Sam. 15:19, the formula is used in violation of holy war. In 2 Sam. 11:27; 12:9, the formula is used against the capricious use of royal power, insisting on the authority of the torah against the king.[20] Thus

---

17. The formula is positive rather than negative. But the point is the same.

18. Both formulas are positive. But the fact that one man regards curse as "right" (*yšr*) and the other regards blessing as "good" (*ṭôb*) suggests the political dimensions of the formula.

19. The juxtaposition of vv. 5 and 12 makes the political point. What is in the "eyes" of Moses is also in the "eyes" of Yahweh. The *transcendent referent* and the *political authority* are identical in the use of power. Such an identification is at the heart of our argument. The theological claim of the formula embodies crucial political realities.

20. Cf. 7:14. See Gerhard von Rad, "The Beginnings of Historical Writing in Ancient Israel," in *The Problem of the Hexateuch and Other Essays* (New York: McGraw Hill, 1966), 198–204. It is curious that this formula has been singled out as a sophisticated theological statement, whereas the parallel use in Gen. 38:7, 10 would

while the formula of Judges clearly makes a theological appeal, it employs a formula that relates to the defense and maintenance of a particular form of social order.[21]

2. The second part of the formula concerns punishment in the form of social oppression given for violation of social order. Here the formulas are more uniform. They include (*a*) a theological statement: "[T]he anger of Yahweh is kindled" (2:14, 20; 3:8; 10:7), and (*b*) the political consequence of subjugation, "sell into the hand" (2:14; 3:8; 4:2; 10:7), or "give into the hand" (2:14; 6:1), "strengthen the enemy" (3:12). Again the variation does not seem to be important, for they all point to the same reality, with the juxtaposition of theological claim and political reality.

Of these two parts, the first, dealing with the anger of Yahweh, is the more interesting. Several episodes suggest that the anger of Yahweh is closely linked with the leadership of Moses. That is, Yahweh is angered when Moses is not obeyed (Exod. 32:10, 11, 22;[22] Num. 11:1, 10,[23] 33; 12:9; 32:10, 13). Four other passages seem especially important: (*a*) Num. 25:3 uses the term especially for syncretism;[24] (*b*) 2 Sam. 24:1 relates it to the census of David, that is, the emergence of royal power; (*c*) Isa. 5:24-25 links it to the rejection of the torah; and, most important, (*d*) Hos. 8:5 uses the term in relation to the mention of kings in 8:4. It is unlikely that the institution of monarchy is rejected in principle.[25] But clearly the anger of Yahweh relates to a wrong embrace of political authority. And linked to polit-

---

scarcely be regarded the same way. In both cases, the formula is employed to insist upon and underscore a view of social reality.

21. On the social function and use of such theological formulas in the service of a social order and therefore a political authority, see Peter Berger and Thomas Luckmann, *The Social Construction of Reality* (Garden City, N.Y.: Doubleday, 1966), 71 and passim; and Peter Berger, *The Sacred Canopy* (Garden City, N.Y.: Doubleday, 1969), especially chaps. 1 and 2. On the political element in the formula, see the shrewd comments of Dennis McCarthy, "The Wrath of Yahweh and the Structural Unity of the Deuteronomistic History," in *Essays in Old Testament Ethics*, ed. James L. Crenshaw and John T. Willis (New York: KTAV, 1974), 100–104.

22. In v. 19, it is the anger of Moses that is kindled. Again there is nearly identification of the anger of Yahweh and the anger of Yahweh's agent, Moses.

23. This verse offers a striking hint of our formula. It employs two of our phrases, "anger kindled" and "evil in the eyes of." But one is assigned to Yahweh, the other to Moses.

24. See George Mendenhall (*The Tenth Generation* [Baltimore: Johns Hopkins Univ. Press, 1973], 105–21) on a plausible sociological setting for the episode. He locates the crisis in terms of syncretism and the problem of legal systems. Hans Walter Wolff ("The Kerygma of the Yahwist," *Int* 20 [1966]: 133, 153–55) locates the episode in the traditioning process.

25. Cf. Hans Walter Wolff, *Hosea*, Hermeneia (Philadelphia: Fortress, 1974), 139.

ical authority is the mention of "calves," a hint about a wrong social order.[26]

The other formula, concerning political subjugation, calls for little comment (cf. Deut. 32:30; 1 Sam. 12:9). There is no doubt of political implication. The same figure is used with reference to Egypt because of its pride (Ezek. 30:12) and the Philistines because of their maltreatment of Israel (Joel 4:8; Eng. 3:8).[27] With both Egypt and the Philistines, it is for acts of political and social exploitation that the "selling" is announced.

Thus it appears that the anger of Yahweh is the middle term between "evil" and "selling." It is clear that the anger of Yahweh is a way of speaking about the price assessed in the historical process for the wrong order of society and the rejection of the right ordering of society.

3. The simplest articulation of this two-membered formulation is expressed in the three statements:

> And the people of Israel again did what was evil in the sight of the Lord; and the Lord strengthened Eglon the King of Moab . . . because they had done what was evil in the sight of the Lord. (3:12)

> And the people of Israel again did what was evil in the sight of the Lord, after Ehud died. And the Lord sold them. (4:1-2)

> The people of Israel did what was evil in the sight of the Lord; and the Lord gave them into the hand of Midian. (6:1)

In none of these is the middle term of anger used, though its presence does not change the simple structure. In these there is no embellishment, no intensification by more elaborate rhetoric.

The indictment is that Israel has adopted a way of political decisions antithetical to the northern "royal ideal."

26. Perhaps the reference to "calf" links this text to Exodus 32. The reference to kings here and the obvious struggle for leadership in Exodus 32 indicate how our formula is related to political control and social order. In Hos. 8:1-6, two members of our formula ("cry" in v. 2, as well as "anger burns" in v. 5) are used. The connections between our fourfold formula and this passage are worth pursuing. Wolff (*Hosea*, 141) suggests these are a "fixed part" in the narratives of apostasy and paraenesis.

27. Note the use of "requite" or "turn back" in 4:7 (Eng. 3:7), a term important for the construct of "deed-consequence." Cf. Josef Scharbert, "ŠLM im Alten Testament," in *Um das Prinzip der Vergeltung in Religion und Recht des Alten Testaments*, ed. Klaus Koch, Wege der Forschung 125 (Darmstadt: Wissenschaftliche Buchgesellschaft, 1972), 300–325; and the basic article of Koch, "Gibt es ein Vergeltungsdogma im Alten Testament?" in ibid., 130–80.

The simple formula is an expression of the teaching of the close correspondence of deed and consequence,[28] which we may characterize as one of the primary intellectual constructs of Israel.[29] These conclusions on this formula seem appropriate:

   a. The twofold formula has no necessary linkage to the other parts of the "Deuteronomic" fourfold formula of repentance and deliverance. It is independent and expresses its own teaching.

   b. The action and involvement of Yahweh (either implicit or explicit) between evil and selling are evident. We are not dealing with an automatic sphere of destiny but with a highly theologized version of retribution.[30]

   c. It is doubtful if this simple formulation can be regarded as a "lawsuit," though the fuller forms of 6:7-10 and 10:10b-14 may qualify. Thus the standard Judges formula is not lawsuit but a simple "deed-consequence" assertion, which means it lives in a different setting. There is no necessary connection between this formula and the lawsuits that Beyerlin has identified, though the more expanded passages permit such an interpretation.

II

Our main interest is to consider the sociology of the deed-consequence teaching presented here. While attention has been given to that teaching in the sapiential materials, it can hardly be regarded as a wisdom construct. It is equally assumed and utilized in the Prophets and elsewhere in the literature. Wherever it is used, the teaching reflects a well-ordered, coherent, stable social world in which rules are well established, power is properly legitimized, and consequences are reasonably predictable for the honoring and dishonoring of the stable order, established rules, and legitimated

---

28. Beyerlin, "Gattung," 3–4.

29. That construct has been especially located in wisdom materials. Cf. von Rad, *Wisdom in Israel*, 124–37, and Koch, "Gibt es ein Vergeltungsdogma," 131–40. While the construct surely has close parallels to the teaching of the wisdom teachers, we have found no close relationship to wisdom in the terminology of Judges. The closest analogy may be in Prov. 3:3-4 in structure, but not in wording. The phrase "eyes of God" is also used there, but not in a way significant for our material.

30. Obviously, it makes a difference in our label if this construct is "retribution" or "deed-consequence." Cf. Henning Graf Reventlow, "Sein Blut komme über sein Haupt," in *Um das Prinzip*, 412–31, and the response of Koch, "Gibt es ein Vergeltungsdogma," 432–56, for the distinction.

power. Life makes sense. This formula means both to insist on this and to rely upon it.[31]

To be sure, the deed-consequence teaching can be utilized by more than one societal claim. In every case it insists on some societal claim of a positive kind. It is not used to protest an order or to declare it null and void. On the one hand, it can be used with theological intentionality about the rule of God. But as the references to Moses suggest, the rule of God is never an abstract idea. It is a rule that has historical concreteness and therefore political implications. On the other hand, the deed-consequence construct can also be used for any present social order, which may be legitimated by royal propaganda, justified by the use of power, and serving the interests of the ruling class. This, perhaps, is its function in the Proverbs, if not its intent.[32] It takes no subtle analysis to know that in any stable society the rule of law tends to equate the ordering of God and the ordering of the dominant class.[33] The normality presumed in the simple formula of "evil/sell" is not only an important theological claim. At the same time it is an appeal to a social, political, intellectual coherence from which some peculiarly benefited. That would seem to be the case with Job's friends, who have theological affinity with the formula in the book of Judges.[34] This is not to say they act in bad faith. It is rather that the distance between the ordering of God and the ordering of the present arrangement has been

---

31. That the construct makes life predictable is not seriously qualified by von Rad's stress on mystery in it (cf. *Wisdom in Israel*, 124–33), for the mystery presumes the linkage of deed and consequence. It only seeks to go behind it for the sake of refinement and greater understanding. The mystery is premised on the connection of deed and consequence.

32. Cf. Robert Gordis, "The Social Background of Wisdom Literature," in *Poets, Prophets and Sages* (Bloomington: Indiana Univ. Press, 1971), 160–97; and the judicious statement of Brian Kovacs, "Is There a Class Ethic in Proverbs?" in *Essays in Old Testament Ethics*, 173–89; and George Mendenhall, "The Shady Side of Wisdom," in *A Light unto My Path*, ed. Howard N. Bream, R. D. Heim, and Casey A. Moore (Philadelphia: Temple Univ. Press, 1974), 319–27.

33. Thus every theological claim has at least a temptation toward self-serving ideology. See Karl Mannheim, *Ideology and Utopia* (New York: Harcourt Brace Jovanovich, 1936), and the use made of Mannheim's construct by Paul D. Hanson, *The Dawn of Apocalyptic* (Philadelphia: Fortress, 1975). Robert Merton (*Social Theory and Social Structure* [New York: Free Press, 1957], 114–36) helpfully distinguishes motivation and consequence, or manifest and latent function. Thus the construct of deeds-consequences, willfully or not, orders society in a certain direction. On the social function of wisdom, see Mendenhall, "The Shady Side of Wisdom."

34. Von Rad (*Wisdom in Israel*, 211) reflects on the formula handled by the friends of Job.

collapsed, and the two are identified.[35] That is likely to happen in any use of the construct of "deed and consequence."

In our formula in the book of Judges, several options lie open for its political implication.

1. If the formula is a sanction of an early community of liberation, as Mendenhall argues,[36] then the formula represents right discipline necessary to maintain the movement and resist accommodation. Clearly, then, syncretism has important sociopolitical implications, for it means the erosion of the liberation movement. The honoring of Yahweh is the practice of the politics of liberation. And any apostasy toward another god carries with it the dangers of oppression. The formula assumes a correlation of theological loyalty and political possibility.

2. But the formula has a different use when set in the context of monarchy. Then the formula (even if cast as a theological formula) serves to rationalize, legitimate, and justify the claims of the royal establishment. This is not the function of the formula in Judges, but the formula of deed-consequence in the service of the monarchy is evident in the three cases of Joab, Barzillai, and Shimei (1 Kings 2:5-9). Two are negative and one is positive, but each is set as a consequence for a deed:

(*a*) Joab:	"He did,...he murdered,...he put;	(deed)
	...therefore,...do not let..."	(consequence)
		(vv. 5-6)
(*b*) Barzillai:	"...deal loyally	(consequence)
	...because they met me with loyalty."	(deed) (v. 7)
(*c*) Shimei:	"He cursed me...;	(deed)
	bring down his gray head."	(consequence)
		(vv. 8-9)

There is no statement of anger or even of vengeance. The acts are for transparent reasons of state, that is, to maintain the present order.

---

35. We have observed this in three cases with Moses (Exod. 32:10, 19; Num. 11:10; 32:5, 13).

36. Mendenhall made this suggestion in a lecture given in St. Louis in October 1976. He suggests the formula reflects the discipline of a community of liberation that has learned that any relaxation of discipline (that is, loyalty to the social vision of Yahweh) leads to erosion and eventually reabsorption into the dominant system against which the liberated community is organized. Thus he urges that the formula reflects political experience and realism. See Gottwald, *Tribes of Yahweh*, on the same inclination.

3. It is likely that our formula in the book of Judges is neither the early radical formula of a community of liberation nor the self-serving formulation of the monarchy. Rather it is the delicate posturing of reform teachers who hold for a particular vision of royal reality, tightly disciplined by torah and resistant to syncretism. As is well known, in later Deuteronomistic History, both the discipline of torah and the resistance to syncretism come to be present as the claim of the Jerusalem temple. But that, of course, cannot be presented by the history as the case yet in Judges. It is plausible that the use of the formula in Judges is much more theologically radical and much less politically concrete than are the formulas in Kings. That may be because of the historical casting of the teaching in the pre-Jerusalem period. Thus this theological radicalism by the history is a counterpart for the political specificity of the history's later material in Kings.

The point is that the teaching of "deed-consequence," that is, "evil/sell," is a formula in which an order holds. There is no slippage in the *nomos*.[37] It is not in doubt that consequences follow evil or good in the eyes of Yahweh; nor is it in doubt that evil causes subjugation.[38] This world is reliable, predictable, and coherent and has gifts to give those who will live in it. It need be explored no further. And, therefore, this passionate theological conviction can be given concrete institutional expression and can be dealt with by explicit, deliberate, and intentional conduct. The conduct of Israel need not be experimental, exploratory, or precarious (see Deut. 4:5-8; 30:11-14). It may proceed with confidence. And even when negative behavior causes negative results, there need be no puzzlement. There is still ground for confidence, for the world has not collapsed. The proponents of this theological vision undoubtedly had in mind a rather specific quid pro quo political and social world that could also be trusted (see 2 Kings 22–23).

---

37. Here I use *nomos* as social norm. Cf. Merton, *Social Theory*, chap. 6, in his discussion of anomie.

38. Von Rad (*Wisdom in Israel*, 129) suggests a movement from experience to doctrine. There is no doubt that our formula in the book of Judges is on the way to doctrine. But if it grows out of a genuine liberation community, it is not yet doctrine remote from experience. It may well have been experienced that departure from the radical social vision of Yahwism leads to oppression.

III

The second part of the formula of Judges is "cry out/deliver."
1. The first member of this formula is consistently "cry out"
(*zāʿaq, ṣāʿaq;* 3:9, 15; 4:3; 6:6-7; 10:10-14). It remains constant and
is not developed. It is a plea to be delivered from oppression. In
current interpretation of the Deuteronomistic History, the term "cry
out" has been understood in terms of repentance.[39] That, however,
seems doubtful in its general use or in the usage in Judges. The term
may refer to a formal complaint against or a protest against injustice
(Gen. 4:10; 18:20; Exod. 22:22; 2 Sam. 13:19; Prov. 21:13; Neh. 5:1;
Isa. 5:7). When so used, it is an appeal to a higher authority against
an offender. Or it may be simply a cry of desperation, hoping for deliverance (Deut. 22:24, 27; Isa. 42:2). Or it may be a general outcry
against an unbearable situation in which it is not a plea addressed to
anyone, but it is simply an undirected grieving (Isa. 14:31; 15:4; Jer.
48:4, 34; 50:46; 51:54; Esther 4:1).

In the uses in Judges, only in 10:10-14 is there a development.
It is used in this passage in three ways. First, in verse 10, it is indeed used as repentance, but this appears to be the only such case
in Judges. However, that meaning is carried not by the term itself
but by the words that follow. Second, the term is used in historical
review (v. 12), to cite past acts of Yahweh's responsiveness. And then
in verse 14, Israel is challenged to seek an alternative source of help,
which Israel rightly refuses (v. 15). In the unit of verses 10-14, the
topic is repentance, but that motif belongs to the total wording and
not to the term *zāʿaq.*

On the one hand, the term refers to the deliverance from Egypt
(Exod. 2:23; 3:7-9; 14:10-15; 15:25; Num. 20:16; Deut. 26:7; Josh.
24:7). The exodus has become a paradigm for the needful call of
Israel and the caring, powerful response of Yahweh. The other primary usage is in the Psalms (9:12; 22:6; 34:18; 77:2; 88:2; 142:2, 6),
which concerns more intimate personal matters, though the intent
and the appeal are the same.

---

39. See Wolff, "The Kerygma of the Deuteronomic Historical Work," 87–88, and
cf. E. Janssen, *Juda in der Exilszeit,* FRLANT 51 (Göttingen: Vandenhoeck und
Ruprecht, 1956), 74-76, more generally on "Umkehr" in the Deuteronomistic History. Cf. Richter, *Die Bearbeitungen,* 18–20, on *zāʿaq.* As far as I can determine, in
his more general study of "Umkehr," Wolff ("Das Thema 'Umkehr' in der alttestamentlichen Prophetie," in *Gesammelte Studien zum Alten Testament* [Munich: Kaiser,
1964], 130–50) nowhere is concerned with the terms *zāʿaq, ṣāʿaq.*

So far as I can determine, only in Jon. 3:7-8 is the term used explicitly in relation to repentance. But again that is more weight than can be placed on the term itself. The meaning of "repentance" can perhaps be deduced for the word when Israel is accused of not crying to Yahweh (Hos. 7:14) or is invited to appeal to idols (Isa. 57:13) or when Yahweh refuses to listen to the cry (1 Sam. 8:18; Mic. 3:4; Jer. 11:11-12; Hab. 1:2; Lam. 3:8; Job 19:7; 35:9-12; Isa. 46:7). But the total usage suggests a much more limited intent. The concern characteristically is limited to a situation of need and danger and an action seeking escape from it. While Yahweh may have more in mind in the call to "cry," the voice of Israel tends to focus on extrication from a situation of oppression and/or distress. The term itself implies very little in relation to the one addressed by the call.

2. The other part of this second formula is (as in the first formula we have considered) more concrete in its political intent. The term "deliver" is used in the formula in 2:16-17; 3:9.15; 10:10-15. Of course, there are many other uses in the book of Judges because of the general subject matter and the easy exchange of *yāša'* and *šāphaṭ*. For our purposes we may focus on the thematic statement of 2:16:

> Then the Lord raised up judges, who saved them out of the power of those who plundered them.

The characteristic statement shows that the formula speaks of Yahweh as a source of political power who will liberate from another, lesser political power that oppresses.

3. In order to analyze this second half of the fourfold formula of Judges, it is important to recognize that the combined formula "cry out/save," taken by itself, is an intellectual construct in Israel of primary importance for the religion of Israel.[40] To be sure there are uses of each term alone, but it is their juxtaposition that is crucial for their function here. In Judges that juxtaposition is found in 3:9, 15; 10:10-12. The other formulary texts offer some variation, but these are the decisive uses.

It is clear that the construct of "cry out/save" originated neither in the Deuteronomistic History nor in the book of Judges. It reflects an old and fundamental claim of biblical faith, characterizing the

---

40. Cf. Claus Westermann, *Elements of Old Testament Theology* (Atlanta: John Knox, 1982), 153–57; Westermann, "The Role of the Lament in the Theology of the Old Testament," *Int* 28 (1974): 20–38; and Walter Brueggemann, "From Hurt to Joy, from Death to Life," *Int* 28 (1974): 3–19.

relation between Israel as a people in need and Yahweh as the God who powerfully responds.[41] That juxtaposition is found in:

a. the psalmic traditions of personal lament (Pss. 9:13-15; 22:6;[42] 34:7, 18; 88:2; cf. Hab. 1:2);

b. the various texts surrounding the exodus (Exod. 14:10-13; cf. also 2:23-25);[43] the reference of 1 Sam. 9:16 refers to the Philistines and is derivative from the model of exodus (cf. Neh. 9:27-28);

c. the anecdotal report on 2 Kings 6:26-27, which does not appear to be influenced by the Deuteronomistic History;

d. a negative form in Jer. 11:11-12; Isa. 46:7; see also the negative counterpart to our formula in Judg. 12:2; these uses will be important for the argument to follow;

e. stylized statements that are a shorthand form of the basic claim of Israel's faith; in such uses, the formula has lost most of the radical dimension that belongs to its primary uses (cf. Ps. 107:13, 19;[44] Neh. 9:27; 2 Chron. 32:20-22). In Isa. 19:20, the same structure is given a curious and bold turn.

IV

The formula of "cry out/save" expresses a major intellectual construct of Israel's faith. However, the social world of faith and power it reflects is in tension (if not antithesis) to that reflected in the construct of "evil/sell" we have already considered. This second formula of Judges is in no way relevant to the social situation of "deed-consequence" in which both theological order and political authority are clear, reliable, and well established.

Indeed, this second construct of "cry out/save" reflects persons and community in a situation in which the stable, ordered reliability has failed and been found wanting. Theologically, we may say it is the end of the world of *nomos*.[45] There are no known modes of conduct

---

41. Karl Barth (*Church Dogmatics* [Edinburgh: T. and T. Clark, 1960], 3/3:267–71) urges that asking and petitioning are the heart of biblical prayer.

42. The term here is *mlṭ*, but see vv. 2 and 22.

43. The term *yšʿ* is not used, but see *nṣl* in Exod. 3:8.

44. Verses 6 and 28 have the same construct but with different terms. Cf. Ps. 145:19.

45. On the social process and significance of the collapse of *nomos*, see Berger and Luckmann, *Social Construction*, 119–21; Berger, *Sacred Canopy*, 47–51; and Merton, *Social Theory*. Merton (*Social Theory*, 218–19) offers a list of indicators of anomie

that will produce the desired consequences. There are no assured authorities who preside over an order and who keep their word.[46] To the extent that the torah has been reduced to a "system" that can be "worked," this formula means that the torah can no longer be relied upon to produce a world of secure blessing. It is not only that the outcome of blessing is not received but that the system—theological and political—is now experienced as dysfunctional. This formula is a response to the very world of "deed-consequence" reflected in the first formula of "evil/sell." (Set in the context of the Deuteronomistic Historian, who uses an older formula, this suggests the inadequacy of Josiah's reform, which appeals to "deed-consequence," and it illuminates Jeremiah's rejection of newness by way of reform as inadequate.)[47]

That the formula is a theological invitation in the face of a collapsed life-world is evident in both its primary settings. We have seen that the formula in Israel is especially linked to the exodus event. That is, by the use of this formula, Israel moves from the epistemology and promises of Egypt to cast its lot with this other One who is always something of an unknown quantity. The system of Egypt can be "worked," that is, can be reduced to "deed-consequence." And as the exodus is a departure from that system with Yahweh, so the yearning to return (Exod. 16:3; Num. 14:2-4) is a desire to reenter the imperial world of "deed-consequence." The choice is between a safe world of "deeds-consequences" that crushes and Yahweh's own version of "save" (cf. Exod. 17:4-6; Num. 12:13-14).

The situation is not different in the other primary use of the lament psalm. There also the speaker has experienced the deep failure of the system. He is at a loss to make the system work. Now he must make an appeal to an alternative form of hope and help.

Let us consider the situation of those who must utilize the construct of "cry out/save." They are in distress in the Psalms, for the other systems of support and reward have failed (see the extreme

---

that may illuminate Israel's rejection of an alien *nomos*. "The end of the *nomos*" may be a shattering or a liberation, depending on one's benefit from that ordering of reality.

46. Such a rejection of the system is perhaps reflected in Jeremiah's programmatic word *šqr*. Cf. T. Overholt, *The Threat of Falsehood*, SBT, n.s., 16 (London: SCM, 1970).

47. On Jeremiah's attitude toward the reform, see the old but judicious statement of John Skinner, *Prophecy and Religion* (Cambridge: Cambridge Univ. Press, 1963), chap. 7. See the summary of Harold H. Rowley, *Men of God* (London: Nelson, 1963), 158–68, and the bibliography of José Miranda, *Marx and the Bible* (Maryknoll, N.Y.: Orbis, 1974), 74 n. 37.

statement in Job 30). Or alternatively they are the slaves of the Egyptian empire who look for an appeal against pharaoh. Either way, they are those for whom the "deed-consequence" frame of reference has failed or even become hostile. And they must, at some risk, entrust themselves to this alternative life-world where things are much more precarious. But the alternative (if I have correctly understood the contrast of the constructs of "deed-consequence" and "cry out/save") admits of new possibility. We may thus summarize the former formula as reflecting a well-ordered and predictable world of law (*nomos*). The latter is a world that relies on the freedom of Yahweh and looks to Yahweh's faithful but unpredictable graciousness. This second formula breaks with the old *nomos*. Its speaker is in a *"pre-nomos"* situation of dangerous grace (*yš'*) that has both theological and political dimensions.

Our argument is that this is not simply a theological issue. It is rather a distinction between life-worlds[48] with contrasting political possibilities, epistemological commitments, and modes of certitude. Any attempt to understand the formulas theologically apart from such a political dimension misunderstands the claim and function of the formula.

In that light, then, we must understand those who use "cry out/save" as a way of existence—they stand outside the managed world of "deed-consequence."

Such a move from the one life-world to the other recognizes that the managed world of "deed-consequence" has failed and cannot keep its promises. Thus it embodies an important critique of the "system," asserting that it cannot be trusted. Appeal to "cry out/save" is a rejection of the other mode. Thus, in Exod. 10:29 and 11:8, Moses will appeal to that mode of existence no longer. Such a rejection may reflect an awareness that it is weak and ineffectual, that deeds simply do not produce consequences (so Job). Or it may go deeper to see that it is not disinterested but inequitable, so that it is biased for some, against some others (thus the critique of the system of "deed-consequence" in Isa. 5:20-23; Amos 5:7, 10-12; Job 9:13-23).

The shift of formulas from "deed-consequence" to "cry/save" is a decision to move from one court of appeal to another, to turn from the failed, now rejected authority to an alternative au-

---

48. See Peter Berger (*The Precarious Vision* [Garden City, N.Y.: Doubleday, 1961]) on the plurality and tension of life-worlds. Note especially his three-dimensional titles on "Egypt, Zion, and Exodus," terms pertinent to our argument.

thority (Yahweh) who may be more responsive, fairer, and more compassionate.[49]

The shift in formulas thus reflects a changed model of power relations. To "cry out" and look for saving implies withdrawal from the old system of "deed-consequence."[50] Thus the "cry/save" mode of reality delegitimates the world of "deed-consequence." It asserts that the system upon which Israel relies has become a source of oppression and exploitation. At different times that rejected system may be (1) the Egyptian empire, (2) Israel's monarchy, (3) Israel's torah, or (4) the power and claim of Babylon.

V

Thus the four-member formula of Judges combines two contrasting intellectual constructs, that of "deed-consequence," reflecting an ordered world of stability, and that of "cry/save," a daring departure on the basis of Yahweh's responsiveness. The two constructs had independent development and only later were formed into a unity. The one is marked by a presumption of control, the other by risking trust. We do not know when or in what way the two formulas were combined. But we conclude it was a remarkably bold and imaginative theological achievement.

If the formula reflects the early liberated community before the monarchy,[51] our analysis suggests the formula urges movement from the world of imperial oppression with a managed epistemology[52] to the new world of trust, freedom, and, hopefully, justice. The use of

---

49. Probably too much should not be made of the verb "sell" in another context. But the Yahweh of liberation (Lev. 25:42) is one who does not "sell" his people. Perhaps the saving God of the "cry out/save" construct is to be contrasted with all the lords of the "deed-consequence" construct (including the Yahweh of the establishment) who "sell" their people (cf. Amos 2:6). On the juxtaposition of theological and social implications of the Jubilee, see John H. Yoder, *The Politics of Jesus* (Grand Rapids: Eerdmans, 1972), chap. 3.

50. George Mendenhall ("The Hebrew Conquest of Palestine," in *The Biblical Archaeologist Reader* [Garden City, N.Y.: Doubleday, 1970], 3:100–120) has urged that the liberated community of early Israel is one that withdrew from and denied the authority of the system, and in so doing formed an alternative.

51. This early placement is argued by Mendenhall on sociological grounds and is permitted by Beyerlin's literary analysis. It is not impossible that Beyerlin's lawsuit interpretation can be understood in fresh ways in terms of the sociology of withdrawal and liberation.

52. See Walter Brueggemann, "The Epistemological Crisis of Israel's Two Histories (Jer. 9:22-23)," in *Old Testament Theology: Essays in Structure, Theme, and Text* (Minneapolis: Fortress, 1992).

the entire formula summons Israel to shift from one life-world to another, with its alternative theological, epistemological, and political claims.[53]

This suggests that repentance as a change of life-worlds, both political and theological, is not in the third element ("cry out") but occurs *between the two systems,* that is, between the second and third elements of the formula. That is, the act of "cry[ing] out" reflects a changed orientation that is already accepted. The decision has been made to take a new risk. The "cry" acknowledges not only a new authority but also a new awareness of the situation. Now it is recognized that the world of "deed-consequence" is untenably oppressive. Until that is recognized, there will be no "cry." Thus the new act of "cry[ing] out" involves a new theological commitment and new political awareness.

The use of the formula by the Deuteronomistic History may be much more radical than has been recognized. It may mean that in the late seventh century or early sixth century, this theology urged Israel to reject a mode of reality that assumed coherence and offered a system of security. If, with Frank M. Cross,[54] the Deuteronomistic History in its major part is dated before 587 B.C.E., it may be a radical critique of monarchy and even of the Mosaic covenant as a source of hope, when it had become a legal system to be "worked." If, with Hans Walter Wolff,[55] the formula is used in the exile, it may be a call to Israel to awaken to its true situation in which it has no recourse except to rely on Yahweh. Either way such a summons requires a rejection of all alternative forms of loyalty and security.[56] Such a radical call may be concerned with reliance on royal modes of reality, on torah-centered obedience, or even on the seductive promises of Babylon. The shift from "deed-consequence" to "cry out/save" is in-

---

53. See J. N. M. Wijngaards, "Death and Resurrection in Covenantal Context (Hos. VI 2)," *VT* 17 (1967): 226–39.

54. Frank M. Cross, *Canaanite Myth and Hebrew Epic* (Cambridge, Mass.: Harvard Univ. Press, 1973), chap. 10.

55. Wolff, "The Kerygma of the Deuteronomic Historical Work."

56. Such a political-theological summons illuminates the exclusiveness of Deut. 6:5, which is programmatic for Deuteronomy. Cf. S. Dean McBride, "The Yoke of the Kingdom," *Int* 27 (1973): 273–306. He casts his exposition in terms of the political and sociological dimensions of the texts.

Such a radical exclusiveness, when discerned sociologically, may illuminate Jesus' call for discipleship. This is evident in his primal *proclamation* (Mark 1:14-15), which implies a rejection of the other kingdom, and in the *demand* for clear choices between kingdoms, as in Matt. 6:24; Mark 8:15.

deed an expectation of a "new thing," for the "old thing" has failed (cf. Isa. 43:18-19).

Finally, we may observe that by joining the two formulas together and treating them as one "system," what was a bold attempt to place two formulas in juxtaposition has in part served to tone down and domesticate the second formula. Now the "cry out/save" formula functions in continuity with the former. Where the two systems are contrasted, they are as radically in tension as the "deed-consequence" system of Proverbs and the bold protest of Job. But when they can be brought together, they become the managed, comprehensive scheme of Job's friends. It is the tendency of every system of management to "contain" the dangers of real repentance. It is the work of every domesticated religion to make the free grace of God a part of the system. What may have begun as a bold, revolutionary proposal in time becomes a new legalism against which Jeremiah, Ezekiel, Second Isaiah, and the poet of Job each must protest afresh.

The final result gives the appearance of controlled and predictable religion in the service of a well-ordered and managed political vision. That is a far cry from a risky world of surprising gifts of power in which even the spirit can rush (Judg. 3:10; 6:34; 9:23; 11:29; 13:25; 14:6, 19; 15:14, 19; 1 Sam. 10:6, 10; 11:6; 16:13; 18:10).

5

"Vine and Fig Tree":
A Case Study in
Imagination and Criticism

THE PROPHETIC TRADITION in Israel is characteristically double-focused: on the one hand, it announces judgment of what is to be dismantled; on the other hand, it makes promises in anticipation of the newness yet to be given. Most succinctly, this has been summarized in Jer. 1:10:

> to pluck up and to break down,
> to destroy and to overthrow,
> to build and to plant.

One need not be a reductionist to see that these two general tendencies are at work.[1]

The ways of prophetic work are essentially rhetorical. While there may be political interventions and acts, and symbolic, parabolic acts,[2] the primary way of the prophets is by speech. Such speech in Israel (cf. Jer. 1:10) is the use of the word to do both the dismantling

---

1. Ronald Clements ("Patterns in the Prophetic Cause," in *Canon and Authority,* ed. George Coats and Burke Long [Philadelphia: Fortress, 1977], 48–55) has seen that, in its present form, the prophetic literature is organized around "a single theme of Israel's destruction and renewal" (p. 48). In another way, I have sought to speak of the same matter in terms of criticizing and energizing (*The Prophetic Imagination* [Philadelphia: Fortress, 1978]).

2. See Georg Fohrer, *Die symbolischen Handlungen der Propheten,* ATANT 54 (Zurich: Zwingli, 1968).

and the new evoking. Without addressing the matter of the "evocative and effective power of the spoken word,"[3] it is clear that the speech of Israel's poets did play upon the imagination of Israel, both to bring old worlds to an end and to initiate new worlds into their awareness.

The present study examines one such case in which the imaginative speech of the prophet inaugurates a new world of social possibility and in which an alternative use of the same figure calls the old world into question. Specifically, the formula "every man under his vine and under his fig tree" will be examined in its promissory use in Mic. 4:4 and in its critical use in 1 Kings 4:25 (Hebr. 5:5). It is the premise of the essay that the two uses have some intentional linkage, even though the precise connection is obscure. That is, the usage in 1 Kings 4:25 cannot be fully understood apart from its primary and normative use, either in Mic. 4:4 or in a poetic, promissory tradition behind that use. We hope to show here that the two uses (Mic. 4:4; 1 Kings 4:25) must be taken together for either of them to be fully appreciated in terms of its imaginative power to pluck up and break down, to build and to plant.

I

The poem of Mic. 4:1-5 is an example of imaginative use of concrete and anticipatory metaphor to evoke an alternative world in the consciousness of Israel. On critical grounds, it cannot be determined how old this promise-oracle is or what its precise relationship is to the parallel use in Isa. 2:2-4. Most commentators are agreed that the oracle is not from the hand of Micah.[4] Here it is assumed that the oracle belongs to an older tradition of promise, clearly oriented to Zion.[5] That it may not be from the mouth of the man Micah does not detract from the fact that it has now been placed

---

3. Cf. Anthony C. Thiselton, "The Supposed Power of Words in the Biblical Writings," *JTS* 25 (1974): 283–99.

4. See the summary of scholarship by J. M. Powis Smith, *Micah, Zephaniah and Nahum,* ICC (Edinburgh: T. and T. Clark, 1911), 83ff., and the comments of James L. Mays, *Micah,* OTL (Philadelphia: Westminster, 1976), 95 n. a. As Mays indicates, however, a case has been made for derivation from the prophet Micah.

5. This is the judgment of Brevard S. Childs, *Introduction to the Old Testament as Scripture* (Philadelphia: Fortress, 1979), 435. I do not find arguments for late dating convincing, as in E. Cannawurf, "The Authenticity of Micah IV 1-4," *VT* 13 (1963): 26–33.

into the Micah tradition. And because of its juxtaposition to 3:9-12, we may conclude that it has been most carefully placed.[6] That is, 3:9-12 and this passage together bespeak the plucking up of old Zion and the emergence of a new Zion. The connection between the two may be editorial, but the connection is more than an external one based on catchwords. Rather, the juxtaposition in the present form of the tradition concerns the end and the new beginning of Israel.

But beginning our study with this passage is not based on literary-critical grounds. Rather, it is based on a theological judgment: (1) Israel's primal speech is promise. The initiating communication of this faith takes the form of promise that is never justified or explained but only asserted. (2) Israel's primal mode of articulation is poetry. It is poetry that cannot be reduced or administered but is simply left as a subversive possibility.

So our beginning point with this text is that Mic. 4:1-5 is a radical assertion of a poetic promise,[7] designed to lead Israel to an alternative reality. Admittedly, this is not a political strategy or a concrete action. It is only a practice of imagination that presents an unthinkable, underived future. Those who heard this oracle (as well as those who spoke it) were called to realities they could not see or identify. Nor could they discern how such an anticipation could become a reality.

The practice of such imagination performs two rhetorical functions. On the one hand, it introduces a sphere of freedom. Israel is invited to think about inexplicable futures that God may yet give, that are beyond human engineering. On the other hand, the promise subverts the present. It announces that the present system is not absolute and that the managers of the present (Zion) system have not spoken the last word or fully co-opted all the energies at work in life.

The oracle can be divided into two main parts, identified by four uses of the name of God. The rhetorical claims of the text are matched by the deliberate uses of the name of the deity. The first *inclusio* begins in verse 1 and is answered in verse 2b:

---

6. See Mays, *Micah*, 94, on the delicacy of this placement.
7. It is clear that v. 5 is somewhat disconnected from the preceding. It is clearly a summons, likely liturgical, for a response to the promise. In the parallel of Isa. 2:2-4, there is also such a summons, but somewhat weaker. It is also the case that Mic. 4:4 is missing in the parallel of Isaiah 2. This rather striking departure is important to our argument.

> the mountain of the house of the Lord (v. 1b) ...
> the mountain of the Lord ...
> the house of the God of Jacob ... (v. 2b)[8]

This *inclusio* portrays the dramatic procession of world powers, that is, self-contained systems of security and meaning. Those self-contained systems here yield their authority and claims to power to the God resident in Jerusalem, the God of Israel. Thus the drama here enacted for the (liturgical?) imagination of Israel presents a shift of royal/theological power. A reassignment of roles among the nations is done by the coming of the nations to Zion. And implicitly, the coming of the nations means a yielding of the gods identified with those nations. That is, the nations no longer identified with sundry gods, but now with the God of Jerusalem. Thus the enthronement of Yahweh here celebrated carries with it a dethronement of all other gods. The correlation of submission and delegitimation is evidenced in the anticipations of verse 2c:

> that he may teach us his ways,
> and we may walk in his paths.[9]

The statement means a rejection of other ways and other paths (see below on v. 5). This conclusion stands outside the *inclusio* as such. The effect of this added line is to show the consequences of the dramatic yielding just presented. There has been a shift in royal/heavenly power. And in verse 2c, there is an anticipation of its political results.

The second part of the oracle matches the first. Again, there is an *inclusio* based on the references to God:

> For out of Zion shall go forth the *torah*,
> and the *word of the Lord* from Jerusalem. ... (v. 2d)
> For the *mouth of the Lord* of hosts has spoken. (v. 4b)

Thus the oracle in its main parts is crafted around two sets of *inclusios*. But they are very different in their themes. The first has to do with the residence and presence of God (mountain/house). The second concerns God's word and will. The first concerns royal domicile,

---

8. Mays, *Micah*, 94, has observed how these formulas also link the unit to 3:9-12.

9. On the word "walk," see below on v. 5. On the political implications of this vision, see Norman Gottwald, *All the Kingdoms of the Earth* (New York: Harper and Row, 1964), 200–203.

divine sovereignty. I suggest that it asserts a new ordering of heaven, that is, a new rule among the gods who preside over the nations. The second concerns the torah and anticipates a new arrangement on earth, that is, among the nations. Thus the structure of the oracle is theologically self-conscious. It is a new ordering in heaven that makes possible a new arrangement on earth. The power shift among the gods is expressed as new policy now to be implemented on earth.[10]

Inside the second *inclusio* of verses 2b-4d are two metaphors articulating a possible new society, made possible because of the shift among the gods in the first *inclusio*. The first metaphor is the well-known image of disarmament:

> They shall beat their swords into plowshares,
>   and their spears into pruning hooks;
> nation shall not lift up sword against nation,
>   neither shall they learn war any more.

But what is envisioned is not just the end of arms. The sweep of this oracle, I submit, concerns the end of such public policy, such propaganda, such education and psychology. What is envisioned is both a transformed public policy and a transformed human consciousness.[11] And all this happens because of a new word from Yahweh, premised on the submission and legitimation in verses 1-2a.

The transforming of arms is the first metaphor in the second *inclusio,* and the best known. But we must give special attention to the second metaphor, which provides a countertheme to this subversive vision:

> But[12] they shall all sit under their own vines and under
>   their own fig trees. (NRSV)

---

10. The linkage between the two, religious power and social policy, is indicated by Mays, *Micah,* 93: "[T]he appearance of YHWH's reign on earth will inaugurate an imperial peace that transforms the conditions of life for nations and individuals." The linkage between Yahweh's appearance and conditions of life is much more intentionally expressed by Norman Gottwald, *The Tribes of Yahweh* (Maryknoll, N.Y.: Orbis, 1979). Implicit in Mays's comment is the very connection Gottwald urges, a connection that rejects every "idealistic interpretation."

11. Norman Gottwald (*The Church Unbound* [New York: Lippincott, 1967], 72–73) has provided a helpful comment on the passage: "Nations *learn* war. War is not blind fate. It is learned. It is an instrument of social change in which many of our unconscious and unadmitted instincts find expression. Those instincts can find other outlets; war can be *unlearned.*"

12. An adversative is used for a contrast to the armed world.

The poet is in touch with deep agrarian dreams. He presents what must be Israel's most elemental social hope. That hope is not simply for a disarmed world. It is much more personal. What one wishes for is to be secure enough to produce and enjoy produce unmolested, either by lawlessness or the usurpation of the state. While our inclination may be to imagine the threat to this personal dream to be lawlessness, in what follows I hope to show that it is, in fact, usurpation of the state that is the main threat.[13]

The poet ends on this most personal and intense hope, together with the guarantee, "none to make afraid." The phrase seems to appeal to the old blessing tradition of Lev. 26:6, _'ên maḥărîd,_ "none to terrify."[14] By using that formula, the poet links the coming, disarmed society to the oldest hope of Israel. The anticipated new society will keep the promises Israel has cherished longest.

But the structure of this second _inclusio_ is not romanticism or rootless imagination. The poet places back-to-back a large royal dream of disarmament (v. 3) with a personal agrarian dream of well-being (v. 4a). The poet sees that there will be no personal well-being, no lack of terror, until there is an end to the public policy of war. The mad pursuit of security by war, the mad pursuit of energy for weapons, the reliance upon imperial administration of resources—all that must be dismantled in order for the personal dream to come true. Obviously, there can be no such personal well-being as long as

---

13. By contrasting the program of "swords and spears," which reflects an imperial war system, with that of "vines and fig trees," which reflects a peasant economy and peasant perception of reality, we may discern in this poem a dramatic conflict of social systems. As Norman Gottwald has made clear ("Were the Early Israelites Pastoral Nomads?" in _Rhetorical Criticism,_ ed. Jared J. Jackson and Martin Kessler [Pittsburgh: Pickwick, 1974], 254–55), we may trace two economic systems in the ancient world, the one enjoying concentration of surplus wealth for some at the expense of others, the other based on equal consumption of wealth by the immediate producers of wealth. In this passage, "vines and fig trees" represent the produce of a peasant economy that is threatened by an alternative economy dependent on military power and based on the power of the state to usurp. Gottwald follows Eric R. Wolf in characterizing the peasants as the ones who must rely upon and protect their own produce from its subsequent use by others. In that context, the much used formula, "build houses and dwell in them, plant vineyards and drink their wine" (stated both positively and negatively; cf. Amos 5:11; 9:14; Isa. 65:2; Jer. 29:28; Deut. 28:30), warrants new investigation. Negatively and positively, it speaks about the safety of the peasants in the face of the usurpation of the state. On the peasants in Israel, see the summary of Gottwald, _Tribes of Yahweh,_ chap. 46. In this same regard, see Albrecht Alt, "Micha 2, 1-5 GES ANADASMOS in Juda," in _Kleine Schriften zur Geschichte des Volkes Israel_ (Munich: C. H. Beck, 1959), 3:373–81.

14. For other uses of the formula, see Jer. 30:10; 46:27; Ezek. 34:28; 39:26; Zeph. 3:13; and negatively, Deut. 28:26; Isa. 17:2; Jer. 7:33.

there is war and threat of war. But what denies that personal hope is not simply hostility and the threat of hostility. Rather, the main threat to "vines and fig trees" is the economics that sustain and require war. What usurps vines and fig trees is not just invading armies but the tax structure and the profit system that are both cause and effect of military dangers. The poet envisions not simply a cessation of war but the dismantling of the war apparatus and, undoubtedly, a major economic displacement. Thus this may be an idyllic vision, but it contains political realism at its center. The oracle offers not only a grand dream but a realistic hint of what is required. There will be no peace without a lowering of consumerism to match the banishment of arms. For the arms serve primarily either to usurp what belongs to others or to guarantee an arrangement already inequitable. The arms cannot be given up without abandoning swollen appetites as well. There is here no desire to claim this oracle for Micah in the eighth century, but to observe that such an interpretation fits well with Micah's strictures against the surplus-value practice of the royal economy (see 2:1-5; 3:1-3).[15] The hope for an alternative matches the rhetorical dismantling of the present arrangement.

Thus the oracle is a practice of knowing, subversive political imagination: (1) It is expressed as promise, as a critique of the present. (2) The promise touches on ultimate religious symbols, for the gods are delegitimated and the nations submit to Yahweh (first *inclusio*). (3) The promise touches public policy. It appeals to a deep personal hope as a lever on changed social policy that may dismantle the so-called security system of swords and speakers (second *inclusio*). And in that connection, it is clear that the social implications involve not only disarmament. The promise also anticipates lowered economic expectations. It anticipates a modest life-style of not having more than one's own produce and therefore a respect for the produce of others. It implies being ready to settle for one's own vines and figs without yearning for or coveting the vines and figs that others produce. The poet knows that the vines and fig trees of others will be safe only when the powerful are content with the grapes and

---

15. That this contrast should occur especially in Micah is illuminated by Hans Walter Wolff, "Micah the Moreshite," in *Israelite Wisdom*, ed. John G. Gammie et al. (Missoula, Mont.: Scholars Press, 1978), 77–84; and more fully his "Wie verstand Micha von Moreschet sein prophetisches Amt?" in *Congress Volume: Göttingen*, VTSup 29 (Leiden: Brill, 1978), 403–17. Wolff has argued that Micah speaks for the elders of the village who hold to a view of reality in conflict with that of the Jerusalem royal apparatus. Thus it makes sense that verse 4 on "vines and fig trees" should occur in Micah and not in the parallel of Isaiah.

figs they themselves produce. Thus, this radical vision understands that a dismantling of the military machine carries with it a break with consumeristic values.

Taken as a unit, the poet combines the subversion of promise, the transformation of religious symbols, and a radical alternative social policy. Taken together, these factors invite Israel to a dangerous and liberated imagination of how life may yet be ordered. The oracle is as radical and realistic in social anticipation as it is bold in theological affirmation. And the linkage between the social anticipation and theological affirmation is in the torah that stands just between the two *inclusios* in verse 2.

II

The other task of the prophets of Israel is to "pluck up and break down," that is, to mount an effective criticism of the present arrangements. The rhetoric of faithful Israel is to work an assault on such arrangements to discredit and delegitimate their claims upon the people.

The criticism regularly mounted in ancient Israel is against present arrangements that terrify and usurp the life-goods from one table to put them on another, more fortunate, table. We have seen that such criticism is implicit in the promise. But we can be more precise. The criticism mounted in Israel tends not to be a technical discussion of this or that material or strategy. Rather, it is a fundamental critique of the system that claims too much. The system criticized tends to contain all possibilities, to know everything and promise everything. The criticism is to assert that the system is a poor replica for the sovereignty of Yahweh, who stands over against every such pretension. It is the way of the royal system in Israel to domesticate promises and contain imagination so that everything "imaginable" is already given in the present order.

It is widely agreed that Solomon is the paradigm of such a comprehensive systems-approach to reality in ancient Israel.[16] In the late united monarchy, in imitation of ancient Near Eastern counterparts, the Solomonic pretense sought to be completely comprehensive. The text reflective of that system studied here is 1 Kings 4:20-28

---

16. See Frank M. Cross, *Canaanite Myth and Hebrew Epic* (Cambridge, Mass.: Harvard Univ. Press, 1973), 237–73; George Mendenhall, "The Monarchy," *Int* 29 (1975): 155–70.

(Hebr. 4:20-5:8). The text appears to be a straightforward narrative account. It may be divided into two parts:
The first part is a brief generalization:

> Judah and Israel were as many as the sand by the sea; they ate and drank and were happy. Solomon ruled over all the kingdoms from the Euphrates to the land of the Philistines and to the border of Egypt; they brought tribute and served Solomon all the days of his life. (vv. 20-21 [Hebr. 4:20—5:1])

The statement reports unprecedented well-being for Israel based on broad dominions and the resultant taxes from subservient peoples. The juxtaposition of motifs is telling: well-being/dominions/subservience/taxes!

The second part (vv. 22-28 [Hebr. 5:2-8]) gives the particulars to illustrate the main claim of verses 20-21. Thus verse 20 asserts peace and prosperity. That is described in verses 22-25 (Hebr. 5:2-5):

> Solomon's provision for one day was thirty cors of choice flour, and sixty cors of meal, ten fat oxen, and twenty pasture-fed cattle, one hundred sheep, besides deer, gazelles, roebucks, and fatted fowl. For he had dominion over all the region west of the Euphrates from Tiphsah to Gaza, over all the kings west of the Euphrates; and he had peace on all sides. During Solomon's lifetime Judah and Israel lived in safety, from Dan even to Beer-sheba, all of them under their vines and fig trees. (NRSV)

Verse 21 (Hebr. 5:1) describes the dominion and taxes that make it all possible. That is characterized in detail in verses 26-28 (Hebr. 5:6-8) with special attention to armaments. Thus the whole of verses 22-23 may be summarized:

verses 22-23 (Hebr. 5:2-3)	prosperity at the king's table, that is, for the vast imperial apparatus;
verse 24a (Hebr. 5:4a)	broadness of dominions that shows that the old land-promises are now fulfilled;
verses 24b-25 (Hebr. 5:4b-5)	a picture of idyllic peace and well-being;
verses 26-28 (Hebr. 5:6-8)	administrative arrangements for collection of taxes and deployment of arms.

On the face of it, we are given a comprehensive picture of an affluent, secure, self-sufficient, promise-keeping regime. Perhaps that is all that is intended in the narrative. But when this report is considered in light of the promise of Mic. 4:1-5, one may ask if this is a simple narrative report, or if it is criticism couched in subtle and high irony, subtle enough to escape the vigilant censors and high enough not to be missed by those who hold other visions.

We may identify irony at three points. First, in verse 20, "Judah and Israel were many...; they ate and drank and were happy." The claim is for a high standard of living. But we know there is only so much material, energy, and consumer goods. And when some have so much, someone else is paying. So "Judah and Israel were...happy." But, we may ask, "Which ones?" "Which citizens?" "Which Judahites and which Israelites?" Certainly not all. When some live so extravagantly, others must have paid. And, of course, the benefactors are the ones in the royal system, the ones regarded as first-class citizens, well-connected, privy to how it all works.[17] But that does not include everyone. The evidence is disputed. But there is evidence. In 1 Kings 9:22, Israel is carefully excluded from the forced labor policy. (And forced labor is an imperial way of having some produce "surplus value" for the high standard of living by the others.) But 1 Kings 5:13 appears to be more candid, even if less carefully loyal to Solomon. Perhaps we cannot decide between these two kinds of evidence.[18] But it does not matter. Either way, the point is that prosperity and abundance in such extravagance are based on slave-labor policy. It could not be otherwise. Affluence and security are linked to oppression and domination. Some share the dream ful-

---

17. George Mendenhall ("The Shady Side of Wisdom," in *A Light unto My Path*, ed. Howard N. Bream, R. D. Heim, and Casey A. Moore [Philadelphia: Temple Univ. Press, 1974], 321–25) has a trenchant characterization of the development of this "class" in society. Brian Kovacs ("Is There a Class-Ethic in Proverbs?" in *Essays in Old Testament Ethics*, ed. James L. Crenshaw and John T. Willis [New York: KTAV, 1974], 171–89) and Robert Gordis (*Poets, Prophets and Sages* [Bloomington: Indiana Univ. Press, 1971], 160–97) have made a beginning in tracing the vested interest in the teaching of this class. But I do not think we have fully grasped the connection between the *intelligence* of this group and the *economic interest* that it sustains and legitimates. That connection, I submit, is evident in this text from Solomon. Glendon E. Bryce (*A Legacy of Wisdom* [Lewisburg, Pa.: Bucknell Univ. Press, 1979], chaps. 6–8) has offered a helpful review of the political function of wisdom in Solomon's court.

18. John Bright (*A History of Israel* [Philadelphia: Westminster, 1972], 281) notes the problem and draws a conclusion including Israel in the program. See his n. 92 on the counteropinion by Noth. Martin Noth (*The History of Israel* [New York: Harper and Row, 1960], 211) concludes, "[I]t would have been a monstrous infringement of their legal rights on the king's part to have compelled them to do forced labor." But that is precisely the point.

filled. Others pay for it. And it does not matter greatly if these others are Israelites. Such a consuming enterprise with such a gargantuan appetite is not likely to discriminate. The "peace and prosperity" system of Solomon is surely a system of exploitation, as is evident in 1 Kings 11–12. And that makes us alert to the possible irony in verse 21 (Hebr. 5:1).

Second, there may well be irony in the curt note of verse 24 (Hebr. 5:4): "peace on all sides." Again it appears that Lev. 26:5 is invoked. That is, Solomon is the embodiment of all the oldest, most previous promises. The old promise had been for "peace on every side." And now Israel under Solomon has it. But this uncritical "realized eschatology" is undoubtedly for some at the expense of others. The irony in the text suggests that we ask about such systems of security and meaning: Who benefits? Who eats well? Who has peace? That is, *cui bono?*

We have seen that the old promise of Lev. 26:6 is at play in the promise of Mic. 4:4. And it likely is used in 1 Kings 4:25 (Hebr. 5:5), "Judah and Israel lived in safety," *lābeṭaḥ* (cf. Lev. 26:5). Thus both Mic. 4:4 and 1 Kings 4:25 (Hebr. 5:5) appeal to the promise of Lev. 26:5-6, where the blessing is "peace on all sides" and "dwell in safety." The statements of Micah 4 and 1 Kings 4 are not completely parallel. But they are close enough to indicate that both draw on the same tradition of blessing. And it may well be that this ironic text is not unfamiliar with the promise tradition reflected in Mic. 4:1-4.

But it is the third indication of irony that claims our attention. The very dream of Mic. 4:4 is reiterated here:

> During Solomon's lifetime...all of them under their vines and fig trees...

The quintessential dream used by the promise-oracle to protest statism (that is, systems of swords and spears) is now co-opted by the propaganda of the state. The elemental dream of liberation from state usurpation is now preempted to support the very ideology of usurpation by the state. That is, the very same metaphor is now taken in a reverse way to support the system it was intended to criticize. It is strikingly odd to find this irenic vision now set in verse 25 (Hebr. 5:5) bounded in verse 24 (Hebr. 5:4) by a report of imperial boundaries and in verse 26 (Hebr. 5:6) by a reference to forty thousand horses and twelve thousand horsemen. And the whole is rounded off in verses 27-28 (Hebr. 5:7-8) with a recipe for the acquisitive society.

The irony is complete. The foundation of personal well-being in a stable, equitable society had been affirmed in Mic. 4:1-4[19] at the cost of acquisitive "social security." That is, to have a vine and fig tree, one must give up swords and spears. Now that radical, subversive, alternative imagination is reduced to an imperial slogan.

The formal construction of the ironic statement is evident. It consists in taking this statement about "vines and fig trees" (which I judge to be old and familiar) and setting it in the utterly incongruous context of Solomonic arms and oppression. That formal device is confirmed by the substance of the irony. The state practices greed, usurpation, and exploitation. It is an embodiment of crass impingement upon personal well-being.[20] It is not anarchy but state policy that leaves everyone unsure and terrified. It is the state system that claims and consumes and devours every fig from every personal fig tree and every grape from every personal vine.

By any objective criterion, the state system is organized against the fundamental dream of Mic. 4:4. The present royal, prosaic practice is diametrically opposed to the poetic future of the prophetic oracle. And yet the royal system manages to co-opt the very thing it opposes. It pretends to guarantee the very thing it refutes.

Finally, of course, we cannot know if 1 Kings 4:20-28 (Hebr. 4:20—5:8) is a serious statement of state policy or if it is heavyhanded propaganda or if it is subtle, critical irony. What is clear is that by such shrewd manipulation, the propaganda of the state promises the very thing it cannot give because it is in principle opposed to it. And the remainder of the Solomonic narrative makes the point: it cannot secure personal vines and fig trees for its citizenry because it is fundamentally devoted to a rapacious use of those very products. It

---

19. Gottwald (*Tribes of Yahweh*) has used the term "egalitarian" to characterize this society. It is most plausible that "vines and fig trees" embody the notion of an egalitarian society. But as Gerhard Lenski (*Power and Privilege* [New York: McGraw-Hill, 1966]) has made clear, an egalitarian society is incompatible with an economy based on surplus value. Thus a criticism of the Solomonic enterprise invites a move not only to equal distribution but also to much more modest production and much more modest consumption.

20. See again the statement of Noth cited in n. 17, above. He terms it a "monstrous impingement." The Solomonic arrangement is to be understood in terms of the radical shift of economic arrangements and benefits. This is especially evident in the program of redistricting in 1 Kings 4:7-19, which envisioned and accomplished an important economic realignment. Already in 1965, G. Ernest Wright (in an SBL paper) argued that the report must be understood *economically* in terms of the concentration of great wealth in the hands of the bureaucracy. Gottwald (*Tribes of Yahweh*, 368) speaks of "bureaucratic rationality."

cannot give up that rapacious use without at the same time abandoning its pretense of being an inclusive system that can keep every promise.[21]

III

The argument of this discussion depends upon and points to the juxtaposition of these two texts. Their relation cannot be firmly established on critical grounds. But a case can be made for their deliberate juxtaposition on grounds of theological probability. It is evident, I think, that the promise passage, whenever it is dated, must be prior to the narrative report on Solomon. The strident claim of 1 Kings 4:25 (Hebr. 5:5) makes sense only if it is an appeal to a traditional promise.

So, my argument is a very simple one. The use of the "vine and fig tree" metaphor in Mic. 4:1-4 shows a poet in Israel practicing bold imagination, evoking an alternative community yet anticipated. And on the basis of that, the narrative of 1 Kings 4:20-28 (Hebr. 4:20—5:8) is an example of ironic criticism, designed to show that the present royal order, absolute and comprehensive in its claims, cannot keep its promises. Thus the juxtaposition of the texts shows juxtaposition of imagination that describes (and evokes) an alternative future and criticism that exposes the pretense of present ideology. The two texts together point to the unmistakable incongruity of the claims of the Solomonic system.

Micah 4:1-4 shows the deep, irrevocable opposition between swords and spears, on the one hand, and vine and fig trees, on the other. Israel cannot have both, not both the old peasant vision and, at the same time, the new vision of statism. The hard question Israel's faith asks of every system of security and meaning is whether it can give reality to deepest hopes, or if it is in principle diametrically opposed to such promises.

"Vines and fig trees" are modest, peasant dreams. They do not ask for much. They are not royal dreams. The issue posed by this

---

21. It is beyond question that the Solomonic enterprise disintegrated because of oppressive social policy and labor practice. For our purposes, it is important that these policies are not careless aberrations but are the goal of the system. The final result of exploitation is based on the combination of a consumer economy and a class-defending "wisdom." As Bryce (*A Legacy*, chap. 8) has indicated, such wisdom not only is propaganda for others but also is the articulation of a self-deceiving legitimation.

juxtaposition in Israel is about the modest claims and the new state promises. The royal system always promises "more." And that is contrasted with the lower expectations of the deep dream that refuses great oppressive instruments for fulfillment. It appears the criticism in this juxtaposition is not just that the means are wrong but that the goals are also wrong. With the goals inevitably come inequitable and oppressive means.

The juxtaposition of the imagination of Mic. 4:1-4 and the criticism of 1 Kings 4:20-28 (Hebr. 4:20—5:8) permits an observation of incongruity. In our society (and one may hazard it is regularly so), it is the case that those who hold to the most intimate dreams of personal vines and fig trees (that is, "get the government off our backs") are also those who hold most passionately to a war system to create an umbrella of security. These texts together point to the fundamental contradiction in such a posture. It is contradictory to cherish freedom from state usurpation and at the same time to hold for a war system of protection; for the war system can exist only by confiscating the very thing it claims to protect. The prophetic tradition of Israel, among other things, pointed to that contradiction. The contradiction survived only by a delicate balancing act, balancing that got out of kilter at the death of Solomon. And for a moment, the old dream was liberated from the ideology of the state (cf. 1 Kings 12:16).

The juxtaposition leads me to make three methodological observations:

1. Of course, I have taken a bold risk in linking these texts when the critical basis for doing so cannot be established. I do not argue finally that the texts ought to be arranged in this way, though I believe that the promise tradition must be very old or appeal to it would not be made in 1 Kings 4:25 (Hebr. 5:5). But my methodological point is that there is enormous heuristic value in such a juxtaposition even though it is based only on the recurrence of the same formula in both texts. The pursuit of such a formula admits only a provisional linking of texts, but, nonetheless, a very telling linking.

2. The interface of Mic. 4:1-5 and 1 Kings 4:20-28 (Hebr. 4:20—5:8) confirms the dialectic of imagination and criticism. Only a radical practice of imagination, the characterizing of alternative futures, provides ground for criticizing the present. Only the sharp articulation of "things hoped for" permits awareness of how the best hopes have become instruments of oppressive policy. The hope is reduced to a strategy for administrative hopelessness. Prophetic

imagination seems to liberate Israel's hopes from ideological systems that have co-opted the hopes.

But the dialectic works the other way as well. Only the discernment of the ideological dimension of present policy and present power arrangements can let us see how radical, dangerous, and subversive are the genuine visions of this faith. Only the recognition of vested interest at work permits us to see the boldness of a genuinely disinterested vision.

Criticism must begin in imagination. The report of 1 Kings 4:20-28 (Hebr. 4:20—5:8) can be understood only in light of the poem of Mic. 4:1-5. Israel (in the poetic, prophetic tradition of imagination) understood that such radical sketches of hope are the only ground from which to resist the ideologies that devour the grapes and sell the figs for more chariots.

3. Though it has not been my primary concern, my juxtaposition of texts raises the question of the political function of the promissory oracle. It is suggested that the promise has a political function, even if it is not always intentional. Its function is to criticize closed systems of meaning and security that dominate and comprehend the present. That subversive action is done by evoking in the imagination alternative scenarios of how it might be and how it is going to be. Such an act of imagination makes one hold the present arrangement much more provisionally and tentatively.

That observation may be an important one for method. It is worth noting that the dominant scholarly tradition has regarded most such promissory oracles as late. To be sure, that has been done on literary-critical grounds. But the tacit assumption informing such a critical judgment is that hope belongs to times of trouble, that is, exile. The negative counterpart is that hope is unnecessary (or impossible) in times of prosperity. And so hope is banished from situations of well-being. That is, on "critical grounds," the subversion of hope is silenced, and the ideology of the closed systems of prosperity and oppression is left without critique. And when hope is banished, criticism has no base.[22] Specifically in this case, if the oracle of Mic. 4:1-5 is "late," then perhaps one cannot detect any critique in the narrative report of 1 Kings 4:20-28 (Hebr. 20:5-8).

---

22. Mendenhall ("The Shady Side of Wisdom," 323) observes: "For it is true that the products of technical specialization are intended to impress: to neutralize or overcome any possible exercise of critical faculties on the part of those who are not part of the specialized group."

Against a presupposition that in the end is ideological, we have urged that in terms of well-being such hope is urgent. This does not dictate a revision of our critical judgments about promissory oracles, but it may lead to a review of the presuppositions that have informed critical judgments. It may be, as in the time of Micah, that hope is precisely for times of well-being when the closed systems of meaning and security have preempted the field. That theological possibility suggests a different basis for critical judgments.

IV

One other text that uses the formula of vines and fig trees may be cited.[23] I cite it because, in terms of function, it may be placed midway between the imagination of Mic. 4:1-5 and the criticism of 1 Kings 4:20-28 (Hebr. 4:20—5:8). The formula occurs in 1 Macc. 14:4-15, specifically in verse 12. The climate of 1 Maccabees is, of course, very different from either the radical, critical hope of Mic. 4:1-5 or the ideological or ironic report on Solomon in 1 Kings 4:20-28 (Hebr. 4:20—5:8). This is a victory narrative by an oppressed community recently liberated, a minority community for a moment given its own way in history. This text is a buoyant, even strident celebration of Simon, the one who brought victory. The text has echoes of the celebration of Solomon and proceeds in the same way. In verse 12, our phrase occurs:

> All the people sat under their own vines and fig trees,
> and there was none to make them afraid. (NRSV)

---

23. The formula "vine and fig tree" is used in various other contexts. In Jer. 5:17, the threat is that the foreign nation will devour the produce of Judah. In Hos. 2:12 (Hebr. 14), Yahweh will destroy the produce. In Joel, the metaphor is used both negatively (1:12) and positively (2:22) for the destruction by the locusts and the deliverance from them. In Hag. 2:19, the phrase is a general formula for blessing; and in Zech. 3:10, it is a way of speaking about the well-being to come with the arrival of the Branch.

The most interesting and telling use is in the Assyrian proposal of surrender (2 Kings 18:31 = Isa. 36:16). The Assyrian emissary offers that policy as an alternative to the failed policy of royal Judah. That idyllic promise is held out but is immediately followed by an announcement of deportation, to an even better situation. Thus the oldest peasant dream of well-being is not only used by the propaganda of Solomon, but is also placed in the mouth of the invaders. The incongruity of promise and promise-maker is intensified when the phrase is in an Assyrian mouth. (For what it is worth, the fig tree is linked to the practice of "messianic imagination" in John 1:48-50: "You shall see greater things than these.")

And this claim is supported by the statement of verse 8:

> They tilled their land in peace,
> the ground gave its increase,
> and the trees of the plains their fruit. (NRSV)

The text, as noted above, is important for our purposes because it seems to stand midway between ideological claims of the kind made for Solomon and the promissory imagination of Mic. 4:1-5. On the one hand, it is no longer imaginative hope because it does not anticipate. It celebrates what is, in fact, in hand, a new distribution of freedom, power, and goods. History has already turned, even if briefly, to fulfill expectation. The threat of foreign taxes and exploitation has been ended.[24] There is safe space for personal vines and fig trees. The metaphor is used to speak both of a political turn wrought by the Maccabees and of an act of God.

On the other hand, this text is not yet ideology, as the Maccabean movement so soon became. There is nothing here yet of the crass militarism, exploitation, and self-serving stance that so soon infected the Hasmoneans. The text, however, is at the brink of ideology, as is evidenced by the military strutting that is reported:

> Old men sat in the streets;
> they all talked together of good things;
> and the youths donned the glories and garments of war. (v. 9)

The latent militarism here bespeaks a coming oppressive ideology. But there is still only a hint. This text lives at the precarious, precious moment just after promissory imagination and criticism and just before ideological stridency.

This celebration of Simon is important. It gives us a rare glimpse of a text in movement as it slides quickly from critical imagination to conventional ideology. And Israel in the prophetic tradition understood that it is in that moment that faithfulness is to be practiced.

---

24. Martin Hengel (*Judaism and Hellenism* [Philadelphia: Fortress, 1974], 1:28) concludes: "These excessive tax demands will have helped the Maccabean independence movement and are perhaps the real cause for the smouldering of revolt after the death of Judas Maccabaeus."

V

Finally, we make one more return to Mic. 4:1-5, this time to consider verse 5. That verse is likely a cultic formula of summons asking for a response on the part of the community at worship. The parallel use in Isa. 2:2-4 also contains a summons, but a much weaker one. It appears there is much more at stake in the Micah version:

> For all the peoples walk
>   each in the name of its god,
> but we will walk in the name of the Lord our God,
>   forever and ever.

The formula is constructed around two uses of the verb "walk."[25] The contrast of the two uses is sharp and clear. The poet knows there are alternative gods. And he knows that alternative gods bring with them alternative social systems. He knows that the gods and nations who reject Yahweh's kingship (cf. the first *inclusio* of vv. 1-2a) are accompanied with alternative social systems that practice swords and spears, that resist plowshares and pruning hooks, that confiscate vines and usurp fig trees (cf. the second *inclusio* of vv. 2c-4). That is, the summons about the "walk" understands that a choice for a god is also a choice for a social system. And, therefore, a change of gods, to which Israel is called, is a radical disengagement from an absolutist system of meaning and security. It is the "alternative walk" in verse 2 that stands between the two *inclusios*. And that distinctive "walk" is according to torah.

The statement about walking in the name of Yahweh is a decision about religious loyalty but also a decision about alternative social practice, radical disarmament, trust in plowshares and pruning hooks, reliance on simple produce, and rejection of the gifts given by the royal war-machine. The summons of verse 5 is dangerous and polemical—dangerous, because it rejects the gifts given by the absolute royal system; polemical, because it exposes the system as one incapable of doing what it says. The choice is pressed because the oracle affirms that swords and spears are an utterly impossible route to vines and fig trees, which Israel so craves. This, it appears, is the intent of this summons, if it is taken as a judgment drawn from the preceding promissory oracle.

---

25. For a general discussion of the theological motif of "walk," see James Muilenburg, *The Way of Israel* (New York: Harper and Brothers, 1961), 33–38.

It cannot be shown, of course, that verse 5 is to be linked closely to the Solomonic enterprise. But the juxtaposition of Mic. 4:1-5 and 1 Kings 4:20-28 (Hebr. 4:20—5:8) permits a suggestion in that direction. And the suggestion is that the summons of verse 5 may provide a clue to the shape of the Solomonic narrative. We have suggested that the Solomonic narrative is shaped in ironic fashion. Now we may press one specific possibility.

In 1 Kings 3:3, as is well known, the narrative begins, "Solomon loved the Lord." And in 3:14, that he loved the Lord is concretized as "walk in all my ways" (cf. 9:4). Thus Solomon is prepared to walk faithfully, as the summons of Mic. 4:5 suggests. (The "walk" in Mic. 4:5 refers to torah [v. 2] as surely as the "walk" in 1 Kings 3:14 refers to statutes and commandments.)[26]

In contrast, at the conclusion of the Solomonic narrative when the empire is about to disintegrate, the narrator concludes, "Solomon loved many foreign women" (11:1), a knowing antithesis to 3:3. And this is concretized in 11:5, 10, where he walked after many foreign gods (cf. 9:6), which resulted in domination and oppression. Thus we may summarize the next juxtaposition:

loved Yahweh (3:3)...walk in my ways...[yields well-being].
loved foreign women (11:1)...walked after foreign gods...[yields oppression].

The point may not be pressed that Mic. 4:5 in any direct way is related to Solomon. And indeed the word "walk" is too much used to claim anything. But the juxtaposition is a telling one to link even more tightly the imagination of the promise and the criticism of the narrative. The summons of Mic. 4:5 is to decide about alternative walks, walks that have to do with loyalties among the gods and with the implementation of social policy. Solomon begins with a passion for Yahweh's torah (1 Kings 3:14; cf. Mic. 4:2) and ends with other gods, which leads to chariots and horsemen, swords and spears (cf. Mic. 4:3).

The linkages should not be pressed. But attention to the metaphor of "vines and fig trees" suggests a remarkable juxtaposition. It also suggests that attention to social function and vision, social

---

26. On the significance of v. 14 for the entire passage and on the intent of "walk" as a form of obedience, see the careful analysis of Helen Ann Kenik, *Design for Kingship: The Deuteronomistic Narrative Technique in 1 Kings 3:14-15*, SBLDS 69 (Chico, Calif.: Scholars Press, 1983), 163–69.

interest and power, is important in our reading of the text. The poetic claims of the oracle function in political, subversive ways. And they permit the possibility that in the midst of propaganda, we may discern critical irony.

6

At the Mercy of Babylon:
A Subversive Rereading of the Empire

BIBLICAL THEOLOGY as a study of Israel's faithful speech may be said to revolve around two organizing questions. The first question of biblical theology is, "How does Israel speak about God?" Israel characteristically does not speak about God unless it speaks at the same time about the world in which God is present and over which God governs. For that reason, the second question of biblical theology is, "What else must Israel talk about when it talks about God?" It belongs decisively to the character of this God, as artistically rendered in Israel's text, always to be engaged in ways that impinge both upon God and upon God's "other." One aspect of that God–other engagement that is typical of Israel's theological speech is God in relation to the nations. The God of Israel is a God who deals with the nations, and the nations inescapably deal with the God of Israel. Together they form a common subject in Israel's theological speech.

I

The great powers, north and south, dominate Israel's public life and policy.[1] In this chapter, I will pay attention to one of the great

---

1. On the bipolar geopolitical situation of Israel, see Abraham Malamat, "The Kingdom of Judah between Egypt and Babylon: A Small State within a Great Power Confrontation," in *Text and Context,* ed. Walter Claassen, JSOTSup 48 (Sheffield: Sheffield Academic Press, 1988), 117–29.

northern powers, Babylon, and the way in which Babylon enters into Israel's speech about God. While Babylon may be regarded as simply one among several great powers that concern Israel, it is also clear that Babylon peculiarly occupies the imagination of Israel. Babylon goads and challenges Israel's theological imagination in remarkably varied ways. As a theological metaphor, Babylon is not readily dismissed or easily categorized. Indeed, in the postexilic period, it is Babylon and not Persia that continues to function as a powerful theological metaphor for Israel. Babylon operates in a supple way in Israel's theological speech because Babylon is a partner and antagonist in Israel's political life and is perceived as a partner and antagonist worthy of Yahweh. As Yahweh cannot be settled or reduced in Israel's discernment, so Babylon cannot be settled or reduced, but remains as a tensive, energizing force in Israel's faith and imagination. Moreover, if the experience of exile was decisive for the canonizing process, as seems most probable, then it is equally probable that Babylon takes on imaginative power that is not simply historical and political but canonical in force, significance, and density.

By considering the theological function of Babylon, we are concerned with the question, What happens to *speech about Babylon* when it is drawn into the sphere of speech about God? In a lesser fashion, we will also ask, What happens to *speech about God* when God is drawn into the sphere of speech about the empire? In posing these questions, it is clear that we are taking up issues of artistic construal that are not fully contained in historical and political categories. As George Steiner has said of great art in general, we are dealing in the Bible not simply with a formulation but with a reformulation and a rethinking.[2] We are concerned with a canonizing process whereby Israel voices its normative, paradigmatic construal of imperial power. Israel's rhetoric at the interface of God and empire is a concrete attempt to hold together the inscrutable reality of God (which is at the center of its rethought world) and the raw power of the empire (which is a daily reality of its life). Israel's self-identity, presence in the world, and chance for free action depend upon how these two are held together.

By joining speech about God to speech about Babylon, Israel's faith radically rereads the character of the empire, consistently

---

2. George Steiner (*Real Presences* [Chicago: Univ. of Chicago Press, 1989], 44) writes of "un-ending re-reading" and reevaluation.

subverting every conventional reading of the empire in which complacent Babylon and intimidated Israel must have colluded. That is, Babylon presented itself as autonomous, invincible, and permanent. When Israel entered fully into the ideology of Babylon (and abandoned its own covenantal definitions of reality), it accepted this characterization of Babylon and, derivatively, its own fate as completely defined by Babylonian reality. This is a classic example of the phenomenon, noted by Marx, of the victim willingly participating in the ideology of the perpetrator.[3] This conventional collusion about power practiced by perpetrators and victims is controverted, however, in Israel's alternative reading, which is deeply and inherently subversive. When Israel, in a Yahwistic context, could discern that Babylon was not as it presented itself, then Israel did not need to define its own situation so hopelessly. Thus Yahwistic faith makes an alternative to imperial ideology available to those who live from this counterrhetoric.

II

I have selected six texts concerning Babylon on which to focus. These texts are: Jer. 42:9-17; Jer. 50:41-43; Isa. 47:5-7; 1 Kings 8:46-53; 2 Chron. 36:15-21; and Dan. 4:19-27.[4] My thesis, which I will explicate in relation to these texts, is that when Israel's speech about Babylon is drawn into Israel's speech concerning God, the power of the empire is envisioned and reconstructed around the issue of mercy (*rhm*).[5] The intrusion of the rhetoric of mercy into the realpolitik of Babylon derives from the uncompromising character of God. It also arises from the deepest yearning of the exilic community, which must have mercy to live, which expects mercy from God,

---

3. See Karl Marx and Friedrich Engels, *The German Ideology, Part One*, ed. C. J. Arthur (London: Lawrence and Wishart, 1970), 64–68.

4. The texts on Babylon that I will not consider include Isaiah 13–14; materials in Isaiah 40–55; references in the Ezekiel collection of oracles against the nations; 2 Chron. 30:6-9; and Dan. 1:5-9.

5. In the texts I will consider, there are two exceptions to the use of the term *rhm*. In 2 Chron. 36:15-21, the term is *hml*. In Dan. 4:24, the term used is *hnn*. Both these terms, however, belong in the same semantic field as *rhm*. On the political, public dimensions of *rhm*, see Michael Fishbane, "The Treaty Background of Amos 1:11 and Related Matters," *JBL* 89 (1970): 313–18; and Robert B. Coote, "Amos 1:11: RHMYW," *JBL* 90 (1971): 206–8. On the intimate, interpersonal nuances of the term, see Phyllis Trible, *God and the Rhetoric of Sexuality*, OBT (Philadelphia: Fortress, 1978), 31–59.

and which by venturesome rhetoric dares to insist that the promised, yearned-for mercy cannot be ignored by the empire.

1. *Jeremiah 42:9-17.* In its final form the book of Jeremiah has a decidedly pro-Babylonian slant, mediated through the Baruch document and perhaps powered by the authority and influence of the family of Shaphan.[6] The sustained urging of the text is that the people of Jerusalem must stay in the jeopardized city and submit to the occupying presence of Babylon and not flee to Egypt. This announcement reflects a political judgment and a political interest that cooperation with Babylon is a safer way to survival. This voice of advocacy also concluded that cooperation with Egypt would only cause heavier, more destructive Babylonian pressure. That political judgment, however, is given as an oracle of God. The urging, therefore, is not simply political strategy but is offered as the intent of God for God's people. Thus the oracle is not simply speech concerning the empire but also speech about God.

The oracle of Jeremiah 42 is cast in two conditional clauses: one positive, "if" you remain in the city (vv. 10-12); the other negative, "if" you flee to Egypt (vv. 13-17). The positive conditional clause is cast as a promise that God will repent of evil and issues in a salvation oracle:[7]

> Do not fear the king of Babylon
> of whom you are afraid.
> Do not fear him, says the Lord, for I am with you
> to deliver you from his hand. (v. 11)

The Jeremiah tradition takes a conventional speech form, the salvation oracle, and presses it into new use. The conventional form is "do not fear," followed by an assurance. Here, however, the form is daringly extended to identify the one not to be feared, the king of

---

6. Christopher R. Seitz (*Theology in Conflict: Reactions to the Exile in the Book of Jeremiah,* BZAW 176 [Berlin: de Gruyter, 1989]) has discerned the conflicting and competing ideologies concerning exile present in the book of Jeremiah. On the peculiar and decisive role of the family of Shaphan in the Jeremiah tradition, see J. Andrew Dearman, "My Servants the Scribes: Composition and Context in Jeremiah 36," *JBL* 109 (1990): 403–21.

7. On the theological implications of this text, see Terence E. Fretheim, *The Suffering of God,* OBT (Philadelphia: Fortress, 1984), 138–44; and Francis I. Andersen and David N. Freedman, *Amos: A New Translation with Introduction and Commentary,* AB 24A (New York: Doubleday, 1989), 659–63.

Babylon.[8] Moreover, the speech form is utilized exactly to juxtapose the fearsome power of Nebuchadnezzar and the resolve of the Lord, "Do not fear him. . . . I will deliver." The oracle counters the empire with God's good resolve. The assurance of God continues:

> I will grant you mercy [*raḥamîm*]
> that [*wᵉ*] he will have mercy on you,[9]
> and let you remain in the land. (v. 12)

The connection between "I" and "he" (the king of Babylon) is elusive, bridged only by a waw consecutive. The oracle does, however, insist upon this decisive, albeit elusive, link between Yahweh's resolve and anticipated imperial policy. The oracle asserts that Babylon can indeed be a source of mercy to Jerusalem when the empire subscribes to God's own intention. The negative counterpart of verses 13-17 indicates that if there is flight to Egypt and away from Babylon, the same Babylonian king who is capable of mercy will indeed be "the sword which you fear" (v. 16).

Our historical-critical propensity is to say that the oracle of Jer. 42:9-17 simply reflects a wise, pragmatic political decision. Such a reading, however, ignores the casting of the speech in which the "I" of God's mercy directly shapes the "he" of Nebuchadnezzar's policy. That rhetorical linkage is crucial for the argument of the whole of the tradition. This rhetorical maneuver recasts the empire as an agent who is compelled, under the right circumstance, to show mercy. The speech practice of the Jeremiah-Baruch-Shaphan tradition includes Babylon in the sphere where mercy will be practiced as a public reality.

2. *Jeremiah 50:41-43.* Scholars tend to read these "oracles against the nations" as a separate literary unit and in terms of historical, political developments. In distinction from the Greek, the Hebrew text places the oracles against the nations, and especially chapters 50–51 against Babylon, at the end of the book; this arrangement invites us to pay attention to their canonical intention, that is, to move beyond

---

8. See Edgar W. Conrad, *Fear Not Warrior,* BJS 75 (Chico, Calif.: Scholars Press, 1985), 48–51.

9. The LXX reads the second verb in the first person, "I will have mercy on you," thus removing the tension that is crucial to our argument. That rendering makes the text irrelevant to the interface we are seeking to identify. Recent major commentaries consistently prefer the MT reading. See the comment of John Bright, *Jeremiah: Introduction, Translation, and Notes,* AB 21 (Garden City, N.Y.: Doubleday, 1965), 256.

historical, political concerns to notice the connection between these oracles and other parts of the Jeremiah tradition.[10] In this ordering of materials, the midterm verdict of the book of Jeremiah is that Nebuchadnezzar will triumph and rule, even in Jerusalem (25:8-11; 27:5-7b). That midterm verdict, however, is overcome by the final verdict of the Hebrew book of Jeremiah (see also 25:12-14, 27:7b). In the end, it will be God and not Nebuchadnezzar who prevails in the historical process. Again, we can read this assertion simply in relation to the politics of the nations, so that we anticipate (in retrospect) that the Persians will have defeated and succeeded the Babylonians.

Israel's way of speaking, however, is not rooted simply in historical analysis. The ominous verdict against Babylon in Jer. 50:41-43 is rather an intentional rhetorical effort that intends to answer and resolve the so-called Scythian Song of 6:22-24. This is not simply a conventional recycling of poetic images, but this reuse of poetic material intends to counter and refute the first use. The purpose of the Scythian Song (6:22-24) is to invoke in the most threatening fashion the coming of the intruder from the north. The coming threat is portrayed in this way:

> They lay hold on bow and spear;
> they are cruel and have no mercy [*rḥm*]. (6:23)

In contrast to the anticipated Babylonian accommodation of chapter 42, the poetry of 6:23 knows there will be "no mercy" from the invading army. The coming of the invader with "no mercy" in chapter 6 is God's resolve to punish recalcitrant Jerusalem.

Chapter 50 uses the same rhetoric to reverse the earlier verdict of 6:23. Now the threatening intruder from the north is not Babylon, but one who comes against Babylon. This coming people, like Babylon, is savage in its invasion:

> They lay hold on bow and spear;
> they are cruel and have no mercy [*rḥm*]. (50:42)

---

10. The alternative placement of these texts by the LXX after 25:14 anticipates the debate about whether Nebuchadnezzar's massive power is temporary (MT chaps. 27–28) and whether Jerusalem will indeed be given a future (MT chap. 29). See William L. Holladay, *Jeremiah 2: A Commentary on the Book of the Prophet Jeremiah, Chapters 26–52*, Hermeneia (Minneapolis: Fortress, 1989), 312–14. Note the abrupt "until" in 27:2, 11. Moreover, 25:12-14 anticipates the demise of Babylon and asserts that the Babylonians will in time be reduced to the status of slavery (cf. Isa. 47:1-4).

The ones who come against Babylon have "no mercy." Thus the poem threatens and destabilizes Babylon with the same phrasing that authorized Babylon in 6:22-23.

The use of the same phrasing in 6:22-24 and 50:41-43 greatly illuminates the way in which Yahweh relates to the nations. On the one hand, Yahweh is in both situations the one who takes initiative, the one with authority. On the other hand, Yahweh's purpose is multidimensional, so that in different times and circumstances, the rule of God may be evidenced both for Babylon and against Babylon. In both postures, the way of Yahweh is the implementation of a policy of "no mercy."

The prose commentary that follows this oracle in 50:44-46 interprets the poetry. It makes a sweeping theological claim: God has a plan (*'ṣh*) and a purpose (*mḥšb*) and can appoint and summon "whomever I choose" (v. 44). The retention and exercise of imperial power are tentative and provisional. Even the great Nebuchadnezzar, the rhetoric asserts, is subject to the rule of Yahweh, which concerns the practice of "mercy" and "no mercy." Thus the oracle of Jeremiah 50–51 at the end of the canonical book asserts the rule of God over international affairs. The reuse of 6:22-23 is, for our purposes, particularly important. The double use connects the dispatch of Babylon by God with "no mercy," and then the destruction of Babylon with "no mercy."

Two things strike us in this construal of Babylon's destiny. First, God deals directly with Babylon and Persia, without any reference to Judah or Jerusalem. God is indeed the God of the nations. Second, the exercise of God's sovereignty concerns matters of mercy and no mercy. The destiny of Babylon turns on Yahweh's various initiatives with mercy. Thus the rhetoric of Israel reconstitutes the geopolitics of the Fertile Crescent with reference to mercy.

The sequence of 6:22-24 (which anticipates Babylon) and 50:41-43 (which dismisses Babylon) stands in an odd relation to the salvation oracle of chapter 42. The editing of the book of Jeremiah is complex, so that we may indeed have different editorial hands. In the text as we have it, the Baruch document promises mercy from Babylon, though that mercy is conditional (42:9-17). The poetic units, both the "early" poem (6:22-23) and the oracle against the Babylonians (50:41-43), refute the option of mercy. Yet in all of the texts, whatever their origin, the rise and fall of empires has been drawn into the language of mercy. The tradition insists—as regards Babylon, Persia, Jerusalem, and God's assurance—that the play of power around the city of Jerusalem raises the question and the possibility of mercy.

3. *Isaiah 47:5-7.* Because we do not know when to date the Jeremiah materials, we do not know about the relative dating of Jeremiah 50 and Isaiah 47.[11] I take up Isaiah 47 after the Jeremiah text because conventionally, Second Isaiah is placed after Jeremiah, though Jeremiah 50 may indeed be later. In any case, Isaiah 47 permits a more comprehensive and reflective commentary on the mercy questions posed in the Jeremiah tradition. In brief form, Isaiah 47 offers one of the most comprehensive statements of Israel's theology of the nations. God's dealing with the empire is elaborated in four stages:

a. The first element is:

> I was angry with my people. (v. 6a)

The tradition insists that the destruction of Jerusalem was not an accomplishment of Babylonian policy but happened at the behest of God (cf. Jer. 25:8-11; 27:5-6; Isa. 40:1-2). The destruction is a sovereign act of God, only implemented by Nebuchadnezzar.

b. The second element is:

> I profaned my heritage;
> I gave them into your hand. (v. 6b, c)

It is God who submits Jerusalem to the invasion of Babylon. These first two elements of the speech of God constitute a conventional prophetic lawsuit. Israel is indicted for its failure to obey God. Israel is placed under the judgment of foreign invasion. The coming of the invader is God's stance of "no mercy" toward Jerusalem.

c. The third element of this oracle is unexpected and moves well beyond the conventional lawsuit speech:

> You [Babylon] showed no mercy (*rḥm*). (v. 6d)

---

11. The current options for dating the materials are reflected in the commentaries of William L. Holladay, *Jeremiah 1: A Commentary on the Book of the Prophet Jeremiah, Chapters 1–25*, Hermeneia (Philadelphia: Fortress, 1986); and idem, *Jeremiah 2*; and Robert P. Carroll, *Jeremiah: A Commentary*, OTL (Philadelphia: Westminster, 1986). The dating of the materials is not important for our argument about rhetoric but would illuminate the sequence in which the texts might be taken up.

The text offers no grammatical connection between this statement and what has just preceded. We expect "but" or "however" or "nevertheless," but we get nothing.[12] d. This parataxis then leads to a rebuke of the empire:

> You said, "I will be mistress forever,"
> so that you did not lay these things to heart
> or remember their end. (v. 7)

The first two elements in Isa. 47:5-7, then, are conventional: God is angry with Israel. God punishes Israel by summoning a punishing nation, in this case Babylon. We are not prepared for the third and fourth elements, however. The speech is constructed as though Nebuchadnezzar (and Babylonian policy) was all along supposed to have known that mercy toward Jerusalem was in order and expected, appropriate even in light of God's anger. I imagine that inside the drama of the text, Nebuchadnezzar could react to these third and fourth elements in God's speech by saying in indignation, "Mercy? You never mentioned mercy!" Of course, Nebuchadnezzar is not permitted to speak at all, except in the poetic self-indictment of verse 7a.

The turn in the third element of Isa. 47:5-7 is precisely pertinent to our thesis. "Mercy" readily intrudes into political talk where it is not expected. Mercy impinges upon the policies and destiny even of the empire. In conversation about God and empire, mercy operates as a nonnegotiable factor. Nebuchadnezzar should have known that Yahweh is that kind of God. From the beginning, Yahweh has been a God of mercy, and mercy is characteristically present where Yahweh is present. In the end, even the empire stands or fails in terms of God's resilient commitment to mercy. Ruthless power cannot circumvent that resolve of God.

It is clear that rhetorically, something decisive has happened between the second and third elements of this oracle. The first two phrases look back to 587 and echo the predictable claims of lawsuit, long anticipated by the prophets. In the third and fourth phrases, however, the poet has turned away from conventional lawsuit claims, away from 587, away from destruction and judgment. Now the poet looks forward, out beyond the exile. Now God's very tool of exile has become the object of God's indignation. In this moment, God's

---

12. On the function of such parataxis, see G. B. Caird, *The Language and Imagery of the Bible* (Philadelphia: Westminster, 1980), 117–21.

old, old agenda of mercy reemerges (cf. Exod. 34:6-7). The practice
of this rhetoric, in the horizon of the poet, destabilizes the empire.
Israel's speech knows that empires, in their imagined autonomy, will
always have to come to terms with God's alternative governance.[13]
The empire is never even close to being ultimate but always lives
under the threat of this rhetoric that rejects every imperial compla-
cency, every act of autonomy, every gesture of self-sufficiency. The
poem of Isaiah 47 ends with an awesome verdict emerging from this
exchange about arrogant autonomy and mercy: "There is no one to
save you!" (v. 25).

4. *1 Kings 8:46-53.* This text is commonly taken to belong to the
latest layer of Deuteronomistic interpretation.[14] It is cast as part of
the prayer of Solomon. It is structured as an "if-then" formulation,
echoed in 2 Chron. 30:9. The petition anticipates a conditional exile. It contains an "if" of repentance in exile (v. 48) and a "then"
followed by four imperatives addressed to God on the basis of
repentance:

> [H]ear thou in heaven…,
> maintain their cause,
> and forgive thy people;…
> grant them mercy [*rḥm*]. (vv. 49-50)

A motivation is offered to God in verse 51; an additional petition is
voiced in verse 52; and a final motivational clause is given in verse 53.

What interests us is the fourth imperative of petition in verses
49-50:

> Grant them compassion [*rḥm*] in the sight of those who carried them
> away captive, that they may have compassion [*rḥm*] on them.

It is clear in the prayer that it is God and only God who gives mercy.
God is the only subject of the verb, *ntn*. God must grant (*ntn*) mercy
if any is to be given. The last word of the petition adds, however,
"that they [the captors] may have compassion [or mercy]." Again
the inclination of God and the disposition of Babylon are intimately
related to each other. It is not doubted that the Babylonian empire

---

13. See, for example, Isa. 37:22-29, and the comments of Donald E. Gowan, *When
Man Becomes God* (Pittsburgh: Pickwick, 1975), 31–35.

14. See Hans Walter Wolff, "The Kerygma of the Deuteronomic Historical Work,"
in *The Vitality of Old Testament Traditions,* by Walter Brueggemann and Hans Walter
Wolff (Atlanta: John Knox, 1982), 95–97.

could be a place of mercy. The exile can be a place of compassion, but that can only be because God hears prayers and attends to the needs of the exiles. The empire is a place where God's inclination for mercy can indeed be effected in a concrete, public way. Babylon can enact what God grants.[15] The claim of this text is close to the affirmation of Jer. 42:12.

5. *2 Chronicles 36:15-21.* This text is the penultimate paragraph of 2 Chronicles. In these verses, the Chronicler gives closure to the narrative and engages in a sweeping retrospective. The term "mercy" (*ḥml*) occurs twice in this concluding and ominous statement. First, the God of Israel is a God of mercy who has practiced long-term, persistent mercy toward Israel:

> The Lord, the God of their fathers, sent persistently to them by his messengers, because he had mercy [*ḥml*] on his people and on his dwelling place. (v. 15)

The whole history of prophecy is an act of mercy. In this usage, however, mercy is not rescue but warning, to deter Jerusalem from its self-destructive action. Israel, however, refused and resisted, until God's wrath arose and there was "no remedy" (*'ên rāpā'*, [v. 16]).

This passage is constructed so that Babylon does not appear in the text until God's mercy is spent. Only then does the empire enter the scene:

> Therefore, he [God] brought up against them the king of the Chaldeans, who slew their young men with the sword in the house of their sanctuary, and had no mercy [*ḥml*] on young man or virgin, old man or aged; he gave them all into his hand. (v. 17)

It was the designated work of Babylon to destroy, reflective of God's exhausted mercy. The statement is framed so that the active subject at the beginning and end is God; only in between these statements is the king of Babylon permitted as an active agent. Thus far the argument with the double use of "mercy" closely parallels the first two elements of the argument in Isaiah 47.

It is to be recognized that the key term in this text is *ḥml* and not *rḥm*, as elsewhere in our analysis. However, the explicit reference

---

15. Richard Nelson (*First and Second Kings*, Interpretation [Atlanta: John Knox, 1987], 54–55) suggests that the promise of mercy from "your captors" "is the thinnest possible offer of a chance at return for the exiles, one the narrator dares not even whisper" (cf. Ps. 106:46).

to Jeremiah in verse 21 suggests that this text in the Chronicler is an intentional development of the Jeremiah tradition.[16] The Chronicler reiterates the assertions of the Jeremiah tradition that justify the catastrophe of 587. Yet the Chronicler also moves beyond the reflections of the Jeremiah tradition. Thus, the text of Jeremiah is cited as an anticipation that now comes to fresh fulfillment. This penultimate paragraph with the double, albeit negative, reference to "mercy" prepares the way for the final paragraph of verses 22-23, which moves dramatically beyond judgment to God's new act of mercy among the nations:

> Now in the first year of Cyrus, king of Persia, that the word of the Lord in the mouth of Jeremiah might be accomplished, the Lord stirred up the spirit of Cyrus the Persian so that he made a proclamation throughout all his kingdom and also put it in writing. (v. 22)

Even this new world power is to fulfill the word of Jeremiah. Now begins the new phase of Jewish history with Cyrus. It is a new beginning to which Jeremiah 50 has made negative reference and to which Isaiah 44–47 makes positive reference. Our pivotal point of interpretation juxtaposes *the exhausted mercy of Yahweh* and *the lacking mercy of Babylon.*

These texts from Jeremiah, Isaiah, 1 Kings, and the Chronicler seem to be intimately connected to one another in a sustained reflection on the destiny of Israel vis-à-vis Babylon and the workings of God. The salient point is that mercy from God and mercy from Babylon live in an odd and tense relation; neither will work effectively without the other. That is, when Babylon has mercy, it is derivative from the mercy of God. Conversely, when God has no mercy left, there will be none from Babylon. This straightforward connection, however, is disrupted by the discernment of Isa. 47:6. It is this text that creates tension between the mercy of heaven and the mercy of earth. The tension occurs because the empire can indeed exercise autonomy. That autonomy characteristically is self-serving, against mercy, and sure to bring self-destruction, even upon the empire.

In all these texts, Israel is now prepared to move toward the newness embodied in Cyrus the Persian. Thanks to Second Isaiah, the Persian period, contrasted to that of the Babylonians, is perceived

---

16. On this text as an example of intertextual reading, see Michael Fishbane, *Biblical Interpretation in Ancient Israel* (Oxford: Clarendon, 1985), 481–82.

as a new saving action of God that permits the survival and modest prosperity of Judaism. Yet Persia never takes on the imaginative power or metaphorical force of Babylon. In the Old Testament, the theological struggle concerning public power and divine purpose remains focused on the reality, memory, experience, and symbolization of Babylon.

6. *Daniel 4:19-27.* When we come to the book of Daniel, we see that Israel's theological reflection cannot finally finish with Babylon. It is clear that by the time of the Daniel texts, we have broken free of historical reference; Nebuchadnezzar now looms on the horizon of Israel as a cipher for a power counter to the Lord.[17] It is evident, moreover, that Babylon is not a reduced or flattened metaphor, for then Nebuchadnezzar could be defeated and dismissed in the literature. Nebuchadnezzar, however, is kept very much alive and present by the rhetoric of Israel.

The narrative of Daniel 4 concerns the dream of Nebuchadnezzar that the "great tree" will be cut down. As Daniel interprets this dream, it anticipates Nebuchadnezzar's loss of power. Two assumptions operate for the narrator that make the story possible. First, it is proper, legitimate, and acceptable for Jewish lore to entertain a story about Nebuchadnezzar. As we might expect, such a story is told in order to mock and deride the great king. As we shall see, the narrative is not finally a mocking or dismissal of Nebuchadnezzar but in fact portrays his remarkable rehabilitation. Thus, the horizon of the Bible does not flatly dismiss the empire but entertains its possible transformation to an agent of obedience.

Second, the narrative assumes that the great king and his governmental apparatus are dysfunctional. In the end, the great king must step outside his own official circles of power and influence for the guidance he needs. On one level the narrative is a rather conventional contrast between the stupid wielder of power and the shrewd outsider who is able to turn the tables. As we shall see, however, the narrator moves in a different, somewhat unexpected, direction. This story is not primarily about how a Jew prevails over Babylon. It is a story, in the end, about the well-being of Babylon and its power.

Daniel's interpretation of the dream of the king turns on three

---

17. On the freedom of the Daniel text from historical reference, see W. S. Towner, "Were the English Puritans 'the Saints of the Most High?' Issues in the Pre-Critical Interpretation of Daniel 7," *Int* 37 (1983): 46–63; and, more programmatically, Brevard S. Childs, *Introduction to the Old Testament as Scripture* (Minneapolis: Fortress, 1979), 618–22.

crucial affirmations. First, "It is you, O king" (v. 22). The interpretation by Daniel brings the dream into immediate political risk with rhetoric that recalls Nathan's indictment of David (2 Sam. 12:7). Second, the purpose of the dream is that the king will "know that the Most High has sovereignty over the kingdom of mortals, and gives it to whom he will" (v. 25). This formula dominates the narrative, occurring in verses 14, 22, 29, and, with greater variation, 34. Moreover, the formulation contains an echo of Jer. 50:44, to which we have already made reference (cf. 49:19):

> I will appoint over him whomever I choose. For who is like me? Who will summon me? What shepherd can stand before me? Therefore, hear the plan which the Lord has made against Babylon.

In the Jeremiah usage, the transfer of power away from Babylon to "a people from the north" is sure and settled.

In the Daniel narrative, however, there is a third point that leads the narrative in a surprising direction. At the end of his interpretative account, Daniel says,

> Therefore, O king, let my counsel be acceptable to you; break off your sins by practicing righteousness and your iniquities by showing mercy [ḥn] to the oppressed. (v. 24)[18]

Daniel's counsel to the king is unexpected in this context. We have been given no reason to anticipate this narrative development. Daniel ceases here to be an interpreter and becomes a moral instructor of and witness to the great king. For our purposes, it is important to recognize that the empire is understood by the narrative as a potential place of mercy; Nebuchadnezzar is presented as a ruler who is capable of mercy to the oppressed and would be wise to practice such mercy and righteousness.

In the unfolding of the narrative, we are never told that Nebuchadnezzar heeded Daniel and practiced righteousness and mercy. We are later told, however, that his "reason [minda'] returned" (v. 34). He submitted in praise to the Most High (vv. 34-35). Thus, it is legitimate to imagine that the narrative understands the "return of reason," the capacity to praise, and the restoration of majesty and

---

18. As indicated, the term here is not *rḥm* but *ḥnn*. On the cruciality of the old creedal formulation in which they are closely related, see Hermann Spieckermann, "Barmhherzig und gnädig ist der Herr...," *ZAW* 102 (1990): 1–18.

splendor to Nebuchadnezzar (v. 36) as evidence of the practice of mercy as urged by Daniel. We may now consider the sequence of texts we have discussed concerning the recurring interplay of God, mercy, and the destiny of the empire:

a. In Jer. 6:23 and 2 Chron. 36:15, there is no mercy because God intended that there should be no mercy.

b. In Isa. 47:6, there is no mercy, and Nebuchadnezzar is sharply admonished for this lack that violates God's intention.

c. In Jer. 42:12 and 1 Kings 8:50, Babylon is judged to be capable of mercy, and Jews legitimately expect mercy.

d. In Dan. 4:27, which is a late, perhaps climactic word on Babylon in the Old Testament, the hope of Daniel again counts on the mercy of the empire, as that mercy is anticipated in Jer. 42:12 and 1 Kings 8:50.

To be sure, this good word about Nebuchadnezzar and Babylon may be simply part of a Jewish strategy of political quietism and co-operation. We should not, however, neglect the theological force of Dan. 4:22 and its fruition in verses 34-37. The theological claim of the narrative, regardless of what it may mean for Jewish conduct and hope, is that the empire is transformable and can become a place of mercy and righteousness. This transformation happens when the God of Israel is accepted as the Most High, that is, when the empire is brought under the rule of the Lord. Thus, the nations, given this example of Babylon, are redeemable, transformable, and capable of salvage for the humane purposes of God. Moreover, the narrative of Daniel 4 is a warning to all would-be Nebuchadnezzars that the exercise of power uninformed by righteousness and mercy will lead to insanity and loss of authority. The empire is a place that may host mercy. It is a place that, in its self-interest, must host mercy. There is no alternative strategy for royal power that can possibly succeed.[19]

---

19. In addition to the several texts that juxtapose "mercy" and "Babylon," there are a large number of texts dated in and around the exilic period that speak of God's mercy: see Isa. 14:1; 49:13-15; 54:7-10; 55:7; 60:10; Mic. 7:19; Jer. 12:15; 30:18; 31:20; 33:26; Lam. 3:22, 32; Hab. 3:2; Zech. 1:12, 16; 10:6. These texts suggest that "mercy" became an extremely important theological issue in a time when Israel's relation to God appeared to be in jeopardy. These texts, however, lie outside the scope of this study because they do not explicitly concern the empire and because the mercy is promised after the exile by the empire, and not in the midst of it.

III

At the outset, I offered two questions that may focus the task of theological interpretation: (1) How does Israel speak about God? and (2) What else must Israel talk about when it talks about God? The answer to the first question, given our topic, is that Israel talks about God in terms of the reality of mercy. The answer to the second question, I have suggested, is that when Israel speaks of the mercy of God, it first speaks of the nations, specifically *Babylon*, more specifically, *the mercy of Babylon*. To say that Israel's speech about God entails speech about the mercy of the Babylonian empire evidences the delicate, daring enterprise that Israel's theological speech inescapably is. In its theological speech, Israel recharacterizes God. At the same time, it recharacterizes the empire and the meaning of worldly power.

Israel's speech about God requires and permits Israel to say that the empire is not what it is usually thought to be. It is not what it is thought to be by Israelites who fear and are intimidated by the empire. Conversely, it is not what it is thought to be by the wielders of power themselves, in their presumed self-sufficiency. Negatively, this claim of mercy asserts that imperial rule is not rooted simply in raw power. Israel, when it is theologically intentional, will not entertain the notion that "might makes right." Positively, this claim asserts that political power inherently and intrinsically has in its very fabric the reality of mercy, the practice of humanness, or as Daniel dares to say to Nebuchadnezzar, the care of the oppressed (Dan. 4:27). This daring rhetoric, which follows from Israel's speech about God, does not mean that the holder of power will always accept this characterization of power. Israel, nonetheless, refuses to allow any enterprise of power to exist and function outside the zone of its theological rhetoric.

This claim about imperial power is even more stunning when the subject of such speech is characteristically Babylon. The same playful, ambiguous, venturesome rhetoric of Israel is also employed concerning Egypt and Assyria, but perhaps not as extensively. While Babylon functions in this regard as a metaphor for all such power, no doubt Babylon, in and of itself, occupies a peculiar and distinctive role in Israel's theological horizon. In the Bible, Israel would never finish with Babylon, and therefore its speech about Babylon is of peculiar importance.

We may suggest two reasons for this odd focus. First, there is good historical reason for such an insistence concerning Babylon.

The deportation of the Jerusalem elite required honest and alarming theological reflection by the makers of Judaism. It was Babylon that had the capacity to create a situation in which God's mercy was experienced as null and void; Israel was left to wonder what that nullification signified (cf. Lam. 5:20-22). Second, there is surely canonical reason for such a focus on Babylon. It is most plausible that the process of displacement in the sixth century not only was decisive for the community that experienced it but also became, through the process of canonization, a decisive and paradigmatic reality for continuing generations of Jews.[20]

Thus the exile became paradigmatic for all Jews, including the God of the Jews. Jews and the God of the Jews must come to terms with the definitional role of Babylon. It was exactly the experience and metaphor of *Babylonian exile* that made the question of *mercy* so acute. It was exactly the mercy of God, remembered, experienced, and anticipated, that made a redefinition of Babylon so urgent and so problematic.

Israel's rhetoric accomplished a stunning claim. It asserted that no savage power in the world could separate Israel from God's mercy. It did more than that, however; it also asserted that no savage power, no matter its own self-discernment, can ever be cut off from the reality of God's mercy. It is for that reason that the burden of mercy is repeatedly thrust upon Nebuchadnezzar; and for that reason, Daniel finally, at the end of this literature, has Nebuchadnezzar's "reason return" (Dan. 4:31). Now Nebuchadnezzar "knows."[21] What he knows is that power is held by the God who gives it as God wills.[22] Moreover, "God wills" always toward mercy. No amount of cunning or force can escape this intentionality of God. The rhetoric of Israel about the nations is rooted in the very character of Israel's God. The very character of God, however, lives in this rhetoric that

20. Jacob Neusner (*Understanding Seeking Faith* [Atlanta: Scholars Press, 1986], 137–41) has shown how the displacement of the sixth century became a shaping paradigm for the self-understanding of all Judaism, a paradigm only loosely connected with the historical realities.

21. The term usually rendered as "reason" is from the root *yd'*. Thus, the "reason" of Nebuchadnezzar is the acknowledgment that the world is indeed shaped through the intention and governance of Yahweh. Though the term *yd'* is here removed from the notion of "covenantal acknowledgment," it still participates in that covenantal reality, whereby "knowing" consists in reckoning with in loyal obedience (cf. Jer. 22:16). See H. B. Huffmon, "The Treaty Background of Hebrew *Yada'*," *BASOR* 184 (1966): 31–37.

22. On this phrase, see the comments of Gowan, *When Man Becomes God*, 121–28 and its use in Jer. 50:44.

is not negotiable. The rhetoric assures that God is bound to Babylon even in the work of mercy. The rhetoric assures as well that Babylon is bound to mercy because it is the purpose of this God who gives power to whom God wills. Nebuchadnezzar persistently has refused this reality of God's powerful resolve for mercy. His rule culminates in sanity, praise, majesty, splendor, and more greatness, however, only when he accepts God's rule of justice and abandons the option of autonomous pride. Nebuchadnezzar's reason is his "knowing," knowing the truth of Israel's rhetoric and knowing the one who is the primal subject of that rhetoric.

IV

I want now to situate my comments in relation to two addresses given by past presidents of the Society of Biblical Literature. I suggest that a contrast between the presidential addresses of James Muilenburg and Elisabeth Schüssler Fiorenza will illuminate the claim I am making for the theological intentionality of Israel's rhetoric.

On the one hand, James Muilenburg delivered his remarkable and extremely influential address on rhetorical criticism in 1968.[23] It was Muilenburg who both noted and, in my view, enacted the decisive methodological turn in the guild toward literary analysis. One can hardly overstate the cruciality of what Muilenburg accomplished in his address and more generally in his work.

Nonetheless, it is fair to say that Muilenburg's presentation of the importance of speech and of rhetoric was quite restricted. There is no hint in his presidential address of an awareness that speech is characteristically and inevitably a political act, an assertion of power that seeks to override some other rhetorical proposal of reality.[24] One can rightly say of Muilenburg's horizon either that he was not interested in such issues or that the whole critical awareness of the political dimension of speech came much later to the discipline of biblical interpretation. In any case, it is time to move beyond such innocence in rhetorical criticism, as many in the field have done, to an awareness that the text entrusted to us is a major act of power. Our

---

23. James Muilenburg, "Form Criticism and Beyond," *JBL* 87 (1969): 1–18.

24. On the political dimension of all rhetoric, see Terry Eagleton, *Literary Theory: An Introduction* (Minneapolis: Univ. of Minnesota Press, 1983); and Richard Harvey Brown, *Society as Text: Essays on Rhetoric, Reason, and Reality* (Chicago: Univ. of Chicago Press, 1987). Eagleton insists that traditional literary criticism has always refused to think of "the 'aesthetic' as separable from social determinants" (p. 206).

own interpretation is derivatively an act of power even as we pose, or perhaps especially as we pose, as objective in our interpretation. One can detect Muilenburg's lack of interest or attention to this issue at the end of his address, when, in juxtaposition to T. S. Eliot's phrase "raid on the inarticulate," he speaks of a "raid on the ultimate." I suggest that such a formulation bespeaks a kind of untroubled transcendentalism. Of course, Muilenburg was not untroubled, and he knew the text was not untroubled. Nonetheless, he moves directly from the text to "the ultimate." Given what we know of the political power of rhetoric, we dare not speak of a "raid on the ultimate" unless we first speak of a "raid on the proximate."[25]

There is available to us a variety of theories of speech and rhetoric. The move beyond Muilenburg's innocent analysis of rhetoric can benefit from Jean-François Lyotard's presence in the conversation.[26] Lyotard suggests that speech is fundamentally agonistic, that it intends to enter into conflict with other speech-claims. One figure he uses for this agonistic understanding is that speech is like the taking of tricks, the trumping of a communicational adversary, an assertively conflictual relation between tricksters.[27]

Without following Lyotard's complete postmodern program, I suggest that in the guild of scholars, we shall more fully face the danger and significance of the texts entrusted to us if we notice how these texts enter into conflict with other rhetorical options. Concerning my theme of *mercy and empire*, the several texts I have cited and their shared rhetorical claim do not constitute an innocent, neutral, or casual act. In each case the text is a deliberate act of combat against other views of public reality that live through other forms

---

25. Eagleton (*Literary Theory*, 205) writes: "Rhetoric, which was the received form of critical analysis all the way from ancient society to the eighteenth century, examined the way discourses are constructed in order to achieve certain effects.... [I]ts particular interest lay in grasping such practices as forms of power and performance." Muilenburg's focus on the "ultimate" may not give sufficient attention to "power and performance."

26. Jean-François Lyotard, *The Postmodern Condition: A Report on Knowledge* (Minneapolis: Univ. of Minnesota Press, 1984), cxi, 10, 16, and passim.

27. Lyotard's strictures are aimed especially against Jürgen Habermas's theory of "communicative action." On the latter, see Habermas, *Knowledge and Human Interests* (Boston: Beacon, 1968), and the utilization of Habermas by Richard J. Bernstein, *Beyond Objectivism and Relativism: Science, Hermeneutics, and Praxis* (Philadelphia: Univ. of Pennsylvania Press, 1983). Lyotard holds that speech is much more adversarial than Habermas allows. I am suggesting that such an adversarial perspective is helpful in understanding what the rhetoric of Israel does concerning great concentrations of political power and the mandate of mercy. The texts we have considered are in no way innocent about their claims.

of rhetoric. Thus, the "trump" of this rhetoric seeks to override the assured autonomy of Babylon that dares to say, "I am and there is no other" (Isa. 47:10). Conversely, this rhetoric enters into combat with Israel's rhetoric of complaint, which asserts that "there is none to comfort" (Lam. 1:2, 17, 21), that "the hand of the Lord is shortened" (Isa. 50:2; 59:1), and that "my way is hid from the Lord, and my right is disregarded by my God" (Isa. 40:27). Both the arrogance of autonomous Babylon and the despair of doubting Israel generate, authorize, and commend a politics of brutality and intimidation.

The rhetorical trajectory I have traced refuses to leave either Israel or the empire at peace in its mistaken rhetoric. This counter-rhetoric, this "strong poetry," that seeks to reread the empire and the faith community is a radically subversive urging.[28] Aside from the specific argument I have made about empire and mercy, I suggest that our scholarly work requires a theory of rhetoric that is more in keeping with the relentlessly critical, subversive, and ironic voice of the text, which sets itself endlessly against more conventional and consensual speech. Thus, we are at a moment not only "beyond form criticism," which Muilenburg had judged to be flat and mostly sterile, but also beyond rhetorical analysis that is too enamored of style to notice speech as a means and source of power.[29]

On the other hand, in 1987, nineteen years after Muilenburg, Elisabeth Schüssler Fiorenza delivered a major challenge to the Society of Biblical Literature.[30] Alluding to the presidential addresses of James Montgomery in 1919, Henry Cadbury in 1937, and Leroy Waterman in 1947 as the only exceptions in presidential addresses,[31] Schüssler Fiorenza protested against scholarly detachment and urged that members of the society have public responsibility in the midst of their scholarship. She proposed that attention to

---

28. My reference here is to Harold Bloom, *Anxiety of Influence: A Theory of Poetry* (New York: Oxford Univ. Press, 1973). See William H. Rueckert, *Kenneth Burke and the Drama of Human Relations* (Minneapolis: Univ. of Minnesota Press, 1963), 8–33, on Burke's early notion of rhetoric as counterstatement and counterdiscourse.

29. In reflecting on my critique of Muilenburg, it occurred to me (and may to others) that my own statement appears to be an attempt to "trump" his influence and thus to enact the force of rhetoric as Bloom and Lyotard suggest. That is far from my intention, but I am not unaware of that dynamic.

30. Elisabeth Schüssler Fiorenza, "The Ethics of Interpretation: De-centering Biblical Scholarship," *JBL* 107 (1988): 3–17.

31. The addresses to which Fiorenza alludes are James A. Montgomery, "Present Tasks of American Biblical Scholarship," *JBL* 38 (1919): 1–14; Henry J. Cadbury, "Motives of Biblical Scholarship," *JBL* 56 (1937): 1–16; and Leroy Waterman, "Biblical Studies in a New Setting," *JBL* 66 (1947): 1–14.

rhetorical rather than scientific categories of scholarship would raise ethical-political issues as constitutive of the interpretative process. Moreover, she observed that no presidential address since 1947 had made any gesture in the direction of public responsibility.

It is not my purpose to enter directly into an assessment of previous presidential addresses. It is, however, my purpose to reflect on the task and possibility of biblical theology. The dominant line of scholarly argument has insisted that biblical theology must be a descriptive and not normative enterprise. Or to put it with Krister Stendahl, it must be concerned with what the text "meant" and not with what the text "means."[32] In my judgment, that urging contains within it not only a considerable fear of authoritarianism but also a decision about "strict constructionism" concerning the text, a preoccupation with "authorial intent," and a positivistic notion of rhetoric, of image, of metaphor, and, finally, of text.

If we move in Muilenburg's direction of rhetoric and in Schüssler Fiorenza's direction of public rhetoric, and if we understand that the rhetoric of a classic text is always and again a political act, then it is, in my judgment, impossible to confine interpretation to a descriptive activity. The text, when we attend to it as a serious act of rhetoric, is inherently agonistic and makes its advocacy in the face of other advocacies.

The trajectory of texts I have cited may be taken as a case in point. There is no doubt that the primary references in these texts are the God of Israel and the Babylonian empire, a datable, locatable, identifiable historical entity. There is also no doubt, however, that the term "Babylon" has become a metaphor for great public power and that the term spills over endlessly into new contexts. A primary example of such spilling over is the power of the metaphor "Babylon" in the book of Revelation. The Babylon metaphor has exercised enormous influence in the church's thinking about "church and state." There is no doubt that that spilling over happens in the text itself and, as W. Sibley Towner has shown, that spillover has continued in any but the most flattened historical interpretation.[33] Thus

---

32. Krister Stendahl, "Biblical Theology, Contemporary," in *IDB* 1:418–32. See the careful and critical response to the categories of Stendahl by Ben C. Ollenburger, "Biblical Theology: Situating the Discipline," in *Understanding the Word* ed. James T. Butler et al., JSOTSup 37 (Sheffield: JSOT Press, 1985), 37–62; and, more fully, idem, "What Krister Stendahl 'Meant'—A Normative Critique of Descriptive Biblical Theology," *HBT* (June 1986): 61–98.

33. Carroll (*Jeremiah*, 832) observes that Babylon has become "the symbol of

we never have in the text the concrete historical reference to Babylon without at the same time the potential for spillover into other contexts. That spillover, I suggest, is not evoked simply by willful, imaginative interpreters but is also rooted in the metaphors and images themselves, which reach out in relentless sense making.[34]

Thus, we have before us in these six texts concern for the God of Israel, who is the God of mercy, and the empire, which must be endlessly concerned with mercy. In attending to these texts, we seek to enter Israel's rhetoric and to notice Israel's agonistic intent in this set of metaphors. We read the text where we are. We read the text, as we are bound to read it, in the horizon of China's Tiananmen Square and Berlin's wall, of Panama's canal and South Africa's changing situation, of Kuwait's lure of oil. Or among us, when we are daring, we may read the text in relation to the politics of publication, the play of power in promotion and tenure, the ambiguities of acquiring grants, and the seductions of institutional funding. We inevitably read the text where we sit. What happens in the act of theological interpretation is not an "application" of the text, nor an argument about contemporary policy, but an opening of a rhetorical field in which an urgent voice other than our own is set in the midst of imperial self-sufficiency and "colonial" despair.[35] We continue to listen while the voice of this text has its say against other voices that claim counterauthority.

Thus, the agenda that Schüssler Fiorenza proposes is not extrinsic to the work of the Society of Biblical Literature. The spillover of the text into present social reality is not an "add-on" for relevance; rather, it is a scholarly responsibility that the text should have a hearing as a serious voice on its own terms. One need subscribe to no

---

hubristic opposition to Yahweh." For an amazing example of such a spillover into contemporaneity, see Octavio Paz, *One Earth, Four or Five Worlds: Reflections on Contemporary History* (New York: Harcourt Brace Jovanovich, 1985), 151. In commenting on the power of the United States in the Latin American countries, Paz writes: "This contradiction revealed that the ambivalence of the giant was not imaginary but real: the country of Thoreau was also the country of Roosevelt-Nebuchadnezzar."

34. On the concept of spillover, I am utilizing the notion of Paul Ricoeur (*Interpretation Theory: Discourse and the Surplus of Meaning* [Fort Worth: Texas Christian Univ. Press, 1976]) concerning "surplus." The term "surplus," as a noun, is too static, however, and so I have chosen an active verb to suggest that the text actively moves beyond its intended or ostensive meaning to other meanings.

35. Mary Douglas and Aaron Wildavsky (*Risk and Culture: An Essay on the Selection of Technical and Environmental Dangers* [Berkeley: Univ. of California Press, 1982], 83–125) provide convenient phrasing for this context in their formula, "The center is complacent, the border is alarmed."

particular ideology to conclude that our public condition is one of deep crisis. And since we as biblical scholars have invested our lives in these texts, one may ask directly how or in what way this text is an important voice in the contemporary array of competing rhetorics. Or less directly, one may ask if we want to be the generation that withholds the text from its contemporary context, the generation that blocks the spillover that belongs intrinsically and inherently to the text. It is possible that we would be the generation that withholds the text from our contemporary world in the interest of objectivity and in the name of our privileged neutrality. Such an act, I should imagine, is a disservice not only to our time and place but also to our text. Such "objective" and "neutral" readings are themselves political acts in the service of entrenched and "safe" interpretation.

It can, however, be otherwise. Without diminishing the importance of our critical work, it is possible that the text will be permitted freedom for its own fresh say. That, it seems to me, is a major interpretative issue among biblical scholars. The possibility of a fresh reading requires attentiveness to the politics of rhetoric, to the strange, relentless power of these words to subvert and astonish.[36] When our criticism allows the rhetoric of the text to be voiced, the way mercy crowds Babylon continues to be a crucial oddity, even in our own reading. Those of us who care most about criticism may attend with greater grace to readings of the text that move even beyond our criticism.

---

36. On fresh and liberated readings, see William A. Beardslee, "Ethics and Hermeneutics," in *Text and Logos: The Humanistic Interpretation of the New Testament,* ed. Theodore W. Jennings (Atlanta: Scholars Press, 1990), 15–32. Beardslee concludes his proposal for a reading of the text that will permit a "relational, participatory view of justice" with this comment: "This path will move away from the rigid image of hermeneutics as 'translation,' which presupposes a fixed element to be re-expressed. It will contribute to the formation of a hermeneutics that can fully recognize the strangeness of the text, which offers no 'pure' disclosure, and yet can release the ethical power that successive generations have found in an encounter with the New Testament." Beardslee's proposal is congruent with what I see happening in these "mercy/Babylon" texts.

7

A Poem of Summons (Isaiah 55:1-3) and a Narrative of Resistance (Daniel 1)

THE POETRY OF ISAIAH 40–55 is enormously generative for Israel's future.[1] That visionary poetry generated powerful religious hope and political courage for the life of Israel after 540 B.C.E. That poetry also evoked subsequent texts, the clearest case being the text of Isaiah 56–66. Thus Joseph Blenkinsopp can assert that "passages in Isa. 56–66 can be shown to relate to passages in Isa. 40–55 as commentary to text."[2] In this chapter I wish to investigate a different example of "commentary to text," considering Daniel 1 as a midrashic commentary on the text Isa. 55:1-3.[3]

---

1. See the summary comment of Paul D. Hanson, "Israelite Religion in the Early Postexilic Period," in *Ancient Israelite Religion*, ed. Patrick D. Miller Jr. et al. (Philadelphia: Fortress, 1987), 501–3. The evocative power of Second Isaiah operates literarily and theologically, even if we proceed with a canonical understanding of the book of Isaiah. The current discussion about canonical criticism does not affect our present argument.

2. Joseph Blenkinsopp, "Second Isaiah—Prophet of Universalism," *JSOT* 41 (1988): 95.

3. On the midrashic character of the Daniel narratives, see André LaCocque, *The Book of Daniel* (Atlanta: John Knox, 1979), 1–2. See also Gerhard von Rad, *Old Testament Theology* (San Francisco: Harper and Row, 1965), 2:313–15. On the more general interpretative practice of midrash, see Michael Fishbane, *Biblical Interpretations in Ancient Israel* (Oxford: Clarendon, 1985); I. L. Seeligmann, "Voraussetzungen der Midrashexegese," in *Congress Volume: Copenhagen*, VTSup 1 (Leiden: Brill, 1953), 150–81; Jacob Neusner, *Midrash as Literature: The Primacy of Documentary Discourse* (New York: Univ. Press of America, 1987). Neusner (*What Is Midrash?*, Guides to Biblical Scholarship [Philadelphia: Fortress, 1987]) has also provided a convenient introduction to and definition of midrashic study. The clearest succinct statement

I

The text of Isa. 55:1-3, part of the conclusion of the poetry of Isaiah 40–55, issues a summons that is in fact a promise. The summons is expressed in an extended series of imperatives dominated by the verb "come":

> come ... come ... buy ... eat ...;
> come ... buy [v. 1];
> hearken ... eat ... delight ... [v. 2.];
> incline ... come ... hear. (v. 3)

This massive imperative assault suggests urgency and presses the listening community to an immediate and crucial decision.

The decision urged is to abandon sources of nourishment and sustenance that do not feed or satisfy (v. 2a, b). The questions in verse 2 function as disputational speech intended to dismiss the negative option now to be rejected. The main rhetorical force of the poetic lines, however, is in the series of positive imperatives that frame the questions of verse 2. These imperatives present to the listeners an alternative that will indeed nourish and satisfy.

The promissory character of the summons is clear in verse 3b. After the three imperatives of verse 3 (incline, come, hear), the promised possibility is that the listeners' *nephesh* will live. The *nephesh* of Israel (singular noun, plural pronoun) is in jeopardy from starvation; now a freely given alternative is possible. This programmatic promise is then extrapolated in two phrases that express the main concern of the entire poetic piece: (1) God offers an "everlasting covenant," one not abrogated even by the reality of exile; and (2) God asserts "steadfast, sure love for David."[4] That is, the promise

---

concerning this mode of interpretation is offered by Michael Fishbane, "Inner Biblical Exegesis: Types and Strategies of Interpretation in Ancient Israel," in *Midrash and Literature*, ed. Geoffrey H. Hartman and Sanford Budick (New Haven: Yale Univ. Press, 1986), 19–37. Fishbane concludes: "The most characteristic feature of the Jewish imagination, the interpretation and rewriting of sacred texts, thus has its origin in the occasional, unsystematized instances of exegesis embedded in the Hebrew Bible, examples of which it has been my effort to recall" (p. 36).

4. On the reformulation of the Davidic promise in this text, see Otto Eissfeldt, "The Promises of Grace to David in Isaiah 55:1-5," in *Israel's Prophetic Heritage*, ed. Bernhard W. Anderson and Walter Harrelson (New York: Harper and Row, 1962), 196–207. My argument in this chapter concerns the claim that Daniel 1 appeals to the "old text" of Isa. 55:1-3; here it is clear that Isa. 55:1-3 also appeals to an older text of Davidic theology (such as 2 Samuel 7). It offers a reinterpretation of that earlier text as Daniel 1 subsequently offers a reinterpretation of the poetic

that "your _nephesh_" will live is interpreted to refer to God's continuing covenantal loyalty and attentiveness in a situation of enormous threat and discontinuity. It is the covenant solidarity of Yahweh that makes life possible for Israel, life that is not possible while Israel spends its money, energy, and loyalty for what is not bread and what does not satisfy.

In recent commentary on this passage, scholarly attention has been given primarily to the identification of the voice and genre of the summons. We may identify the following hypotheses concerning the identity of the voice of summons:

1. Joachim Begrich has offered the dominant hypothesis, followed by many scholars, that this is the summons of "Dame Wisdom" to her banquet as an alternative to foolishness that destroys.[5] It is the banquet of wisdom that gives life.

2. James A. Sanders has utilized the motif of banquet somewhat differently. He suggests that the invitation is issued by a king who invites his subjects to a banquet to celebrate the king and his enthronement.[6] This suggestion pays attention to the mention of David in verse 3, which draws the poem toward royal imagery.

3. Claus Westermann has set alongside the notion of the banquet of wisdom the summons as the voice of a vendor in the marketplace offering a sale to a prospective buyer.[7] Characteristically, Westermann finds the antecedents in the daily, secular life of the community. This hypothesis is a variation of an older hypothesis of Franz Delitzsch that this is the voice of a "water seller."[8]

4. Richard J. Clifford has suggested, utilizing Ugaritic parallels, that the summons is the presence of God in the temple, "proximity to the deity in the deity's shrine."[9]

---

rendering in Isaiah 55. Fishbane ("Inner Biblical Exegesis," 20) suggests that the "foundation text [may be] *already* an interpreted document." In our case, Isa. 55:1-3 is already interpreted from the older Davidic materials but is again reinterpreted in Daniel 1.

5. Joachim Begrich, *Studien zur Deuterojesaja*, TBü 20 (Munich: Kaiser, 1969), 59–61. See the appeal to the hypothesis by James Muilenburg, "The Book of Isaiah, Chapters 40–66, Exegesis," in *IB* (Nashville: Abingdon, 1956), 5:643; and Claus Westermann, *Isaiah 40–66*, OTL (Philadelphia: Westminster, 1969), 281–83.

6. James A. Sanders, "Isaiah 55:1-9," *Int* 32 (1978): 291–95.

7. Westermann, *Isaiah 40–66*, 282–83.

8. Franz Delitzsch, *Biblical Commentary on the Prophecies of Isaiah* (Edinburgh: T. and T. Clark, 1890), 2:325.

9. Richard J. Clifford, "Isaiah 55: Invitation to a Feast," in *The Word Shall Go Forth*, ed. Carol L. Meyer and M. O'Connor (Winona Lake, Ind.: Eisenbrauns, 1983), 27–35.

5. A more theological interpretation, as, for example, in Calvin, suggests that the summons of the poem is to the gospel, which may in Christian interpretation be given a christological or eschatological accent.[10]

Helpful as these various proposals are, I suggest that such interpretations miss the poignancy of the voice and the cruciality of the decision to which the poet now summons Israel in exile. That is, these several interpretations lead away from the concrete crisis of the text itself. Thus, we may consider three elements of interpretation that may open the text beyond these explanations:

1. The hypotheses we have mentioned identify the "voice of summons" either in terms of generic interest (wisdom, vendor) or as a theological generalization (cultic proximity, royal banquet, the gospel). Neither such a literary antecedent nor a theological generalization, however, would seem to touch the unmistakable urgency, expressed in the series of imperatives. This is indeed an immediate, life-and-death decision. The identification of the voice should not lead us away from the textual moment given us. The voice in the text is not that of a generic vendor or of undifferentiated wisdom, but rather that of a pastoral poet addressing real people in a crucial moment. The summons is not just to cultic presence but also to a more hazardous and more marvelous option concerning food, sustenance, and life. The real-life situation of the poem is in the midst of an empire where newness is being enacted (see 43:18-19) and where that newness is being resisted (see 45:9-13). Thus, we are obligated to listen more closely to the text itself than these several hypotheses permit us to do.

2. In identifying the voice of summons by way of literary antecedent or theological generalization, scholars have not paid much attention to the negative force of verse 2. That verse issues two questions that are in fact accusations. The negative force of "not bread" and "not satisfy" is central. That negative, however, is almost skipped over by scholars in their zeal to get to the positive religious affirmation. James Muilenburg notes a general accommodation to

---

10. John Calvin, *Commentary on the Book of the Prophet Isaiah* (Grand Rapids: Baker Book House, 1979), 155–57. Calvin recognizes that "waters, milk, wine, bread" are metaphors that include "all that is necessary for spiritual life." Moreover, the "metaphors are borrowed from those kinds of food which are in daily use amongst us. As we are nourished by 'bread, wine, milk, and water,' so in like manner let us know that our souls are fed and supported by the doctrine of the Gospel, the Holy Spirit, and other gifts of Christ."

Babylonian surroundings but, along with other scholars, soft-pedals the costly and total change that is called for.[11] The negative alternative here rejected, I submit, is the entire imperial world of Babylon that cannot keep its promises and cannot give life. The negative rejected by this poetic voice is Babylonian religion, which makes an offer of life it cannot keep. The Jews addressed by this poet are situated in Babylon and are called to reject and deny the best religious promises offered by Babylonian religion and, with them, the legitimacy, safety, and stability that are available in the empire.[12]

3. A little at a time, we are learning to ask sociopolitical questions of texts.[13] In recent discussion of this text, almost no attention has been given to the sociopolitical dimension of Israel's faith and life in exile. Clearly, the Babylonian religion criticized by the poet did not exist in a vacuum but was linked to and legitimated Babylonian socioeconomic and political definitions of reality and organization of power.[14] Westermann has noted that the reference to bread and milk means that a split of spirit and material is not permitted.[15] That refusal to "split" must be taken more seriously in interpretation. It means that the criticism made by this urgent, imperative poetic voice is not only a theological but also a sociopolitical summons. It is not only a summons away from Babylonian theological loyalty and an invitation to the covenant of Yahweh; it is also a summons away from Babylonian socioeconomic and political reality and an invitation to the historical possibility of Yahwism that is the socioeconomic and political restoration of Judaism.

---

11. Muilenburg, "The Book of Isaiah," 644.

12. The poetry of Second Isaiah maintains a constant and harsh critique of the religious enterprise of the Babylonian empire. This is evident in the disputation speeches of 41:1-5, 21-29, and in the mock song of chap. 46. The lyrical dismissal of Babylonian religious legitimacy is essential to the liberation of Jewish imagination for the sake of homecoming.

13. The decisive contribution thus far has been the work of Norman Gottwald. David Jobling ("Sociological and Literary Approaches to the Bible: How Shall the Twain Meet?" *JSOT* 38 [1987]: 85–93) has offered a discerning critique of Gottwald's work and has identified the most important contributions of Gottwald. For a concrete example of a sociopolitical reading of the text that bears upon our discussion, see John Goldingay, "The Stories of Daniel: A Narrative Politics," *JSOT* 37 (1987): 99–116.

14. On the connection between theological and sociopolitical dimensions of Israel's textual tradition, see Ronald S. Hendel, "The Social Origins of the Aniconic Tradition in Early Israel," *CBQ* 50 (1988): 365–82; and Walter Brueggemann, "Old Testament Theology as a Particular Conversation: Adjudication of Israel's Socio-Theological Alternatives," in *Old Testament Theology: Essays in Structure, Theme, and Text* (Minneapolis: Fortress, 1992), 118–49.

15. Westermann, *Isaiah 40–66*, 282–83.

Thus, the summons in Isa. 55:1-3 is to wholesale resistance to Babylonian options, both religious and political. That imperial option, both religious and political, must be resisted in all its parts because it robs exiled Israel of hope and finally of identity (that is, *nephesh*). It numbs Israel's imagination and robs Israel of its chance for life. Babylon is to be resisted because it will destroy the *nephesh* of Israel. The poetry invites Israel to say no to every form of Babylonian nourishment that denies every Jewish possibility of life. Scholarly preoccupations with antecedents and generalization have largely led us away from the concrete and urgent issues of resistance present in the text, resistance necessary for the liberation of the community of Yahweh.

II

The story of Daniel 1, I propose, is a narrative rendition of the summons and promises of Isa. 55:1-3. It is a tale of *resistance* (thus enacting the summons of the poem) and of *success* (thus receiving and exhibiting the promise of life offered in the poem).

The story of Daniel 1 moves from seduction through resistance to liberated success in three scenes. The action is dated in the narrative with reference to Nebuchadnezzar, the end of whose regime Second Isaiah celebrates (cf. Dan. 1:1-2).

At the outset of the narrative, we are given a glimpse of the Jewish life (scene 1, vv. 3-7). The entire scene happens because "the king commanded" (v. 3). There is no countervoice, no uncertainty, no hesitation. There is only one decisive voice. It is the voice of Nebuchadnezzar.

The narrative quickly lays out the three important dimensions of the plot: (1) The recruits for royal civil service are to be Jewish youths who are in every way "competent" (vv. 3-4). This royal commission evokes the crisis of the narrative. (2) The youths selected are to be inducted into the knowledge, skills, and intelligence of the empire, that is, "the letters and language of the Chaldeans" (v. 4). Clearly their Jewishness is to be radically subordinated to the claims and interests of the empire. (3) The Jewish recruits are to be nourished on the rich food of Babylon, perhaps as a reward, but more obviously in order to make them acceptable physical specimens for standing before the king (v. 5). They are to be chosen in the first instance because they are already handsome and without blemish; nonetheless, rich imperial food will make them more so.

The scene is one of *imperial seduction,* in which Jewish youths are pressed into a service that contradicts their Jewishness. In this seduction, however, there is no bad faith on the part of the king. It is assumed that any Jewish boy will be responsive to the opportunity of upward mobility into the court. The king who commands perceives his order as no threat to Jewishness, as Jewishness is not a factor on his horizon. There is, nonetheless, subtle irony in the awareness that the king who would never acknowledge Jewishness as a factor singles out Jews for his service. The narrator offers no comment on this odd fact but only reports the royal action.

The imperial seduction evokes *Jewish resistance* (scene 2, vv. 8-17). Daniel is clearly the subject and champion of the narrative. Daniel understands immediately what in fact is happening. The invitation to training and service in scene 1 is presented in the narrative as a neutral, "innocent" offer. Only a discerning, faithful Jew can notice that the offer of such imperial food, given to qualify for the king's presence, is in fact "defilement." Daniel introduces into the narrative a partisan Jewish notion that would have been a surprise to Nebuchadnezzar and no doubt to the contemporaries of the narrator to whom the narrative is addressed.[16] What is offered by Nebuchadnezzar is simply "rich food" and "wine." What is refused by Daniel, however, is imperial "defilement."

Daniel is politically shrewd, cooperative, and discerning; all his deftness, however, is in the service of his foundational theological commitment, which lies outside the empire. Thus while the chief of the eunuchs and the steward are cooperative with Daniel, we are told early that "God gave Daniel favor and compassion" (v. 9). In the first scene, only Nebuchadnezzar acts. In scene 2, the scene of Jewish resistance, God is the decisive, albeit unseen, actor who in fact dispatches the imperial officers to do God's work. Daniel's courageous resolve is implemented to provide safeguards for frightened

---

16. This literature bespeaks the "sectarian strategy" that Stanley Hauerwas has championed. On the strategy of the book of Daniel, Lynne Sharon Schwartz ("Daniel," in *Congregation: Contemporary Writers Read the Jewish Bible,* ed. David Rosenberg [New York: Harcourt Brace Jovanovich, 1987], 420–21) writes: "Well, how do such exiles manage? By dreaming, they serve their masters in good faith, with their special kind of divided integrity—a contradiction in terms. Certain things, things of the spirit, they do not, cannot compromise. What they hate most of all is coercion. The flesh they permit to be coerced, but not the spirit. What they believe, they cling to with fortitude, and with an earthly tenacity that both saps their strength and replenishes it. They will not worship false or frivolous gods, for then they would no longer be who they are."

royal officers; these functionaries of Nebuchadnezzar do not understand that one other than Nebuchadnezzar in fact dispatches them in this narrative. Thus there is nothing excessively abrupt or disruptive in Daniel's resistance. It takes place inside the structures and procedures of the royal design. His action is resistance nonetheless. Daniel's alternative to the rich food and wine of the empire is vegetables and water (v. 12). The preliminary test of the alternative program, made to reassure the royal functionaries, is effective (vv. 14-16). The Jewish boys on the lean, nondefiling diet are "better in appearance" and "fatter in flesh." The lean Jewish diet of defiance works better than the rich imperial diet.

The culmination of *liberated success* is a vindication of Daniel's firm resolve (scene 3, vv. 18-21). Nebuchadnezzar had determined scene 1 and was completely absent in scene 2. Now the king reappears in the narrative to give the crucial verdict in scene 3. The verdict given by the king surprises no one. It does not surprise Daniel, man of faith. It does not surprise the royal officers who had already had a preview. Moreover, the verdict does not surprise Nebuchadnezzar, who is innocent of Daniel's faith and Daniel's stratagem. In every regard, Daniel and his friends are "ten times better" (v. 20). No wonder Daniel is ensconced in royal service for a long time to come (v. 21)!

Note the reticence of the narrative in telling the tale. Yahweh was not present in scene 1, which belongs completely to Nebuchadnezzar. Yahweh is decisive in scene 2 but unseen and unacknowledged by the characters. In scene 3, Yahweh is again invisible, not even mentioned in the narrative. Any external observer might have perceived Nebuchadnezzar controlling matters on his own terms. The narrator does not tell us otherwise. He does not explicitly challenge Nebuchadnezzar's dominance in the third scene. We are left to draw the conclusion that God's favor and compassion, explicit only in verses 9 and 17, in fact not only govern scene 2 but also determine the outcome of scene 3. Nebuchadnezzar had imagined scene 3 to be his triumphant scene, but the listener moves to a very different conclusion.

Daniel is offered to the listeners of the story as a model for resistance.[17] His is a fine and careful blend of cooperation and resistance.

17. See W. Lee Humphreys, "A Life-Style for Diaspora: A Study of the Tales of Esther and Daniel," *JBL* 92 (1973): 217–23. See the splendid analysis of Daniel 1 by W. Sibley Towner, "Daniel 1 in the Context of the Canon," in *Canon, Theology, and*

With discipline and integrity, he knows where to draw the line for Jewishness (that is, trust in God's favor and compassion) and against imperial "defilement." Notice how Daniel has drawn this line. He has refused to labor for that which is not bread, for that which does not satisfy. He has taken food and water without imperial price tags attached.[18] He has delighted his life in fatness. He has cast himself on the faithfulness of Yahweh, relying on the "steadfast, sure love" of Yahweh. He has indeed accepted the summons of the poem of Isa. 55:1-3 and received its promise of life. He has received life and avoided the defilement of submitting his Jewishness to imperial domination. The summons is honored. The promise is kept.

III

I propose that the interrelation of Isa. 55:1-3 and Dan. 1:1-21 is that of text and commentary. The text of Isa. 55:1-3, according to critical consensus, is securely dated and located at the end of the exile, at the demise of the Babylonian hegemony. The poetry of Isaiah 40–55 asserts the freedom and capacity of Jews to depart the empire. Israel's invitation and authorization to leave the empire, while reflecting changed political realities, are cast by the poet as a theological issue concerning Yahweh's sovereignty over Babylon. That claim of sovereignty is asserted by the poet and calls for a decision on the part of listening Israel. The poet presents the large and dangerous theological decision for Yahweh's sovereignty as an act of concrete resistance to the seductive nurture of the empire. The large theological act of departure depends on the specificity of daily food.

Growing scholarly attention to "inner-biblical" interpretation permits us to understand both of these texts in fresh ways. Historical-critical study has been concerned to place each text firmly in its context of origin. Concerning the narratives of Daniel, historical criticism has given its primary energy to the placement of the narratives in the Maccabean crisis of the second century, far away from

---

Old Testament Interpretation, ed. Gene M. Tucker et al. (Philadelphia: Fortress, 1988), 285–98. Note as well his reference to Joyce Baldwin on p. 293.

18. Jürgen Moltmann (*Theology and Joy* [London: SCM, 1973], 54) writes of this verse: " 'It's all *for nothing* anyway,' says the nihilist and falls into despair. 'It's really all *for nothing*,' says the believer, rejoicing in the grace which he can have for nothing, and hoping for a new world in which all is available and may be had *for nothing*." The contrasting perspectives on "for nothing" bespeak the faith of the community and the despair of the empire.

the sixth century, when its reported events purportedly happened. The result of such a historical-critical interest has been to downplay the powerful symbolism of both Nebuchadnezzar and Babylon in the Daniel text. Moreover, the sociotheological issues addressed in the text concerning displacement, oppression, and resistance have been neglected, and affirmative and theological alternative and political possibility have been unnoticed. That is, historical criticism distracted interpretation from noticing the main theological and sociopolitical issues in the text.

However, once it is recognized that both the poem of Isaiah 55 and the narrative of Daniel 1 address issues of resistance and alternative, the two texts may be related to each other in ways not allowed by pure historical criticism. Without denying that the narrative of Daniel 1 may be much later than the poem of Isaiah 55, it is cogent to see the close connection between poem and narrative as text and commentary. This connection does not necessarily draw the Daniel narrative into the sixth century, but it does draw both texts into the typological issues of resistance and alternative that repeatedly concerned the community of early Judaism.

The move from historical-critical study to inner-biblical exegesis permits connections between texts that we may term "midrashic." Such connections are not precise according to the measures of historical criticism. They may be much more impressionistic, reflecting enormous interpretive freedom and imagination. The identification of such imaginative connections, however, permits us to see afresh not only the "new text" derived from the foundational text but also the foundational text in new configuration.[19]

Concerning Daniel, John Gammie has explored these matters in most detail, but as far as I can note, he has not suggested the specific connection discussed here.[20] Following Gammie, W. Sibley Towner concludes: "We seem to be on safe ground in asserting that one function of the stories of Daniel 1–6 is to assure Jews that the visionary hopes and promises of Isaiah 40–55 are indeed capable of realization among the obedient and wise of Israel."[21]

---

19. A basic study in this regard is that of Paul D. Hanson, *The Dawn of Apocalyptic* (Philadelphia: Fortress, 1975). Hanson does not carry his work as far as the literature of Daniel. He has, however, shown how Second Isaiah stands at the beginning of a literary-theological trajectory that continues to develop and generate new literature and new modes of literature.

20. John G. Gammie, "On the Intention and Sources of Daniel i–xi," *VT* 32 (1981): 282–92.

21. W. Sibley Towner, *Daniel*, Interpretation (Atlanta: John Knox, 1984), 27. Von

Once we have opened the possibility that the poem of Isa. 55:1-3 may receive daring rearticulation and reappropriation into new contexts,[22] it is not difficult to identify some of the connections between our two texts. In these several connections, then, I suggest that the interpreting tradition of Daniel took up the text of Isa. 55:1-3, which urges resistance in a Babylonian situation, and reinterpreted it for the sake of Jews under assault in the Maccabean context. The connections between the two texts include the following:

1. *The wisdom motif* may indeed be present in both texts, given the hypothesis of Begrich concerning Isa. 55:1-3. Daniel is clearly offered as a model wisdom figure.[23] Inside the story Daniel is presented as a wise character; and the narrative itself champions wisdom as a mode of life. If Begrich is right, the summons in Isa. 55:1-3 is the voice of wisdom, summoning Israel precisely to the kind of action undertaken by Daniel. Wisdom, then, is the capacity to discern the true character of one's context as a place where death threatens, where life is offered, and where Yahweh can be trusted to give life. Foolishness is to seek life from other sources that can only yield death (cf. Prov. 8:32-36).[24]

2. *The Babylonian connection* is central in both texts, though that reference need not be read historically, that is, as a sixth-century reality. "Babylon" can be taken dramatically and metaphorically as an option for life that is clearly false and that will rob one of one's *nephesh*. Taken dramatically and metaphorically, there is no impediment in reidentifying Nebuchadnezzar as Antiochus, as the oppressed community presumably did.[25] However construed, the fig-

---

Rad (*Old Testament Theology,* 2:314 n. 29) suggests that parts of Daniel might be described as a *pesher* on Isaiah. See also LaCocque, *The Book of Daniel,* 1 n. 1, where the same judgment is expressed. On the relation of these literary traditions, Klaus Baltzer ("Liberation from Debt Slavery after the Exile in Second Isaiah and Nehemiah," in *Ancient Israelite Religion,* 480) concludes: "It has often been observed how vague the details regarding the situation of the exiles are in Second Isaiah. About this subject we learn a great deal more from a line of literature running from Jeremiah 29 through the Book of Ezekiel to Daniel 1–6. These are texts describing captivity in Second Isaiah."

22. On the reinterpretative process in relation to Daniel, see Brevard S. Childs, *Introduction to the Old Testament as Scripture* (Philadelphia: Fortress, 1979), 618–22.

23. Humphreys ("A Life-Style for Diaspora") has shown not only the wisdom intent of the narrative but also how the wise walk a fine line between accommodation and defiance.

24. On wisdom's gift of life, see Roland E. Murphy, "The Kerygma of the Book of Proverbs," *Int* 20 (1966): 3–14.

25. W. Sibley Towner ("Were the English Puritans 'The Saints of the Most High'?" *Int* 37 [1983]: 46–63) has shrewdly explicated the way in which these historical

ure of Nebuchadnezzar and the presence of Babylon are necessary
to provide a foil for the invitation and offer of Yahweh.

3. More obvious than the function of wisdom and the cruciality of Babylon in both texts is the *concreteness of food* in both texts.
"Food" here may be taken metaphorically as referring to much more
than the diet of harassed Jews. It should not, however, be spiritualized away from the concreteness of nourishment and sustenance.
Food is a metaphor that does not lose its concrete vehicle. It does
indeed so refer to sustenance, life-support, and livelihood, which the
empire would gladly give, but at great price. The price for such food
and wine is the cost of one's *nephesh.*[26] To spiritualize the alternative
food of the poem, as commentators are prone to do, is to diminish
the concrete danger and the daily urgency of the choice offered. To
be sure, the food in the Daniel narrative cannot so easily be treated
as metaphor as in the Isaiah poem. Nonetheless, both texts address
real-life issues fraught with danger and risk, concerning both the
possibility of historical survival and the survival of faith, freedom,
hope, and imagination.

4. The common elements of wisdom, Babylon, and food lead us
to see that both texts concern *resistance,* what Towner calls "this magnificent refusal."[27] The two texts belong to a sustained concern in
postexilic Judaism that the community of faith must intentionally resist being bought off and seduced when it is offered life on terms
other than the covenantal offer of Yahweh.[28] The issue of *resistance*

---

names become ciphers to be filled with various interpretative identities. Towner
("Daniel 1 in the Context of the Canon," 291) suggests that Daniel 1 is a "refraction"
of 2 Kings 25:30. If this is plausible, the narrative is drawn more closely into the
Babylonian crisis of the sixth century that preoccupied the poet of Isaiah 55.

26. In both these texts, Babylonian food robs Israel of its *nephesh.* This is an
oddly telling notion because in other contexts, it is food that restores one's *nephesh*
(cf. 2 Sam. 16:14). See Hans Walter Wolff, *Old Testament Anthropology* (Philadelphia:
Fortress, 1974), 10–22.

27. Towner, *Daniel,* 23.

28. John G. Gammie ("The Classification, Stages of Growth, and Changing Intentions in the Book of Daniel," *JBL* 95 [1976]: 191–204) has demonstrated that
the literature of Daniel cannot be linked exclusively to the Maccabean crisis. Thus
it is the sociotheological situation of exile rather than a concrete historical placement that is important for reading the text. Schwartz ("Daniel," 424) observes: "In
truth, as unearthed by research and archaeology and linguistic analysis, the author
of Daniel was of another, later time, another place, and obsessed with other events
entirely. He was indulging in a clever and now familiar tactic, using the Babylonian
exile to illuminate the destiny of Israel in his own day." Just as the precritical link
to the sixth century is not defensible, so the critical link to the second century
need not be held too closely. What counts is the social paradigm and the task of
reinterpretation.

and alternative, so crucial to the character of Judaism, is focused precisely in the recognition that the "alternative food" is indeed real food, even while it alludes to much more. Said in other language, resistance to the empire requires a theological-spiritual decision, but also a concrete, intentional political act. The narrative of Daniel 1, perhaps many generations after the poem, asserts and attests that the poem of Isaiah 55 is true. Life reliant on alternative sustenance is embraceable and livable, albeit with risk. Only with this risk can there be homecoming for the exiles. Indeed, only with this risk can there be a community counter to the empire.

IV

Claus Westermann has worked incessantly to clarify matters of scholarly method with particular reference to form criticism. This essay evidences in a small detail the way in which new methods are developing from Westermann's magisterial work in form analysis. On the one hand, the connection I have proposed between the two texts depends on the traditioning process of constant reinterpretation, so that texts are endlessly commentaries on earlier texts. Thus, intertextual reading has emerged as a new methodological possibility. On the other hand, the posing of sociopolitical questions (inchoate in Westermann's work) leads us to focus on futures generated by the text.

The heuristic value of seeing these two texts as "text and commentary" is to show that the narrative of Daniel 1 is not only a "new text" but also an old poem rearticulated. It is, further, to show that the poem of Isa. 55:1-3 is not only a marvelous offer but also an invitation to resistance. The homecoming offered here, so crucial to Judaism, is at an enormous cost.[29] It matters, therefore, that the voice of summons and promise (that shows up hiddenly in Dan. 1:9) is indeed the voice of the faithful God of Israel. This voice, which sounds variously like a vendor, like wisdom, like an invitation to the shrine or to a royal banquet, is the voice of the God who orders wisdom, governs empires, manages alternative diets, and sustains a community of faithful obedience.

---

29. On the paradigmatic significance of exile and homecoming for Jewish faith, see Jacob Neusner, *Understanding Seeking Faith* (Atlanta: Scholars Press, 1986), 115–49. Neusner has shown how the language of crucifixion and resurrection has served Jewish speech about exile and homecoming.

Part Three

A Social Reading of Particular Issues

8

Israel's Social Criticism
and Yahweh's Sexuality

THE ISSUE of the masculinity/femininity of God is a difficult question for theology in general and for biblical interpretation in particular. It is not clear how much of the long-standing practice of masculine imagery is due to unreflective custom and how much of it derives from deliberate conviction. The linguistic questions reflect complex substantive issues. No discipline has contributed so much in shaping the issue of language and imagery as has Old Testament study with its vigorous assertion of the masculinity of God and its polemical resistance to Canaanite fertility goddesses; for no discipline is more at stake in terms of the basic perceptions that govern research. Perhaps Old Testament studies have a peculiar response to make to the question. The following discussion is an attempt to assess some aspects of the problem as they impinge upon and are influenced by Old Testament studies.

I

Old Testament studies in the United States have largely been shaped in recent decades by a construct of *faith against culture*. Following

William F. Albright,[1] G. Ernest Wright[2] has given the most popular and effective expression of this stance of interpretation. The "againstness" of Wright's program applies to two concerns. First, it articulates Israelite faith in relation to Canaanite religion, so that the distinctiveness of Israel's faith is asserted. Wright builds on the programmatic statement of Albright[3] concerning the nature of Yahweh:

> The belief in the existence of only one God, who is Creator of the world and giver of all life; the belief that God is holy and just, without sexuality or mythology; the belief that God is invisible to man except under special conditions and that no graphic nor plastic representation of Him is permissible; the belief that God is not restricted to any part of His creation, but is equally at home in heaven, in the desert, or in Palestine; the belief that God is so far superior to all created beings, whether heavenly bodies, angelic messengers, demons or false gods, that He remains absolutely unique; the belief that God has chosen Israel by formal compact to be His favored people, guided exclusively by laws imposed by Him.[4]

Albright[5] delineates this God as one without sexuality or mythology and not, as is often presumed, as a masculine God. The asexuality of Yahweh is presented as an essential mark of Yahweh in contrast to the gods of Canaan. It is clear that the contrast Albright and Wright wish to establish concerns the distinctively covenantal character of Israel's God and the temptation to syncretism that ancient Israel always faced.[6] Thus, the againstness asserts discontinuity between Israel's faith and the religion of its neighbors.

A second concern of Wright (not so often noticed) is the rejection of nineteenth-century evolutionism, especially associated with the name of Julius Wellhausen.[7] Indeed, Albright's major work was

---

1. William F. Albright, *Archaeology and the Religion of Israel* (Baltimore: Johns Hopkins Univ. Press, 1956); idem, *From Stone Age to Christianity* (Baltimore: Johns Hopkins Univ. Press, 1957).
2. G. Ernest Wright, *The Old Testament against Its Environment*, SBT 2 (London: SCM, 1959); idem, *The Old Testament and Theology* (New York: Harper and Row, 1969).
3. Albright, *Archaeology*, 116.
4. Wright, *The Old Testament and Theology*, 29.
5. Albright, *Archaeology*, 110–19; idem, *Yahweh and the Gods of Canaan* (Garden City, N.Y.: Doubleday, 1968).
6. Wright, *The Old Testament against Its Environment*, 62–63.
7. Ibid., 15.

intended to refute the entire evolutionary paradigm as an adequate intellectual frame of reference for Scripture study.[8]

These two concerns—(1) Israel *against* Canaan, and (2) covenant theology *against* cultural evolutionism and developmental understandings of religion—while both important, have not always been distinguished as they need to be. For that reason it is likely that some of the rhetoric of "Israel against Canaan" is in fact a stricture against cultural evolutionism and the assumption of natural continuity between faith and culture in our own time. Thus the *ancient* controversy of Israel/Canaan is used to present a *contemporary* hermeneutical conflict. The intent of Wright may well be missed unless his program of "againstness" is seen as a critique of contemporary cultural religion, embodied in Old Testament studies under the name of Wellhausen.

As we consider the issue of fidelity and sexuality in Yahweh, two matters need to be distinguished. First, the problem, as Albright announced it, concerns not the masculinity or femininity of God but the asexuality of God. The concern is to dissociate this God from all cultural forms of growth, productivity, and continuity, to express God's otherness and therefore God's sovereign freedom from and over all cultural claims.[9] Thus, asexuality is a function of God's free sovereignty.

Second, while a statement of God's asexuality is a clear way of expressing God's sovereign freedom, asexual imagery entails its own problems. In a search for effective symbols, we are inevitably drawn into the issue of *masculine/feminine* symbolism, which must be differentiated from that of the question of *asexual/sexual* symbolism. While we may wish to stay with this latter question, it is not possible. We are inevitably drawn into the issue of masculine/feminine imagery. It is likely that this second discussion of masculine and feminine

---

8. Albright, *From Stone Age to Christianity.*

9. Patrick D. Miller has put the issue well in a private communication: "The presumed dangers in use of feminine language and imagery lie in two areas: a) thinking of God in the image of sexual relations (intercourse), and b) thinking of God as giving birth, procreating. It seems to me that neither of these is totally ruled out in masculine imagery. (We have hung eroticism on the female rather than the male, which is ridiculous.)" We are not protected from the dangers of the sexuality of God by insisting on masculine images. The point at issue clearly is to maintain Yahweh's independence from creation and to assert the sharp discontinuity between God and culture. This requires imagery that denies that God either births or begets culture. There is no evidence that masculine imagery is more effective than feminine imagery in this regard. (This essay has benefited greatly from the suggestions and criticisms of Miller.)

symbols still concerns the same issue, that is, faith and culture. The "againstness" of Wright's program must be seen in the context of a confessional biblical theology movement that sought to combat religious liberalism often linked to Friedrich Schleiermacher. Thus, the ancient issue of syncretism has an overlay of an urgent contemporary issue. The same overlay of a contemporary issue is evident in the current discussion of the masculinity/femininity of God. The battle line between those who urge a new rhetoric of sexuality and those who champion traditional masculine imagery also appears to concern the interface between faith and culture.

The heritage of "againstness" in scholarship has left us with two very different issues: (1) the asexuality of Yahweh as a way of asserting God's freedom and sovereignty against every form of culture religion; and (2) the problem of masculine/feminine imagery in the quest for a responsible interface between faith and culture. The double problem exists because even for those who most strongly assert the asexuality of Yahweh, some imagery about "him" seems unavoidable. Thus while we may wish to assert the asexuality of Yahweh, the problem of language and symbolism in reality transposes the question to one of masculine and feminine imagery.

II

Wright's statement of "againstness" has been constant in his work, but the issues have been defined somewhat differently over a period of time. His position was articulated quite early and in a context that included a polemic against Schleiermacher.[10] Various scholars have more recently articulated the issue in ways that require revision of a position of simple againstness.

Anticipating a new perspective, Walter Harrelson raised the question of the positive values of syncretism. Albright had shown that wholesale borrowing of Canaanite culture had occurred already in Israel's formative period. Harrelson discerned that such borrowing is never fully intentional, not unambiguously bad, and often unrecognized. Therefore, resistance to borrowing and maintenance of "purity" are not likely to be single-minded and effective. Syncretism, according to Harrelson, is not to be understood as a willful perversion nor as a sudden decision, but as a long process of the gradual

---

10. G. Ernest Wright, *The Challenge of Israel's Faith* (Chicago: Univ. of Chicago Press, 1944).

transformation of perception, so that even the resisters are a part of the change.

> In short, the prophets use the mythology of the ancient Near East to portray the coming of a wrathful God against his people. And here is my point: as they do so, they are practicing what could be called reflective syncretism. They deliberately use imagery that is "in the air"; they shape it to their own ends; but they are not intimidated from using such imagery by the fact that others use it and that they do so in the worship of other gods than Yahweh.[11]

The strong and single-minded againstness that has been urged as a dominant paradigm is probably too clean to reflect the ways in which cultural forms and perceptions impinge upon and influence one another.

Later, Harrelson[12] sought to articulate an alternative to the sharp againstness in a book that reflects a more subtle and dialectical understanding of the impact of cultural context on Israel's faith. He argues for a different frame of perception that recognizes and affirms the essential *continuities* between Canaanite and Israelite forms of faith. While Harrelson does not urge return to a paradigm of evolutionary continuity, he recognizes that the paradigm of againstness claims too much. His book appeals for an alternative construct in which continuities and discontinuities may be seen as much more fluid and complex. Frank M. Cross has also noted the delicate issue of continuity with Canaanite culture. He observes "the tendency of scholars to overlook or suppress continuities between the early religion of Israel and the Canaanite (or Northwest Semitic) culture from which it emerged. There has been a preoccupation with the novelty of Israel's religious consciousness."[13]

If we are to think afresh about the issue of masculine/feminine imagery for God, it is important to (1) recognize that the issue is tangled in very large faith/culture issues and cannot be separated from them and reduced simply to the issue of sexuality, and (2) see that this fundamental faith/culture issue permits different positions and nuances that in part have to do with one's hermeneutical paradigm. The issue requires careful discernment about the

---

11. Walter Harrelson, "Prophecy and Syncretism," *ANQ* 4 (1964): 10.
12. Walter Harrelson, *From Fertility Cult to Worship* (Garden City, N.Y.: Doubleday, 1969).
13. Frank M. Cross, *Canaanite Myth and Hebrew Epic* (Cambridge, Mass.: Harvard Univ. Press, 1973), vii–viii.

hermeneutical paradigms that operate because they will be informative if not decisive when the question of masculinity and femininity is addressed. Bertil Albrektson has argued that the "God who acts in history" theme is not distinctive to Yahwism but is one way in which various cultures have understood their gods.[14] Such an argument, if it can be sustained, does not preclude the conclusion that Yahweh acted differently, that is, more freely, more graciously, more fully sovereignly, as Albrektson himself concedes.[15] But if he is correct, we are warned against too easy assertions about distinctiveness and too great an emphasis upon againstness.

Claus Westermann has urged the important distinction of salvation and blessing.[16] Salvation is understood as an *intrusive* event, blessing as *abiding* sustenance discernible in the structure and governance of life. Westermann does not wish to overstate the difference or to develop a sharp antithesis. He does, however, correlate salvation with historical traditions and blessing with creation-wisdom traditions.[17] On the basis of his work, it may be possible to do an analysis of the sociology that is behind each of these faith expressions. It surely is the case that the proponents of "against" have stressed salvation to the neglect of the blessing tradition. And now the matter must be redressed if serious biblical theology is to be done.

The salvation/blessing images may be correlated with two different views of faith in relation to culture, which in turn might be correlated with symbolizations of God in masculine and feminine terms. Patrick D. Miller has provided another important expression of the issues articulated by Albrektson and Westermann in exploring a faith/culture model that is not so one-sidedly focused on discontinuity.[18] He suggests that scholars in the tradition of Albright and Wright (as Miller himself is) are indeed reassessing the complexities and possibilities that have been screened out by a paradigm of againstness. This is particularly evident in the explorations of the

---

14. Bertil Albrektson, *History and the Gods* (Lund: Gleerup, 1967).
15. Ibid., 114.
16. Claus Westermann, "The Way of Promise through the Old Testament," in *The Old Testament and Christian Faith*, ed. Bernhard W. Anderson (New York: Harper and Row, 1963); idem, *Blessing in the Bible and the Church* (Philadelphia: Fortress, 1978); idem, "Creation and History in the Old Testament," in *The Gospel and Human Destiny*, ed. Vilma Vajta (Minneapolis: Augsburg, 1971).
17. Westermann, "The Way of Promise," 210; idem, "Creation and History," 30.
18. Patrick D. Miller, "God and the Gods," *Affirmation* 1 (1973): 37–62.

myth of the Divine Warrior by Cross, Miller, and Paul Hanson.[19] Miller's discussion suggests that if the large faith/culture issue as it is focused on continuity/discontinuity permits several readings and needs to be rethought, then the derivative issue of the sexuality of God may also require new consideration.

In a later article, Miller examined the blessing of Num. 6:22-26 and, following Westermann, considered the meaning of blessing as it is distinct from salvation.[20] It is even clearer in the work of Miller than that of Westermann that in the distinction of blessing and salvation, there are theological resources and challenges that have been neglected because of our preoccupation with the salvation-history traditions. The stress on discontinuity has in fact resulted in a "virile" if not masculine God.

So far as I am aware, neither Westermann nor Miller has gone beyond the polarities of blessing/salvation and creation/redemption to the issue of images of sexuality. From their work, nevertheless, such a polarity as salvation/blessing might also be understood in terms of a correlation of blessing with femininity, of salvation with masculinity. As both Westermann and Miller have presented it, salvation has to do with a forceful authoritative *thrust* to alter a situation, whereas blessing has to do with sustaining *embrace*. I do not urge this more than tentatively, but it cannot be unimportant that the distinctiveness of the "God who acts" is expressed in terms of intrusive saving deeds. "He" may be asexual, but "his" manifestations are presented in decisively masculine ways. Thus, Wright speaks of God who is living, active, powerful.[21] He asserts, "Hence, anthropomorphism in Old Testament religion was the very reason for its dynamic and virile character." First, we should note that anthropomorphism is affirmed as essential to Israel's understanding of Yahweh, and obviously asexual anthropomorphism is a contradiction. Wright's own statement leads one to suspect that Israel's anthropomorphism does not exclude the dimension of sexuality. Second, it is striking that he uses the word "virile." While his subject is the Old Testament, it surely is clear that he means Israel's understanding of Yahweh who is virile. But neither Yahweh nor the Old Testament can at the same time be virile and asexual. It is likely that the assertion of an

---

19. Cross, *Canaanite Myth*, 1–194; Patrick D. Miller, *The Divine Warrior in Early Israel*, HSM 5 (Cambridge, Mass.: Harvard Univ. Press, 1973); Paul D. Hanson, *The Dawn of Apocalyptic* (Philadelphia: Fortress, 1975).

20. Patrick D. Miller, "The Blessing of God," *Int* 29 (1975): 240–51.

21. Wright, *Challenge of Israel's Faith*, 66.

asexual God is here transformed in the interest of another agenda. Interestingly, one meaning of the term "virile" is "capable of procreation." We should not hold Wright accountable for too much with one word, but it indicates how slippery are the issues of distinctiveness and continuity. And if in such a context we may speak of "virility," we may ask if there is theoretically a possibility of "fecundity" in characterizing the God of Israel. My point is not to urge such imagery but to observe how exceedingly difficult it is to prevent *asexuality* from in fact being the imagery of *masculinity*. One would not seem to be more problematic than the other if one must choose between "virility" and "fecundity." In discussing the problematics of anthropomorphism, Phyllis Trible[22] notes the need for developing "gynomorphisms." Thus even to speak of "anthropomorphisms" is already a decision on the question before us, a decision made even by those who affirm Yahweh's asexuality. Trible speaks of "anthropomorphic and gynomorphic images."[23] Derivatively, the "God who acts" tradition has found the wisdom traditions problematic precisely when the deity does not intrude but sustains and nourishes (see Isa. 55:1-3, most likely a sapiential tradition). Thus anthropomorphic images are preferred in this tradition of interpretation to the neglect of images of embrace.

In various ways, the work of Harrelson, Albrektson, Miller, Cross, and Westermann suggests that the one-sided paradigm of againstness is precarious in terms of considering the data. And when againstness cannot be affirmed with such single-mindedness, the issue of asexuality may need to be expressed in imagery both masculine and feminine.

We may suggest some correlations in interpretative paradigms that may illuminate our work:

faith against culture	faith sustaining culture
↓	↓
salvation	blessing
↓	↓
a masculine image of God	a feminine image of God

---

22. Phyllis Trible, "Depatriarchalizing in Biblical Interpretation," *JAAR* 41 (1973): 33.

23. Phyllis Trible, "God, Nature of, in the Old Testament," in *IDBSup* (New York: Abingdon, 1976), 368–96.

It is not likely that either set of correlates will account for all of the data. Rather, what is urged is that all of these issues converge in the development of an interpretative model. While the influential paradigm of Albright and Wright was singular in its commitment, more recent scholarship suggests several possible models that may well coexist in the texts.

III

The covenant/syncretism issue as Wright has articulated it has much to commend it both in terms of textual evidence and in terms of a paradigm for interpretation. Israel is always placed in a struggle both "to be like the nations" (1 Sam. 8:5, 20; 2 Kings 17:8) and to be *'am qādôš*, a people holy to the Lord (Deut. 4:6-8; 7:6-11). Israel will avoid a choice on this question in every possible way. Thus, while there is a concern for againstness, the evidence shows that Israel tried often to be on both sides of the covenant/syncretism question (1 Kings 18:21).

In this section, I wish to urge that while the covenant/syncretism issue has not been reduced in importance by recent scholarship, it has been set in a new context and discerned in new categories, especially by the work of George Mendenhall and Norman Gottwald.[24] The issues that led to Wright's posture of againstness are now ex-

---

24. George Mendenhall, *Law and Covenant in Israel and the Ancient Near East* (Pittsburgh: Biblical Colloquium, 1955) (reprinted in *The Biblical Archaeologist Reader* [Garden City, N.Y.: Doubleday, 1970], 3:3–53); idem, "The Hebrew Conquest of Palestine," *BA* 25 (1962): 66–87 (reprinted in *The Biblical Archaeologist Reader* [Garden City, N.Y.: Doubleday, 1970], 3:100–120); idem, *The Tenth Generation* (Baltimore: Johns Hopkins Univ. Press, 1975), 1–31, 174–226; idem, "The Conflict between Value Systems and Social Control," in *Unity and Diversity*, ed. Hans Goedicke and J. J. M. Roberts (Baltimore: Johns Hopkins Univ. Press, 1975), 169–80; idem, "The Monarchy," *Int* 29 (1975): 155–70; idem, "Samuel's Broken Rib: Deuteronomy 32," in *No Famine in the Land*, ed. James W. Flanagan and James M. Robinson (Missoula, Mont.: Scholars Press, 1975), 63–74; idem, "Migration Theories vs. Culture Change as an Explanation for Early Israel," in SBLSP, ed. George MacRae (Missoula, Mont.: Scholar Press, 1976), 135–44. As to Gottwald's work, see Norman Gottwald, "Domain Assumptions and Societal Models in the Study of Premonarchic Israel," VTSup 28 (1974): 89–100; idem, "Were the Early Israelites Pastoral Nomads?" in *Rhetorical Criticism*, ed. Jared J. Jackson and Martin Kessler (Pittsburgh: Pickwick, 1974), 223–55; idem, "Biblical Theology or Biblical Sociology?" in *Radical Religion* 2 (1975): 46–57; idem, "Early Israel and the Asiatic Mode of Production," in SBLSP, ed. George MacRae (Missoula, Mont.: Scholars Press, 1976), 145–64; idem and Frank Frick, "The Social World of Ancient Israel," in *The Bible and Liberation* (Berkeley: Community for Religious Research and Education, 1976), 110–19.

pressed primarily in terms of economic and political matters rather than in the categories of myth and religion.

Recent sociological study of ancient Israel urges that Israel represents in the ancient world a radical social mutation that can be understood only in terms of the liberating activity of the heretofore unnamed God. That is, the disclosure of Yahweh (and consequently Israel) as known in the early traditions of exodus, Sinai, and "conquest" cannot be extrapolated from already existing social reality. This radical social mutation in the ancient world consists of two elements. First, there is a new understanding of God as one who is not at home with the establishment structures of the day and whose action is expressed as solidarity with the poor and disenfranchised. This God is to be sharply contrasted with the gods of the establishment, who legitimate the status quo and sanction social oppression. (This much agrees with the "againstness" as Wright has presented it.) Second, the mutation of Israel is sociologically significant as the emergence of a radically different social organization, not around the coercive power and valuing of establishment law, but around the covenanting activity of this God with the disenfranchised, who then establish alternative public institutions to give durability to covenantal relations.[25] The two parts of the paradigm thus speak of (1) the emergence of a covenant-making, covenant-keeping God who calls a people to covenant with God, and (2) the establishment of social organizations, institutions, and ideology that give historical concreteness to the presence and rule of this new God. The social criticism involved in this scholarship has focused on the close and crucial connection between the *character of God* and *legitimated social institutions.* On the one hand, the gods of the establishment belong appropriately with oppressive social institutions. On the other hand, the unexpectedly liberating God belongs appropriately with covenantal social institutions that redistribute political power and rearticulate human dignity and value.

Mendenhall had already made a strong case for the peculiarly covenantal character of Israel.[26] Unfortunately, his presentation was understood to focus on parallels to nonbiblical political treaties. While scholars have been preoccupied with that question, there has been general neglect of Mendenhall's identification of the impulse to social revolution in Israel's new model of social reality, whether or

---

25. Mendenhall, "Value Systems and Social Control," 174–75.
26. Mendenhall, "Law and Covenant."

not it was paralleled outside Israel. It is this latter that is likely the crucial element in Mendenhall's hypothesis.

In his later work, Mendenhall has been primarily concerned with the social theory and organization Israel deduced from the liberating, covenant-making character of Yahweh. Thus, Mendenhall has proposed that out of this perception of the new liberating God have come the energy and authority to mount a social revolution that enabled the peasants to throw off tyrannical city-kings and establish new forms of social reality.[27] The character of Israel and the character of Yahweh both stand as a challenge to Canaanite religion and Canaanite politics. The socially revolutionary movement of Israel is oriented to a kind of democratic freedom.

Gottwald even more strongly has presented the againstness of Israel in sociological terms by seeing the connection between the character of God and the character of social reality.[28] He asserts that the notion of gods/goddesses having sexuality makes the natural processes the source of life and vitality. And since those natural processes are controlled by the priestly/royal establishment, the power to life is monopolized precisely by the forces of affluence and order that inevitably will be oppressive. Thus, Gottwald is able to show sociologically what is at stake in the question of the sexuality/asexuality of God. The issue is not at all whether God is masculine or feminine. The issue is rather whether this God works in *sexual* ways so that God is continuous with the normal social and natural processes, or whether this God works in *covenantal* ways and is discontinuous both from natural processes and the social apparatus.[29] The one way (which is the way of every self-justifying culture in Israel's time and in our own) denies the freedom of God and eliminates every appeal to radical transcendence and with it every possibility of social protest, and revolution. The other way (which is the way of the radical mutation of Yahweh with Israel) affirms the freedom of God over against every social structure and makes possible appeal to a transcendence

---

27. Mendenhall, "Hebrew Conquest" and "Migration Theories."

28. Gottwald, "Biblical Theology."

29. In this proposition, important questions may be raised about the intent of so-called process theologies that in some sense see God as continuous with the process. On the one hand, such a perspective seems not to require a break with the dominant rationality of the academy. On the other hand, we may doubt if such a hermeneutic of continuity can generate any serious or radical ethical critique. Thus when *process* and *covenant* are placed in juxtaposition, important hermeneutical issues are raised. One may wonder about liberationists who attempt to move from a process hermeneutic.

that gives a basis for social criticism, protest and revolution. Gott-wald argues that the sexuality of God (masculine or feminine) finally leads to social conservatism and the legitimatization of hierarchy and its implicit oppression. The asexuality of Yahweh means that social cohesion happens not naturally but only by intentional, historical covenanting. This means that every social reality can be criticized, and new social realities can emerge through the process of covenant-ing. Thus, the sexuality/asexuality issue is linked to that of *oppressive social necessity* and *liberating social possibility.*

Mendenhall has traced the sociopolitical implications of this con-trast. Israel's vision of reality tends to a society that values human persons, whereas Canaanite perceptions could never do so:

> If the kings of the Late Bronze Age regarded their dominions as something delegated to them from the divine world, it needed only the introduction of an ethic to see that the divine world itself could rule without the extravagantly expensive prestige, symbols of the temple, palace and military establishment of the kings. The Mosaic covenant provided this ethical system, and it created a new people out of the ashes of the Late Bronze Age cultures. The history of Western man is a history of the alternatives between the ethical principle and the technological-political one. This is the battle between Yahweh and Baal; the Lord of the All Powerful State, the source of all prosperity and security, the Lord of Heaven and Earth, but actually the ancient monument to the primitive tribal mentality which was at least for a short time abolished and transcended in the Mosaic monotheism of ancient Israel. But though Baal dies, he perpetually rises again....
>
> It was the Mosaic period which constituted revolution; with Sol-omon the counterrevolution triumphed completely, only to collapse under the same weight of political tyranny and arrogance which had so much to do with the troubles of the pre-Mosaic period.... The real issue was a fairly simple one: whether or not the well-being of per-sons is a function of a social monopoly of force, or the consequence of the operation of ethical norms, which are values determining the behavior of persons in society.[30]

It will be clear that the againstness issue of Wright has been mea-surably advanced by Mendenhall and Gottwald. The issues of faith/culture and of covenant/syncretism continue to be crucial, as they have been to Wright. But now the sociological issues have come to the fore so that it is no longer a question of mythological against

---

30. Mendenhall, *The Tenth Generation,* 173, 196–97.

historical religion but a question of hierarchical, oppressive social reality and the possibility of covenant. Thus, in terms of the correlations we have suggested, we may now include the element of social organization:

faith against culture	faith sustaining culture
↓	↓
salvation	blessing
↓	↓
a free God as asexual (conventionally presented in masculine image)	a sexual god naturally linked to social process (polemically characterized as feminine)[31]
↓	↓
a possible *novum* of social reorganization, shaped by covenant and organized democratically	a necessary social organization celebrative of status quo, shaped by natural necessity and hierarchically

It will be evident that there is a major problem with this schematization, and it is the major problem related to the entire issue of Yahweh's sexuality. On the one hand, the masculine image of God with his intrusive capacity to shatter and make new is conventionally seen as more apropos than the feminine image of God, polemically characterized as embracing of what is and blessing things as they are. These images thus suggest a contrast between a *promissory* and a *conserving* notion of God, and, in that respect, one can easily prefer the one to the other. On the other hand, the radical criticism offered by Mendenhall and especially Gottwald has not contrasted masculine and feminine in God but has restated the issue in the more radical terms of sexuality/asexuality. Thus all imagery about God that suggests any continuity between God and the natural, social world is placed in question. We must face the central problematic of this tradition of scholarship and of the Bible itself—namely, it intends to speak of God in asexual terms but rather consistently uses masculine images to do so. The issue has been transformed now so that our discernment of God has to do with a *covenantal* model that has

---

31. In a lecture in St. Louis on February 4, 1977, Claus Westermann distinguished between the God who saves and the God who blesses. His telling conclusion was that the God who blesses "cannot fail or suffer."

important social implications or a *noncovenantal model* that has other social implications. And we must explore how Israel found it possible to speak about that covenantal decision concerning God. The decision is a crucial political as well as linguistic one. It requires a reexamination of what has been treated *conventionally* (to identify masculinity with the freedom of God) and what has been treated *polemically* (to identify the captive god with femininity).

IV

The problem of affirming the asexuality of Yahweh and speaking of Yahweh in masculine terms suggests two things concerning the recent development of scholarship. First, it is clear that "againstness" cannot be so simply sustained. Purity from cultural contamination and syncretistic use of cultural forms involves a dialectical process. Thus the use of asexuality as a way of understanding Yahweh is important in terms of radical covenantal faith. But at the same time, it is clear that Israel's texts sometimes used feminine language and that at other times masculine language is used in protest against Canaanite religion. Thus the faith/culture issues that lie behind the language are complex, and we must avoid reductionism on the basis of a single hermeneutical decision. Clearly a covenantal understanding requires personal language, but it is precisely personal language that poses the problem.

Second, the projected interpretative program of Mendenhall and Gottwald suggests that the issues of distinctiveness and againstness in the future will increasingly be expressed and understood in terms of sociological issues. That is, what Israel has to say about God will be more intentionally presented in terms of competing social visions. Wright had not been unaware of these matters, but the stress of his work is upon mytho-religious rather than sociopolitical questions. What is at issue, then, is not the sexuality of God but the way in which *different gods* are understood to sanction *different social visions*.

In that context and as a facet of the general problem, we may reconsider the theme of "God as Father" as it is used in Israel. From what we have thus far concluded, we may anticipate that the use of this language is an attempt to speak of Yahweh in terms that express freedom from, sovereignty over, and yet involvement with both natural and historical processes.

Wright had concluded that the Old Testament characteristically prefers royal, political categories for Yahweh and tends to avoid the terminology of fatherhood because that language would more easily be interpreted in terms of sexuality, links to the fertility process, and syncretism in general.[32] However, newer evidence and shifting nuances of the hermeneutical discussion permit a fresh consideration of the data. Wright had concluded that in the process of syncretism, "the 'fatherhood' of a God must have been conceived as more of a *physical* than a personal and ethical relationship."[33] Wright's consuming attention to the problem of syncretism apparently led him to read the imagery in only one way. However, it is likely that "Yahweh as Father" can be read as well in terms of political-covenantal relations as in terms of physical-sexual relations. Thus it seems probable that Wright's conclusion is dictated as much by his hermeneutical program as by the evidence. In moving beyond Wright's strictures, the discussion concerns not simply the interpretation or reinterpretation of any particular text, but reconsideration of againstness as the single hermeneutical concern that controls interpretation.

More recent studies by Dennis McCarthy and F. Charles Fensham,[34] anticipated by John L. McKenzie,[35] suggest that the term "father" need not be consigned to fertility imagery, as Wright had presumed even as Wright himself later questioned.[36] In many cases, the language can as well be interpreted in terms of the imagery of treaty-covenant, that is, in terms of sociopolitical reality. Thus the image need not suggest physical begetting or sexual continuity but may speak of a transcendent freedom standing over against a social reality, over against both in terms of *criticism* and in terms of life-giving *involvement*. Said another way, language that in some contexts surely has sexual implications can also be utilized to speak of a covenantal relationship. This is not to suggest that every trace of sexual connotation is purged, for that is not the way in which lin-

---

32. G. Ernest Wright, "The Terminology of Old Testament Religion and Its Significance," *JNES* 1 (1942): 404–14; idem, "How Did Early Israel Differ from Its Neighbors?" *BA* 6 (1943): 1–20.

33. Wright, "Terminology," 411.

34. Dennis McCarthy, "Notes on the Love of God in Deuteronomy and the Father-Son Relationship between Yahweh and Israel," *CBQ* 72 (1965): 144–47; F. Charles Fensham, "Father and Son as Terminology for Treaty and Covenant," in *Near Eastern Studies in Honor of William Foxwell Albright*, ed. Hans Goedicke (Baltimore: Johns Hopkins Univ. Press, 1971), 121–35.

35. John L. McKenzie, "The Divine Sonship of Israel and the Covenant," *CBQ* 8 (1946): 320–31.

36. Wright, *The Old Testament and Theology*, 117–18.

guistic images function. Rather, even the sexual connotation may be co-opted for covenantal use and therefore radically redefined.

In Jeremiah, for example, father imagery is used boldly in covenantal ways. No prophet is more attentive to the dangers of syncretism with fertility practice. Nor is there any prophet who more boldly utilizes the imagery. Nor is any prophet more singularly committed to covenantal categories of discernment. Thus, he does not flinch from speaking in that language:

> I thought how I would set you among my sons,
>   and give you a pleasant land,
>   a heritage most beauteous of all nations,
> and I thought you would call me, My Father,
>   and would not turn from following me.
> Return, O faithless sons,
>   I will heal your faithlessness. (Jer. 3:19)[37]

Clearly, the term "Father" is used for covenantal purposes, and there is here nothing of the Canaanite connotations, either of physical begetting or of manipulation. This is not to suggest that the terms "evolved" from nature to history. Rather, it is to insist that these words, all words, must be understood in the context of their historical usage according to the fundamental presuppositions of the community using them. Paul Ricoeur observes the change and evolution of the image:

> Thus the evolution of the father figure toward a superior symbolism is dependent on other symbols, which do not belong to the sphere of kinship: the liberator of the Hebraic primitive "saga," the lawgiver of Sinai, the bearer of the Name without image, and even the Creator of the Creation myth, none of which has anything to do with kinship. We could even say, in a way that is scarcely paradoxical, that Yahweh is not primarily father; on this condition, he is also father. . . . By the same stroke, fatherhood itself is entirely dissociated from begetting. . . . [I]t is because there is Covenant that there is fatherhood.[38]

---

37. See Walter Brueggemann, "Israel's Sense of Place in Jeremiah," in *Rhetorical Criticism*, ed. Jared J. Jackson and Martin Kessler (Pittsburgh: Pickwick, 1974), 156–58.

38. Paul Ricoeur, *The Conflict of Interpretations* (Evanston, Ill.: Northwestern Univ. Press, 1975), 486–91.

Thus Jeremiah, for example, is not interested in speaking either of the masculinity of God or of the asexuality of God, for which he presumably has no words. Rather, he is interested in asserting a particular nuance of the covenantal understanding of God, which is fundamental to everything he had to say to his contemporaries who had fallen into dangerously noncovenantal perceptions of reality. The interface between *covenantal reality* (which surely governs these texts) and *a broad range of images* (including sexual imagery) is much more subtle and delicate than a simple "againstness" might suggest. The problem, of course, is that the issue cannot be decided on the basis of exegeting individual texts, but only by facing the presuppositions lying behind the texts and behind the interpreter. The tradition of Wright worked with a presupposition of againstness as it addressed particular texts. An alternative is that the texts make a much more dialectical assumption about the use of this language and every language to advance a covenantal discernment of reality. The interpretative problem concerns the overriding claim of covenant in relationship to the freedom and play of every linguistic image.

Thus it seems likely that Wright has discerned the key issues that we must continue to face. He has seen that there is real distinction between the *perceptual world of Israel* and its environment, and he has also seen that *language* must be used carefully to maintain and appreciate that distinction. But he has also contributed to the confusion because he has wanted to affirm discontinuity in order to maintain the freedom of God and has done so by affirming the asexuality of God. That suggestion is very difficult to maintain (1) textually, because the Bible itself does not consistently employ such a practice or safeguard, and (2) theologically, because nothing, even sexuality, can be excluded from a covenantal understanding and the images used to express it. What is important to our use of such language is to recognize that biblical faith requires *a radically different understanding of all of reality* and therefore of language. This surely means a new understanding of justice, power, and law. It means a new understanding of human personality. And no less must it mean a radically new understanding of sexuality in covenantal terms. In speaking of God, the biblical text intends to use a wide range of images, most of them dealing with human, historical interactions that give life and death, discern endings in pain, and announce beginnings in expectation. In utilizing this range of images, the Bible surely does not screen out the images derived from and informed by sexuality because they are images that serve to articulate the new historical, covenantal reality that gives Israel identity and hope.

Covenanting consists not in withholding self for detached freedom and sovereignty (as asexuality might suggest) but in the free disclosure of self and the full commitment and giving of self. The distinctive affirmation of Yahweh is that he is fully with his people, committed to them in ways that bind him to them and permit his life to be impacted by them.[39] His sovereignty is a committed sovereignty. What better way to articulate this entry into the history of the partner than to use relational-sexual imagery to express the suffering, pain, hurt, joy, and caring that belong to his distinctive kind of sovereignty? He is not only the holy one, but "the holy one in your midst."[40] Walther Eichrodt shows that Hosea boldly used dangerous syncretistic language to articulate his radical discernment of Yahweh's power and sovereignty: "He does not shrink back from the dangerous proximity to the erotic divine love of the Baal cult but designates the irrational power of love, which determines the lover in all his expressions and drives unto complete surrender, as the power of God revealed in Israel's election."[41] The poets of Israel must use every possible linguistic image to articulate that *novum*. This *novum* is a radical one in the history of oppressive society and in the history of contained religion. Its articulation requires a bold, radical linguistic act.

This radical linguistic act requires that every image and every metaphor must be transformed by the confessional intent of the community. And since asexual language is problematic, it requires the transformation of both masculine and feminine imagery. Thus the transformation of the language is practiced as the way to deal with the problem of covenantal purity and syncretism. This alternative is selected rather than (1) choosing masculine images over feminine images, or (2) opting for using asexual language, which the Bible presumably cannot do. This decision on the part of the Bible about linguistic images raises important criticism about the posture of againstness that has dominated the scene. That criticism is important at two points. First, the againstness of Israelite Yahwism and Canaanite fertility religion has in much contemporary practice

---

39. J. Gerald Janzen, "Metaphor and Reality in Hosea 11," in SBLSP, ed. George MacRae (Missoula, Mont.: Scholars Press, 1976), 413–45; Jürgen Moltmann, *The Crucified God* (Philadelphia: Fortress, 1975), 69–84.
40. Walther Eichrodt, "The Holy One in Your Midst," *Int* 15 (1961): 259–73.
41. Ibid., 263–64.

become that of the masculinity of Yahweh versus the femininity of Canaanite deities. The hermeneutic of againstness that begins in a claim for the asexuality of Yahweh has become in fact and in practice an affirmation of the masculinity of God. Thus, the "mighty acts of God in history" as a theological program depends on a robust, virile God who can intrude to change things. The intent of the protest is better than the practice, which frequently becomes a well-intentioned defense of the masculinity of Yahweh against the "terrible" feminine deities of Canaan.

Second, such a transition from the asexuality to the masculinity of God appears to be premised on unexamined notions of femininity that are treated negatively, assigned to Canaanite categories, and predictably rejected. Perhaps this suggests an inclination to assign "good" qualities to masculinity (for example, ethical, free, initiative-taking, saving) and "bad" qualities to femininity (for example, unethical, controlling, manipulating). These presuppositions likely are very deep in the consciousness of our culture and perhaps also in the consciousness of ancient Israel, though that is less certain. The evidence is clear that Canaanite fertility religion included not only fertility goddesses but also fertility gods, and all partake in those qualities that are objectionable to covenantal faith. Conversely, it is likely that Israel found occasion to speak of Yahweh, the covenanting God, in images both masculine and feminine. Thus, we are required to affirm the singular covenantal focus of biblical faith and also the freedom inherent in images that serve various nuances to that focus. Unfortunately, in recent discussion, partisans insist on holding either to the single focus or to the variant images to the neglect of the other.

V

Concerning the discussion that has been derived from the work of Albright and Wright, this conclusion may be drawn: the program of againstness is not really interested in the issue of sexuality or sexuality of God as such. Rather, the interest is the contrast between a *covenantal* view of reality and a *noncovenantal* or *anticovenantal* view of reality, each of which depends upon a *notion of God* and each of which contains a *derivative social vision*. On that basis and for the future of the discussion, these hypotheses may be offered to refocus the discussion around issues that are decisive for biblical theology:

1. What is at issue in Israel's polemical and confessional discernment of God does not concern sexuality or asexuality. That concern is an intrusion of modern scholarship concerning ways of speaking about (*a*) Canaanite religion and (*b*) evolutionary developmental approaches to religion. Since Israel did not flinch from bold imagery likening Yahweh to human persons, it is not to be presumed that even this dimension of imagery is by definition problematic. The texts characteristically are concerned for Yahweh's fickleness and faithfulness and not sexuality as such.

2. What is at issue for Israel's discernment of God is not masculinity. Baal is also masculine. Indeed if there is a fertility process in Canaanite religion, it obviously involved both masculine and feminine. Those who insist upon the masculinity of Yahweh as a way of avoiding the temptation of fertility religion misunderstand the role of the gods in the Canaanite religion. This Wright had clearly seen as he resists even the masculinity of Yahweh. Masculinity is as much in question as femininity and cannot be used to express Yahweh's distinctiveness. Yahweh's contrast with Baal does not concern masculinity but covenantal faithfulness. Nowhere is this more evident than in Hos. 2:16-20 (Eng.), in which Yahweh is '*îš* and not *ba'al*. The use of masculine imagery is clear, but it is not the point either to be affirmed or to be denied. The point is the *fidelity* expressed in verses 19-20, which is contrasted with the *fickleness* of Baal in the preceding poetry. In Hos. 11:8-9, the assertion is made that Yahweh is God and not man, but no case can be made that this is a denial of sexuality. Rather, it is a denial of the kind of vengeance that takes form as quid pro quo. Hans Walter Wolff, in commenting on Hosea 2, rightly suggests that the *ba'al/'îš* contrast concerns a deep personal relation in contrast to a legal position as owner.[42] The contrast suggests an important transformation of masculinity.

3. What is at issue for Israel's discernment of God is neither masculinity nor asexuality but covenantal faithfulness. Israel's confession concerns Yahweh's capacity to enter into abiding and enduring relations in which Yahweh's free sovereignty is characteristically risked but reaffirmed and in which new life is created and new history made possible.[43]

4. Covenantal faithfulness as the distinctive mark of Yahweh permits itself to be expressed in a variety of images and in many

---

42. Hans Walter Wolff, *Hosea,* Hermeneia (Philadelphia: Fortress, 1974), 49–50.

43. Karl Barth, *The Humanity of God* (Richmond: John Knox, 1960), 45–65.

different relationships. These images and relationships are borrowed from various places and carry various nuances. But each such image is a vehicle to manifest Yahweh's faithfulness. So far as can be determined, no image or relationship is ruled out as a legitimately possible form of expression for Israel's covenantal imagination.

5. Covenantal faithfulness is the central intention of those texts in which Yahweh is presented as masculine. The texts intend neither to affirm nor to deny Yahweh's masculinity but to articulate peculiar faithfulness. But the masculine imagery is not neutral. It shapes the disclosure and defines the character of faithfulness in a specific way, for example, as effective warrior (Exod. 15:1-3) or as faithful lover (Hos. 2:16). The stress is on *fidelity*, but the image presents it as *masculine* fidelity.

6. Covenantal faithfulness can be expressed in feminine terms. Where that is so, the central intention is covenantal faithfulness. The text means neither to affirm nor to deny femininity but to articulate this peculiar form of faithfulness (for example, Num. 11:11-12). But the feminine imagery is not neutral. It shapes the disclosure and defines the character of faithfulness in a specific way. The stress is on *fidelity*, but the image presents it as *feminine* fidelity.

7. We are required to be more sensitive to the mutual influences flowing between (*a*) the central affirmation of covenantal faithfulness and (*b*) the rich imagery used in various contexts. Certainly covenantal faithfulness redefines and characterizes in fresh ways every image used, including masculine and feminine images. Thus covenantal masculinity is different from masculinity outside of covenant. And covenantal femininity is different from femininity outside of covenant. The proponents of "againstness" have seen that clearly. But it is also true that each image has a voice of its own that is not silent and not lost when used in covenantal ways. Each concrete image shapes covenantal faithfulness for that moment in a peculiar and intentional way. The richness and variety of images suggest that the central theme of fidelity can be turned in a myriad of ways to articulate its many-sidedness. Trible concludes, "Israel knows the inadequacy of all analogies. . . . [T]hat is reason enough for Israel to have a rich variety, for there are always fresh dimensions to covenanting yet to be articulated."[44] Sallie TeSelle has written more broadly on the question of the delicate, reciprocal relation between

---

44. Trible, "God," 369.

image and "truth."[45] She illuminates her point with a consideration of the use of "father" to speak of God. That sensitivity and freedom with image might illuminate the substantive discussion of our theme.

VI

There is no doubt that Israel preferred masculine imagery for God, and that must be recognized and faced. It may well be that such language was used as the normative language for the very reasons Wright suggested. But more recent understandings of the meaning of "father" in covenantal contexts make that questionable. Our current tasks (which move beyond simple "againstness") are (1) to be more sensitive to bold and inventive hints of feminine imagery in ancient Israel that utilize telling and poignant images to express Yahweh's person, and (2) to work more intentionally at delineating the feminine forms of covenantal faithfulness.

P. A. H. de Boer has addressed the theme of the mothering function in the faith of Israel.[46] He suggests that there are hints of the motherhood of God in the Old Testament that either have been missed by later interpreters or have been screened out by subsequent editors. Among the texts he notes are:

1. Numbers 11:12, in which Moses denies he is mother of Israel, with the clear implication that Yahweh mothered Israel.

2. Deuteronomy 32:11-12, the analogy of an eager mother protecting the young. In his comment, de Boer asserts that "in times of disaster the Lord appears to be, in more than an ethical sense, a father and a mother for his believers. . . . There exist, in my opinion, enough indications that ancient Israel and Judah have worshiped motherly aspects of their God."[47]

3. Exodus 19:4, the carrying of small children as a motherly task.

4. Deuteronomy 32:18, "the Rock that bore you."

5. The "we" sections of Genesis 1, which suggest that "father and mother guarantee life and existence."[48] The interpretation of Karl Barth is worth noting:

45. Sallie TeSelle, *Speaking in Parables* (Philadelphia: Fortress, 1975), 44–48.

46. P. A. H. de Boer, *Fatherhood and Motherhood in Israelite and Judean Piety* (Leiden: Brill, 1974).

47. Ibid., 36–37.

48. Ibid., 47.

Humanity which is not fellow-humanity is inhumanity. For it cannot reflect but only contradict the determination of man to be God's covenant partner, nor can the God who is no *deus solitarius* but *Deus triunus,* God in relation, be mirrored in a *homo solitarius.* ... By the divine likeness of man in Gen 1:27f., there is understood the fact that God created them male and female, corresponding to the fact that God himself exists in relationship and not in isolation.[49]

It is not possible here to explore fully such hints of God's femininity that might be identified. But the list of pertinent texts can be expanded. In the exilic poetry of Second Isaiah, all of Israel's traditional themes converge. Here creation and redemption themes are brought together in an effort to speak about the radically new.[50] Certainly in Second Isaiah, salvation and blessing themes are used in rich combination. Might it also be that here feminine/masculine images for God come to share expression in Second Isaiah precisely for the same reason? We may note only two considerations. In Isa. 40:1-11, the poet offers a picture of Yahweh bringing his people back to Zion. The location of this text in the divine council, as indicated by Frank M. Cross, is not affected by the following comments on verses 10-11; what concerns us here is the assignment of the functions of the council to Yahweh in those verses—that is, Yahweh acts the part of the gods who might have been masculine and feminine.[51] In terms of a God fulfilling both functions, Helmer Ringgren refers to an Akkadian text in which Marduk is spoken of as mother and father.[52] It is not impossible that Yahweh, a rival to Marduk in the Babylonian period, is assigned those roles as well, as in our text. R. Norman Whybray has shown how all of the functions of Marduk and his council are taken singularly by Yahweh.[53] Verse 10 presents God in his conquering power, surely masculine. Verse 11, in an abrupt change of mood, speaks of nourishing tenderness:

> Behold the Lord God comes with might,
>   and his arm rules for him;

---

49. Karl Barth, *Church Dogmatics* (Edinburgh: T. and T. Clark, 1961), 3/4:117ff.

50. Carroll Stuhlmueller, *Creative Redemption in Deutero-Isaiah,* AnBib 43 (Rome: Biblical Institute Press, 1970); Rolf Rendtorff, "Die theologische Stellung des Schopfungsglaubens bei Deuterojesaja," *ZTK* 51 (1954): 3–13.

51. Frank M. Cross, "The Council of Yahweh in Second Isaiah," *JNES* 12 (1953): 274–77.

52. Helmer Ringgren, " 'ab," in *TWAT,* vol. 1 (Stuttgart: Kohlhammer, 1970).

53. R. Norman Whybray, *The Heavenly Counsellor in Isaiah xl 13–14* (Cambridge: Cambridge Univ. Press, 1971).

> behold, his reward is with him,
>   and his recompense before him.
> He will feed his flock like a shepherd,
>   he will gather the lambs in his arms,
> he will carry them in his bosom,
>   and gently lead those that are with young.

To be sure, Yahweh is still "he." But the verse may well speak of feminine qualities, of Yahweh's mothering tenderness, so that verses 10-11 together give expression to the abundant fidelity of Yahweh who is powerfully taking initiative and gently bearing and feeding. Thus verses 10-11 show two very different dimensions of covenantal faithfulness—one aggressive leadership, the other protective nourishing.

In Isa. 49:14-15, the poet contrasts Yahweh with a forgetting woman:

> But Zion said, "The Lord has forsaken me,
>   my Lord has forgotten me."
> "Can a woman forget her suckling child,
>   that she should have no compassion on the son of her womb?"
> Even these may forget,
>   yet I will not forget you.[54]

There is, of course, nothing here requiring femininity. But it is clear that the imagery does not flinch from setting Yahweh in such a context. If such a nuance is indeed here, then it may be asked if feminine imagery for Yahweh is particularly appropriate for times of exile, as refuge in time of distress (cf. Matt. 23:37). In that connection, Ps. 27:10 affirms: "When my father and my mother have forsaken me, Yahweh will take me up." Again the nuance must not be pressed, but clearly God is surrogate for both parents.

From these considerations, the following two conclusions may be drawn: (1) Current issues of sexist language in relation to God must be distinguished from the distinctions between Israelite covenant faith and Canaanite religion. (2) The Old Testament prefers masculine language for God, but it apparently was no sufficient way to speak of the faithfulness of God. Moreover, the Bible is able to experiment with feminine images of faithfulness that it does not regard as necessarily dangerous or syncretistic. When these matters are

---

54. Cf. Claus Westermann, *Isaiah 40–66*, OTL (Philadelphia: Westminster, 1969), 219; and Barth, *Church Dogmatics*, 3/4:245–46.

sorted out, it is clear that no simple equation can be made between a masculine God and Israel's covenant faith and between a feminine God and Canaanite religion. Rather, the Bible strains to use every possible image to speak of God's peculiar fidelity. The use of new imagery is always possible, as is especially evident in the crises of Hosea and Second Isaiah, in which new situations require bold new linguistic acts. Considerable freedom is granted in this exploration if the above considerations are correct. That freedom is bounded by these affirmations: (1) A wide variety of images is usable because every image is transformed by the decisiveness of covenantal faithfulness. (2) Covenantal faithfulness is an experience to Israel of such richness and power that no image will express all that must be articulated. The substance of faith outdistances all images that might be used, and so the confession of Yahweh is not fully captured by any of them. (3) While every image is transformed, every image also retains something of its own character and thus brings to covenantal faithfulness a peculiar quality and dimension. The process of traditioning in the Bible itself suggests that fresh imagery is important in speaking of the God of Israel. It is the process of continually speaking faithfully of this God, rather than defense of a closed stock of images, that best informs our present work. Only in the freedom of faithful speaking can the process of social criticism by bold image continue. Without the freedom of such faithful speaking, contained religion and oppressive social vision are inevitable. Thus scholarship concerned with radical social criticism informed by covenant (Mendenhall, Gottwald) needs to be more attentive to the freedom of images and more aware that the various images, in their great variety, do indeed turn the central paradigm in various directions. Conversely, scholarship concerned with the meaning of language and metaphor (TeSelle) needs to be more attentive to the faith that transforms every metaphor and every language in the service of the central paradigm. Covenanting is different when presented in masculine or feminine terms. But masculine and feminine are also radically transformed when presented according to a covenantal understanding. Thus, the metaphor of sexuality can be understood in terms of the social criticism that properly belongs to Israel's vision of reality.

9 *the) god > se*

Theodicy in a Social Dimension

*a system of natural theology
aimed at seeking to vindicate
divine justice in allowing
evil to exist*

THE ISSUE of theodicy in current theological discussion is articulated in three distinct but not unrelated conversations:

1. The most obvious and popular is the pastoral question: Why did this happen to me? That is, the question is focused on a negative experience of a person who seems not to deserve such treatment. This question is effectively posed in the popular book by Rabbi Harold Kushner, *When Bad Things Happen to Good People.*[1] The pervasiveness of the issue is evident in the popularity of the book, even though its argument seems romantic and scarcely adequate.[2]

2. In Old Testament studies, theodicy is conventionally related to the crisis of 587 B.C.E. and the emergence of the relatively miserable situation of exilic and postexilic communities.[3] It is a situation in which the older historic traditions of confession are found wanting. On the one hand, it is conventionally thought that the question is posed in an early form of Habakkuk,[4] in Jeremiah, and in Job. On

---

1. Harold Kushner, *When Bad Things Happen to Good People* (New York: Schocken, 1981).

2. A more solid, reflective discussion is offered by W. Sibley Towner, *How God Deals with Evil* (Philadelphia: Westminster, 1976). However, this book has not captured popular imagination as has Kushner's.

3. On the literature related to these issues in that context, see Peter Ackroyd, *Exile and Restoration* (Philadelphia: Westminster, 1968); and Ralph W. Klein, *Israel in Exile* (Philadelphia: Fortress, 1979).

4. See the pastoral discussion of Donald E. Gowan, *The Triumph of Faith in Habakkuk* (Atlanta: John Knox, 1976).

the other hand, it has been proposed that wisdom, apocalyptic, and creation faith are responses to the issue, when the historical traditions are inadequate. In particular, James Crenshaw has contributed to this conversation in most helpful ways.[5]

3. The reality of the Holocaust has focused the question of God's justice in inescapable ways and has muted old answers.[6] In some ways, the Holocaust is an echo of the dilemma of Job. But Richard Rubenstein[7] and others have shown that the Holocaust is of such unutterable magnitude and irrationality that it violates any parallel with the old tradition. Indeed it is such a unique happening among us that it must be bracketed out provisionally from most discussions. Such a bracketing is not to dismiss the issue but to avoid trivializing it with frivolous comparisons.

I

These three ways of putting the question are all important, and none can be taken lightly. The following discussion, however, attempts to press the issue in a different direction. The notion of theodicy, of course, combines the issues of God (*theos*) and justice (*dikē*). However, the theodic questions are largely treated as speculative questions about the character and person of God, so that the justice issue is too much shaped in religious categories.[8] In fact justice is a social question about social power and social access, about agreed-upon systems and practices of social production, distribution, possession, and consumption. Scholarship has taken a largely idealistic view of the issue, which likely reflects the social location of those in the conversation.[9]

---

5. James L. Crenshaw, *A Whirlpool of Torment* (Philadelphia: Fortress, 1984); idem, *Theodicy in the Old Testament* (Philadelphia: Fortress, 1983); idem, "Popular Questioning of God in Ancient Israel," *ZAW* 82 (1970): 380–95; idem, "The Problem of Theodicy in Sirach," *JBL* 94 (1975): 47–64.

6. Emil Fackenheim (*To Mend the World* [New York: Schocken, 1982]) has provided an excellent statement on the implications of the Holocaust for both Jewish and Christian faith. Of course, the various writings of Elie Wiesel have provided the most helpful and most disturbing commentary. On his work, see the introduction by Robert McAfee Brown, *Elie Wiesel: Messenger to All Humanity* (Notre Dame, Ind.: Univ. of Notre Dame Press, 1983).

7. Richard Rubenstein, *After Auschwitz* (Indianapolis: Bobbs-Merrill, 1966).

8. On the question handled in more speculative, philosophical fashion, see John Hick, *Evil and the Love of God* (New York: Harper and Row, 1966).

9. I am using "idealistic" here in the sense criticized by Norman Gottwald, *The Tribes of Yahweh* (Maryknoll, N.Y.: Orbis, 1979), 592–607.

Here I shall argue instead that the subject of God-justice (that is, theodicy) requires a "materialist" reading of text and experience,[10] for Yahweh functions and is discerned either through a *practice* of social consensus or through a *challenge* to a social consensus still held but under assault. The justice of God cannot be separated from the actual experience of justice in the social process because Yahweh's presence in Israel is known through and against the social process.

It is odd that scholarly characterization of justice, and therefore of theodicy, in the Old Testament is bifurcated. In the eighth-century prophets, for example, justice surely has to do with social practice in which Yahweh is understood to have a crucial concern.[11] We have enough critical data to know that in the strictures of the prophets, the advocacy of justice concerns both the social systems and the God confessed through the practice of the social system.[12] That is hardly in doubt both in the text and in our usual interpretations. The justice questions in the eighth-century prophets clearly concern social goods, social power, social access, and the way those are configured in society.

In contrast to the eighth-century prophets, our conventional handling of Job (and similar materials) tends to disregard those understandings of justice and remove the justice question from the arena of social processes to the reified air of theological speculation. Such an interpretative move tends to make theodicy an odd or pecu-

---

10. It should be clear that "materialist" here does not require Marxist categories but requires taking into account the material basis and the historical context of real social life. The use of the word "material" is not remote from conventional use of the word "history" in Old Testament scholarship, as in the phrase "God acts in history," as long as "history" is understood as the actual social processes of communal interaction that include the process of organization and technology as much as ideology and mythology. On a materialist reading, see Kuno Füssel, "The Materialist Reading of the Bible," in *The Bible and Liberation*, ed. Norman Gottwald (Maryknoll, N.Y.: Orbis, 1983), 134–46; Walter J. Hollenweger, "The Other Exegesis," *HBT* 3 (1981): 155–79; and the essays in *God of the Lowly*, ed. Willy Schottroff and Wolfgang Stegemann (Maryknoll, N.Y.: Orbis, 1984).

11. See the fine article by James L. Mays, "Justice," *Int* 37 (1983): 5–17. For justice in relation to social processes, see Bernhard Lang, "The Social Organization of Poverty in Biblical Israel," *JSOT* 24 (1982): 47–63, and Robert Coote, *Amos among the Prophets* (Philadelphia: Fortress, 1981), 24–45.

12. Gottwald (*Tribes of Yahweh*) is most helpful in showing how Yahwism holds together the agency of Yahweh and the social practice of the community. The two are inseparable, even though many of us are more inclined than Gottwald to maximize the theological rather than the sociological counterpart. On the interface of Yahwism and social practice, see also Robert Wilson, *Prophecy and Society in Ancient Israel* (Philadelphia: Fortress, 1980); and Paul D. Hanson, *The Dawn of Apocalyptic* (Philadelphia: Fortress, 1975).

liar question of exilic and postexilic periods, whereas in fact theodicy
is a regularly functioning presupposition that permeates every text
either as consensus or as challenge. That is, theodicy may be peculiarly in crisis in the Joban literature, but it is not a new social
phenomenon. The entire literature of the Old Testament, since the
exodus narrative, concerns the interface of God and social justice.

This change of our perception of justice from a *prophetic-social
issue* (in the eighth century) to a *speculative theological issue* (in the
sixth century) results in a separation of the God-question from issues of social reality, from the ways of production and distribution
of social goods and social power. Such a separation is hinted at in
James L. Crenshaw's conventional inventory of theodic categories, in
which he lists the dimensions of theodicy as: "moral evil, natural evil
and religious evil."[13] In this chapter I want to urge that social evil is
a crucial, if not central, matter for theodicy in the Old Testament.
Social evil concerns those arrangements of social power and social
process that enable goods and access to be systematically legitimated
by religious ideology though nonetheless unjust. It is an important
fact of the sociology of our scholarship that the enormous concern of Israel for social power and social goods is characteristically
bracketed out when we come to the question of theodicy.

It may be argued that a focus on social evil is not ontologically
serious. But such an argument only presses us to a more basic conversation about God and God's enmeshment in the social processes.
I propose then that social evil (by which I mean unjust power arrangements in society for which God is claimed as the legitimator
and guarantor) is at the center of Israel's reflective thought. This
way of understanding theodicy is an overriding concern for marginal
people whose daily task of survival does not permit the luxury of
more speculative questions. From "the edge,"[14] the justice or injustice of God is encountered in the way social process enhances or

---

13. James L. Crenshaw, introduction to *Theodicy in the Old Testament* (Philadelphia:
Fortress, 1983), 2. Rainer Albertz ("Der sozialgeschichtliche Hintergrund des Hiob-
buches und der 'Babylonischen Theodizee,'" in *Die Botschaft und die Boten*, ed. Jörg
Jeremias and Lothar Perlitt [Neukirchen-Vluyn: Neukirchener Verlag, 1981], 349–
72) has made a formidable argument that the question of theodicy in the poem of
Job represents a social crisis in the Persian period that endangers the conventional
class structure. The parallels he draws to Nehemiah 5 may be too specific, but his
point is congruent with this essay.

14. See Mary Douglas and Aaron Wildavsky, *Risk and Culture* (Los Angeles: Univ.
of California Press, 1982), chaps. 5–8, on "center" and "border." Their use of
"border" may include social marginality.

denies life, and the justice or injustice of God is not otherwise experienced. Thus the issue of theodicy for Israel is not an interesting speculative question but is a practice of social criticism of social systems that do or do not work humanely and of the gods who sponsor and guarantee systems that are or are not just. A god is known by the system it sanctions. Theodicy becomes in fact an irrelevant speculative issue if the God-question is not linked to systems of social access and goods.

II

I propose that we begin a fresh discernment of theodicy by noticing how the concept is used in social analysis, particularly by those who are not interested in the God-question as such. Here I cite the contributions of three scholars whose views are representative in the field.

1. Peter Berger offers a typology of theodicies that runs a continuum of rationality–irrationality.[15] His articulation of the theodic problem includes a reference to a religious dimension, but he makes it clear that theodicy of any type is nonetheless a social agreement about how to handle the "anomic experience" of communal life, that is, how to justify, order, and understand meaningfully the experiences of actual disorder. To some extent theodicy, then, exists to rationalize and make things palatable. Berger suggests that a theodicy may be a "collusion, on the level of meaning, between oppressors and victims."[16] Such an agreement (characteristically not explicit) may be a theodicy of suffering for one group and a theodicy of happiness for the other.[17] Following Emile Durkheim, Berger regards the transcendent dimension of theodicy as central. That is, a concern for justice requires relation to divine symbolization. But it is clear that the transcendent serves to legitimate social power, goods, and access in a certain configuration. The function of God is to establish a kind of givenness about a particular arrangement and to invest it with a quality of acceptability and legitimacy, if not justice. Examples might be the tacit agreement of society that blacks have custodial jobs, that women receive less income than men for

---

15. Peter L. Berger, *The Sacred Canopy* (Garden City, N.Y.: Doubleday, 1967), 53–80.

16. Ibid., 59.

17. Ibid.

comparable work. These are deeply legitimated practices in our society, not much challenged until recently. Such socially accepted inequities presume the *operation* of a theodicy long before the *crisis* of oppression and the yearning for equity become a public act.

2. Robert Merton takes up the same question in less direct and more technical language without a primary religious reference.[18] He offers a sociological analysis of *nomos*,[19] that is, the norms by which a society maintains itself and sets criteria for what is right and wrong, good and evil, what is to be rewarded and punished. *Nomos* thus functions as a set of criteria to govern social benefits and settlements.[20] The positive benefits are for those who meet the norms. Those benefits are made available in certain parameters: "The range of alternative behaviors permitted by culture is severely limited."[21] Obviously, behavior that is deviant from those norms, that violates the reward system, is not rewarded and may be punished.[22] There is no doubt that the system of benefits is in part informed by and grows out of the ontological realities of life. Merton, along with Berger, concedes the legitimating function of ritual in this regard. But Merton's sociological realism is more critical than that of Berger in arguing that the *nomos* is not a gift of heaven but is a contrivance of earth, which requires that the theodic consensus be read critically, as a decision about who will have access to social goods and social power. The extent to which *nomos* is a social contrivance is the extent to which theodicy is an enquiry about social reality, social benefits, and social decisions about reward and punishment. Violation of *nomos* may be regarded as disobedience to God. It also threatens social stability and will not be tolerated extensively.

The argument of this essay, on the ground of Merton's analysis, is that every theodic settlement (including its religious articulation) is in some sense the special pleading of a vested interest. Indeed, it cannot be otherwise because there are no statements about God's justice that are not filtered through a social reality and social voices that have a stake in such social reality. The point to be stressed is that more theoretical and speculative treatments of theodicy have

18. Robert K. Merton, *Social Theory and Social Structure* (Glencoe, Ill.: Free Press, 1957).
19. Ibid., 121–94. Cf. James L. Crenshaw, "The Problem of Theodicy in Sirach: On Human Bondage," in *Theodicy in the Old Testament*, 133–34.
20. Merton, *Social Theory*, 137–38.
21. Ibid., 134.
22. For a particular scriptural example, see Walter Brueggemann, "A Neglected Sapiential Word Pair," *ZAW* 89 (1977): 234–58.

acted as though the discussion can be conducted without reference
to those life-realities. There is no theodicy that appeals to divine
legitimacy that is not also an earthly arrangement to some extent
contrived to serve special interests. This point must be insisted on,
and, derivatively, scholarly consideration of theodicy must recognize
the ways in which *nomos* is mediated through such social reality and
social interest.

3. Most helpful for our purposes is the analysis of Jon Gunnemann.[23] Influenced by Max Weber, Peter Berger, and Thomas Kuhn,
Gunnemann understands social revolution as a shift of paradigms
for theodicy, a different perception of evil. Theodicy is a settlement
made in a society concerning how much evil and suffering is necessary, legitimate, and bearable. It concerns the relative assignment
of suffering to different members and groups in the community.
Theodicy is an agreement on the amount of suffering to be borne in
situations of unequal power and privilege in which some are happy
while others suffer. Theodicy as a crisis occurs when some—usually
the sufferers—no longer accept that reading of evil, that assignment
of suffering, and insist that evil be perceived differently and suffering
be distributed differently. When evil is perceived in new ways, social
power must be distributed differently to redress the unacceptable
arrangements. The odd reality is that a settlement may be long-
standing and only lately rejected, but the crisis is nonetheless acute
when the question is raised. Revolution, then, according to Gunnemann, is not simply a seizure of power but is a change in the rules
through which power and access are apportioned.

What is clear in the analyses of Berger, Merton, and Gunnemann
is that theodicy concerns real power in real social communities. Any
discussion of theodicy that fails to consider this dimension is likely
to be ideology in the worst sense of the word, that is, a cover-up of
social reality. A catalogue of dimensions of theodicy that includes
only the moral, natural, and religious, and excludes the *social*, fails
to address the ways in which evil is not a cosmic given but a social
contrivance. Interpretations of Scripture that are idealistic, that is,
that read theology only in natural, moral, and religious categories
without reference to social, institutional reality, have missed the crucial point. They offer a theological exercise that is irrelevant to real
human life, even if it is a great comfort to the benefactors of present

---

23. Jon P. Gunnemann, *The Moral Meaning of Revolution* (New Haven: Yale Univ.
Press, 1979), 9–50.

disproportions. In the Old Testament, the theodicy issue surfaces as early as the exodus event, which rejects the theodic settlement in the Egyptian empire and makes possible an alternative social arrangement. Israel, in its normative tradition since the exodus, continues to reflect precisely on the social dimension of evil and suffering.[24] Moreover, Israel continues to believe that every theodic settlement is a contrivance that is open to change.[25]

III

The insights of social theory are not unknown in the field of Old Testament study. I note three studies that are well informed by attention to social reality:

1. Klaus Koch[26] has offered an important statement on theodicy in his argument of a deed-consequence system. That system operates as a sphere of destiny without active intervention of an agent. Unfortunately, Koch's analysis does not pursue the sociological implications of his own insights. It is the case that the deed-consequence construct as a system of social rewards and punishments is not ordained in the cosmic ordering of things but is a social construction to maintain certain disproportions, a fact Koch does not take into account. It is when the system of advantage and disadvantage is no longer regarded as legitimate that a crisis in theodicy occurs. Koch makes these statements:

---

24. At the heart of Israel's credo tradition is not speculation but a *cry* against unjust social power (cf. Exod. 2:23-25). It is that cry, which is at the center of Israel's discontent, that Herbert Schneidau (*Sacred Discontent* [Berkeley: Univ. of California Press, 1976]) properly calls "sacred." On the social power of "cry," see the poignant lines of Ernst Bloch, *Atheism in Christianity* (New York: Herder and Herder, 1972), 16–18. Bloch is concerned with a cry that is not heard, a conclusion Israel's credo does not accept.

25. For ancient Israel, all such injustice is open to change and must be addressed to God, who is the guarantor but also the transformer of social order. That is why the credo models shaped out of such a change (the exodus) were wrought through a cry to God. And that is why the credo as a paradigm of social possibility must be taught to each new generation. Cf. Michael Fishbane, *Text and Texture* (New York: Schocken, 1979), 79–83. The "core narrative" is a paradigm that must be in each case related to historical specifics, but the paradigm itself insists that social arrangements can be changed. On that central claim, see Walter Harrelson, "Life, Faith and the Emergence of Tradition," in *Tradition and Theology in the Old Testament,* ed. Douglas A. Knight (Philadelphia: Fortress, 1977), 11–30.

26. Klaus Koch, "Is There a Doctrine of Retribution in the Old Testament?" in *Theodicy in the Old Testament,* 57–87.

> It is when skepticism gained the upper hand that there was a *radical reassessment of the concept that there was a powerful sphere of influence in which the built-in consequences of an action took effect.*[27]

> In the later documents of the Old Testament, Qoheleth and Job show us that *the concept of actions with built-in consequences was shaken to the foundation.*[28]

Koch's statements can easily be related to the categories of social analysis offered by Berger, Merton, and Gunnemann. The first quote concerning skepticism means that the entire system of benefits is in question. The second means that the benefit system is no longer regarded as a cosmic given but is seen as a construction, or, we may say, as a social contrivance. Once seen as a contrivance, its positivistic legitimacy is ended, and it is subject to criticism and revision.

2. Patrick D. Miller[29] has examined the ways in which benefits, that is, rewards and punishments, function in prophetic literature. First, his primary argument concerns the correspondence of sin and judgment. Second, his work carries on an important dialogue with Koch in which he identifies cases in which Koch has used the texts to serve his hypothesis, but in ways that are not the most compelling reading. But it is Miller's concluding statement that concerns us. He concludes:

> The correlation of sin and punishment while effected by Yahweh is not manifest in a capricious and irrational way unconnected to the nexus of events, as if it were an "act of God" in the sense that insurance companies use such a term, a bolt of lightning from the sky that suddenly destroys. There is no such trivialization of the notion of judgment in the passages studied. On the contrary, they reveal a kind of synergism in which divine and human action are forged into a single whole or the divine intention of judgment is wrought out through human agency.[30]

For our purposes the telling phrases are "the nexus of events" and "wrought out through human agency." That is, *benefits occur through social processes,* through control of access, goods, and power. Any critique of God's justice must be a critique of the social agency

---

27. Ibid., 79; italics in the original.

28. Ibid., 82; italics in the original.

29. Patrick D. Miller, *Sin and Judgment in the Prophets* (Chico, Calif.: Scholars Press, 1982).

30. Ibid., 138.

through which that justice is made concrete. Theodicy is not an es-
oteric speculation about God, not a supernaturalism, but concerns
the handling of power through human agency that claims religious
legitimacy. What had been taken as divinely ordered is at least in
part seen to be historically contrived. *Theos* is the legitimator of *dikē*,
but the issues surface always about justice as experienced in the
historical process.

3. David N. Freedman, in his summary of the exilic period, concludes with a section entitled "The Final Response: Second Isaiah."[31]
He states:

> The simplest explanation of Second Isaiah's theology is to say that
> what everyone else thought was the question (Why do the innocent
> suffer?) was in fact the answer to a larger question, How does history
> work?[32]

That shift of the question proposed by Freedman is precisely correct, but I believe Freedman has not carried the shift far enough.
To ask how history works is not a theoretical question about God
but an immediate political question about social power. Thus, for
example, in Isaiah 46 the gods of Babylon are criticized, but this is
joined immediately in chapter 47 by a critique of arrogant political
power. The two cannot be separated.[33] The key interpretative point
for our purposes is the decisive linkage of *divine authority* and *social
power.* While scholarly attention has been on the matter of divine authority, the overriding question in the text itself, I propose, is the
issue of social power. The ways of administering social power are now
deeply criticized, and there is no going back. There is no appeal to
divine legitimacy that can now nullify the criticism. The conversation that Norman Gottwald has boldly mounted concerns precisely
this connection between divine legitimacy and social power, which
cannot be dismissed as Marxist. Israel's critical theological tradition
since the exodus is precisely a protest about and inquiry into the
benefit systems of society in which God is affirmed to be present as
dispenser, legitimator, and guarantor. My concern here is to identify
precisely what is at issue in the matter of theodicy. As soon as the

31. David N. Freedman, "Son of Man, Can these Bones Live?" *Int* 29 (1975):
185–86.

32. Ibid., 186.

33. On the powerful connection between the two, see the essays in *The Idols of
Death and The God of Life*, ed. Pablo Richard (Maryknoll, N.Y.: Orbis, 1983).

fact of social evil is acknowledged, it becomes clear that theodicy is an inquiry into such arrangements that give excessive life to some at the expense of others. It takes no great imagination to see that that is how the theodicy question is posed in our time. I submit it is the way Israel characteristically posed the question.

IV

To test this proposal we take up the two texts commonly cited as most explicitly posing the question of theodicy (Jer. 12:1; Job 21:7).
   1. In Jer. 12:1, the theodic question is articulated as follows:

> Why does the way of the wicked prosper?
> Why do all who are treacherous thrive?

The two pairs of terms here yield a deed-consequence understanding: wicked (rāšāʿ)/prosper (ṣālaḥ), be treacherous (bāgad)/thrive (ṣālâ). Three observations are in order. First, the linkage of "wicked" and "prosper" is indeed a structure of act–consequence. The issue is raised by the poet because the consequence should not follow from the deed. The deed and the consequence contradict each other, which shows that the system of benefits has collapsed. The case is brought before Yahweh because Yahweh is the guarantor that certain deeds yield certain consequences, and certain consequences do or do not follow from certain deeds. The question to Yahweh grows out of concrete experiences of social practice. It is not speculative.
   Second, the decisive term "prosper" (ṣālaḥ) is of special interest to us.[34] On the one hand, the term is tightly tied to obedience in a clear scheme of deed and consequence. This is true in the sanctions of the Torah (Deut. 28:29; Num. 14:41; Josh. 1:8). It is used with reference to the reforming kings by the Chronicler (2 Chron. 14:6; 26:5; 31:21; 32:30). On the other hand, the term also refers to physical, material, social well-being, with an unmistakably eudaemonistic connotation (cf. Gen. 24:21, 40, 42; 39:3, 23; Isa. 48:15; 53:10; 54:17). Those who ṣālaḥ are those who benefit from the best rewards of the social system. It is not thought that the blessings and well-being are given like a bolt from the blue, but are given the way such matters are always administered, through the responsible and reliable

---

34. On the term ṣlḥ, see Robert Davidson, *The Courage to Doubt* (London: SCM, 1983), 21–26.

function of the social system. The term has no special religious connotation but refers to prosperity according to society's capacity and
criteria.

Third, in the text itself (Jer. 12:1) *ṣālah* is exposited by the terms
of verse 2, "they take root, they grow, they bear fruit." There are
visible measures so that one can see for whom the social system
functions. Elsewhere in Jeremiah this material-social dimension is evident: in 2:37, it means (negatively) political well-being; in 5:28, it is
linked with justice and welfare of orphans; and in 22:30, it refers to
longevity of the dynasty.

2. The second text commonly cited with reference to theodicy is
in Job 21:7:

> Why do the wicked live,
>   reach old age, and grow mighty in power?

This surely is a challenge to God, as conventional discussions of
theodicy have recognized. Verse 4 observes that this protest is not
against *'ādām* (humankind) but against God, who presides over the
social system from which *'ādām* benefits. The conclusion of this unit
in verse 16 speaks of prosperity (*ṭôb*) and observes that the wicked
possess prosperity. The issue is the same as Jer. 12:1. But what is
interesting here is that the issue does not revolve around a theological referent. Indeed God is not directly addressed anymore than
'ādām is. God is addressed by implication, but I submit it is not a
theological statement but a critique of a social system of benefits for
which God is at best the invisible, unnamed guarantor. The accent is
completely on the social and economic rewards that ought not to be
but are because the system is skewed. The problem thus is not some
speculative theological argument or an existential anguish about an
intimate relation; the problem is the distribution of social goods.

A variety of texts explicate Job's concern for the social process as
an instrument of God's injustice:

> Their children are established in their presence,
>   and their offspring before their eyes.
> Their houses are safe from fear,
>   and no rod of God is upon them.
> Their bull breeds without fail;
>   their cow calves, and does not cast her calf.
> They send forth their little ones like a flock,
>   and their children dance....

> They spend their days in prosperity [*ṭôb*],
> and in peace they go down to Sheol. (vv. 8-13)

The restatement in verses 23-24 observes that the wicked go to their graves comfortable, untroubled, confident, rewarded:

> One dies in full prosperity ['*eṣem*],
> being wholly at ease and secure,
> his body full of fat
> and the marrow of his bones moist.

They never see recompense (*šillēm*) or destruction (cf. vv. 19-20).

How one reads this text depends upon one's interpretative posture. The conventional existentialist tendency of interpretation[35] can take this simply and directly as a critique of God alone. But if the sociological analysis of theodicy we have outlined has merit, then it is clear that the well-being of the children, houses, bulls, and cows of the wicked is not caused directly by God as though by edict, but that the well-being takes place through the nexus of social processes.[36] Such houses are safe from fear not because some spirit hovers over the house but because the agents of finance, security, and protection are favorably inclined. One's bull breeds without fail not simply because of God's kindness but because one has the best bulls and has the money to secure the most probable successes.[37]

My point then is not an exegetical but a hermeneutical one. Our reading of Job (or any of the theodic literature) depends on our perspective, that is, our social location. It is odd that an existentialist reading goes hand in glove with a kind of supernaturalism that simply overlooks all the functions of social process. But if the text is read with social realism and we ask how it is that the wicked are well off, it is because the networks of social process that govern access

---

35. An existentialist interpretation has been made most attractive through the study of Samuel Terrien. See his *Job: Poet of Existence* (Indianapolis: Bobbs-Merrill, 1957). It is noteworthy how this sort of interpretation tends to shy away from the materialist issues of social justice.

36. See the negation of these same social elements in Psalm 109, also through social processes. See my study of Psalm 109 as a statement about social processes, "Psalm 109: Three Times 'Steadfast Love,'" *WW* 5 (1985): 144-54.

37. James A. Michener (*Iberia* [New York: Random House, 1968]), in commenting on the sociology of bullfighting, concludes that if the Republicans had won the civil war in Spain, bullfighting would have come to an end. Bullfighting requires the luxury of enormous tracts of land, dependent on social monopoly. The point is not without parallel to Job's observation.

and power are inclined and arranged that way. The theodic question addressed to God becomes at the same time skepticism about a social process that is less and less regarded as legitimate. The God of Israel (who is in some ways still linked to the revolutionary memories of the exodus) is never a God apart from social processes but is one who is mediated, experienced, and practiced in those processes.[38] My judgment is that the entire question of theodicy has been misunderstood in our guild because in the name of objectivity we have devised ways of reading and thinking about the question that screen out the problems that are most difficult for the "haves" of society.

I do not want to claim too much or overstate the case, but I suggest that these two questions from Jer. 12:1 and Job 21:7 read differently if read in the presence of those who resent the wicked because the wicked have come to have a monopoly on social goods and social access, on bulls that breed without fail, on houses that are safe, on children who sing and dance and rejoice, and on land that is too large while others are displaced.

V

One other evidence for relating theodicy to social evil needs to be considered. I have noticed how many times in Job the question of land is present. This is noteworthy because our existentialist readings of theodicy do not much concern land. I propose that where land is under debate, questions of God's justice concern not only God but the processes through which land is governed, distributed, taxed, mortgaged, and repossessed. In such contexts, God is the giver and authority of land.[39] At least to some extent the poem of Job asks about land and so shapes theodicy around issues of *social evil.*

1. The book of Job in its present form is bound by two statements concerning property:

Thou hast blessed the work of his hands, and his possessions [*miqneh*] have increased in the land. (1:10)

---

38. Proverbial sayings that lie behind the tradition of Job make connections between God and social process in the direction argued here. See, for example, Prov. 14:31; 17:5; 18:17.

39. Psalm 37 is a remarkable example of wisdom teaching preoccupied with how to secure and hold land. See especially vv. 9, 11, 22, 29, 34, with the wordplay on "cut off" (*kārat*) and "possess" (*yāraš*). Such a perspective in wisdom supports the claim that wisdom teaching does indeed reflect a class interest, on which see Robert Gordis, Brian Kovacs, George Mendenhall, and Glendon E. Bryce.

And in all the land there were no women so fair as Job's daughters; and their father gave them inheritance [*naḥᵃlâ*] among their brothers. (42:15)

The structure of the book as loss and restoration (which has often been noted) is here articulated precisely around the land question, that is, the question of land loss and land restoration. This movement is reflected as well in the formula *šûb šᵉbît* (42:10), which is also a formula of land restoration.[40]

2. The poem between these prose units is, among other things, an inquiry about land and the processes by which it is lost and held. We may begin with two statements that seem to be conclusions reflecting a consensus. In chapter 20, Zophar presents a massive assertion on the fate of the wicked. The wicked, says Zophar, are excluded from the reward system of society and will receive no blessings. The conclusion in verse 29 is:

> This is the wicked man's portion from God,
> the heritage decreed from him by God.[41]

The portion does not refer to communion with God (as in some Psalms) but to land. Zophar's verdict concerns social, economic, political nullification, so that the possessions of the wicked are taken from him (v. 28).[42] The form-critical analysis of Claus Westermann suggests that one loses possessions not by violence but through the agency of law, court, and finance.[43] It is striking that at the end of the cycle of exchange with the friends, in 27:13 Job quotes Zophar's verdict and agrees with him:

---

40. On the meaning of this formula as it relates particularly to land, see John M. Bracke, "The Coherence and Theology of Jeremiah 30–31" (Ph.D. diss., Union Theological Seminary, Richmond, 1983), 148–55.

41. Brevard Childs (*Isaiah and the Assyrian Crisis*, SBT 3/2 [Naperville, Ill.: Alec R. Allenson, 1967], 128–36) has identified this formula as a "summary appraisal." Rhetorically, then, the statement functions to assert a consensus that sociologically means a theodic settlement.

42. On "portion," see Gerhard von Rad, " 'Righteousness' and 'Life' in the Cultic Language of the Psalms," in *The Problem of the Hexateuch and Other Essays* (New York: McGraw Hill, 1966), 260–66; and Walther Zimmerli, *Old Testament Theology in Outline* (Atlanta: John Knox, 1978), 98–99.

43. Claus Westermann, *The Structure of the Book of Job* (Philadelphia: Fortress, 1981). The extensive use of the lawsuit form draws the argument very close to such public processes, even if the usage is only an imitation. The form itself carries those nuances into the discussion.

> This is the portion of a wicked man with God,
> and the heritage which oppressors receive from the Almighty.

The detailed exposition of Job in 27:14-23 speaks, among other things, of loss of children, silver, house, and riches. Indeed the inversion of materials is such that

> he may pile it up, but the just will wear it,
> and the innocent will divide the silver.

3. We may consider what the three friends say about land. Eliphaz, speaking of the man who is reproved by God, says:

> You shall know also that your descendants shall be many,
> and your offspring as the grass of the land. (5:25)

In a parenthetical comment, he says:

> what the wise men have told
> and their fathers have not hidden,
> to whom alone the land was given... (15:18-19)

Verse 20 offers a contrast by speaking of the wicked man who has pain and who must wander abroad for bread (v. 23) precisely because he has no land from which to receive bread. In verse 29, Eliphaz speaks of the wicked:

> He will not be rich, and his wealth will not endure,
> nor will he strike root in the land.

In 22:8, Eliphaz catalogues Job's sins and says:

> The one with power possessed the land,
> and the favored man dwelt in it.
> You sent widows away empty, therefore...

That is, Job is seen as one who deserves to lose the land because he did not conduct his land possession according to the norms of his society.[44]

Bildad asserts that the land is not excessively troubled by the anger of Job (18:4), and then he comments on the wicked:

---

44. Job of course counters this in his statement of innocence in 31:16-17.

> His memory perishes from the land,
>   and he has no name in the street. (18:17)

This verdict apparently means he has no descendants to inherit the land. Concerning Zophar, we have already commented on 20:39 and his verdict.

Clearly all three friends have a theory about land possession: life is organized so that socially responsible people possess land. Clearly God governs so. Clearly as well, the social apparatus is organized to assure this. The destiny of the righteous and the wicked is not simply a heavenly verdict but a social practice. The verdict of God and the practice of the community hold together, and the debate is about both, never about one without the other. The friends are the voice of a particular theodic ideology, and they keep social practice and religious legitimacy in close connection.

4. Job's response to this mode of social interpretation is clear. We have already seen in 27:13 that Job has the same judgment to make as his friends about the distribution and possession of land. Job's speech concerns social loss. He can remember when the system worked. The socially undesirable

> are driven out from among men;
>   they shout after them as after a thief.
> In the gullies of the torrents they must dwell,
>   in the holes of the earth and of the rocks.
> Among the bushes they bray;
>   under the nettles they huddle together.
> A senseless, a disreputable brood,
>   they have been whipped out of the land. (30:5-8)

That is as it should be. The systems of society work so that the socially undesirable should not have a place, and they do not.

But, of course, that is retrospect. The problem is that Job's present experience does not correspond to the theodic ideology of his friends. Most of the land references in the mouth of Job concern the failure of the deed-consequence system to function:

> The land is given into the hand of the wicked;
>   he covers the faces of its judges—
>   if it is not he, who then is it? (9:24)

> He takes away understanding from the chiefs of the people of the land,
>   and makes them wander in a pathless waste. (12:24)

The reference in 9:24 is important because it mentions judges, thus acknowledging human agency in the wrong distribution. The human agency of judges, closely allied with the inequitable God, is the subject in 24:2-4:

> Men remove landmarks;
>> they seize flocks and pasture them.
> They drive away the ass of the fatherless;
>> they take the widow's ox for a pledge.
> They thrust the poor off the road,
>> the poor of the land all hide themselves. (vv. 2-4)

In this text God does not directly exercise a time of judgment. Rather the established network of social practices favors the powerful rich against the helpless poor. The arena of conflict is land, displacement, and the erosion of old boundaries. God is enmeshed in these practices that destroy society, but God's action is intimately linked to the judicial processes (cf. v. 12). God is assaulted not for direct actions but because of the unfair, unreliable social practices and agents God sanctions.

We have already examined the initial question concerning theodicy in Job 21:7. In that same unit, Job asks,

> How often is it that the lamp of the wicked is put out?
> That their calamity comes upon them?
> That God distributes pains in his anger? (21:17)

The verse is of interest because the term translated as "distribute" is *ḥālaq*, to apportion. It is precisely the question of distribution that concerns Job. His question expects a negative answer. Never is the lamp of the wicked put out. Never is their calamity upon them. Never does God distribute pain in anger. Job wishes for God to distribute calamity. But Job does not believe that God will ever do it. Job no longer trusts the social system of rewards and punishment.

Job accepts the fundamental theodic premise of the friends, but he observes that the system has collapsed. Yet, at the same time, Job continues to expect something from that system. In the great climactic statement of innocence in chapter 31,[45] we may observe at the beginning and at the end references to land as the measure of the

---

45. On the chapter, see Georg Fohrer, "The Righteous Man in Job 31," in *Essays in Old Testament Ethics*, ed. James L. Crenshaw and John T. Willis (New York: KTAV, 1974), 1-22.

function of the moral system of benefits. Land, as a blessing from God, is surely given through the social systems of law and finance. Job 31:2, reinforced by verses 3-4, is a statement of innocence and of trust in the conventional processes of reward and punishment. Job in this passage counters the shrill question of 21:7 and affirms the conventional system of reward and ownership:

> What would be my portion [*ḥēleq*] from God above,
>   and my inheritance [*naḥ*ᵃ*lâ*] from the Almighty on high?

The use of *ḥēleq* and *naḥ*ᵃ*lâ* is worth noting. Though the reward is given by God, it is clearly a *material reward* that is given though *social processes*. Thus this assumption and its counter in 21:7 reflect the two theodicies of which Berger speaks. In 31:2-4, we hear the voice of those for whom the system produces happiness. In 21:7, we hear the voice of those for whom the system does not work and produces misery.

At the end of chapter 31 (vv. 38-40), the last conditional self-imprecation concerns land, care for the land, ability to have land, and the risk of what may come upon the land. Job's statement of innocence is, of course, a theological statement concerning blessing from God, but it is also a sociological statement about a system of sanctions. It is not simply a supernatural act of God that some have good land and others have poor land, that some have thorns and briers and others have myrtle and cypress (Isa. 55:13). This statement (31:38-40) is clearly rooted in a conventional curse formula. The curse, however, does not take place in a social vacuum but through social process. The entire chapter—bounded by the references to land in verses 2 and 38-40—assumes a just social system. What is under discussion is not only the good intention of God but also *the reliability of the system of benefits*. It is for that reason that the language of the court is used (vv. 35-37): this is a statement about the workings of the system. Indeed, the inclination of Yahweh is not under review in this chapter, but only the court system that adjudicates claims.

VI

As the poem of Job ends, Job has his material blessings restored and increased (42:10-13), with credit for the rehabilitation given to Yahweh. If the question of theodicy is posed around the issue of *theos*, then the conclusion of this literature asserts that the faithful God of Job answers and intervenes to work justice. But if the question of theodicy is posed around the issue of *dikē*, then one may say that justice is done in the realm of social process. Because Job has spoken what is right (vv. 7-8), he is given twice as much (v. 10).

The way in which Job is given twice as much is important for our theme. To be sure, Yahweh guides the process of rehabilitation. But it is of crucial importance for our argument that the mode of restoration is through visible social channels:

> Then came to him all of his brothers and sisters and all who had known him before, and ate bread with him in the house; and they showed him sympathy and comforted him for all the evil that the Lord had brought upon him; and each of them gave him a piece of money and a ring of gold (v. 11).[46]

Job is given his reward as a just man through the social process. Indeed this human, communal action is stated as a response to God's evil. God may do evil, but redress is done through social process.

To be sure, this human action is matched by and corresponds to the divine blessing (v. 12). But the divine blessing cannot substitute for social process. It is the work of the human community that makes Job's experience of God's justice possible. Indeed, one may believe it is freshly functioning social processes that permit this rehabilitation. Such processes do not displace divine justice but are the means through which it is practiced and experienced. The fidelity and generosity of God and the equity of the social system *both* operate. Indeed they function together. Job's vindication is unmistakably through the social system. Our supernaturalist and existentialist readings of Job have not sufficiently recognized that it is the rehabilitation of the social process that is evidenced along with and as the form of God's equity. Indeed our presuppositions have caused us not even to notice that the rehabilitation happens *through Job's fellows.*

In Jeremiah, to which we have also given attention with respect to theodicy, the same formula of *šûb šᵉbût* (cf. Job 42:10) is used for land restoration and for resumption of a place in the social functioning of the community. There is no doubt that this poetry of rehabilitation bears witness to the fidelity and generosity of God (chaps. 30–31, 33).

---

46. "All who had known him" perhaps refers not only to the three friends but also to that whole company in chap. 30 who treat him with disdain.

For our purposes, what is compelling is the function of reg-
ularized social process through which Jeremiah receives the just
treatment for which he yearns. The narrative is at pains to stress
that the hope of land is implemented through predictable and
trustworthy social practice and social institution:

> I signed the deed, sealed it, got witnesses, and weighed the money
> on the scales. Then I took the sealed deed of purchase, containing
> the terms and conditions, and the open copy; and I gave the deed
> of purchase to Baruch the son of Neriah, son of Mahseiah, in the
> presence of Hanamel my cousin, in the presence of the witnesses
> who signed the deed of purchase and in the presence of all the Jews
> who were sitting in the court of the guard. (32:10-12)

The detailed prose narrative is striking and unexpected after the
rhapsodic poetry of chapters 30–31. In those chapters of consola-
tion, the specific hope is homecoming to the land. But that glorious
promise from God is in this narrative account made concrete in
its specific description of the careful, detailed social practice that
accompanies the reception of land. As is well known, Jer. 32:1-15
is a prose account of a legal transaction whereby Jeremiah, the
righteous complainer who seeks justice and vengeance, receives the
land to which he is entitled. There is no doubt that this quite
personal episode is presented as a theological affirmation about
the restoration of Israel in the land by God. The mode of the
assertion, however, is that this rehabilitation in the land is done
precisely through social, contractual processes, through payment,
signed deed, secured witness, and careful measure.[47] God's hope for
justice is enacted through social processes. The derivative promise of
verses 42-44 presents precisely *social good* as the way Israel will know
God's justice.

The grand promise of verse 15 and the specific historical details
of verses 10-12 are not in any tension. Their juxtaposition only indicates that in this tradition of theodicy, the righting of injustice is
done through the structures and processes of society that make justice possible. To hope in God's future justice requires engagement

---

47. On the historical basis for the narrative of 32:1-15, Robert P. Carroll (*Jeremiah:
A Commentary*, OTL [Philadelphia: Westminster, 1986], 134) refuses to make a judgment. There seems no reason, in my opinion, to deny this narrative account to
the historical experience of Jeremiah, thus permitting it to be a resolution of the
issue raised in 12:1. On the specificity of the legal process, see Gene M. Tucker,
"Witnesses and 'Dates' in Israelite Contracts," *CBQ* 28 (1966): 42–45.

with such historical concreteness. It takes deeds and witnesses and records to implement the promises of God in historical processes. The tradition acknowledges that in the end, the land promises are not fulfilled through supernatural intrusion but through the transformations of historical process.[48]

In both Job and Jeremiah (the two places where the theodicy question is most explicitly posed), the resolution of the theodic crisis is restoration through social processes that are again known as functioning and reliable: (1) Job 21:7 moves to 42:10-13 and restoration by the *community giving*. (2) Jeremiah 12:1 moves to 32:1-15 and rehabilitation by *legal procedures*. The attack on God's justice is resolved through rectified social process, the only rectification in which Israel has an interest.

Three methodological conclusions are hinted at in this argument:

1. Our conventional readings of theodicy through speculative, supernatural, or existentialist lenses may be a misreading. It may be that theodic literature is finally more interested in *dikē* than in *theos*.

2. To the extent that we have settled for a misreading through wrong categories, our habitual approach may be reflective of our social location as scholars, for we tend to be well-placed within the social system and therefore not inclined to let our theological reflection spill over into social criticism. It may be our social location that causes us to agree that theodicy concerns moral, natural, and religious evil, to the disregard of *social* evil. I propose that putting the question differently invites a different reading of the text.

3. This argument may suggest (as I think is hinted by Koch, Miller, and Freedman) that a materialist reading is required. The reality of God's governance is through social processes and not without them. This may make us more open to current exegesis that connects religious matters to issues concerning social power, social access, and social goods. That is, read in relation to the crises of social process, the biblical literature has a different, more radical claim to make.

As noted above, Freedman has tracked the change of the question of theodicy. The question Why do the innocent suffer? is transformed into How does history work? The answer that Israel

---

48. Micah 2:1-5, of course, shows how the gift of land from God takes place through disciplined and formal social processes. See especially Albrecht Alt, "Micha 2:1-5, *Gēs Anadasmos* in Juda," in *Kleine Schriften zur Geschichte des Volkes Israel* (Munich: n.p., 1959), 3:373–81.

knew very well is that history works through social processes (in Job's case through brothers and sisters and all who knew him and in Jeremiah's case through witnesses and court officials). Those social processes are either legitimated or judged by God. They operate either equitably or unjustly, either for the well-being of the community or for its destruction. That is how history works. Yahweh is discerned in Israel, sometimes as the impetus of the social process, sometimes as the norm, and sometimes as the agent for the transformation of the process.

10

The Social Nature of the Biblical Text for Preaching

THE PREACHER stands midway in the process of the biblical text. The process of forming, transmitting, and interpreting the biblical text is a creative task at its beginning, midpoint, and ending. The creative dimension of the process means that the text and its meanings are always being produced. They never simply exist: they are not just "there"; rather, the community is continually engaged in a willful act of production of meaning. That is what is meant by "the social nature" of the text.[1]

The Textual Process

The textual process has three identifiable points, each of which is creative, that is, productive. First, it begins in *the formation of the text,* that is, the way in which the text has reached its settled canonical form. Historical-critical methods of study are concerned with the ways in which the community, through editors, redactors, scribes, and traditionists, has put the text together. Whatever view we have of the creation of the text, we know that human hands and hearts have been at work in its formation.

---

1. On the work of the community in generating the text, see Michel Clevenot, *Materialist Approaches to the Bible* (Maryknoll, N.Y.: Orbis, 1985), esp. chaps. 12–15. Leonardo Boff (*Church, Charism and Power* [New York: Crossroad, 1985], 110–15) has seen the critical implications of this insight of production concerning the ideological control that the interpreting community exercises over the text.

Second, the end of the textual process is *the reception and hearing of the text* that are done by the congregation. We know that such listening is a complex matter because communication in general is exceedingly complex, and reception of the text is a specific moment of communication. No one can imagine any longer that the preaching of the text is heard by members of the community just as it is spoken or just as it is intended by the preacher. The listening is done through certain sensitivities that may distort, emphasize, enhance, or censor, depending on the particular situation of the listening community. The listening community is engaged in a constructive act of construal, of choosing, discerning, and shaping the text through the way the community chooses to listen.[2] The text thus construed may or may not be the text that is the one offered by the speaker. That is, the text heard may be quite different from the one proclaimed.

It is the third identifiable point, *the midway process of interpretation,* that interests us in this essay. Interpretation is all the action between formation and reception that seeks to assert the authority and significance of the text. This interpretative step includes the classical creeds and commentaries, the long history of theological reflection, contemporary scholarship, and contemporary church pronouncements. Above all, it includes the interpretative work of the preacher in the sermon. It is in the sermon that the church has done its decisive, faith-determining interpretation. The sermon is not an act of reporting on an old text; it is an act of making a new text visible and available. This new text in part is the old text and in part is the imaginative construction of the preacher that did not exist until the moment of utterance by the preacher.[3] Like a conductor "rendering" Beethoven so that that particular music exists only in that occasion,

---

2. On the freedom exercised and the choices made in such construal, see David H. Kelsey, *The Uses of Scripture in Recent Theology* (Philadelphia: Fortress, 1975). On a "canonical construal" of the Old Testament, see Brevard S. Childs, *Old Testament Theology in a Canonical Context* (Philadelphia: Fortress, 1986).

3. Michael Fishbane (*Biblical Interpretation in Ancient Israel* [Oxford: Clarendon, 1985]) has shown in a compelling way the dynamic relation between *traditum* and *traditio,* that is, the tradition and the ongoing traditioning process. It is often the case, clearly, that the *traditio* becomes the new *traditum.* See also his more succinct statement of the matter, "Torah and Tradition," in *Tradition and Theology in the Old Testament,* ed. Douglas A. Knight (Philadelphia: Fortress, 1977), 275–300. In this latter work he comments: "Hereby the danger inherent in the dialectical process between a divine Torah-revelation and a human exegetical Tradition has been disclosed. Tradition has superseded the Torah-teaching and has become an independent authority. Indeed, in this case, Tradition has replaced Torah itself" (p. 294).

so the preacher renders a text so that it exists only in that particular form in that particular occasion of speaking.[4]

These three dimensions of the textual process—formation, interpretation, reception—are all creative acts in which the text and its meaning are not only an offer made to the community but also a product generated in the community. Interpretation and listening, as well as formation, are creative acts of construal. This creative aspect of the text is unavoidable and should be welcomed as an arena in which faith is received, discerned, and made pertinent. Some may think such creative possibility in interpretation is an aberration to be avoided. It cannot be avoided. Nor should it be avoided, because it is the way in which God's word is alive among us. Interpretation can and must be creative and imaginative if it is to be interpretation and not simply reiteration. Listening is inevitably an imaginative act of response in which the listener does part of the work of rendering the text.[5]

This entire creative process consists of two factors that are in tension and make our topic both important and difficult. The textual process is at every point *an act of faith*. In faithful interpretation, the entire process is governed by the work of God's Spirit of truth. It is this that permits interpretation to be an act of faith. The promise of faith is the conviction that in its formation, interpretation, and reception the text is a word of life that makes a difference. No part of this process is undertaken on the pretense that this is objective or neutral or a matter of indifference.

Those who formed the text did so because they knew the traditions to be important and they judged them to be true and urgent for the ongoing generations of the community. That is the theological meaning of the canon. The subsequent interpreter who received the text has labored diligently over it, as does the contemporary interpreter, because faith requires interpretation. Interpreters in every generation, even those who have exercised enormous freedom, have intended their work as an effort in fidelity. Finally, those who receive the text, the assembled community of listeners, gather in an act of faith. The church gathers around the text because it takes the

---

4. In the "rendering" of the text, one "renders" God in a new way. On the theme, see Dale Patrick, *The Rendering of God* (Philadelphia: Fortress, 1981).

5. On the methodological possibilities in "reader response," see Wolfgang Iser, *The Act of Reading: A Theory of Aesthetic Response* (Baltimore: Johns Hopkins Univ. Press, 1978), and the collection of essays *The Reader in the Text*, ed. Susan R. Sulieman and Inge Crosman (Princeton, N.J.: Princeton Univ. Press, 1980).

text seriously. It listens eagerly (and therefore imaginatively) to try to hear the nuance in the text that is God's live word now. Participants at every point of the textual process are unembarrassed about the premise of faith. All parts of the textual process are undertaken primarily to ensure the powerful, authoritative presence of the word among members of the community.

It is also the case, however, that every part of the textual process is *an act of vested interest.* Exegetical study is now learning this insight from sociological criticism.[6] The textual process does not proceed objectively or neutrally but always intends to make a case in a certain direction. Just as there is no "exegesis without presuppositions,"[7] so there is no textual activity that is not linked to a vested interest. The formation of the text itself has been an act of vested interest. Certain pieces of literature are selected, gathered, shaped, and juxtaposed in different ways to argue certain points. We know, for example, that the early community around Moses authorized certain texts that served the interest of liberation.[8] The exodus narrative is surely put together by proponents of a radical, liberating faith. In the time of Solomon, other texts were celebrated because they legitimated the concentration of power in the monarchy and served to enhance the inequality of the status quo.

In like manner, the interpretative act is notorious for being an act of vested interest. There is no doubt that "liberation communities" in the Third World approach every text with an inclination that tilts interpretation in a specific direction. We are coming to see that even what we regarded as the objective scholarship of the historical-critical method has not been objective but has served certain social interests and enhanced certain epistemological biases.[9]

---

6. For brief introductions to this method of study, see Robert R. Wilson, *Sociological Approaches to the Old Testament* (Philadelphia: Fortress, 1984), and Norman Gottwald, "Sociological Method in the Study of Ancient Israel," in *Encounter with the Text,* ed. Martin J. Buss (Philadelphia: Fortress, 1979), 69–81.

7. See Rudolf Bultmann, "Is Exegesis without Presuppositions Possible?" in *Existence and Faith* (Cleveland: World, 1960), 289–96. Given our current sociological inclination, the formula has come to have different, and perhaps more radical, implications than originally suggested by Bultmann.

8. This is a central argument of Norman Gottwald, *The Tribes of Yahweh* (Maryknoll, N.Y.: Orbis, 1979). See, for example, chap. 13 where he speaks of substructure and superstructure and narratives as "objectifications of the tradition superstructure."

9. This point has been well argued by Elisabeth Schüssler Fiorenza, *Bread Not Stone* (Boston: Beacon, 1984). For startling examples of tendentious interpretation, see Robert Ericksen, *Theologians under Hitler* (New Haven: Yale Univ. Press, 1985).

We are coming to see that what we thought was objective has in fact been the "class reading" of male, Euro-American theology. Richard Rohrbaugh has offered stunning and convincing evidence that many of the great American preachers of the last generation handled texts so that the sharp and disconcerting social dimension that questioned our economic commitments was ignored. As a result, the text was interpreted in other directions that probably were serious distortions.[10] This was not intentional distortion on the part of the preacher. It was simply a function of the fact that our faith is regularly embodied in a vested interest that we ourselves are not always able to discern.

Finally, listening to the text and its interpretation is an act of vested interest. Over time we select the mode and substance of interpretation that we want to hear. We select our interpretative tradition. We read certain books, subscribe to certain journals, even join or avoid certain churches in order to find a textual interpretation that is congruent with our vested interests and that we can receive and hear and to which we can respond.[11]

The textual process of formation, interpretation, and reception is therefore always a mixture of faith and vested interest. To study "the social process" is to pay attention to that vexed combination. That the textual process is skewed by interest requires a hermeneutic of suspicion.[12] That the textual process is an act of serious faith permits a hermeneutic of retrieval. Despite the identification of these two hermeneutics, the matter remains complicated and problematic because we cannot practice one hermeneutic first and then the other. We cannot first sort out vested interest and then affirm faith, because vested interest and faith always come together and cannot be so nicely distinguished. We must simply recognize the fact that the two always come together, even in the midst of our best efforts of discernment and criticism.

---

10. Richard L. Rohrbaugh, *The Biblical Interpreter* (Philadelphia: Fortress, 1978).

11. On the neutralizing effect of much scholarship, see José Cárdenas Pallares, who has observed the power of "guild scholarship" to avoid the central interpretative issues. He writes, "Today, Sacred Scripture is studied with the benevolent approval of the *pax imperialis;* no exegetical activity disturbs the tranquility of the 'empire' for a single moment. What biblical periodical has ever fallen under suspicion of being subversive? Biblical specialists have curiously little to suffer from the Neros and Domitians of our time" (*A Poor Man Called Jesus* [Maryknoll, N.Y.: Orbis, 1986], 2).

12. The notion of a hermeneutic of suspicion has been normatively presented by Paul Ricoeur, *Freud and Philosophy* (New Haven: Yale Univ. Press, 1970). See the programmatic use made of it by David Tracy, *The Analogical Imagination: Christian Theology and the Culture of Pluralism* (New York: Crossroad, 1981), 346–73 and passim.

The creative act of formation–interpretation–reception *produces a text*. As it produces a text, it forms an imaginative world in which the community of the text may live. That production of a text is a willful, intentional act generated by faith and vested interest. That the text is "produced" means a different text could have been formed, interpreted, or received. This means that the produced text is never innocent or disinterested. But it is this text, never innocent or disinterested, that we take as the normative text for our faith. The text that has been produced and made canonical is the only one we have. It is to that text we must obediently and critically attend.

When the community has thus produced a text, it is the task of the community to *consume the text,* that is, to take, use, heed, respond to, and act upon the text. The entire process of the text then is an act of production and consumption whereby a new world is chosen or an old world is defended, or there is transformation of old world to new world.[13] The purpose of using the categories of production and consumption is to suggest that the textual process, especially the interpretative act of preaching, is never a benign, innocent, or straightforward act. Anyone who imagines that he or she is a benign or innocent preacher of the text is engaged in self-deception.[14] Preaching as interpretation is always a daring, dangerous act in which the interpreter, together with the receivers of the interpretation, is consuming a text and producing a world.

The world so produced is characteristically a world made possible by faith, but it is a world mediated through vested interest. Thus the text never only says; it also does. What it does is to create another world of perception, value, and power that permits alternative acts. Great attention must be paid to vested interest and its impact on perception, value, and power because vested interest has an enormous power to guide the textual process in certain directions. It is this dangerous, inevitable drama of the text that is referred to under the rubric "social nature." As both member and leader of the community, the preacher is necessarily involved in this dangerous,

---

13. On production and consumption in relation to texts, see Kuno Füssel, "The Materialist Reading of the Bible," in *The Bible and Liberation: Political and Social Hermeneutics,* ed. Norman Gottwald (Maryknoll, N.Y.: Orbis, 1983), 134–46.
14. The preacher characteristically and by definition uses words in a performative manner. Cf. J. L. Austin, *How to Do Things with Words* (Cambridge, Mass.: Harvard Univ. Press, 1962). On the definitional impossibility of a "neutral pulpit," see Walter Brueggemann, "On Modes of Truth," *Seventh Angel* 12 (March 15, 1984): 17–24.

problematic production and consumption of texts through which worlds are chosen and life is transformed.

The Classic Tradition of Sociology

The classic tradition of sociology illuminates the lively shaping action of the community upon the text.[15] It is important to recognize that sociology arose as a distinct discipline in response to a specific social crisis. That is, sociology is not simply the general study of human community, but from its beginning was a discipline preoccupied with a particular set of awarenesses and problems.[16] The startling changes in human consciousness that came in the seventeenth, eighteenth, and nineteenth centuries and that are associated with the Enlightenment and modernity have made us aware that the world in which we live is a social contrivance that carries with it important costs and gains. Sociology is essentially a critical discipline that has exposed the deceptive notion that the social world is an absolute given arrangement; it has accomplished this exposure by bringing to visibility the ways in which society continually constructs itself. At the outset, sociology as criticism was aimed against traditional notions of the absolute givenness of social life that were legitimated by religious orthodoxy. These notions, as sociological study made clear, also brought with them the legitimacy of an absolutist economic and political orthodoxy.[17]

Sociology was therefore initially addressed to the mystification of a religion that claimed and pretended the world was a given. At the same time, however, sociology tended to be blind and inattentive to a scientific orthodoxy that posited a new social given, this time objective, rational, neutral, and technological—all the things we have come to label as positivistic.[18] Critical sociology emerged to deal intentionally with the naive positivism of much social science; it has

15. C. Wright Mills (*The Sociological Imagination* [New York: Oxford Univ. Press, 1959]) exhibits the categories of discernment that have been generated and nurtured by sociology.

16. See Robert A. Nisbet, *The Sociological Tradition* (New York: Basic Books, 1966), for a survey of the characteristic themes of classical sociology.

17. This is, of course, the focus of Marx's critique of religion. It is important that this critique be taken in a specific context and not as a general statement. For a positive sense of Marx's critique of religion, see José Miranda, *Marx against the Marxists* (Maryknoll, N.Y.: Orbis, 1980).

18. See Robert N. Bellah, "Biblical Religion and Social Science in the Modern World," *NICM Journal for Jews and Christians in Higher Education* 6 (1982): 8–22.

become clear that the new "objective" world is as confused as the old religious world and as incapable of seeing the workings of its own ideology.[19] Critical sociology can help us see that the vested interests and ideological defenses of "scientific objectivity" are as dangerous and dishonest as the old absolutes of religion.

This shift from the old world of religious tradition and convention to the new world of technical control is a theme that has preoccupied the classical tradition of sociology. This theme has been articulated in various forms. We may mention its appearance in the three progenitors of the classical sociological tradition.

1. Karl Marx addresses the social alienation caused by capitalism and the role of religion in legitimating social structures that are exploitative and dehumanizing.[20] Marx's great insights are that economic arrangements are decisive for all social relationships and that religion functions primarily to legitimate economic arrangements. Clearly Marx was preoccupied with the shift in economic relations that tore the economic dimension away from the general fabric of social life.[21] He saw that this shift was deeply destructive of the possibility of human community. The emergence of alienation as a central product of the modern world is at the center of Marx's analysis. The textual tradition entrusted to the preacher has as a task the discernment of that alienation and the consideration of alternatives to it. The preacher must pay attention to the ways in which the text and its interpretation participate in the process of alienation.

2. Max Weber sought to provide an alternative to Marx that did not identify economics as the cause of everything.[22] Weber paid particular attention to the new forms of social control and administration and the emerging power of bureaucracy. It would be a

---

19. See Alvin Gouldner, *The Coming Crisis of Western Sociology* (New York: Basic Books, 1970).

20. The writings of Marx are complex and not easily accessible. The best access point I know is the introduction by David McLelland, *The Thought of Karl Marx* (New York: Macmillan, 1971). On alienation in Marx in relation to religious questions, see Arend van Leeuwen, *Critique of Heaven* (New York: Scribner's, 1972); idem, *Critique of Earth* (New York: Scribner's, 1974); and Nicholas Lash, *A Matter of Hope* (Notre Dame, Ind.: Univ. of Notre Dame Press, 1982). See also René Coste, *Marxist Analysis and Christian Faith* (Maryknoll, N.Y.: Orbis, 1985).

21. On the emergence of "laws of the marketplace," which are regarded as detached from social pressures and values, see Karl Polanyi, *The Great Transformation* (Boston: Beacon, 1957).

22. Max Weber's works are scattered, but a useful sourcebook is *From Max Weber: Essays in Sociology*, ed. H. H. Gerth and C. Wright Mills (New York: Oxford Univ. Press, 1946). For an accessible introduction to Weber, see Frank Parkin, *Max Weber* (London: Tavistock, 1982).

mistake, however, to interpret Weber (against Marx) as a friend of modernity. Like Marx, Weber saw the heavy toll that the structures and values of modernity would continue to assess against the possibility of humanness. The emergence of new forms of rationality preoccupied Weber. The emergence of destructive forms of rationality is also a struggle in the Bible, where covenantal modes of rationality are regularly offered against the temptations of naturalism and nationalism. In our present social situation, the connections Robert Bellah has made concerning managerial rationality offer a suggestive critical insight for the preaching office.[23]

3. In a more conservative mode, Emile Durkheim was interested in the requirement of social cohesion for the survival of society.[24] In his classic study of suicide, Durkheim observed what happens in societies where the fabric of value and cohesion is exhausted and persons must live in a context of normlessness.[25] Durkheim's critique can cut two ways. On the one hand, ours is a society that lives at the edge of normlessness; on the other hand, we react to normlessness with a heavyhanded emphasis on conformity. The crisis of normlessness and conformity in our culture sounds strangely reminiscent of the Mosaic crisis about freedom and obedience and the problematic of the law as Paul understood it. The preacher is cast in a social role as a voice of normativeness, in a society bereft of norms.

There are great differences among these three spokespersons for social possibility and pathology, but they all focus on the fact that societies have ways in which to articulate and distort certain kinds of truth that make human life possible or problematic. Social structure, order, and value are not objective givens. But they also are not simply connections that can be willfully and artificially wrought. They are, rather, the slow, steady work of formation, creation, and transformation by which a community orders its life of perception, value, and power.[26]

---

23. See Robert N. Bellah et al., *Habits of the Heart: Individualism and Commitment in American Life* (Berkeley: Univ. of California Press, 1985), 44–51.

24. Robert K. Merton (*Social Theory and Social Structure* [New York: Free Press, 1957], chaps. 4 and 5) has articulated well Durkheim's attentiveness to the crisis of normlessness.

25. Emile Durkheim, *Suicide: A Study in Sociology* (New York: Free Press, 1951). More generally on Durkheim, see Kenneth Thompson, *Emile Durkheim* (London: Tavistock, 1982).

26. For a general critical survey of more recent sociological thought, see Robert W. Friedrichs, *A Sociology of Sociology* (New York: Free Press, 1970).

Interpretation as Social Construction

The act of interpretation takes seriously both the old treasured memory and the new demand of the situation. Interpretation seeks to mediate between tradition and situation. On the one hand, interpretation is always *responsive* to the situation, that is, commenting on the new social realities that are already established. On the other hand, interpretation is always *assertive*, saying something genuinely new and challenging the community to rethink and reperceive the newly established reality in light of the tradition. In modes of both response and assertion, interpretation is an imaginative act that articulates reality in a new way impossible until the moment of speech. It is the speech that creates the possibility.

Sociology shows us that society is constantly reconstructing itself. While great attention therefore needs to be paid to the manipulation of power and the management of economic and political forces, we know that the primary mode by which a community reconstitutes itself is by its interpretation, by its reflection on ancient memory and tradition, and by its recasting of that memory and tradition in new ways resonant with the new situation.[27] All communities are always engaged in the process of interpretation. This is what ideology, propaganda, mass media, and civil religion are about. They are responses and assertions, more or less creative, that seek to mediate a newness juxtaposed between tradition and situation.

In order to arrive at a better understanding of interpretation as a social act of reconstruction, several dimensions of critical exposition are peculiarly important.

1. Interpretation is unavoidably a communal activity. The whole community is involved in the process. Interpretation must take place if the community is to live and continue. Interpretation inevitably does happen because it is a main activity of the community. Sociology has helped us see that communities are always engaged in interpretative acts of reconstitution and reconstruction. That act of interpretation is characteristically a mixture of faith and vested interest.

With the coming of the Enlightenment and the rise of modernity, many have failed to understand the inevitability of interpretation. The fascination with so-called objectivity led to the mistaken notion that reality did not need to be interpreted. As reality did not

---

27. See Fishbane, *Biblical Interpretation*, 1 and passim.

need to be interpreted, it was mistakenly concluded that the biblical text could be read in a straightforward manner without interpretation. This is also the mistaken notion of those who want the U.S. Supreme Court to be "strict constructionists," that is, not to engage in interpretation. The kind of interpretation that denies it is interpretation is indeed interpretation of the most dangerous kind because it attempts to establish itself as unavailable for criticism.

2. The interpretative act of social reconstitution is what the biblical text itself is all about. That is, the text is not simply a factual reporting about what happened. In each of its statements it is an act of interpretative mediation whereby ancient Israel and the early church seek to reconstitute the community in the face of a new danger or crisis.[28] In ancient Israel, the new situation is characteristically the new concentration of power and knowledge in the monarchy or the loss of monarchal power and knowledge in the exile.[29] In the New Testament, the characteristic new situation is the interface between Jewish and gentile Christians and the derivative problems of ethics and organization. In each case, the new situation requires a total recasting of the memory in order to sustain the identity of the community.

The texts are not only response, however, They are also bold assertions in the face of the new situation. For example, in the Old Testament the Yahwistic theologians do not simply conform to the new social reality but make a strong case that in the new situation Israel must understand itself as the bearer of a blessing.[30] In the New Testament, for example, Luke-Acts offers bold suggestions about how the church must understand itself and order its faith. That the Old and New Testament texts are both responsive and assertive means

---

28. Narrative is essentially this act of recasting and interpreting the memory to meet a new crisis. Unfortunately, narrative theology has been frequently presented as a relief from Enlightenment modes of historicity, without attention to the dynamic, positive act of reconstitution. On the power and significance of story, see James Barr, "Story and History in Biblical Theology," in *The Scope and Authority of the Bible* (London: SCM, 1980), 1–17; and Tracy, *Analogical Imagination*, 275–81. On the cruciality of narrative, see Fred B. Craddock, *The Gospels* (Nashville: Abingdon, 1981): "A writer has in the sources available the sayings and the events for a narrative about Jesus Christ. A church has needs to be addressed. The intersection of the two is called a Gospel, a literary work of immense courage and freedom" (p. 27).

29. Gerhard von Rad (*Old Testament Theology* [New York: Harper and Row, 1962], 1:36-85) has shown how these two crises are pivotal for Israel's interpretive action.

30. See Hans Walter Wolff, "The Kerygma of the Yahwist," in *The Vitality of Old Testament Traditions*, by Walter Brueggemann and Hans Walter Wolff (Atlanta: John Knox, 1975), 41–66.

that they are deeply imaginative. They proclaim a social reality that did not exist until that moment of articulation. Moreover, because the text is deeply imaginative, it is probable that each such requesting of social reality is a mixture of faith and vested interest. Thus the J writer is concerned to maintain a human vision against a monarchal enterprise of self-aggrandizement. Luke seems to have been concerned lest the early church become a sect aligned against the empire. The community over time has judged the vested interests of the texts (for example, J and Luke) to be faithful vehicles for faith and not acts of distortion. As a result, these specific texts have been judged authoritative and designated as canonical.

In the Pentateuch, the documentary hypothesis of JEDP has been much misunderstood and maligned. It is an attempt to characterize the ongoing interpretative act of mediation that was underway in ancient Israel.[31] The J material, according to the dominant hypothesis, is an attempt to mediate the old memory in the affluent situation of Solomon. Similarly, the P tradition is an attempt to mediate the old memory in the despairing situation of exile.[32] These two moments, united monarchy and exile, require fresh interpretative acts or the old tradition will have been in vain. In the cases of both J and P, one can detect that this interpretative act is indeed a response to a social crisis, an assertion in the face of the crisis, and is a remarkable act of imagination. It takes very little insight to see that in each case the mediation is a mixture of faith and vested interest.

In like manner, the Synoptic Gospels are mediations of the old memory of the early church.[33] The Gospel of Mark faces the challenge of Roman imperialism; Matthew takes up the question of the relationship between Christians and Jews, or perhaps Jesus and the Jewish tradition; and Luke struggles with the gospel in a gentile world. These statements are clearly not theological absolutes (or we would not have these three variants), nor are they factual descriptions of what happened, but they are mediations that make available a new world in which the community may live joyously and faithfully.

3. In the creative, imaginative act of construction of reality, the interpreters, those who process the text, are dangerously engaged in

---

31. See more generally Brueggemann and Wolff, *The Vitality of Old Testament Traditions.*

32. On the exile as a situation requiring and permitting bold interpretation, see Ralph W. Klein, *Israel in Exile* (Philadelphia: Fortress, 1979).

33. On the canonical process and its significance in the New Testament, see James D. G. Dunn, "Levels of Canonical Authority," *HBT* 4 (1982): 13–60.

two ways.[34] On the one hand, they are so engaged because they inevitably make responsive, assertive mediations in the midst of their own mixture of faith and interest. Interpreters are never interest free but always present reality in partisan ways and, indeed, cannot do otherwise. On the other hand, in the act of interpretation they also have their own world remade. They do not stand outside this process but are being self-interpreted in the very act of biblical interpretation. In this act of mediation, hermeneutics then makes a new world possible. In hermeneutics as mediation, we thus bring the "process of the text," which includes formation, interpretation, and reception, together with the sociology of world making through which the community reconstructs itself.

The key hermeneutical event in contemporary interpretation is the event of preaching. The preacher either intentionally or unintentionally is convening a new community. This recognition will help us see why preaching is such a crucial event not only in the life of the church but also in our society. We must interpret to live. There is almost no other voice left that is honest, available, and open to criticism and that can do the interpretation on which society depends. Most of the other acts of interpretation that are going on in our midst are cryptic and therefore not honest, not available, and not open to criticism. The preaching moment is a public event in which society reflects on what and who it will be, given the memory of this church and given a postmodern situation in society.[35]

4. In the handling of the text by the preacher as interpreter and by the congregation as receiver, the hermeneutical work of world-constitution is going on. The interpretative work is done through the preacher's mixture of faith and interest while the congregation is listening and responding in its mixture of faith and interest. All parties to this act of interpretation need to understand that the text

---

34. For a formidable introduction to the issues, see Anthony C. Thiselton, *The Two Horizons* (Grand Rapids: Eerdmans, 1980). See also Richard E. Palmer, *Hermeneutics: Interpretation Theory in Schleiermacher, Dilthey, Heidegger, and Gadamer* (Evanston, Ill.: Northwestern Univ. Press, 1969). Unfortunately both Thiselton and Palmer are confined to the tradition of Heidegger. This tradition needs to be carefully criticized by a political hermeneutic rooted in Marx, as suggested by Ernst Bloch and the Frankfurt School. A more balanced view that takes into account the liberation trajectory is offered by David Tracy, *Analogical Imagination,* chap. 5 and passim.

35. On the shape of religious problems and possibilities in a postmodern context, see William Beardslee, "Christ in the Post-Modern Age," in *The Post-Modern Condition: A Report on Knowledge,* ed. Jean-François Lyotard (Minneapolis: Univ. of Minnesota Press, 1984); and Mark C. Taylor, *Erring: A Post Modern A-Theology* (Chicago: Univ. of Chicago Press, 1984).

is not a contextless absolute or a historical description but is itself a responsive, assertive, imaginative act that stands as a proposal of reality to the community. As the preacher and the congregation handle the text, the text becomes a new act that makes available one mediation of reality. That new mediation of reality is characteristically an act of fidelity, an act of inventiveness, and an act in which vested interest operates. Moreover, the preacher and the congregation do this in the midst of many other acts of mediation in which they also participate, as they attend to civil religion, propaganda, ideology, and mass media. They are incessantly involved in a complex of various interpretative, constructive acts, while claiming the interpretative act authorized by the Bible to be the normative one.

The Congregation and the Crisis of Modernity

The congregation that engages in interpretation (and with the interpretation embraces a certain refraction of the text) is not a contextless, undifferentiated entity. The congregation, as a community in crisis, gathers to decide one more time about its identity and its vocation. The people gathered have been bombarded since the last gathering by other voices of interpretation that also want to offer an identity and a vocation. In what follows, I am focusing broadly on the typical mainline North American congregation, either Protestant or Catholic. I assume such a congregation because that is the context in which I characteristically do my interpretation. Certainly other congregational settings could be assumed, and I do not imagine that this one is normative or even preferable.

A different statement might be made in a different context, such as in post-Christian Western Europe, in a totalitarian state, or in oppressive El Salvador, but our congregation is not yet post-Christian, is not in a totalitarian context, and is not faced with direct oppression. This congregation is a gathering of people who have been largely enveloped in the claims of modernity. It is a community with a memory and with a present reality. In the midst of this memory and this reality, the act of interpretation is undertaken one more time.

The memory is the memory about God and God's people, about the summons of ancient Israel and the baptism of the early church, about Jesus and the people of Jesus from his time until our time. That memory is about births given to barren women, bread given to desperate peasants, shepherds given to scattered sheep, forgiveness given to those immobilized by guilt. It is about deep inversions and strange power for daring obedience. This memory and the text that conveys this memory are the source and subject of our preaching. But the memory around which the congregational gathering takes place is also somewhat distorted. In my own work I have studied the memories of David to show how those memories have been variously cast and how they have been articulated to accommodate various social settings and social possibilities.[36] The memory may be enmeshed in a nostalgic longing for normalcy and "the good old days" when life was simple and agrarian, settled, and well ordered. That nostalgia is all intertwined with evangelical memory, so that the nostalgia has a vague religious feeling about it. There is a need to sort out the normative memory from this other vague yearning.

The present situation of the congregation needs careful attention. It is usually a situation of considerable affluence (even if some present are not affluent). The affluent ones are the ones who are competent and know how to generate income and move through the chairs to the seats of power. But the affluence and competence we treasure so much are matched by a profound fear—that the dollar will collapse, that the bomb will explode, that we will be overrun by immigrants. The affluence-competence factor invites us to "stand tall" and be secure; the fear syndrome undermines our confidence, and we live our days in an inarticulate uneasiness. This interface of affluence-competence and fear distorts public issues. The matters of compassion and "justice for all" that are embedded in our public conscience have become shriveled. Our fear drives us to selfishness, greed, and vengeance. Along with public failure, we find an erosion of our personal sense of life, a restlessness that generates anxiety that drives us to greed and finally to despair that things won't really work out. Our actual experience of our common life is not remote from the alienation of Marx, the technical rationality of Weber, and the normlessness of Durkheim.

There are many things to celebrate in this new world of competence and technical security. It boggles the mind to think how different we are from our grandparents and how much better off we are. But we are dimly aware that this new mode of life we value so much has caused us to jettison much that we previously valued. It is odd that the old festivals of solidarity wane, yet there is a persistent hunger for such occasions of solidarity. Old patterns of familial and

---

36. Walter Brueggemann, *David's Truth* (Philadelphia: Fortress, 1985).

liturgical gatherings are less and less compelling in our society. Our young people ask about roles and careers, but vocation seems like an obsolete idea. We surprise ourselves when we entertain brutality as a policy option in the world, and vengeance now seems acceptable if aimed at the right people. We have become people we did not intend to become, and we are not fully convinced that this is who we want to be. Given our perception of the world, however, that is who we need to be if we are to "succeed" according to the norms we have embraced.

Such a community gathers for the act of interpretation. Even if we have never heard of the word "modernity," we sense in inarticulate ways that we embody much that is "modern." Much has been lost to us, even if much is gained. We gather to see if we can hold the gain and yet recover what is lost. We gather to see if the world of vocation and tradition, of birth and bread, of shepherds and forgiveness can be mediated to us in the midst of our disproportionate affluence and fear. We do not want to discard the old memory, as our modern world wants to do, but we do not want a flat reiteration of the old memory that pretends we are not affluent and not afraid. We do not want simply a nostalgia that does not touch any of the real problems, the ethics of our affluence and the moral dilemma of our fear. We yearn for a responsive, assertive, imaginative act of interpretation that recasts the memory in bold ways that will transform our situation.

Our discussion thus far suggests a convergence of four major factors in the act of interpretation. These reflect, on the one hand, our present general intellectual situation and, on the other hand, the specific situation of the church. I find it remarkable that these four factors, which are drawn from very different aspects of contemporary thought and life, should so powerfully intersect in relation to our interpretative responsibility.

1. *The textual process* itself is an act of regular recasting that includes both faith and vested interest.

2. *The sociological tradition* in its classic presentations concerns the problem of alienation (Marx), the problematic of rationality (Weber), and the emergence of normlessness (Durkheim). All of these conditions are part of the modern world, and we know them all firsthand.

3. *The task of interpretation* is the task of the community to mediate the tradition in ways that construe a new world, that permit a new ethic among us.

4. *The congregation is gathered* to see if the old memory can be articulated in ways that reconfigure our present social reality of affluence and competence, of fear and brutality, of restlessness and despair.

The preaching moment is a moment of great complexity, great danger, and great possibility. Present in that moment are the textual process, the sociological realities, the act of interpretation, and the waiting congregation. Such a moment requires a strategy through which a new community might be summoned to a fresh identity and a bold vocation.

Options in Social Construction

The preacher in the act of interpretation and proclamation of the text is engaged in world making. I find it most helpful to appeal to the phrase of Peter Berger and Thomas Luckmann, "the social construction of reality."[37] The community authorizes special persons to head and oversee the process of social construction. In our context, the minister (usually ordained) is authorized to lead the community of faith in its construction of reality. Such an act is an ongoing process of education and nurture, especially in liturgy.[38] This liturgical articulation is presented as objectively true. When it is also received in this way, this liturgically presented world may be internalized by members of the community as "mine." Thus the process of appropriation includes the public action of the community and the personal internalization by the individual members who participate in the liturgy.

The second awareness from Berger and Luckmann is that the "life-world" so constructed is always underway and must be modified. New data, fresh perspectives, new experiences, and changed circumstances require recasting the life-world to keep it credible. If it is not regularly recast, the "old world" becomes disengaged from experience so that it must either live in protected, uncritical space (where it will be irrelevant) or be jettisoned as dead. It is the ongoing act

---

37. Peter L. Berger and Thomas Luckmann, *The Social Construction of Reality* (New York: Doubleday, 1966).

38. On constructive work in education, see Jack L. Seymour, Robert T. O'Gorman, and Charles R. Foster, *The Church in the Education of the Public* (Nashville: Abingdon, 1984), 134–56. More generally on the constructive work of imagination, see Paul W. Pruyser, *The Play of Imagination* (Madison, Conn.: International Universities Press, 1983), chap. 4 and passim.

of interpretation that recasts the life-world to keep the text credible. The preacher is engaged with the biblical texts in both elements, to sustain *the act of appropriation* and to engage in the ongoing *recasting* to keep the text credible.

This means that the purpose of interpretation and preaching is to present a life-world that is credible, that can be appropriated, and out of which the community is authorized and permitted to live a different kind of life. As the text itself is a responsive, assertive, creative act, so the interpretation of the text is also a responsive, assertive, creative act. The purpose of the sermon is to provide a world in which the congregation can live. Indeed, the preacher is intentionally designated precisely to mediate a world that comes out of this text that endures through the generations. That world the preacher mediates is one possible world out of many that could be offered. The offer of this world competes with other offers made by capitalism, by militarism, by psychology of various kinds, by health clubs, by automobiles, by beers, and so on. Moreover, it is a possible world among many that might be articulated out of the Bible, so it makes a difference if the text mediated is a Mosaic or a Solomonic text.

Scholarship has found it helpful to speak of a typology of interpretative postures. We may speak of a primary decision, so that the interpretative act is either transformative or stabilizing, in the service of discontinuity or in the service of equilibrium.[39] The basis for that model is rooted in the social history of ancient Israel and is evidenced textually in the Old Testament tension between the transformative vision of Moses, which belonged to the earliest voice of liberated Israel, and the stabilizing tendency of royal theology, which sought to build institutions and establish a reliable social structure.[40] When the texts are read sociologically, this interpretative issue of transformation/equilibrium is enormously helpful. This Old Testament paradigm (as Norman Gottwald has shown)[41] has important parallels to a Marxist class analysis, to Weber's construct of charisma

---

39. Friedrichs (*A Sociology of Sociology*) shows how the tension of transformation and equilibrium has operated in sociology. Concerning Old Testament study, see Walter Brueggemann, "A Shape for Old Testament Theology, I: Structure Legitimation," *CBQ* 47 (1985): 28–46; idem, "A Shape for Old Testament Theology, II: Embrace of Pain," *CBQ* 47 (1985): 395–415 (both are reprinted in Walter Brueggemann, *Old Testament Theology: Essays in Structure, Theme, and Text* [Minneapolis: Fortress, 1992], chaps. 1 and 2).

40. See chap. 1, above.

41. See Gottwald (*Tribes of Yahweh*, chap. 50) on the interface between his method and the classical traditions of sociology. See my presentation of the paradigm

and bureaucracy, and, I should suggest, also to Ferdinand Toennies's typology of *Gemeinschaft* and *Gesellschaft*.[42] The text itself in the Old Testament reflects this tension. The radical vision of Mosaic faith is in deep tension with the royal enterprise subsequently developed. The tension exists between texts with different social locations.[43] The act of interpretation can and inevitably must deal with the ways in which the text destabilizes and transforms or the ways in which the text stabilizes and gives equilibrium. How the text is interpreted by the preacher and how the text is received in the congregation may depend on the vested interest of both preacher and congregation, which may or may not adhere to the position of the text itself. Texts may transform *and* stabilize. Sometimes the same text may function either to transform *or* stabilize, depending on context, interest, and interpretation. Text and/or interpretation offer a world of transformation or equilibrium that enhances or diminishes a particular view of social reality. It is in the nature of the act of interpretation and therefore of preaching to participate in these world-making acts, either knowingly or unwittingly.

In what follows, I present a typology of texts through which various texts will be interpreted. It is, of course, the case that the texts themselves are never as clear and unambiguous as is the typology. The typology is useful only to the extent that it helps us see specific texts afresh; it should never be imposed on texts.

The text can be an act of good faith because both transformation and stabilization are faithful acts of God and both meet deep human yearnings, but the mediation of either comes through the vested interest of the preacher. Whether the preacher will mediate a world of transformation or equilibrium depends on many things, including what the preacher reads, with whom the preacher eats, the economic history of the preacher, and much else.

The texts will be received by the congregation as an act of faith. People do come to church to hear and respond. The reception of a mediation of either transformation or equilibrium happens through the interpretative receptivity of the congregation. What happens,

of the two trajectories in tension, Walter Brueggemann, *The Prophetic Imagination* (Philadelphia: Fortress, 1978).

42. Ferdinand Toennies, *Community and Society*, trans. C. P. Loomis (1887; reprint, New York: Harper and Row, 1963).

43. Robert R. Wilson has pursued the same textual paradigm with a typology of central and peripheral prophets. Following Wilson's language, one may say there are texts that are "central" and those that are "peripheral" (*Prophecy and Society in Ancient Israel* [Philadelphia: Fortress, 1980]).

what the text can "do," depends on the propensity of the congregation. That will be determined by many factors, but they include where and how the congregation is socially situated; what travels have been taken; what part of the world has been seen; how many members have experienced poverty, unemployment, crime, and all sorts of social disruption; or, conversely, the strength of the social equilibrium in the experience and horizon of the congregation. All of these factors impinge in powerful, subtle, and complex ways upon the interchange of text, preacher, and congregation. In the midst of the interchange, a new world may be mediated.　·

In presenting the world of the text to the congregation, the preacher has, according to this typology, four possible strategies. The typology assumes that the text may be an offer of transformation or stability and that the congregation is likely to be in a situation of transformation or stability. The available strategies in establishing an interface between the text-world and the congregation are these:

1. To present "a world of transformation" to those who yearn and hope for transformation. This is done when oppressed or marginalized people are invited to hope for the basic changes of social reality that are given in the texts of transformation.

2. To present "a world of equilibrium" to those who wait and yearn for transformation. This is done when oppressed or marginalized people are invited to accept and participate in the present regime as their proper duty and their only hope. The present order is then presented as the best chance for any change, but it will be change within that order that is accepted as nonnegotiable.

3. To present "a world of transformation" to those who value the status quo and do not want the world changed. This is when those who benefit from present social arrangements are called, in the face of that benefit, to submit to change as the will and work of God.

4. To present "a world of equilibrium" to those who crave equilibrium and regard the present social world as the best of all possible worlds, a world decreed by God. This is done when religion becomes a comfortable endorsement of the status quo.[44]

Each of these strategies is possible, and each reflects a decision about the thrust of the biblical text and how that thrust is to be related to the actual situation of the church.

---

44. The presentation of a religious world of equilibrium to those who crave equilibrium is what Marx referred to with his famous characterization of religion as "the opiate of the people."

Each of these four strategies is possible, and, on formal grounds, each is biblical. It is equally clear that the gospel gives criteria to sort out the various strategies and to see that all the possible strategies are not equally legitimate for genuine evangelical proclamation. The preacher is summoned by the gospel to present an imaginative word that lives "out beyond" and challenges the taken-for-granted world of the congregation.

In presenting this typology, I am aware that the actual situation of any congregation is enormously complex. In every congregation there are those who welcome change, those who resist change, and those who are unsure. Moreover, there are various kinds of changes, each of which needs to be critically assessed. In addition, various preachers and pastors are inclined either to welcome or to resist change, and that helps shape interpretation and preaching. My discussion intends not to deny or disregard all of that complexity, which must be honored and taken seriously.

For purposes of clarity, however, in what follows I have chosen to deal only with the third and fourth elements of this typology. My sense is that these dimensions of interpretation bear particularly on the typical North American congregation. A church that does not want the world changed will be offered either a text-world of transformation that calls the present into question (no. 3 above) or a text-world that celebrates equilibrium (no. 4 above). To be sure, there are times in such a congregation when equilibrium is legitimate and a genuine offer of the text, but for now we have posed the question in another way. The preacher thus may appeal to texts that offer either equilibrium or transformation and in doing so must pay attention to the possible hearing of the gospel that will occur in the congregation if the text is heard as an abrasion or as an assurance.

The important interpretative point is that the text should be kept in conversation with what the congregation already knows and believes. At times, the purpose of interpretation is to evoke fresh faith for another world from that which the community already knows and believes. In the typical North American situation, it is often the case that the text should be interpreted to make available an imaginative world out beyond the one to which the congregation now clings. More often this is so because such congregations tend to be ideologically trapped in a social world at odds with the gospel. But this interpretation that calls for newness may, nevertheless, appeal to the deep and serious faith latent in the church.

In a world of war and violence, for example, equilibrium is not objectively true but is in fact an imaginative act of interpretation that has been established and accepted as true. The interpretative issue is whether to ally the gospel with that already accepted, mediated world or to propose an alternative that may "ring true" but also will surely evoke conflict.

The strategy of the preacher then is to use texts in ways that legitimate the present perceived life-world or to present a life-world that puts people in crisis by offering a challenge to their present view and posing an alternative. Both are needed, but different emphases probably need to be made in various circumstances.

Whatever strategy is undertaken, it is most important that the preacher—and hopefully the congregation—is aware that good preaching (which is an act of inventive world-construction) is fundamentally opposed to two tendencies in our culture. It is opposed to a false kind of objectivity that assumes the world is a closed, fixed, fated given. That assumption of objectivity is a great temptation to us, whether the claim is given in the name of religious orthodoxy or in the name of technological certitude. An evangelical understanding of reality asserts instead that all of our presumed givens are provisional and open to newness, a newness that may be enacted in the event of preaching.

The other tendency to which good preaching is opposed is a kind of subjectivity that assumes we are free or able to conjure up private worlds that may exist in a domesticated sphere without accountability to or impingement from the larger public world. Such a powerful deception among us seems to offer happiness, but it is essentially abdication from the great public issues that shape our humanness.

The preaching task is to be critical and challenging in ways that expose our present life-world as inadequate, unfaithful, and finally flat. This is to be done, however, in ways that neither become ideological nor simply terminate the conversation. Preaching is aimed not simply at this or that ethical issue but seeks to cut underneath particular issues to the unreasoned, unexamined, and unrecognized "structures of plausibility" that are operative in the congregation. Such preaching is also to offer reassurance about the coherence of reality, but a reassurance that is not a legitimation of present arrangements but an act of hope about another life-world available in the gospel. That life-world could offer the joy for which we yearn, which the present life-world cannot give. This offer of another world is the primary work of the gospel, for the gospel is news of another world. The articulation of that other world is unavoidably a critique of and challenge to every present world. This "other world" that is announced in and mediated by the gospel is not other-worldly in the sense that it is in the remote future, in heaven, after death, or "spiritual." Rather, the other world is now "at hand" (Mark 1:15). It refers to the present rule of God that calls us to a new obedience now and that releases us from every other obedience in the here and now, for the sake of God's sovereign rule.

Texts of equilibrium are important to the formation of a new lifeworld. The creation narrative-liturgy of *Gen. 1:1-2:4a* is such a text. It asserts that the world is ordered, is good, belongs to God, and is therefore reliable. When, according to critical study, that text is set in the exile as an affirmation to Israelites and a polemic against Babylonian imperialism and Babylonian gods, the social function of that equilibrium emerges. The Genesis text asserts that the world belongs to God and therefore not to Babylon, not to its gods or its rulers. Moreover, God rests and Israel is mandated to rest. That mandate asserts that Israelites in exile need not be endlessly anxious and frantic to become secure or to please Babylon but can rest in God's sure rule. Thus the text offers a world of well-ordered stability and equilibrium, in which Israel is invited to live. That well-ordered stability is not neutral, however, but is a counterequilibrium that invites Israel to break with seductive Babylonian offers of stability and equilibrium that cannot be true because the world does not belong to Babylon. The community that lives within this text is given stability but also is summoned to a freedom outside Babylonian definitions of reality. That is, by an act of imagination, creation theology becomes a warrant for what the empire would regard as civil disobedience.[45] The capacity of exiled Israel to act freely depends on its acceptance of the world of this text. The text responds to exile, asserts against Babylon, and imagines an alternative world of faith in which life is possible. The congregation may be invited to sense what an uncommon act of imagination this text is that dares to say that the world belongs to Yahweh who is a God of rest and order, dares to say it even to exiles whose life is disordered and restless.

Texts of transformation are equally important for a new lifeworld. The healing-feeding narrative of Elijah in *1 Kings 17:8-24* is such a text.[46] It is a text of disruption. It tells about this strange for-

---

45. Fishbane (*Biblical Interpretation,* 322–26) has shown how Second Isaiah is a reinterpretation of Genesis 1 for quite specific purposes in a polemical situation.
46. On the text, see chap. 11, below.

midable man of inexplicable power who comes into the life of a poor widow. He deals with her poverty by giving her food. He deals with death by raising her son to life. And the widow, the narrator, and finally we perceive him as a bearer of the power for life. This text evokes a question about this power, where it is available, and on what terms. The narrative asserts that power for life is not given through the royal regime but by this uncredentialed outsider.

This story destabilizes. It shatters the poverty-stricken, death-ridden world of the widow. It breaks her assumptions and her habits. If we listen attentively to the story when it is well told, it will also break our conventional assumptions, for it announces that the world is not the way we thought it was. The critical effect of the narrative is to delegitimate the king and his deathly rule and to invite us to another rule under the God of life. But the story of disruption also turns out to be a story of affirmation. It asserts that power is available, that life can be given, that food is offered.

Thus the story responds to the failure of Ahab and his governance. It asserts an alternative reality against Ahab's world. By an act of imagination, a story of feeding and a story of healing have been mobilized as vehicles for a different life-world. The narrative invites the listening community into a new arena of existence in which God's power for life has enormous vitality for new possibility, even though it is untamed and unadministered and we cannot harness and manage it on our terms.

Every text proposes a life-world that may counter ours. Texts of equilibrium are needed to give people a sense of order, but such texts as Gen. 1:1-2:4a turn out to be invitations to transformation. Texts of transformation are needed to give people hope that there is possibility outside present circumstances. But such texts as 1 Kings 17:8-24 turn out to be invitations to a new equilibrium wrought only by the gospel. Texts of both equilibrium and transformation are needed. Both cases require not only the capacity to respond and assert but also the capacity for imagination in order to let these texts become truly effective. Characteristically they invite the listening community out beyond the presumed world to a new world of freedom, joy, and obedience.[47]

---

47. The original publication of this essay included a sermon on 1 Kings 8:1-13, 27-30, together with exegetical comments and postsermon reflections.

11

The Prophet as a
Destabilizing Presence

BOTH TRADITIONAL CONSERVATIVES and conventional liberals misunderstand the prophetic dimension of Israel's faith. The former, in my judgment, tend to make too much of the predictive element, as though the prophets are forecasting, with particular reference to Jesus. The latter tend to understand the prophets primarily in terms of social action and righteous indignation. Both misunderstandings have an element of truth. It is true, on the one hand, that the prophets do care about the future, and they do believe that in the future, God will bring the historical process to obedience. On the other hand, the prophets do care intensely about the moral shape of society, so they assault every social disorder. I have tried to articulate an alternative understanding of the prophets that reflects the current inclinations of scholarship[1] and that I hope is useful for the practice of pastoral ministry in our own context.

The Prophets

My impression is that the most helpful study of the prophets just now is an analysis of the social systems of ancient Israel that "construct reality" in various ways. That is, the prophets are not isolated

---

1. For statements on the inclinations of scholarship, see the excellent books by Joseph Blenkinsopp, *A History of Prophecy in Israel* (Philadelphia: Westminster, 1983); and Klaus Koch, *The Prophets: The Assyrian Age* (Philadelphia: Fortress, 1982).

individuals but can best be understood in terms of the organization of society and the performance of certain social roles.[2] Although the implications of what I have to say apply to the prophets generally, I take as my text the Elijah narrative. I am primarily concerned with the ways in which this narrative reflects, serves, and challenges social organization.

1. As the prophets understand it, society consists in *an organization of social power*. This may refer variously to land, money, hardware, technology.

2. The organization of social power is derived from and dependent on *the management, control, and articulation of social symbols* that, in our day, may be understood as access to the media. In that day, this process was largely managed and controlled by the temple community, which was the center of symbolic life. Thus, the priests held enormous power, perhaps analogous to the power of the media in our context. *similar in function but not in origin or structure*

3. The organization of *social power* and the administration of *social symbols* were intimately linked together. Each reinforces and legitimates the other. The two together constitute a *social system* that orders, defines, values, and legitimates all life. It seeks to contain and monopolize all social meanings and all social possibilities. It inclines to be effective at delivery of a "good life" for those who participate in and support the system. Such support is given through a variety of modes: political conformity, economic solidarity, ritual commonality, epistemological assent, moral coherence. The system works well for all those who accept its definitions of reality.

The upshot of such a social achievement (which it is) is that "the system is the solution" for all social needs and hopes. Indeed, nothing of worth falls outside the system, so that the social system comes to be identified as being equivalent to reality. This is particularly evident in creation theology, which speaks of "creation" but often seems to refer to a certain social system that is assigned ontological status as the embodiment of what the creator intended.[3] Both the managers and the benefactors of the system tend to absolutize the system, to

---

2. An important book on the subject is Robert R. Wilson, *Prophecy and Society in Ancient Israel* (Philadelphia: Fortress, 1980). Scholars are increasingly noticing that as one talks about "organizations of society," one may observe that a variety of things can be "organized" in partisan ways. Note the suggestive titles by Bernhard Lang, "The Social Organization of Peasant Poverty in Biblical Israel," *JSOT* 24 (1982): 47–63, and Gary Alan Herion, "The Social Organization of Tradition in Monarchic Judah" (Ph.D. diss., University of Michigan, 1982).

3. See Walter Brueggemann, "A Shape for Old Testament Theology, I: Struc-

preclude alternative notions of reality. Indeed, alternative notions of reality constitute a threat, for they assert that this way of organizing social power and social goods is not an absolute given but only a historical contrivance. The goal of the managers and benefactors is to stabilize the system so that it is not noticed that it is a system, so that it seems it is the only *reality*, the only possible, thinkable reality. And if no other social reality is thinkable or possible, then criticism of this one tends to be precluded. Thus, most participants in and benefactors of the system do not notice that it is a managed, contrived system to which there are alternatives. They notice only that there is a reality to be trusted, valued, and adhered to. The result is that there is a kind of positivism that treats the social organization of power and symbols as an absolute given, "as it was in the beginning, is now, and ever shall be." That system is deeply valued because it comes to its adherents as though the only alternative to this system is chaos, which is experienced practically as the loss of advantage.

Destabilizing Presence

The prophetic task in such a social world is to maintain a destabilizing presence, so that the system is not equated with reality, so that alternatives are thinkable, so that the absolute claims of the system can be criticized. Thus, the destabilizing effort of the prophets takes as its responsibility the attempt to counter the powerful forces of stabilization that are at work among the participants and benefactors of the social system.

One may identify a *ground* and an *impetus* for this vocation of destabilization. The ground for such destabilization is not that the prophets are simply "angry young men," filled with righteous indignation, who like to "go off" on people. The ground is that they have an alternative perception of social reality that they insist is true and for which they want to create working space and allow for social possibility to emerge. That alternative perception of reality puts the presumed world of the regnant system in jeopardy. Such an alternative perception serves, by definition, to destabilize precisely when the alternative is stated or acted with clarity, so that the contrast is sharp. The contrast may be between the rule of God who liberates and the

ture Legitimation," *CBQ* 47 (1985): 28–46 (reprinted in Walter Brueggemann, *Old Testament Theology: Essays on Structure, Theme, and Text* [Minneapolis: Fortress, 1992]).

rule of idols that enslave, between the coming reign of God that invades and the present regime that sustains, between the yearning for justice and the experience of injustice. But note well, the prophetic is not understood primarily as denunciation or rejection, unless it is clear that there is a positive alternative available that, in fact, is true, gives life, and really functions.

The destabilization that results from such a powerful contrast may or may not be overt political action. On occasion, the prophets did speak directly about policy issues (perhaps most noticeably, Isaiah). But most often, the prophets issue a gesture or word that intends to play on the imagination of the community.[4] The preliminary point I want to make here is that prophecy is not in any overt, concrete sense political or social action. It is rather *an assault on public imagination,* aimed at showing that the present presumed world is not absolute, but that a thinkable alternative can be imagined, characterized, and lived in. The destabilization is, then, not revolutionary overthrow, but it is making available an alternative imagination that makes one aware that the presumed world is imagined, not given. Thus, the prophetic is an alternative to a positivism that is incapable of alternative, uneasy with critique, and so inclined to conformity.

The ground for such an alternative picture of reality is the sovereign rule of God. The prophets, skilled as they are with word pictures, relentlessly insist that the entire world must be imagined differently because of God's sovereignty.

Now it may seem that I have staked out a modest claim for the prophetic, that I have given away most of the great ideas for which "prophetic ministry" is embraced. My response is that first we need to look at what the poets of Israel do, and then we need to look at what is going on in our society. The truth is that because of the enormous fear in our social context, our government and its allies have constructed for us a fanciful world of fear, threat, security, and well-being that has little contact with the data at hand. But because we are managers and benefactors of the system, we find it easy and natural to accept this imagined world as real.

So the ground for prophetic destabilization is the alternative truth about the rule of God that gives the lie to our presumed worlds. The immediate *impetus* for much of the prophetic is the visible and daily presence of powerless and disenfranchised people.

---

4. I have explored some of the implications of this in *The Prophetic Imagination* (Philadelphia: Fortress, 1978).

Robert Wilson, among others, has explored how this factor generates voices of destabilization. The socially critical point is that the social system that claims to be the solution is, in fact, a solution for some at the expense of others. As the system empowers and secures some, it renders others powerless and marginalizes them. The ideological claim of the system is that it cares for all and provides for all. So the president can assert that a man losing his job in South Succotash is "not news." Or, the president's aide can say that he knows of no real data concerning hungry children. The system not only creates such disproportion, but then it also creates a set of lenses so that we look and genuinely do not see (Isa. 6:9-10).

Israel's sense of the historical process is that the voices of the excluded cannot be silenced. They can be administered for a long time, but they will not be silenced. They can be administered for a long time, but they will not be finally nullified. They will cry out. And when they cry out, they constitute an attack on the system and in fact a delegitimation, for they assert that the system is not working, is not giving life, is not keeping its promises.

The prophets of the Old Testament discern a peculiar linkage between the truth of God's rule and *the voice of the marginal*. The former gives the long-term *ground;* the latter gives the immediate *impetus*. That ground of God's sure rule and the impetus of a voice of marginality constitute the alternative world of the prophets. When this is mobilized against the dominant imagination, it makes a powerful alternative. The prophets intend that the participants in the dominant system should hear enough to transform the system. But their characteristic experience is that assault on imagination drives system people only deeper into their closed imagination.[5] The helplessness of the prophets is that they cannot penetrate this dominant imagination when it is finally hardened. Then the question is simply whether that closed imagination can finally fend off the truth of God and the cry of neighbor. In every particular circumstance, this question is always quite open and yet to be decided.

---

5. A. Vanlier Hunter (*Seek the Lord* [Baltimore: St. Mary's Seminary and University, 1982]) has demonstrated that consistently the prophets do not appeal for repentance. What appears to be such an appeal is characteristically reference to an earlier appeal that has been rejected. The old appeal for repentance regularly leads to a conclusion of judgment. In the present form of the prophetic text, it is the speech of judgment that overrides every possibility of serious repentance.

The Elijah Narrative

Now with that general background, we may consider three episodes from the Elijah narrative. The Elijah narrative is a remarkable piece in 1 Kings (17–21), with accompanying pieces on Micaiah (1 Kings 22) and Elisha (2 Kings 1–10). These narratives form a distinct corpus in the literature of 1 and 2 Kings, clearly contrasted both to the usual royal formula and to the Deuteronomistic editing, for there is almost no such marking on these texts. It is commonly presumed, as I do here, that these narratives are older than their royal-historiographic context.[6] It is likely that they were preserved and treasured in something of a folk culture and reflect such a community of storytelling. But I should also insist that the stories in their very character are not simply for entertainment but in fact perform an important critical function. That is, the rather primitive quality of the narrative not only reflects a socially primitive community. It also reflects a socially marginal community that has kept its distance from the reason, language, and epistemology of the dominant culture. It has, I suggest, fashioned a reason, a language mode, and an epistemology resonant with its social, political, and economic situation. These narratives, in their very mode, enact marginality. They perform an important social function, to state an alternative reality apart from the dominant reality. That social function is not created by placing these narratives in the context of the book of Kings but was the point of the narratives in their very first telling. The narratives are told, treasured, and practiced precisely in this community that wants to keep its freedom from the cultural perceptions of the royal system.

Now in saying this, I am urging that we read these texts with a kind of social responsiveness not honored by the historical-critical methods. Ask not what these texts mean, or even what they say, as though one may arrive at a conclusion and then summarize. Rather, ask what these texts *do,* in their inception and each time in their

---

6. Among the important studies of the Elijah narratives are the following: L. Bronner, *The Stories of Elijah and Elisha,* Pretoria Oriental Series 6 (Leiden: Brill, 1968); Georg Fohrer, *Elia,* ATANT 53 (Zurich: Zwingli, 1968); Odil H. Steck, *Überlieferung und Zeitgeschichte im der Elia-Erzählungen,* WMANT 26 (Neukirchen-Vluyn: Neukirchener Verlag, 1968); and R. S. Wallace, *Elijah and Elisha* (London: Oliver and Boyd, 1957). Two books that are not so critically disciplined but that are important for the sort of argument made here are Jacques Ellul, *The Politics of God and the Politics of Man* (Grand Rapids: Eerdmans, 1972), and Davie Napier, *Word of God, Word of Earth* (New York: United Church Press, 1976).

retelling. I argue that they propose to us an alternative world in which to live. They invite us to try it and for the moment to withdraw our intense allegiance to the world defined by the system. The stories have as their function to loosen our tight commitments to the life-world of our vested interests and for a moment to perceive the world differently.

The use of these stories by the Deuteronomistic presentation of 1 and 2 Kings is complex. I have drawn the conclusion that the Deuteronomistic editors were not fully contained in the royal world but mount a massive criticism against it.[7] One ground for that massive criticism is precisely these stories that hold out an alternative. Thus, even the Deuteronomistic Historian may have understood that these narratives function to unmask and debunk the royal system. It may be for that reason that they occupy such a prominent place in the historical account.

One of the interesting questions for scholarship today is that these are prophetic *texts*.[8] Our usual way is to take the personality of the prophet as an example of what we are to do. So, in the case of Elijah, we consider how, in our situation, we may act like that prophet. There may be something in that approach. The problem that scholars now detect is that it is an appeal of the example of a person when in fact what we have is the model of a text. Current scholarship wants to argue that our role, insofar as these texts are concerned, is not that we should replicate the person of Elijah but that we should handle the text so that it can have its say in the community.

The faith of the church is not vested in the person of Elijah. But it is staked very much on the claim of the text. So one will want to keep in mind that our tradition does not summon us to be prophets but to let the prophetic text have its continued say among us. To let this text have its continued say is to let it be a continuing voice of destabilization in a tightly ordered system, for that was its primary and original function. This leads me to a consideration of three episodes in three texts that characterize three dimensions of prophetic destabilization.

---

7. See my expository comments in *I Kings* (Atlanta: John Knox, 1982) and *II Kings* (Atlanta: John Knox, 1982).

8. The most important impetus in this direction comes from canonical criticism, especially the work of Brevard Childs, *Introduction to the Old Testament as Scripture* (Philadelphia: Fortress, 1979), but it also reflects the increasing importance of literary theory for Old Testament study.

Transformative Gestures of Solidarity

The first text, as a model of prophetic destabilization, is in *1 Kings 17:9-24*. The narrative falls into two parts, verses 9-16 and 17-24. It is introduced in a striking way with two significant elements:

1. The word of the Lord came to him,

2. "Arise, go to Zarephath, which belongs to Sidon, and dwell there. Behold, I have commanded a widow there to feed you."

Notice how abrupt and unaccommodating is the directive. The narrator has no interest in accommodating the listening community, in providing context or continuity. It is blurted out in all its powerful discontinuity. The text is destabilizing in its form because it offers a clean break. The initiative of the story holds two things in juxtaposition. The entire action is by the word. It is not explained but is under compulsion. There is agency within the narrative that is not attributable to the prophet. The word, however it is to be explained phenomenologically, is theologically presented as destabilizing. It breaks and it disorders life.

The second element is curious next to this awesome word. Elijah is sent outside, outside his people, outside his normal traffic pattern, outside the system. The *word* notices what lies outside the *system*. Elijah is sent to the widow. He is sent there to be fed by the widow. He is driven outside normal support systems. He is not sent there with resources for her. He is sent there to receive, to be given life precisely by this one whom society has defined as having no life-resources. It is not said that this is a testing of Elijah. But clearly, what the sovereign word of Yahweh does is to drive the prophet out beyond everything conventional and safe, perhaps to push him to "faith alone."

The widow, by definition, is poor. "Widow" is a legal category for those without social power. She has no representative in the village council, in the market, in the court. She is a genuine nobody, one whom the system is quite skillful in discounting and nullifying. Yet Elijah is to be fed by her. The story is remembered explicitly in Luke 4:26, where Jesus talks about the reach of God beyond the social system. The text seems to be strangely echoed in John 4, where Jesus receives water from the unacceptable, disreputable woman at the well.

So why tell the story? Well, likely it was told among widows and people like that. They did not regard themselves as without life-resources. The system thought so, but they knew better. Such communities at the margin do have strange ways in which to give life. By being sent there, Elijah is in an act of disengagement from the dominant support system. The story functions to assert, both in the community of the marginal and against the system, that the system does not have a monopoly on life. Elijah is sent to find life precisely outside the system.

This juxtaposition of *word* and *widow* is important for the prophetic. It is echoed in Isa. 57:15:

> For thus says the high and lofty One
>   who inhabits eternity, whose name is Holy:
> I dwell in the high and holy place,
>   and also with him who is of a contrite and humble spirit,
> to revive the spirit of the humble,
>   and to revive the heart of the contrite.

The God of the word dwells on high. This God speaks and it is commanded. But this same one sojourns with the widow and all those outside the system. The word does not leave one at rest in a safe system but drives one outside to the other place where God dwells.

So Elijah goes (v. 10). He is immediately obedient to the destabilizing word. We need to learn to read the text in terms of systems analysis. The imperative of Yahweh and the response of Elijah are a direct counter to the worldview of the dominant system. This woman and all like her have been nullified. They do not exist. They are nonpersons, invisible, without rights and without power. The social system does not notice or reckon with her. Probably King Ahab and his advisers had a government memo floating around showing that there really were no destitute widows. But the word noticed. (If there is a sound of laughter lurking behind these words, it is because it is there!)

In this act of the commanding word and the responding prophet, official reality is countered. These two together, Lord and prophet, declare official reality to be a lie. The woman does exist. There really are widows. And in an odd way, they have social power that the regime cannot nullify. They can be a source of life.

So Elijah goes to her. She is gathering sticks (or picking greens) or whatever it is that marginal people do to stay alive on marginal land. And Elijah says, "Fetch me a little water" (cf. John 4:7). It is an incredible act of solidarity and certainly not do-good liberalism, for he undertakes no action on her behalf. He is present to her at the point of her possibility, which officialdom had denied her. Then he ups the asking: "Give me bread." She pleads utter poverty. She had no bread, only a handful of meal, a little oil, and no prospect of any more. She knows she is to die. The system has fixed her fate in that way. Now read it as a systematically destabilizing narrative. It is an assertion that this is social reality in Israel. There really are people like this. They really are going to die. Her poverty is not because of her wickedness. There is no hint of that. Rather, it is because the social system has marginalized her and failed to provide a life-support system. Obviously then, as now, life-goods are given in adequate supply only to the competent, the productive, the well connected. She is none of these. So the gas has been turned off in her house. She shares what she has. But it is precious little.

Now we have seen that Elijah, in obedience to the word, has made a striking gesture of solidarity. He has come to be with her. He submits himself to her circumstance. Her poverty is not glorified, but it is entered into as real. He quests in her circumstance to find a source for life. But his solidarity with her is more than a gesture of sympathy. It is a transformative gesture. His transformative act is in this speech: "Do not fear, use the little you have." The little, in the act of using it, is transformed and redescribed. In verse 14, the little is described according to the promise of God: "The jar of meal shall not be spent, and the cruse of oil shall not fail." And verse 15 ends tersely, "She went and did as Elijah said; and she...ate for many days."

Now there is something mysterious, odd, primitive, and inscrutable here. It may be only a wonder tale that only simpleminded people can tell. The story explains nothing. And neither shall I. The outcome is that the life-world of the widow is utterly changed. What had been a world of death becomes a season of life. Characteristically, such narratives cannot be explained. They can only be told and heard, decided on, and perhaps believed. It is not the person of Elijah that is prophetic for us. It is the narrative. It is the narrative that asserts that the world is not closed and the system is not absolute.

We recognize, of course, that this story has parallels to the feeding miracles of Jesus. That does not explain anything either. But the stories bear witness to the same subversive reality. The prophet is one who has the power, the authority, and the freedom to commit acts of life in a world that has been defined by death. When the prophet calls the woman to "fear not," he wrenches her out of the world of

fear, fear that was a product of her marginality. What is she afraid
of? Well, of death. But also of being despised, of being emptied of
power and dignity, of marauding soldiers and foreclosing lawyers and
snooping social workers and loan sharks. She is set in a social world
of terror. She is without friend, without advocate, utterly exposed,
and at the mercy of social agents whom she cannot understand.

In the middle of all this, there is holy power at work in Elijah.
But let us not spiritualize. What Elijah does is to break the death
grip of the dominant system. He acts against the social monopoly of
those who control the means of production. The king is supposed to
control bread and oil. Energy must be properly administered. With
the king, it was all routine. He was the only source. But he had failed.
That is what the whole narrative presumes, already with the drought
in 17:1. The king could not cope with the energy crisis. The narrative
destabilizes because it asserts that the official forms of power not
only are dysfunctional but in fact also bring death. Life will have to
be sought and found elsewhere, outside the system that has failed. So
a transformative gesture of solidarity turns out to be destabilizing. It
declares that the dominant definition of reality is null and void. The
king cannot give life. There are, however, sources of life that the king
does not administer. Those have been retained by God alone. Every
time this narrative is rightly told and faithfully heard it reenacts and
replicates this nullification of the social system. One can tell that
it continued to have such a power and attractiveness because Jesus
uses it in Luke 4 and assumes that his listeners will catch the point.
In Luke 4, Jesus is also seen as a destabilizing agent who renders the
known world null and void. It is no wonder that they tried to stone
him, because he enacted the destruction of their known world.

So a practical digression. Every community, every family, every
congregation, every person has arranged a settlement of power and
weakness. We know who has social power in a family.[9] We know in
ordering our lives which sorts of things are honored and credited.
We learn to compensate and adjust so that we "lead from strength."
We live in those patterns so long that they appear absolute. The prophetic action is to speak a "fear not" at the point of weakness. When
that "fear not" is sounded, one begins to notice new sources of life
where none was noticed, new vitality that had been declared null
and void. We can now notice on a clear day that some forms of so-

---

9. See the discerning analysis of R. D. Laing, *The Politics of the Family and Other
Essays* (New York: Pantheon, 1971).

cial power we had trusted are in fact deeply dysfunctional. My point is that prophetic ministry is not limited to public policy and social action. It belongs to the liturgy and to pastoral care. It consists in finding life at the weak, discounted points of existence. When life is spotted there, the presumed power arrangements are threatened and destabilized because the monopoly is broken. The narrative invites us into a crisis in which old power arrangements are failed and new ones are being honored and found functional. And it is wrought by a "fear not" spoken at the moment of helplessness, a speech-promise that opens an alternative world.

Well, Elijah should have left then. He would have been ahead. But he did not get away in time. Soon the mother comes with her final loss. Now she has lost not meal or oil, but her only son, probably her only reason to scratch for life from day to day. She blames the prophet. Maybe you are good at giving meal and oil, she says. But you must also be the one who is a child-killer. It is odd reasoning. Perhaps the mother is hysterical. Or perhaps she senses what a destabilizing force he is and does not like it that close to home. Anyway, the agenda is now not hunger. It is death, as it always finally is with the marginal. The prophet is put in a situation of death to see if he can work life. Indeed, the entire narrative sets him against death and challenges his power. The question is, Who has the power of life? Those who have the forms of power do not have the power for life. King Ahab never raised anyone from the dead!

Elijah does not flinch. He takes the body of the boy. He seems to engage in some kind of physical gesture, perhaps artificial respiration. But what he finally does is pray. In the first scene, he addressed the woman, "Do not fear." Now he does not address the woman. Now he addresses God, the God who must be addressed in seasons of death. In verse 20, he cries out in anguish to God. He accuses God, even as the mother has accused him. In verse 21, he petitions God to let this child have life. He prays to God against the coldness of death because he does not believe that death is the last word. Notice how unencumbered and unarmed is this prophet. He has no resource, only prayer. Only the capacity to invoke the God of life in a season of death.

The narrative ends by having the prayer answered. God hears. The child lives. The woman trusts. This narrative, then, is an episode of *rehabilitation*,[10] which is the counterside of *destabilization*. The

---

10. Erhard Gerstenberger (*Der bittende Mensch: Bittritual und Klagelied des Einzel-men im Alten Testament* [Neukirchen-Vluyn: Neukirchener Verlag, 1980], 107–69) has

prophet engages not simply in an act of solidarity. He is not only willing to be there in this season of death. He transforms. He has power and authority to change circumstance because he trusts utterly the sovereign rule of Yahweh against the power of death. Now I do not want to overinterpret, but let me suggest this way of reading the text. Perhaps the story concerns the question, Who has power for life? The conventional answer that all of us give almost automatically and certainly uncritically is, "The system." That is what the system claims, and that is what it exists for. But, of course, this widow has no access to that. The system is not for her. She receives no life from the royal apparatus of the legal establishment or the temple machinery. So her crisis is to see if there are forms of life available that fall outside administered forms. The narrative makes it unavoidable. The power for life is loose in the world. It is not contained by the king, who can cause no rain. But other kinds of folks, especially this prophet, have access to power for life.

That is how pastoring may be prophetic: to assert, to act on, and to live out the assurance that the power for life is worked by God in our midst and will not be contained by our vested interests. The power for life is not controlled and contained in the normal, official channels. The monopoly is broken. The medical community does not control healing. The bureaucratic church does not govern grace. The agents of arms do not really preside over the possibilities of peace. The world is much more open than that to the invasion of God's life-giving power, granted to the unqualified.

One can recognize the echo of this story in Jesus' handling of the daughter of Jairus (Mark 5:22-24, 35-43). Of course, where Jesus is, the power for life is loosened. It will not be denied or monopolized. Every society has agents who imagine that they control and can dispense the power of life and that such a monopoly lends stability. This prophetic tale is destabilizing because the power for life turns up in odd and unexpected places. Indeed, that is what the resurrection of Jesus is about. It concerns the shattering of the monopolies around which life is organized and dispensed. So the early church can say that God raised up Jesus because it was not possible that the bindings of death should hold him (Acts 2:24). We need to learn to read these life-surprising narratives with much more systemic awareness.

---

argued that Israel had ways in which to conduct "liturgies of rehabilitation," even though these escape our rationality of modernity. Perhaps the work of Elijah here is in the context and according to the accepted form of such an enterprise.

They bear witness to the power for life at work in those undeserving places where we could not choose to administer life. Elijah seems to bear in his person the power for life that is always destabilizing in a world that has all things channeled in controlling ways. So the theological assertion is that God's power for life comes. The sociological statement is that the ones accustomed to administering life-goods do not control this. That evokes hostility because the marginal, when enlivened, pose a social threat to those who benefit excessively from the present arrangement.

The Audacious Clarification of Sovereignty

The second episode is better known to us, the contest at Mount Carmel (1 Kings 18–19). Now Elijah is not dealing with the poor. Now he is face-to-face with the regime, the king, the priests, the prophets, the professionals, the credentialed types. The crisis is a practical one that, on the face of it, does not seem to be theological. The problem is the drought. The drought hangs over the entire Elijah cycle, announcing that the royal enterprise is inept and dysfunctional. So the issue is, How do we get rain? Who has the capacity to make rain? Or, if you like, Is the government capable of handling the energy crisis? (The lack of rain, after all, means failed energy.) So there is an acute anxiety about rain because that now becomes the issue of life and death. Likely, the polls revealed that 62 percent of the people regarded the threat of the drought to be the overriding public problem. It is somewhat analogous to the problem of security in our time. Not too long ago, at least 62 percent of the people indicated that the nuclear threat was the primary public issue. We have great debates about how to get security, who has the capacity to make us secure, and whether the government is capable of handling the matter.

We know how the narrative advances. It becomes a contest. Elijah is at his most audacious. He is so utterly convinced of the truth of his cause, of his God, that he dares to mock royal religion, to make fun of the sponsors, agents, and benefactors of the dominant system. He goes to extreme measures to set them up, all the more to humiliate them. For Elijah, for the narrator, and for the listening community, the outcome is never in doubt; it is only dramatically suspended. The outcome is sure.

Elijah begins by mocking their incapacity. He means to articulate that the system cannot deliver and cannot keep its promises. The king of the system, the priests and the prophets of the system, and finally the gods of the system cannot deliver (see the parallel startling conclusion on the Egyptian technicians in Exod. 8:18). The system cannot deliver, cannot keep its promises. Then he makes his own task as difficult as possible by pouring water on the fire before his prayers.

What the narrator has Elijah do is to see that the question of rain and energy is in fact a theological question of sovereignty. The question about the system is, *Can the gods of the system give life?* Is there an alternative source of life? Now the urging I make is that prophetic faith must be theologically intentional and explicit, knowing that the God-question is both open and urgent. That does not fit our stereotypes of the prophetic. But it is so. Conservatives tend to regard the God-question as settled and capable of reduction to a few formulas. Liberals tend to regard the God-question as trivial and unimportant. Elijah rejects both the liberal trivialization and the conservative reductionism because he believes that theology is important. To be sure, Elijah is not a systematic theologian spinning out theoretical tomes. But he is doing theology. He believes that in the thick of social conflict, the God-question is crucial because everything follows from it. My sense is that any of us who would be prophetic must take on ourselves the task of hard-nosed, intellectually disciplined theological work, because finally the real issues concern the question of sovereignty.

The poignant center of this episode is Elijah's question in 18:21: "How long will you go limping with two different opinions? If the Lord is God, follow him; but if Baal, then follow him." Prophetic faith holds for an either/or at the base of life. What is at issue here is not simply a theological label, as though the simple name of God matters. But we have rather a discussion about the relation between *the processes of life* and *the source of life.* Canaanite religion, Baalism, and indeed every civil religion, argues and presumes that the processes of life contain and are identical with the source of life. Being able to manage the process gives one control over the source. Now what this means practically is that the establishment—political, religious, or scientific—has access to the processes and can secure its own existence by mastering the processes. Baalism is a religion that believes that the mystery of life has now been put at our disposal and that we have life on the terms we might like.

In the ancient world, when the temple was thought to be the

seat of life, the priests were regarded as controllers of the sources of life. They were characteristically in the service of the king. Indeed, the history of the church reads in like manner with its tight control of sacraments as the access point of life, security, and well-being. In Jesus' time, the torah was thought to be the source of life, and so arguments about the torah became discussions on how to secure life on one's own terms. In the modern world, the seduction of scientism and technology is that we have the capacity finally to administer life on our own terms. The arms race was a spin-off of that, for arms are an attempt to have our technology secure us. Every attempt at containing life, including some forms of process theology, runs the risk of this confusion of source and process.

Against all that, the hard-nosed Yahwism of Elijah makes a radical distinction between source and process. The processes of rain, energy, and life may be discernible. But the source is hidden, inaccessible, and inscrutable. Rain will not be gotten by manipulation but only by reference to the holy sovereign God, who is jealous. Therefore, all the techniques of religion, ritual, piety, morality, dogma, science, economics, whatever, are finally in vain. Because God will not yield to that. God has God's own person. God is not simply our own policy interests expressed in exaggerated form. God is an identifiable, known person, known in the liberating memory of the exodus. This God will give gifts, the gifts of life, but always on God's inscrutable terms that mock the pretensions and the mechanisms of the regime.

So the center of this prophetic act may be found in 1 Kings 18:36-37, where Elijah again resorts to prayer: "O Lord, God of Abraham, Isaac, and Israel, let it be known this day that thou art God in Israel, and that I am thy servant, and that I have done all these things at thy word. Answer me, O Lord, answer me, that this people may know that thou, O Lord, art God, and that thou hast turned their hearts back." As in the case of the dead child, the critical act is prayer, yielding, submitting, acknowledging. The result is a response (v. 38) that leads to praise and confession (v. 39). Finally, it is not technique, but petition. It is not management, but trustful asking that matters. Out of it emerges the awareness that God is not available and useful. The God of this prophet has no utilitarian value and cannot be harnessed into schemes for rain, for energy, for life, for security.[11] Now

---

11. See the striking statement of Ellul, "Meditation of Inutility," in *Politics of God*, 190–99. Ellul's analysis concerns the inutility of human effort, but the implied coun-

this prayer should not be trivialized. It is not an act of "spirituality." It is referring to life outside the system. It is driving the life-question back behind the processes to the source that is inaccessible. In such prayer, Elijah redescribes the world for himself and his contemporaries, and he enacts a claim for sovereignty that means to refute every false claim to sovereignty.

So prophetic faith has a stake in articulating the otherness, awfulness, holiness, sovereignty, and jealousy of God, to keep final meanings at some remove from management practice and technical capacity. Indeed, it is God at some remove who permits critical reflection and the reception of an alternative. Note well that the prophet is an alien in the world of his contemporaries, for he fails to live inside their rationality. Indeed, were he to concede their rationality, his capacity to pray and have power for life would surely be lost.

Prophetic faith resists the temptation to reduce God to a *technique*. God does not belong in any phrases that are concerned with "how to." In the ancient world, God is treated as though God were a technique for rain. In the modern world, God is treated as a technique for keeping families together, for keeping middle-class morality functioning, for maintaining the well-being of the Western alliance, for maintaining the free-market system, for the soothing of a troubled psyche, and so on. Elijah's assault on Baalism is to assert that there is no essential or reliable linkage between the sovereign God and any technique for securing our existence or our well-being.

The push of prophetic faith is always to force a decision. The decision to be faced is not always immediately evident because the decision most often seems to concern something other than theology. Prophetic faith is concerned to redefine the relation between heaven and earth, between God and creation, to insist that God is not an echo of creation or a client but is in fact a free agent about whom a decision must be made.

It is worth thinking about technique and usability in our time. The pastor has access to many places in our common life where the truth of things is reduced to technique—about money, about relationships, about sexuality. In the world of technique, there is this audacious clarification of sovereignty. Life-issues are about sovereignty. The question concerns what is finally real, to which

---

terpart that resonates with Ellul's analysis is the inutility of God for every human agenda.

everything else must be referred. And that, in this age of relativism, is so difficult because we prefer to think that there is no overriding reality, but only a series of little realities that we choose and like and fashion for ourselves. Sovereignty in any language—inclusive or exclusive—is so difficult for us because we are dealing with a reality who has no analogy anywhere in our experience.

To articulate this holy one as really true is audacious because it flies in the face of so much obvious pragmatism and utilitarianism. One must speak against the presumed data, for all the data are against this. But the data must be transformed to fit the claim. So Elijah's prayer returns to the roots. It goes back to the old tradition of Abraham, Isaac, and Jacob. The God addressed is the one who has always violated pragmatic reason. This God violated pragmatic reason in giving a birth to barren Sarah,[12] in freeing the slaves. Quite clearly, Elijah believes that this violation of technique and pragmatic reason is necessary to resolve the energy crisis.

Is it not clear that such an audacious clarification of God's sovereignty is destabilizing? You see, this theology is serious stuff. We have treated theology as a leisure-time activity. But this theology serves to delegitimate the main claims of the royal system. The exposure of Baalism as gods who cannot give life is equivalent to nullifying the political, cultural authority of the regime. Prophetic theology concerns the unmasking of the idols that keep the system functioning. Prophetic ministry has these exposures to make. There are false claimants to power who must be delegitimated in order that the true God can have a say. So again I make the point: prophetic ministry destabilizes to permit a newness that must be thoughtful and disciplined, a hard intellectual effort. The evidence that such an act is destabilizing is the resolve of Jezebel against Elijah: "So may the gods do to me, and more also, if I do not make your life as the life of one of them by this time tomorrow" (19:2). Who asserts the sovereignty of Yahweh asserts that *processes* do not give access to *source*. Who asserts sovereignty clashes with all the pseudosovereigns. But the reality of Yahweh's sovereignty has persuasion. It permitted people to make a life-receiving decision in 18:29. It did not, of course, persuade the regime, as indeed it hardly ever does.

---

12. See my essay "'Impossibility' and Epistemology in the Faith Tradition of Abraham and Sarah (Gen. 18:1-15)," *ZAW* 94 (1982): 615–34.

Unseemly Interventions
in Presumed Power Arrangements

The third dimension of Elijah's prophetic presence is in the well-known story of Naboth's vineyard (1 Kings 21). The narrative falls into two oddly related parts. In the first part, verses 1-16, the key actors are Naboth, Ahab, and Jezebel. Elijah is nowhere mentioned. It is possible to have narratives in Israel in which prophets are not present. But according to this tradition, when that happens, dimensions of humaneness disappear. The triangular interaction of the landowner, the king, and the queen is not to be read as a personal struggle about greed. We shall understand the narrative more faithfully if we see that it is about the clash of land-tenure systems. Naboth embodies and is faithful to a system that is governed by patrimony, which assures him the inalienable rights, privileges, and responsibilities of his family inheritance. This vineyard could not be without Naboth belonging to it. Naboth could not be without this land. That close and inalienable land linkage is likely reflected in the jubilee practice (Leviticus 25), a social, institutional guarantee that this connection of land and family is indispensable for the functioning of society. It is less directly also a statement about the *materiality* of the human process. Human persons are intended to have land and turf as well as the social power that goes with them. When human persons lack land and social power, their persons are by that much diminished.

Conversely, Jezebel embodies a different land system, called prebendal.[13] We may in this context take that as a conventional Canaanite land system, perhaps specifically related to Tyre, from whence she came. This view sees land as a tradable commodity. But finally land is in the right of the king. There are no safeguards against the rapacious social policy of the strong against the weak. Obviously, the linkage of land and person is not inalienable, but a historical accident. All safeguards of egalitarianism are lost. Social power is distributed as one can seize it. This view offers a sharp contrast in economic theory to the view held by Naboth. Perhaps it finally offers a contrasting reading of human reality at the base in which some are entitled to social power over others, especially a monarch over the other landowners.

---

13. Robert B. Coote (*Amos among the Prophets* [Philadelphia: Fortress, 1981], 24–45) has well summarized the data from a sociological perspective.

So the issue of the story is this: Who is entitled to what kind of social power in the form of land? Jezebel's ruthless and cunning action against Naboth shows that the release of rapacious possibility leaves none safe. Ahab is a pitiful figure in the middle. He is not an agent but only a passive recipient. He knows better than does his queen about the rights of patrimony and how sacred they are in Israel. But he has neither the will to act on his own, nor the will to safeguard the practice of patrimony, nor the will to curb Jezebel.

So the story works out its course. It ends with Naboth dead for having resisted the unbridled will of the throne. And the last statement is closure, in verse 15: "Arise, take possession of the vineyard of Naboth the Jezreelite, which he refused to give you for money; for Naboth is not alive, but dead." Then the narrator concludes laconically, "As soon as Ahab heard that Naboth was dead, Ahab arose to go down to the vineyard of Naboth the Jezreelite, to take possession of it." End of story—it ends in death. Too many stories end that way, in death, usurpation, confiscation. The narrative ending in death tells not only about a clash of land systems but also about how it turns out. It is always death for the weaker at the hands of the stronger. The narrative describes a set of power relations that have stability and legitimacy. All parties assumed that the narrative was over and that it had ended on royal terms. It seems to be over for Naboth. Ahab and Jezebel also think it is over. The narrative seems ended. The land seems claimed. History seems closed. Everything seems so.

But Elijah is so unseemly. In fact, just as the narrative seems to end, this unseemly one starts the narrative underway again. Now in the second part of the narrative (vv. 17-29), things begin abruptly in a way that the royal partners did not suspect and could not resist: "Then the word of the Lord came to Elijah the Tishbite, saying, 'Arise, go down to meet Ahab.'" The word from Yahweh is quite explicit. It commissions Elijah to speak an entire lawsuit form, complete with indictment and sentence. Where there is a prophet, history can continue. Where there is a prophet, the narrative can continue, although now the narrative takes on a conflictual tone. Until verse 17, everything had been managed and covered over in seeming harmony. Now the same matters are unclosed, disclosed, and shown to be in deadly dispute.

Until this moment in the narrative, the presumed power arrangements had all been in favor of the royal couple. Nobody raised serious questions—until the word, until the prophet. Elijah's speech, which is unseemly, if not treasonable, does not for a moment accept those power schemes. Elijah considers them illicit and in fact already nullified. The indictment puts it this way: "Thus says the Lord, 'Have you killed, and also taken possession?'" (v. 19). The question is rhetorical, the answer clear. This is followed by the sentence: "In the place where dogs licked up the blood of Naboth shall dogs lick your own blood" (v. 19). The lawsuit is dumped right into the middle of the narrative, even as the lawsuit is dumped inescapably into the middle of life. The abrasiveness of the lawsuit disturbs the presumed power arrangements. The premise of royal power is that there is no voice or agent bold enough to posit a lawsuit. Indeed, the speech of Elijah is only a rhetorical act. He seems to have no proper authority to make such a claim. But it turns out immediately to be a rhetorical act with immense destabilizing power. Its power is that, on the face of it, it is true. No party in the narrative seems to doubt its validity. Jezebel is kept silent and invisible by the narrator. Ahab is moved to repentance. The truth of the lawsuit is so simple, yet so urgent. It asserts that Yahweh, not Jezebel, not Ahab, not Baal, nor the gods of Tyre, in fact, orders life. If Yahweh orders life, then in Israel this always refers one back to torah. The lawsuit asserts that power must answer to covenantal rule. Specifically, there are in the torah prohibitions of a nonnegotiable kind against murder and against usurpation (coveting). The power of the state is not absolute. The power of the powerful is not excessively regarded. The dominant system may have power to fashion its own world. But that fashioned world is always relative, always under scrutiny, always in jeopardy.

Power now, in the second part of the narrative, is deployed differently. It is not simply throne against Naboth. Now Yahweh intrudes as the key power agent in the narrative. Where Yahweh enters, the power of the others seems irrelevant. The calculus is all shifted. Naboth has no ally who will save his life; it is too late for that. Naboth and his folk now have an avenger who will see that the blood of Naboth is honored in retaliation (cf. Gen. 9:6).

Regimes that absolutize their power tend to freeze the historical process and order life absolutely. There power of a social kind seems transcendent and beyond challenge. But power relations, so the prophet insists, are never as clean and simple as we imagine. The prophetic task is to reopen the power question, to ask, Who needs to have a say in this matter? This applies not only to the great public issues. I suggest that there is no pastoral encounter in which the redefinition of power relations is not an open problem. We are so caught up in our presuppositions that we fail to notice. But in so many ways, Elijah gives a paradigm that asserts that the cry of the "bruised reed" and the "dimly burning wick" (Isa. 42:3) is never silenced, even as the cry of Abel from the ground is never silenced (Gen. 4:10), precisely because such folk have an advocate who will not quit. Elijah brings to speech the presence of that powerful, relentless advocate who will not let such deathliness go unanswered.

The narrative then moves to an exposition of the lawsuit, which is somewhat cryptic. But in verses 20-24, Elijah makes it plain, harshly plain. The lawsuit means the end of the dynasty, an ignoble end. The wonder may be that Ahab is still enough in touch with the tradition that he can repent (v. 27). But the repentance does not override the judgment. It only delays the matter one generation. The judgment is sure against such a false set of power relations.

Implications for Pastoral Ministry

Now Elijah is not the whole of the prophetic tradition. But for our context he offers some remarkable pointers for a pastoral ministry that is prophetic. I have focused on three narratives that suggest three characteristic prophetic agendas:

1. *Transformative gestures of solidarity,* in which Elijah brings life to a marginal widow, in a season of death.

2. *Audacious clarification of sovereignty,* in which Elijah mocks the theological claims of the established power and permits a time of obedience to the true God.

3. *Unseemly intervention in presumed power relations,* in which Elijah, by his powerful speech, shatters the closed power system and opens life to the relentless holiness of God.

Throughout this process of study I have asked myself, How was Elijah able to do this? Where did he get the courage, the freedom, the stamina, and the authority to enact such a ministry? We know that in 19:4-18 he was in a deep depression because his great efforts seemed to make no difference, except to make him an exposed outcast. I do not minimize the problem, but I state it squarely so that we understand the "map" of prophetic ministry and are not surprised that it leads here. If I have rightly discerned the categories, this ministry of destabilization brings hostility as part of the territory. And I have suggested that all three of these acts are acts of destabilization.

I have a modest observation on the resources that are available to Elijah. At the outset of this narrative (17:3-6), in Yahweh's first address to him, he is given this initial command: "Depart from here and turn eastward, and hide yourself by the brook Cherith, that is east of the Jordan. You shall drink from the brook, and I have commanded the ravens to feed you there" (vv. 3-4). And the ravens did as commanded. At the outset, Elijah is commanded to the wilderness, to the same place where John the Baptist and, later, Paul went, to a place not unlike the setting for the temptations of Jesus.

So I suggest this: from the beginning, Elijah is commanded *to disengage from royal definitions of reality.* He is not to think the thoughts of the royal establishment. He is not to eat their food, hope their hopes, fear their fears. He is not to share their perceptions or participate in their rationality. He is to be one who lives in a different social rationality that is defined by the power and purpose of Yahweh. Elijah's freedom and authority stem from the fact that he did not perceive the world through royal categories. He owed no such allegiance and had no fear of conflict because he had arrived at a different perception of truth. Surely, the key issue is withdrawal from that rationality. But the beginning point is *economic:* a different food supply (cf. Daniel 1; Mark 8:15). The key factor is not to be beholden economically, for then if one is not cared for and fed by the royal system, one may more likely be free of the controlling perception of reality. I suggest that for all of us in our affluent society who yearn for the freedom and authority to be prophetic, we will find different modes of living only insofar as we disengage, intellectually and economically. After all, that disengagement from royal definitions of reality is what Jesus called for in summoning disciples and in proclaiming the kingdom. And it is what we claim is at issue in baptism when we renounce loyalty to the rulers of this age.

Finally, I must make explicit what I have implied about pastoral care. I know well that "frontal" prophetic ministry of a stereotypical kind is not our agenda. Maybe it should be, but it is not. I hope that what I have said relates to pastoral care broadly conceived in all its dimensions. So let me say it two ways.

First, I argue that the agenda of Elijah is the agenda of all serious pastoral ministry, which includes, but is not limited to, pastoral counseling. Much pastoral ministry has been preoccupied, in my judgment too singularly, with psychological matters. But there is now a move away from that in the field. The urging I make is that these three issues of solidarity with the *marginal,* clarity about *sovereignty,* and *renewed power relations* belong to a biblical understanding of

health. Any pastoral care that shrinks from these matters is likely to
be romantic, trivial, and irrelevant to the real health issues facing us.

One can ask about marginality in one's own person (cf. the use
made of such an analogy in 1 Cor. 12:14-25). One can pursue power
relations in marriage or in any other social unit. One can reflect on
sovereignty in any part of one's personal or interpersonal life. These
are not alien categories. But they are categories of concern that have
been neglected by modernity. And yet they will not go away, because
they are the real issues. What matters is that the claim of covenant
with the Holy God gives us a different agenda from self-help and adjustment theories of well-being. My sense is that in U.S. society we
have adopted models of psychological health that will finally destroy
us. There is in this a discernment of human reality that gives us peculiar access to the real issues and, I dare say, peculiar resources for
responses that are genuinely healing and restorative.

Second, the modes in which this textual material may be helpful
are many and varied. I do not suggest that one ought (or can) stand
up and announce prophetic lawsuits. Indeed, I have insisted from
the beginning that our work is not to replicate Elijah but to let these
texts have their full say. My hunch is this: if we get clear on what the
real issues are—marginality, sovereignty, power relations—we will begin to see many ways in which these issues can be pursued. Pastoral
care requires enormous intentionality, so that in every circumstance
of preaching, liturgy, public prayer, wherever, the real human issues
are raised.

The dichotomy of prophetic and pastoral is a misunderstanding
of both. I can think of no one in our tradition who is more intensely engaged in pastoral care than Elijah. He practices it with
the widow by being present in her need. He practices it with the
false prophets by exposing their fraud and permitting a faithful confession. He practices it with the king by telling the truth. And in
each case, as Yahweh's sovereignty is celebrated, the power for life is
present—even to Ahab. The unleashing of the power for life in this
world bent on death depends on pastoral work that is rigorous and
prophetic work that is passionate. But such pastoral-prophetic work
requires being fed by ravens, not at the king's table.

12

The Social Significance of Solomon as a Patron of Wisdom

THE RELATIONSHIP between Solomon and wisdom is much disputed in recent scholarly discussion. A part of the dispute concerns the categories in which to consider the relation of Solomon to wisdom. It makes a great deal of difference if the question is treated in terms of literary, historical, or sociocultural categories.

The Problematic of Historical Evidence

The literary evidence for Solomon as a patron of wisdom is not extensive, nor is it difficult to identify. First, the literary evidence concerns texts embedded in the "history of Solomon" as it is portrayed in the Deuteronomistic account of 1 Kings 3–11. Four texts are important: (1) 1 Kings 3:3-14, Solomon's inaugural dream and prayer in which Solomon prays for wisdom to govern; (2) 1 Kings 3:16-28, a narrative in which Solomon is reported to exercise wisdom in the execution of royal justice; (3) 1 Kings 4:29-34 (MT 5:9-14), in which Solomon is credited with the production of encyclopedic proverbs; and (4) 1 Kings 10:1-13, concerning the visit of the Queen of Sheba in which Solomon's wisdom is closely related to his power and wealth.[1]

---

1. The grouping of wisdom, power, and riches is reflected in Jer. 9:23-24 (MT vv. 22-23). On the significance of this text, see my essay "The Epistemological Crisis of Israel's Two Histories (Jer. 9:22–23)," in *Israelite Wisdom*, ed. John G. Gammie

A literary analysis of these texts requires close attention to the question of genre. It is immediately clear that we are dealing with narratives that reflect common narrative tendencies and strategies, so that the events reported are to be regarded as stereotypical, marked by literary convention, with evidence of legendary or fictional development or both. Thus, for example, the first narrative belongs to the genre of inaugural dream;[2] the second is a standard and recurring example of juridical cunning; and the fourth is filled with propagandistic comparisons between competing royal figures. It may well be that none of these narratives will carry the weight expected of a factual historical report on a concrete event. In any case, whatever happened historically is cast in a narrative form that makes factuality precarious.

R. B. Y. Scott (closely followed by James L. Crenshaw) has concluded that these texts provide no substantive basis for linking Solomon historically to the enterprise of wisdom.[3] Moreover, each of these texts likely serves an interest other than the assertion of a sapiential function, that is, the legitimacy and success of the monarchy. In short, they are rendered imaginatively and function intentionally as propaganda. Indeed if the propagandistic element were absent, they would fail in their function. Such intentionally overstated material provides poor evidence for factuality. Finally, because these narratives bear some marks of Deuteronomistic influence, they are likely later and not to be regarded as historically reliable.

The second cluster of evidence is found in three superscriptions in the book of Proverbs that apparently introduce distinct collections of proverbs (Prov. 1:1; 10:1; 25:1). The first of these may be regarded as a late designation by the framers of the book of Proverbs as canonical literature.[4] The second is perhaps a late designation for an earlier, precanonical collection. The third, Scott believes, bears witness to the time and activity of Hezekiah, but not the time

(Missoula, Mont.: Scholars Press, 1978), 85–105 (reprinted in Walter Brueggemann, *Old Testament Theology: Essays on Structure, Theme, and Text* [Minneapolis: Fortress, 1992]).

2. On this text, see Helen A. Kenik, *Design for Kingship*, SBLDS 69 (Chico, Calif.: Scholars Press, 1983).

3. R. B. Y. Scott, "Solomon and the Beginnings of Wisdom in Israel," *VTSup* 3 (1955): 262–79 (reprinted in *Studies in Ancient Israelite Wisdom*, ed. James L. Crenshaw [New York: KTAV, 1976], 84–101). James L. Crenshaw, *Old Testament Wisdom* (Atlanta: John Knox, 1981), 42–54.

4. See Brevard S. Childs, *Introduction to the Old Testament as Scripture* (Philadelphia: Fortress, 1979), 551–52.

of Solomon. In any case, these three superscriptions provide no basis for historical judgment, important as they are for canonical understanding.

Third, I mention in passing that in the canonical presentation, Ecclesiastes and the Song of Solomon are credited to Solomon.[5] However, no critical scholar takes such connotations as evidence of authorship. While these connections to Solomon may be important for canonical intention and interpretation, they provide no clue to tenth-century historical realities. Subsequent postcanonical tradition and legend add to this ongoing later tendency to assign sapiential matters to Solomon, but none of these adds to the data for a historical judgment.

Thus the literary evidence is of a fanciful kind, surely marked by legendary tendencies, useful for canonical consideration, but out of which no certain historical judgment can be made. The direct textual evidence for my topic is precarious and is judged by some scholars as nonexistent.

Solomon as a Social Mutation in Israel

However, to pose our question in such categories is itself open to question. An approach that moves directly from literary analysis to matters of facticity proceeds on too narrow a basis because it assumes a simple correlation between literary evidence and historical judgment. If this topic must be treated on that basis, there is little ground for discussion. It is, however, methodologically inadequate to proceed on the basis of a simple correlation between literary evidence and historical judgment. Therefore, one must not so quickly accept the negative judgment of Scott and Crenshaw, but must attend to more than literary analysis of isolated texts and historical conclusions based on that literary analysis. The text never happens in a vacuum, so that, as best one can, one must attend to the social processes and transactions that were operative and likely decisive in the formation and transmission of the text. It is more helpful to view this as a sociopolitical problem rather than as simply a literary-historical one. Indeed my topic invites such a sociocultural approach

---

5. See the comments of Childs (*Introduction*) on Ecclesiastes (p. 584) and on the Song of Songs (pp. 573–75). Childs characteristically urges a move from historical to canonical questions. It will be clear in the end that my argument is congruent with that of Childs.

because of the word "patron" in the title, which opens up a variety of questions concerning social power, social interest, ideology, and intentionality. I am not here concerned with a historical question about whether Solomon was a wisdom teacher, but with a much larger question of the rationality and intellectual commitments of the world of which Solomon is both sponsor and benefactor. I shall not arrive at historical precision, and that is not the nature of this issue.[6]

I begin with the observation that the Deuteronomist (1 Kings 3–11), the formulators of the book of Proverbs (and some of the antecedent collections in the book), and the canonical shapers of Ecclesiastes and the Song of Solomon appealed to some abiding memory of the connection between Solomon and wisdom. While that memory may not be very precise, may not be recoverable by us in detail, and may not be available in factual terms, it seems plausible to assume that the connection between Solomon and wisdom is remembered and not invented—remembered, to be sure, in a quite impressionistic and imprecise way. Even if the various texts to which I have referred are later, the tradition refers back to something in asserting and assuming this connection.

I pose the question in this way: What is it that the traditionists remembered about the Solomonic enterprise?[7] (One can never be certain about historicality, and the question may alternatively be asked: What did they postulate about the Solomonic enterprise? But because I take the traditioning process with seriousness and as having integrity, I pose the question in terms of *remembering* rather than *postulating*.) It seems plausible, given the evidence at hand, to suggest that the traditionist remembered with something like astonishment and perhaps with some dismay that Solomon represents and embodies an important *novum* in the history of Israel—a *novum* anticipated by David but visible, consolidated, and legitimated only

---

6. I shall argue that the canonical reading in the end has it right. The argument, however, is not based on historical precision but on an understanding of the social dynamics related to Solomon. The canon makes the judgment that the role of Solomon understood sociologically is in fact who he is for the Israelite tradition and for generating its sapiential dimension.

7. "Solomonic enterprise" is a carefully chosen phrase. "Solomonic" refers to a large cultural movement and not simply the person of the king. To call it an "enterprise" means that what happened around Solomon is an identifiable "project" that has some social intentionality and is a deliberate departure from the pre-Solomonic world of Israel's faith.

with Solomon. That is, Solomon is not simply a historical person but something of a sociocultural mutation in Israel.[8] The notion of a Solomonic *novum* has been, in a general and not very precise way, characterized by Gerhard von Rad as an "enlightenment."[9] By the term "enlightenment," von Rad refers to a shifted intellectual presupposition about the world, a freshly articulated structure of human plausibility. This proposal by von Rad has been criticized and largely dismissed by Crenshaw on two grounds.[10] First, the wisdom texts are largely legendary, if not fictional. Second, the move from "sacral" to "secular" understandings cannot be sustained by means of a simple contrast before and after Solomon. I have no intention of defending von Rad's hypothesis, except as an important step to our present sociological understandings of the question before us. Concerning Crenshaw's first critique, the legendary character of the texts in itself is not important because the argument needs to be based on much broader sociopolitical and economic grounds than simply by reference to a few texts. Second, it is not necessary to draw a clear line between secular and sacral in order to consider a decisive shift in rationality. It is surely the case that "enlightenment" in retrospect is an unfortunate term to use, for it inevitably invites a parallel to the modern European Enlightenment, and that obviously is not what happened in Solomon's time.

I would insist, however, that what von Rad has grasped, albeit inchoately (and what Crenshaw has neglected), are the modifications in public life, political power, social organization, ideology, and technology and its management that accompanied, permitted, and required a shift in intellectual perspective. What von Rad sensed in

---

8. See Frank M. Cross, *Canaanite Myth and Hebrew Epic* (Cambridge, Mass.: Harvard Univ. Press, 1973), 237–41, and more extensively Gösta W. Ahlström, *Royal Administration and National Religion in Ancient Palestine* (Leiden: Brill, 1982). By using the terms *novum* and "mutation" I am referring to an intra-Israelite development, that is, that Solomon decisively changed the character of Israel. Notice that Norman Gottwald (*The Tribes of Yahweh* [Maryknoll, N.Y.: Orbis, 1979], 489–90 and passim) treats Israel as a *novum* and a mutation in the world of Canaan. I am using the terms in the opposite sense within Israel, but my point is in agreement with Gottwald.

9. Gerhard von Rad, *The Problem of the Hexateuch and Other Essays* (New York: McGraw-Hill, 1966), 69–74, 202–4; idem, *Old Testament Theology* (New York: Harper and Row, 1962), 1:48–56.

10. Crenshaw, *Old Testament Wisdom*, 52–54; idem, "Prolegomenon," in *Studies in Ancient Israelite Wisdom*, 16–20; idem, *Gerhard von Rad* (Waco, Tex.: Word, 1978), 42–52; and idem, review of *Wisdom in Israel*, by Gerhard von Rad, *RSR* 2 (April 1976): 6–12.

terms of a general cultural perspective we now can pursue more confidently in light of more recent social analysis. That social analysis was not available to von Rad, but it is clearly crucial for my general topic. Thus my methodological insistence is that the question of Solomonic wisdom must be explored in terms of a broadly based social transformation, and not on narrow literary or historical-critical grounds.

New Forms of Power/New Modes of Knowledge

A sociocultural approach to my question will not yield historical precision, but it will yield social probability. One important development in Old Testament studies since the enlightenment hypothesis of von Rad and the negative conclusion of Scott concerns the awareness that intellectual (and therefore literary) phenomena in ancient Israel are closely linked to sociopolitical, economic, and technical changes in a social organization of that community. Or to put it more succinctly, economics and epistemology are closely related to each other and decisively influence each other.

Norman Gottwald has offered the most formidable comprehensive hypothesis for understanding the social world in which the Solomonic establishment emerged.[11] He has proposed that ancient Israel in the premonarchal period, that is, from Moses to Samuel, is a radical departure from the conventional state (city-state) modes of organization best known and mostly practiced in Canaan. Israel "withdrew" from that mode of social organization and organized itself in an alternative way as a covenantal-egalitarian social experiment.[12] Not only was Israel a theological oddity, authorized as it was by Yahweh—an odd God in the ancient world—but Israel was also a sociological oddity in a culture characteristically organized in bureaucratic, hierarchical, and therefore exploitative ways. Because conventional orderings of society tend to control and administer

---

11. Gottwald, *Tribes of Yahweh;* and idem, "Early Israel and the Canaanite Socio-Economic System," in *Palestine in Transition,* ed. David N. Freedman and David Frank Graf (Sheffield: Almond, 1983), 25–37.

12. The term "withdraw" was used in the initial hypothesis of George Mendenhall, "The Hebrew Conquest of Palestine," *BA* 25 (1962): 66 (reprinted in *The Biblical Archaeologist Reader* [Garden City, N.Y.: Doubleday, 1970], 3:107). See also Gottwald, *Tribes of Yahweh,* 85, 326, 408, 469; and Marvin L. Chaney, "Ancient Palestinian Peasant Movements and the Formation of Premonarchic Israel," in *Palestine in Transition,* 49. The term and the social proposal behind it are crucial for understanding the social significance of Solomon.

conventional modes of knowledge,[13] this new social reality relies on an alternative epistemology, on "revelation" in the form of torah, that is, directly given guidance about the orderings of communal life. Early Israel thus had no recourse to conventional modes of discernment; that is, it functioned without conventional modes of bureaucratic wisdom. Israel's radical mode of knowledge (revelation at Sinai) is appropriate to the radical substance of guidance, which is an ethos of egalitarianism rooted in the exclusive authorization of Yahweh. The radical mode and the radical substance are appropriate to Israel's peculiar character and self-understanding, which made Israel an essentially alien community in its Canaanite context. Its modes of knowledge are congruent with its modes of power and its social visions.

The emergence of the monarchy, culminating in Solomon, is not to be viewed—as is conventional—simply as a defensive organizational posture to resist the Philistines. Rather, it is reflective of a changed social position that had economic and military roots and that required intellectual, religious legitimation. Frank S. Frick, informed by Frank Crüsemann, suggests that the changes are related to social organization and technology.[14] Thus the direction of social development in ancient Israel is from a segmentary society to a chiefdom. The earlier, socially primitive community is segmented into equal units of power, goods, and leadership, with no central authority and with no power positions that could dominate others. In such a society, in which there are accommodations and associations, there is no mandatory accountability. This means there may be endless splintering into more social units (fission) with lesser or greater autonomy, all equal to each other in authority.

13. See Glendon E. Bryce, *A Legacy of Wisdom* (Lewisburg, Pa.: Bucknell Univ. Press, 1979). It is important and characteristic that in the plague cycle of Exodus 5–11, the power of Egypt is mediated through the wise men of Egypt, the ones who know the techniques to manage imperial power. The alternatives of Moses and Aaron vis-à-vis the imperial wise men are telling for the epistemological crisis of the exodus. On alternative modes of power, see Aaron Wildavsky, *The Nursing Father* (Tuscaloosa: Univ. of Alabama Press, 1984).

14. Frank S. Frick, *The Formation of the State of Ancient Israel* (Sheffield: Almond, 1985). Frank Crüsemann, *Der Widerstand gegan das Königtum*, WMANT 49 (Neukirchen-Vluyn: Neukirchener Verlag, 1978). See also Eckart Otto, "Gibt es Zusammenhänge zwischen Bevölkerungswachstum, Staatsbildung und Kulturentwicklung im eisenzeitlichen Israel?" in *Regulation, Manipulation und Explosion der Bevölkerungsdichte*, ed. O. Kraus (Göttingen: Vandenhoeck und Ruprecht, 1986), 73–87. J. W. Rogerson ("Was Early Israel a Segmentary Society?" *JSOT* 36 [1986]: 17–26) rejects the hypothesis that early Israel was a segmentary society.

In ancient Israel the segmentary society, especially under the
impetus of David, was transformed into a chiefdom, which is the beginning of centralized authority, the assertion of dominant power
supported by military success, and therefore the accumulation of
an economic surplus that began to move toward monopoly. The
introduction of central power and economic surplus entails the systematic introduction of social inequality, in which the chief—the one
who wields the newly formed power—redistributes wealth, power,
and access, and therefore develops a network of supporting alliances
among the powerful and the privileged.[15]

While a chief can discourage but cannot halt splintering movements of independence, that splintered independence is completely
overcome when the chiefdom eventuates in a state in which there is
a strongly centralized authority preempting all other authority and
administering the economic arrangement that is now on its way to
becoming a monopoly.

While these sociological modes of analysis cannot be applied to
ancient Israel with precision, there is a gathering consensus among
scholars that Israel emerged from a segmentary society to a chiefdom
and finally to a state under Solomon. This sociological paradigm
is congruent with the characterization of Solomon's governance
that seems clear in the texts: a social arrangement characterized by
advanced technology, highly developed social organization, and bureaucratic ordering of governmental power.[16] For those who stood at
the center of this arrangement, there was a high standard of living,
a high degree of political security, and a situation of social leisure.

That picture of political, economic, and technical change seems
reasonably secure. The question then is: What happened to Israel's
intellectual life in the midst of this social transformation?[17] Two developments are claimed in the text that are congruent with the social
transformation, and that therefore we take as historically probable.
First, such a social enterprise, which significantly departed from the
old Israelite social commitments, needed religious justification and
legitimacy. Religiously this required the construction of a temple

15. See Frick, *The Formation of the State in Ancient Israel*, 78–86, and Edward
Neufeld, "The Emergence of a Royal-Urban Society in Ancient Israel," *HUCA*
31 (1960): 31–53. See the summary of Norman Gottwald, *The Hebrew Bible: A
Socio-Literary Introduction* (Philadelphia: Fortress, 1985), 323–25.

16. See Ahlström, *Royal Administration and National Religion;* and T. N. D. Mettinger,
Solomonic State Officials (Lund: Gleerup, 1971).

17. See E. W. Heaton, *Solomon's New Men* (London: Thames and Judson, 1974).

and the articulation of cultic practices linking the political apparatus closely to the purposes of God.[18] While one cannot be precise, it is plausible that the practice of divine enthronement begins very early in the Solomonic liturgy, for the enthronement of Yahweh surely carries with it the legitimacy of Solomon and the dynasty.[19]

The religious machinery of temple and cult needed theological, intellectual counterparts, and this is given in "a theology of presence," whereby the God of the covenantal-liberation tradition takes up (permanent) residence in Jerusalem in the temple and becomes patron, ally, and guarantor of the dynasty.[20] This theological adjustment articulates a radically changed definition of Yahweh, from a transformative agent to a guarantor. This theological transformation is congruent with and congenial to the sociological transformation of the community from egalitarian to bureaucratic-hierarchical, in which the economic issues have changed from survival to monopoly, in which the power questions no longer concern marginality but control and domination.

Second, in the context of the theological transformation (in the interest of legitimacy) and the sociological transformation (in the interest of political control and economic affluence), the question of wisdom under royal patronage can be freshly considered. Here one is not dependent simply on a few texts that seem easily disposed of by genre analysis, for one may inquire into sociological probability. What is the likely intellectual climate of the new social situation? What was permitted and required by the new circumstance? To concentrate on sacral/secular distinctions as von Rad (and consequently Crenshaw) has done is not as helpful as focusing on political domination and economic surplus, a focus that requires and permits

18. See Moshe Weinfeld, "Zion and Jerusalem as Religious and Political Capital: Ideology and Utopia," in *The Poet and the Historian*, ed. Richard Elliott Friedman (Chico, Calif.: Scholars Press, 1983), 75–115. On pp. 87–88, Weinfeld writes, "The establishment of the Israelite monarchy thus entailed revolutionary innovation, which in turn required religious legitimation, especially in regards to the concept of dynasty."

19. Thus, Sigmund Mowinckel and A. R. Johnson are surely right (against Hermann Gunkel and Hans-Joachim Kraus) in their argument that the enthronement liturgy was used very early and served a legitimating function for the Jerusalem establishment. On the ideological function of that liturgy, see my *Israel's Praise: Doxology against Idolatry and Ideology* (Philadelphia: Fortress, 1988).

20. On the temple theology of presence, see Samuel Terrien, *The Elusive Presence* (New York: Harper and Row, 1978), 186–213, and T. N. D. Mettinger, *The Dethronement of Sabaoth: Studies in the Shem and Kabod Theologies* (Lund: Gleerup, 1982).

fresh intellectual perspectives. The division of labor that accompanied a bureaucratically ordered community clearly required priests for religious legitimacy and most probably required scribes, sages, and wisdom teachers who functioned as the intellectual brain trust for policy formation, as ideologues for social justification, and as pedagogues for the young who must inherit the monopoly.[21]

Knowledge for Emancipation and Domination

I suggest three social functions performed by such an intelligentsia in the practice of an epistemology congruent with Solomon's new political domination and economic surplus.

1. There is ample evidence that Solomon's ambition was to create an intellectual climate imitative of, and no doubt in touch with and competitive with, the sapiential activity of other state regimes, especially Egypt. Thus it is not accidental that 1 Kings 4:30-31 (MT 5:10-11) mentions wisdom practices outside Israel. Surely these practices were seen, in the purview of Israel's sapiential establishment, both as models and as competitors. It was this intellectual enterprise that emancipated Israel from the categories of Israel's "tribal," "peasant," and "sectarian" modes of knowledge in order to share in more universalizing and perhaps more speculative intellectual activity. Thus accommodation to the international practice of wisdom not only was culturally ambitious in "being like pharaoh" (cf. 1 Sam. 8:5-20) but also may have been emancipatory, the kind of intellectual emancipation needed for a new state eager to operate effectively, legitimately, and prestigiously as a state.[22] Christa Bauer-Kayatz has argued that the wisdom collection of Proverbs 1-9 is very early and closely parallels Egyptian materials in style, substance, and assumption.[23]

21. On the emergence of such an intelligentsia, see R. N. Whybray, *The Intellectual Tradition in the Old Testament*, BZAW 15 (Berlin: de Gruyter, 1974); and S. Yeiven, "Social, Religious, and Culture Trends in Jerusalem under the Davidic Dynasty," *VT* 3 (1953): 149-65, esp. 156. See also Brian W. Kovacs, "Is There a Class-Ethic in Proverbs?" in *Essays in Old Testament Ethics*, ed. James L. Crenshaw and John T. Willis (New York: KTAV, 1974), 173-89; and Mettinger, *Solomonic State Officials*, 140-57. On the priesthood in the monarchy, see Cross, *Canaanite Myth*, 195-215, and Ahlström, *Royal Administration and National Religion*, 44-74.

22. The legendary account of 1 Kings 10:1-13 surely reflects a self-awareness about competing with and being superior to other states. This much is clear even if the account is not taken as historically reliable, which it likely is not.

23. See Christa Bauer-Kayatz, *Studien zu Proverbien 1-9*, WMANT 22 (Neukirchen-Vluyn: Neukirchener Verlag, 1966).

2. The intellectual operation of wisdom, one may imagine, was both congenial to and necessary for such a state. Albrecht Alt has suggested that the notice of 1 Kings 4:33 (MT 5:13) is evidence of a kind of cataloging activity about "natural matters."[24] It is not at all necessary to suggest that such wisdom is "secular" (as opposed to sacral) in order to understand why the royal enterprise would want the cataloging of data. It is now readily agreed that wisdom is "creation theology," which means not only that it is a study of creation ("nature") but also that in this context it is a disciplined marveling at the ordering of the world by God.[25] That is, these teachers can be grateful to the creator, astonished at the delicate and resilient order of the world, but nonetheless deeply curious about how this order works. Amazement is not contradictory to disciplined investigation.

Such an enterprise may be congenial to the new state because politically and economically, the whole world becomes "available" for study and use as it has not been in Israel heretofore. It has not been available because questions of survival limit scope and energy for investigation and because the limited technology of the marginal excludes much of the world from one's horizon. There may well have been, in this new cultural setting, a fresh kind of energy and eagerness to explore, know, and control everything available.[26] Intellectual possibility of a new kind must have been widely recognized, embraced, and pursued. In such a context, there may have been a passion to know in disciplined ways whatever could be known.

But such an enterprise need be not only congenial but also necessary to the new state regime. Crenshaw suggests that such an enlightenment project might be incompatible with Solomon's

---

24. Albrecht Alt, "Solomonic Wisdom," in *Studies in Ancient Israelite Wisdom*, 102–12. While this classifying of "nature" seems like an objective, scientific project, it is necessary to recognize that such an enterprise had important social significance for *ordering*. A wedge must not be driven between social ordering and "natural" ordering. Both aspects of ordering move in a conservative social direction.

25. See Walther Zimmerli, "The Place and Limit of the Wisdom in the Framework of the Old Testament Theology," in *Studies in Ancient Israelite Wisdom*, 314–26; idem, *Old Testament Theology in Outline* (Atlanta: John Knox, 1978), 155–66; idem, *The Old Testament and the World* (Atlanta: John Knox, 1976), 43–52; and Gerhard von Rad, *Wisdom in Israel* (Nashville: Abingdon, 1972), 74–96 and passim.

26. Regarding such energy and eagerness, modern analogies may be found in the sixteenth-century drive in Western Europe for reconnaissance of the "New World" and in the drive of John F. Kennedy in the 1960s to put "a man on the moon." Both these cases represent the drive of genuine exploration, but both have an obviously political-economic motivation, one ending in colonialism, the other ending in a new dimension of military competition.

tyranny, oppression, and greed.[27] On the contrary, such investigation that establishes predictability leads to control, and such control is not incompatible with the fresh assertion of human centrality. Such new knowledge is indeed new power. This need not mean such investigations were undertaken for directly ideological reasons. In our own context, scientists and technologists who work at research and development either for government or for big business need not be directly committed to the use (and misuse) of their findings; they may indeed be those who are genuinely attuned to the wonder, coherence, predictability, symmetry, and finally inscrutability of the world that is the subject of such sapiential investigation. One will not appreciate the use (and abuse) of such wisdom to the regime unless one first notices the emancipatory power of wonder, astonishment, and knowledge that such an enterprise might unleash.

3. Having noted the dimensions of state ambitions and scientific wonder, it is reasonable to match that positive, emancipatory factor with a critical comment about the ideological function of wisdom. Wisdom proceeds on the assumption that life-experience—human life, life in the created order—is a "studiable system." That studiable system has constancy and durability, experienced as regularity and predictability.[28] That is, the proverbs observe and characterize what is continually the same. The constancy and durability of the studiable system are, for those adhering to the royal enterprise, matched by the systemic durability and constancy of the political order and the economic arrangement. Indeed, the political-economic order is experienced, in such a systemic perception, as part of the assumed order that is not questioned or criticized and outside of which questions are not raised.[29]

It is widely held that wisdom, even clan wisdom, represents the interests and perceptions of a landed, established class.[30] The modes

---

27. Crenshaw, *Old Testament Wisdom*, 53.

28. On the theological significance of that ordering of the world, see H. H. Schmid, *Gerechtigkeit als Weltordnung* (Tübingen: Mohr, 1968); and idem, "Creation, Righteousness, and Salvation: 'Creation Theology' as the Broad Horizon of Biblical Theology," in *Creation in the Old Testament*, ed. Bernhard W. Anderson (Philadelphia: Fortress, 1984), 102–17.

29. Ernest W. Nicholson (*God and His People* [Oxford: Clarendon, 1986], 193–210) has understood well the dangerous potential of creation theology when it becomes state ideology. He sees clearly that covenant faith in Israel is a frontal criticism of such state ideology sometimes expressed as creation theology.

30. See Robert Gordis, "The Social Background of Wisdom Literature," in *Poets, Prophets, and Sages* (Bloomington: Indiana Univ. Press, 1971), 160–197; and Kovacs, "Is There a Class-Ethic in Proverbs?"

of knowledge operating in wisdom instruction tend to be conservative and conserving because they seek for reliable and recurring patterns of acceptable behavior. The conserving modes thus tend to buttress the status quo as an order that is to be maintained and not disrupted. Wisdom in the clan is a study about how to maintain and not disrupt the present social arrangement. Thus proverbial wisdom in any family or clan tends to assume the legitimacy and durability of present power arrangements. Knowledge tends not to push outside such interests and such awarenesses.

How much more is this likely to be the case in a royal court setting where political interests are much more visible and intentional and where the entire enterprise depends on the power, access, and the means of the royal budget! Thus it is plausible to suppose that wisdom teachers in the court, wittingly or unwittingly, are committed to the royal arrangement as the prism for wisdom and indeed for reality. Given that prism, the wisdom teachers inevitably perform an ideological function of establishing this present political and social order as an abiding given beyond the flux of historical choice and process.[31]

Thus it is entirely possible that the sages in the service of Solomon may have exercised at times both emancipatory and ideological functions, on the one hand channeling the energies of the regime in bold and exploratory directions, on the other hand justifying present arrangements. While these functions are in tension, they are not mutually exclusive. It is cogent to imagine such court functionaries as being willing to cooperate with the regime (perhaps out of conviction, perhaps not) in order to have a chance for leisure, reflection, and exploration.

If such a sociological enterprise is plausible, I now return to two observations about the Solomonic texts on wisdom. First, this analysis of sociological and epistemological development helps us to understand why the sapiential texts are so carefully placed and carefully controlled by the Deuteronomist in 1 Kings 3–11. In light of the social revolution of 1 Kings 11–12 in which the Solomonic achievement abruptly collapses, it is clear that the ideological thrust of sapiential rationality was uncritical, oppressive, and therefore unacceptable to much of the populace. It may well be that the Deuteronomist

---

31. See Kovacs, "Is There a Class-Ethic in Proverbs?"; and George E. Mendenhall, "The Shady Side of Wisdom: The Date and Purpose of Genesis 3," in *A Light unto My Path*, ed. Howard N. Bream, R. D. Heim, and Casey A. Moore (Philadelphia: Temple Univ. Press, 1974), 319–34.

understood the tension between ideologically prone sages and the uncompromising social claims of the torah. As a result, Solomonic wisdom is characterized by the Deuteronomist in ironic ways to show that it did not work. But that Solomonic wisdom did not work either historically or covenantally/theologically is no warrant for concluding that the regime was not committed to such wisdom. Indeed, it may be an argument that the regime was indeed committed to such an ideological self-deception that brought its own ruin.[32]

Second, if this sociocultural analysis is cogent, one may better understand the claim of the canon about Solomon and wisdom. The canon is not interested in historical concreteness but in the memory that it was Solomon, for better or for worse, who opened Israel's way for such an intellectual enterprise. That in fact is what Solomon did for Israel. Solomon made the larger world "available" for Israel. Canonically then it is sensible to juxtapose the Song of Solomon and Ecclesiastes as derivative articulations of the two poles of Solomonic wisdom. Crüsemann has carefully probed the way in which this text reflects and serves class interests that value social stability.[33] In the interest of maintaining the status quo, the text avoids criticism of an oppressive social order and characteristically supports established order. The emancipatory side of wisdom is reflected in the embrace of creation in the Song of Solomon; the ideological dimension is articulated in Ecclesiastes. Thus I suggest a connection between the sociological-epistemological probability of Solomon and the canonical memory that continued to receive fresh articulation.[34]

---

32. It is instructive that Barbara W. Tuchman (*The March of Folly* [New York: Ballantine, 1984], 8–11) cites the crisis of Israel at the death of Solomon as an early example of "the march of folly." The chapter heading under which she discusses that crisis is "Pursuit of Policy contrary to Self-interest."

33. See the discerning socioeconomic analysis of Ecclesiastes by Frank Crüsemann, "The Unchangeable World: The Crisis of Wisdom in Koheleth," in *God of the Lowly*, ed. Willy Schottroff and Wolfgang Stegemann (Maryknoll, N.Y.: Orbis, 1984), 57–77.

34. On the cruciality of the canonical memory, I am helped by the wonderful phrase of Alan M. Cooper in "The Life and Times of King David according to the Book of Psalms," in *The Poet and the Historian*, ed. Richard E. Friedman (Chico, Calif.: Scholars Press, 1983), 125: "a productive interpretive strategy." Cooper is writing about another canonical shaping of the material, but it applies here as well. That is, to credit Solomon with sponsoring wisdom is not a historical judgment but an interpretive strategy already used in the texts themselves—and now to be used by us. I have argued that this canonical strategy is grounded in sociological possibility, but that it goes well beyond that initial sociological function.

Wisdom as Theology and as Ideology

Finally, I consider the social function of such sages in a context like that of Solomon. It is evident that the concern of the sages is the hidden but discernible orderliness of God's creation, an orderliness that is experienced in terms of the limits of power, the contours of responsibility, and the shapes of freedom.[35] That order concerns ethical realities,[36] but it also concerns the use and misuse of power, and therefore it addresses questions of legitimate power. The juxtaposition of ethical reality and legitimate power causes the wisdom teacher to reflect on deeds and consequences, that is, on justice, righteousness, and equity, on the kinds of behavior (and policies) that are politically permissible and that are tolerable to the non-negotiable perimeters of created order.[37] Because the questions of wisdom concern behavior and policy, it is appropriate that the sages have been regularly characterized as "pragmatic" and "utilitarian." Of course they were!

This sustained ethical reflection, which had all sorts of policy implications, is, in a word, concerned with theodicy.[38] The later sapiential materials, especially Job and Ecclesiastes, are, of course, concerned with the "theodic crisis," with the awareness that the old expectations and assumptions of Israel were no longer adequate. A theodic crisis occurs when the dominant social values, presuppositions, and policies no longer function meaningfully and claim assent, no longer are credited by public opinion as having foundational authority.

Solomon's time was not a time when dominant assumptions were inadequate or when values seemed meaningless. In Solomon's time, everything seemed to work. The creation functioned as did the social system. People in the royal apparatus could discern to some extent how it functioned and could readily observe that it functioned well "for us." Thus there is no theodic crisis. But behind every theodic cri-

---

35. See Bryce (*A Legacy of Wisdom*, 139–62) for a shrewd analysis of Proverbs 25, in which wisdom is hidden and found out, and hidden.

36. See the references in n. 28, above. Schmid has seen that such ordering as the wise discerned not only is "natural" but always has social, political, and moral dimensions. Thus even the encyclopedic wisdom of Solomon's sages is related both to morality and to political power.

37. See Klaus Koch, "Is There a Doctrine of Retribution in the Old Testament?" in *Theodicy in the Old Testament*, ed. James L. Crenshaw, IRT 4 (Philadelphia: Fortress, 1983), 57–87.

38. On theodicy, see the collection of essays edited by James L. Crenshaw, *Theodicy in the Old Testament*.

sis there is a "theodic settlement"—a long-standing consensus about how life works, how society functions, how a system of benefits is allocated, what suffering must be tolerably and inescapably borne, and by whom it must be borne.[39] The theodic settlement that decides who must "rightly" suffer is characteristically a settlement authorized and imposed by those on top of the heap, who benefit from the present social arrangement, so that the system can be legitimated as good, wise, and right. For those who benefit, it is very difficult to notice that the theodic settlement may be for someone else a theodic crisis.[40]

It is my suggestion that long before the theodic crisis in later wisdom, widely recognized today, the Solomonic enterprise of wisdom instituted a theodic settlement that was in fact a rationalization for present systemic inequity and exploitation. People who enjoy the fruits of the present arrangement characteristically have their awarenesses trimmed to and shaped by those interests and experiences. It may be that 1 Kings 4:20-28 (MT 4:20-5:8) articulates a naive, uncritical theodic settlement in which Judah and Israel "ate and drank and were happy" (4:20), in which everyone was secure "under his own vine and fig tree" (4:25 [MT 5:5]). Conversely, 1 Kings 11, with the protest of the prophet (vv. 29-39) and the action of the revolutionaries (vv. 14-22, 23-25, 26-28), and 1 Kings 12, with its hard political resistance (v. 4), articulate a theodic crisis that envisions and requires a deep change in the rules of society. If 1 Kings 4:20-28 (MT 4:20—5:8) and 1 Kings 11–12 stand juxtaposed as theodic settlement and theodic crisis, then the sapiential references in 1 Kings 4:29-34 (MT 5:9-14) and 1 Kings 10:1-13 may be strategically placed to show both how the epistemological settlement was made (1 Kings 4:29-34) and how it was indeed linked to a disproportion of power and wealth (1 Kings 10:1-13).[41] One needs to ask, then, not if this or that text is

---

39. Such theodic settlements, which appeal to "natural law" to keep people in their "right place," are characteristically conservative. Thus in the modern world the "right place" of blacks and women is that they should properly bear disproportionate cost for social order. A blatant case of such a theodic settlement in the church concerns the denial of ordination to women, which is essentially a denial of access to power.

40. Peter L. Berger (*The Sacred Canopy* [Garden City, N.Y.: Doubleday, 1967], 59) observes: "[T]here may be two discrete theodicies established in the society—a theodicy of suffering for one group and a theodicy of happiness for the other." Obviously a society that has two such theodicies will be in endless and relentless conflict.

41. It is clear that in this episode concerning Solomon and the Queen of Sheba, wisdom now has no distinctive function or importance but belongs to the properties

historically accurate but what these texts intend to tell us about "remembered Solomon" in relation to Israel's persistent and recurring question of theodicy.[42]

Conclusion

It is *sociologically probable* that Solomon was a patron of a wisdom that was at once emancipatory and ideological. Only such a conclusion can explain the *canonical memory* of Solomon, both as the one who embraced creation with joy (the Song of Solomon), and as the one who knew despair about the failure of the system of creation (Ecclesiastes).[43] As I have suggested above, Solomon is remembered as a patron of a self-serving theodic settlement that permitted power, wealth, and wisdom in disproportionate measure. Thus, he was a patron of a theopolitical enterprise that did have emancipatory dimensions but that in the end was also ideological.[44] For Solomon was a patron for the justification of a self-serving system that benefitted the patron and those who enjoyed his patronage. Royally formed knowledge inevitably serves royally valued interests.[45] But for all the

of royal prestige. By being contextualized by power and riches, wisdom has been trivialized. The same contextualization of wisdom is evident in the triad of Jer. 9:23-24. Wisdom is then rather like "intelligence" in a superpower, so that knowledge simply serves economic policy and military strategy. That is, it is now instrumental for power and riches.

42. In Israel wisdom and therefore theodicy are never far removed from social reality. See chap. 9, below.

43. Following Cooper ("The Life and Times of King David"), I see in the Song of Solomon and Ecclesiastes productive interpretive strategies of the canon. To reduce these strategies to questions of historical precision would be to ignore what happens in the canonical process.

44. On the power of such an ideological function, see the quotation from François Châtelet in Henri Mottu, "Jeremiah vs. Hananiah: Ideology and Truth in the Old Testament Prophecy," in *The Bible and Liberation*, ed. Norman Gottwald (Maryknoll, N.Y.: Orbis, 1983), 239: "An ideology is a cultural formation (implicit) or a cultural production (explicit) that expresses the point of view of a social class or caste; such a point of view concerns man's relations with nature, imagination, the others, and himself. Ideology presents itself as having a *universal* validity; but in reality it not only expresses a *particular* point of view, but also it tends to *mask* its particularity by proposing compensations and imaginary or fleeting solutions."

45. On the relation of knowledge and interest, see Jürgen Habermas, *Knowledge and Human Interests* (Boston: Beacon, 1971). In the modern world of the Enlightenment, the interest of the dominant class was perceived as objective. While we must not press the analogy of the Enlightenment, it is clear that the wisdom of the royal court in Solomonic time was in the service of the royal interest and the urban monopoly. When interest shapes wisdom, one may expect a "march of folly," which was the course and outcome of the Solomonic enterprise.

skill of that system, Solomon did not escape the "terror of autonomy" in a regime that had violated the old covenantal vision (cf.
Matt. 6:29). The system designed to tame and contain anxiety ended
(perhaps in 922 B.C.E., perhaps in 587) in costly public alienation.

13

Rethinking Church Models
through Scripture

To POSE AFRESH the question of models of the church is itself an important matter. The question suggests a self-critical awareness that we are practitioners of a model that may not be the only or best one and that other models of the church are indeed thinkable. Such a self-critical acknowledgment is a necessary awareness if we are to do any "rechoosing" of our notion of the church.

For this theme, we have before us the influential work of Avery Dulles, *Models of the Church*, which is a thoughtful reflection on the theme from a more systematic perspective; and Paul Minear's *Images of the Church in the New Testament* has provided a shrewd summary of models of the church in the New Testament.[1] These works by Dulles and Minear have come from their sustained involvement in ecumenism, Dulles in a series of bilateral conversations and Minear in his work on the Faith and Order Commission. Undoubtedly the most influential grid of models is that of H. Richard Niebuhr in *Christ and Culture*.[2] That presentation in my judgment, however, has been severely distorted by its many users. Niebuhr's work is a historical study that reflects on the way in which the church, in many different times and circumstances, has had to posture its life in various and different ways. In common usage, however, Niebuhr's typology has

---

1. Avery Dulles, *Models of the Church* (Garden City, N.Y.: Doubleday, 1974); Paul S. Minear, *Images of the Church in the New Testament* (Philadelphia: Westminster, 1960).

2. H. Richard Niebuhr, *Christ and Culture* (New York: Harper and Brothers, 1951).

been taken as normative and has been dehistoricized. The result is that being less historically critical than Niebuhr himself, we are all agreed that "Christ transforming culture" is everywhere and always the normative mode of the life of the church. This amounts to a reductionism that fails to note that both in the Bible and in the history of the church, many other models and postures have been deemed not only necessary but required.

There is no single or normative model of church life. It is dangerous and distorting for the church to opt for an absolutist model that it insists upon in every circumstance. Moreover, we are more prone to engage in such reductionism if we do not keep alive a conversation concerning competing and conflicting models. Or to put it positively, models of the church must not be dictated by cultural reality, but they must be voiced and practiced in ways that take careful account of the particular time and circumstance into which God's people are called. Every model of the church must be critically contextual.

Posing the question about models in this way at this time requires us to think about Christ and culture, to think about the place where God has put us, and to think about an appropriate modeling for our time and circumstance. It is my intention and hope that my exploration in the Old Testament will suggest larger lines of reflection and other characterizations of the church far beyond the Old Testament.

I

In the center of the Old Testament, in the center literarily, historically, and theologically, is the Jerusalem establishment of monarchy and dynasty. It is the royal mode of Israel from David in 1000 B.C.E. to 587 B.C.E. that gives us the core model for the people of God in the Old Testament. This model dominates our thinking even as it dominates the text itself. It is this phase of Israel's life that provides the core of the time line around which we organize all of our thinking about the Old Testament. The test of that reality for me as an Old Testament teacher is that people regularly say, "Well, of course, the Old Testament model of faith and culture does not apply to us, because Israel is both state and church." That statement can refer only to the monarchal period, but it is thought to be *the* model. In fact that convergence of state and church holds true for only a small part of the Old Testament, but it is the part that we take for granted and the part that dominates our interpretative imagination.

My thesis concerning this season in the life of ancient Israel is that as this model dominates our reading of the Old Testament, it has served well the interests of *an established, culturally legitimated church.*[3] I will identify four features of that model for the people of God:

1. There were visible, legitimated, acceptable, stable, and well-financed religious structures with recognized, funded leadership. That is, the temple and its priesthood played a legitimated role in the ordering of civil imagination. The role of the stable temple for this model of church can hardly be overaccented.

2. There was civic leadership in the role of the kings that was at least publicly committed to the same theological discernment as was the stable religious structure of the temple. Indeed, the temple functioned as the "royal chapel." To be sure, the kings of Jerusalem were not so zealous to enact that theological discernment in concrete ways, except for Hezekiah and Josiah; but they were at least pledged to it, so that a critical, two-way conversation was formally possible. It did not seem odd for the priest to be in the palace, and it did not seem odd that the king should respond seriously to the finding of a temple scroll (cf. 2 Kings 22).

3. There arose in this model of the people of God an intelligentsia that was in part civic bureaucracy and in part the lobby of higher education. The sapiential tradition, the sages of the book of Proverbs who permeate and pervade the literature of the Old Testament, likely were influential in establishment thought in this period. This intellectual opinion accepted the formal presuppositions of temple religion. That is, the rule of Yahweh and the moral coherence of the world were assumptions of this community of reflection. This intelligentsia, however, exercised considerable freedom and imagination that drifted toward (*a*) autonomous reason and (*b*) support of state ideology.[4] That is, established religion served well the

---

3. It is not remote from my argument that an analogue exists between the royal-temple establishment in ancient Israel and the Constantinian establishment of the church. Thus the "end of the Constantinian period" in the church is congenial to my argument.

4. For one possible rendering of the social function of the sages, see George Mendenhall, "The Shady Side of Wisdom: The Date and Purpose of Genesis 3," in *A Light unto My Path*, ed. Howard N. Bream, R. D. Heim, and Casey A. Moore (Philadelphia: Temple Univ. Press, 1974), 319–34.

stabilization of power and knowledge for some at the expense of others.[5]

4. Exactly coterminal with stable temple leadership (priesthood) and with civic government that accepted the presuppositions of temple religion (king and sages) was the witness of the prophets, who regularly voice a more passionate, more radical, and "purer" vision of Israelite faith. It may indeed give us pause that the career of the prophets lasts only during the monarchy. That is, this voice of passion is viable only in a social circumstance where established powers are in principle committed to the same conversation.

This pattern of stable religious institution, sympathetic civic leadership, secularizing intelligentsia, and passionate prophecy all come to us as a cultural package. (I dare suggest that this is, *mutatis mutandis,* the governing model of modern, established Christianity in the West.) As is well known, this entire model in ancient Israel was swept away in a cultural and geopolitical upheaval. Moreover, the reason given for its being swept away is that the model had defaulted in its God-given vocation and was no longer acceptable to God.[6] Obviously, I focus on this crisis because I believe we are in a moment of like cultural and geopolitical upheaval that undoes us personally and institutionally. That upheaval in our own time is jarring and displacing and may be why we now reflect on alternative "models." It is worth noting that the collapse and failure of this model in 587 B.C.E. generated in ancient Israel enormous pluralism and vitality, as the community quested about for new and viable models of life and faith.

II

Happily, the temple-royal-prophetic model of the people of God is not the only model evident in the Old Testament. That mode was fitting and appropriate for a time of stable, established power. Israel as the people of God in the Old Testament, however, is not normatively a body of established power. Indeed, one can argue that such power as the Davidic monarchy had was a brief (four hundred years) and

---

5. See J. David Pleins, "Poverty in the Social World of the Wise," *JSOT* 37 (1987): 61–78.

6. This argument is made with greatest clarity and passion in the traditions of Jeremiah and Ezekiel.

passing episode, not to be replicated ever again in the life of this people of God.

Thus my second point is that Israel, prior to the time of David, did very well with another model of its life. If Moses is dated to 1250 B.C.E., then we may say that for the period from Moses to David, 1250–1000, Israel ordered its life and its faith very differently. Five characteristics may be identified for this model:

1. The life and faith of Israel were nurtured and shaped by the exodus liturgy, which confessed that God called for moral, urgent, concrete disengagement from the power structures and perceptual patterns of the day (in this case pharaoh, but later the Canaanite city-states), in order to be an alternative community. That liturgy regularly battled for the imagination of the community that was vulnerable to seduction by the dominant social reality and often succumbed. (Thus the perennial attraction of going back to the fleshpots of Egypt.) There is no way to soften or accommodate the sharp break that stands at the heart of Israel's self-identity that must always be "renerved" for new situations of domestication. The community understands itself, so the liturgy attests, to be a community birthed in a radical and costly break.

2. The meeting at Sinai and the endless process of reinterpretation of torah constitute an enterprise whereby Israel continues to think and rethink and rearticulate its faith and practice in light of its liberation. That practice required endless adjudication among conflicting opinions. If we take Leviticus to be more or less conservative and Deuteronomy to be more or less radical, then the ongoing tension between Leviticus and Deuteronomy already sets the guidelines and perimeters for policy adjudication that is still required of us.[7] This continued torah interpretation exhibits the church seeking to discern the mind and heart of God. It is agreed only that this community (*a*) is shaped in something like a holy covenant, (*b*) is a community liberated by God for new life in the world, and (*c*) refuses the sustenance of pharaoh. All else remained and remains to be decided.

3. Early Israel from 1250 to 1000 had none of the features outlined above for the period of the establishment. It had no stable institutions; it had no sympathetic, stable civic leadership; it had no

---

7. Such a juxtaposition of Leviticus and Deuteronomy is shrewdly rendered by Fernando Belo, *A Materialist Reading of the Gospel of Mark* (Maryknoll, N.Y.: Orbis, 1981), 1–86 and passim.

secularizing intelligentsia; and it had no prophetic voice. Imagine Israel without temple, without king, without sages, without prophets! That is how it was. Early Israel had much more modest means and modes. Indeed, Israel in this period had to make up everything as it went along. It was a community that had to improvise. Its daring, risky improvisation can, on the one hand, be seen as an enormous borrowing from the culture around it. On the other hand, this was a process of deep transformation of what was borrowed, transformed according to its central passion for liberation and for covenant.

4. Unlike Israel in the monarchal period, Israel in this early period was not unified, or we may say, was not rigorously "connectional." It was, as the sociologists say, a segmented community of extended family units and tribes. These units had no central authority or treasury, nor were they blood units. They were communities bound by a common commitment to Israel's central story and its distinctive social passion. It is fair to say that the story of liberation and covenant was inordinately important but became much less important in the period of establishment when the temple made the story less palpable and less urgent. In the early period, lacking visible props, the community depended on the story being regularly heard and told.[8]

5. The community of early Israel was socioeconomically marginal. Its central metaphor is either the "wilderness" or the occupation of marginal land that no one else wanted. In the "wilderness," the community lived by bread from heaven and water from rock, without guaranteed or managed resources. In its marginal land, it depended in its times of threat on the move of the Spirit to give energy, courage, and power sufficient for the crisis. This was a community that lacked the capacity (or perhaps the will) for more stable resources, but managed by a different posture of faith and witness.

I suggest then that in the most radical way possible, Israel was indeed "a new church start." A new church start here means the planting of an alternative community among people who were ready for risk and who shunned established social relations because such resources and patterns inevitably led to domestication and to bondage. It is a new church start that specialized in neighbor priorities and had at its center the powerful voices of Moses and Joshua

---

8. George Lindbeck ("The Church," in *Keeping the Faith: Essays to Mark the Centenary of Lux Mundi*, ed. Geoffrey Wainwright [Philadelphia: Fortress, 1988], 179–208) has argued that "storied community" is the primary identifying mark of Christian ecclesiology.

and Samuel, whose main work is voicing and revoicing and voicing again the liturgy of liberation and the covenant of reshaping communal life, power, and vision.

It may give us pause that the temple model grew increasingly impatient with the voice of Moses, whose leadership was kept in endless jeopardy and under abrasive challenge. It is likely that the narrative of the Golden Calf (Exodus 32), wherein Moses rebukes Aaron, is a partisan assault made by the "new church start" model against the established church model that is too busy generating structure and icon.

III

At the other end of the Old Testament, we may identify yet another model for the community of faith. The temple model came to an abrupt end in 587 B.C.E. To be sure, there was a second temple built after 520 B.C.E., but it never came to exercise a dominant place in the community, nor to capture the imagination of subsequent interpreters. Clearly with the events of 587, the symbiotic relation of king and prophet collapsed. This new circumstance began in exile under the Babylonians and then continued under the patronage of the Persians and finally faced the coming of Hellenization. It is worth noting that, characteristically, Christians know very little about this period, pay little attention to it, and care little for it. Very likely this lack of interest reflects our stereotypes of "postexilic Judaism," which go back at least to the caricatures of Julius Wellhausen. That is, our systemic neglect reflects the anti-Semitic tendency of our interpretative categories. There is at the present time great attention to this period among scholars that requires us to move well beyond our dismissive stereotypes. Recent scholarship suggests that there was a greatly variegated practice of Judaism bespeaking pluralism in this period. It was a pluralism that was theologically serious, with enormous imagination in its practice of faith and vitality in its literary inventiveness.

My suggestion is that this exilic/postexilic period after the collapse of the temple hegemony is one to which we must pay considerable attention for it may, *mutatis mutandis,* be echoed in our own time and circumstance. Five facets of this model may be noted:

1. The community of faith had to live in a context where it exercised little influence over public policy. It is debatable to what

extent the imperial overlords exercised benign neglect so long as they received tax payments and to what extent they were hostile in an attempt to nullify the scandalous particularity of the Jews. The stereotype we have is that the Babylonians were hostile and the Persians were benign, but that may be an ideological construct put together by those indentured to the Persians' government. In any case, after one considers the drama of Elijah versus Ahab, Amos versus Amaziah, and Jeremiah versus Zedekiah, one notices that there is no such confrontation model now available. The reason is, I submit, that there is no one on the side of power interested in such a confrontation, for this community of faith had become politically innocuous and irrelevant.

2. The temptations to cultural syncretism and the disappearance of a distinct identity were acute, particularly in the Hellenistic period. The Maccabean period offers us an example of Jewish boys who were embarrassed about their circumcision and who tried to "pass." In the monarchal period, while there was indeed syncretism, there was no danger of losing an Israelite identity because public institutions supported that identity, and one could afford to be indolent about it. In contrast, in the exilic/postexilic period, because such institutions were lacking and because the pattern of social payouts tended to invite people away from this community of peculiar identity and passion, the deliberate maintenance of a distinctive identity required great intentionality.

3. In the face of political irrelevance and social syncretism, a main task of the community was to work very hard and intentionally at its cultural-linguistic infrastructure.[9] Daniel L. Smith has called that work the development of strategies and mechanisms for survival because the threat was in fact the disappearance of the community of faith into a universalizing culture that was partly hostile to any particularity and that was partly indifferent.[10] Among these strategies for survival, three seem crucial for our reflection.

This community, in the face of sociopolitical marginality, worked at the recovery of memory and rootage and connectedness. The primary evidence of this in the Old Testament is the extended ge-

---

9. I deliberately use the phrasing of George A. Lindbeck, *The Nature of Doctrine: Religion and Theology in a Postliberal Age* (Philadelphia: Westminster, 1984). I believe that the categories of Lindbeck's argument greatly illuminate the practice of ancient Israel when it lacked cultural institutions of support.

10. Daniel L. Smith, *The Religion of the Landless: The Social Context of the Babylonian Exile* (Bloomington, Ind.: Meyer-Stone, 1989).

nealogies, most of which were articulated in this later period. The purpose of genealogy is to connect the threatened present generation with the horizon of reference points from the past. That is, a studied recovery of the past intends to combat the "now generation" and the disease of autonomy and individualism that imagines that we live in a historical vacuum.

4. A second strategy for survival in a community at the brink of despair is the intense practice of hope. The rhetoric of the community filled its imagination with the quite concrete promises of God. In its extreme form, this rhetoric of hope issues in apocalyptic. In our study of apocalyptic, there is much for us to learn about the sociology of our knowledge. When the church is safe and settled and allied with the status quo, it is impatient with apocalyptic. Indeed, most critical scholarship has dismissed apocalyptic as "bizarre." Among the communities of the marginal, however, who find the present laden with hopelessness, apocalyptic is a rhetorical act of power. Thus this literature and this rhetoric belong rightly on the lips of the "world weary" who see this rhetoric as critically subversive of every status quo. It is telling how that apocalyptic rhetoric in our culture appeals to apparently well-off people who are beset by despair.

I believe this is important because satiated young people in the United States (including some of our own children) mostly do not know that something else is yet promised by God. That future is not to be wrought by our busy, educated hands, but by the faithfulness of God. The community at the margin, when it functions at all, is a community of intense, trustful waiting.

5. The third strategy of survival worth noting is that the postexilic community became an intensely textual community. It was busy formulating the text: so it is widely believed that the period around the exile is precisely the period of canonization, the making of normative literature. It was also busy interpreting the text. This is the period of the emergence of the synagogue, which is the place of the text; the formation of the *Beth Midrash*, "the house of study"; and eventually, the appearance of the rabbis, who are teachers of the tradition. Textual study was focused on the imaginative construal of a normative text. This imaginative construal of the text that so characterizes Judaism did not drive toward theological settlement or moral consensus but believed that the act of construal of this text itself is a quintessential Jewish act. Such an act in the midst of marginality did not need a controlled outcome.

With a high and passionate view of Scripture, we must not miss the point concerning social power. The point of sustained textual study is not objective erudition, information, or conclusion. The point is rather to enter into and engage with a tradition of speech, reflection, discernment, and imagination that will prevail over the textual constraints of Persian power and Hellenistic hostility. A textless Jew is no Jew at all, sure to be co-opted and sure to disappear into the woodwork. And my sense is that a textless church is increasingly no church at all.

The *New Yorker*, of all places, has suggested that the United States has had the Cold War as its organizing story.[11] That story has now failed, and our civil community, says the *New Yorker*, is essentially "storyless." So it has always been: the story offered by the dominant empire turns out to be no story at all. These besieged Jews knew that. They knew not only that to keep their young they had to engage the text on its own terms. They also dared to imagine that their particular text was the voice of God among them, and the voice of a true story that would persist in the face of empire and cultural hegemony. This community developed a deep and vibrant confidence in its text, which is what the process of canonization is all about.

Thus it is my conclusion that circumstance required a shift from a temple-royal-prophetic community to a textual community that struggled with the text in all its truth and in all its dangerous subversiveness, continually witnessing to another mode of reality.

IV

I have suggested three models that are intensely reflective of social crisis and historical circumstance: (1) premonarchal model as "new church start"; (2) monarchal model as temple community; (3) postexilic model as a textual community. It is readily clear that the early premonarchal and the late postmonarchal have more in common, and both are easily contrasted with the security and stability of the monarchal model. Finally, then, we may reflect on the dialectic relation of early and late models that had so much in common.

There is no doubt, on the one hand, that the late community went back to the early community. That is, it in fact jumped over the monarchal period to find resources in the early sources that could

---

11. "Notes and Comments," *The New Yorker* (May 21, 1990): 27–28.

sustain it. It did not find in the period of the establishment what it needed and was driven back to more primitive and less stable models. This is poignantly evident in Ezra, the founder of Judaism, who is the second Moses and who replicated the first Moses.

On the other hand, and much more delicately, the late community not only used the early materials but also intruded upon those materials, preempted and reshaped the early traditions for its own use. In the documentary hypothesis concerning the Pentateuch, the Priestly tradition represents a later recasting of early tradition. That is, the late material is not all in the late part of the Bible, but some of the later material is cast as early material. The Priestly tradition is conventionally dated to the sixth or fifth century, either exilic or early postexilic. So when we read the pre-David texts, if we pay attention, many of those texts are postexilic and show not only the needs but also the faith of the later community. Four quick examples demonstrate late material cast as early material:

1. *Genesis 1:1-2:4a,* on the creation, is a Priestly statement that culminates in Sabbath as a sacrament. It is in the late period that Sabbath emerges as a mark of Jewishness, when the Jews in an alien environment had to assert that Jews (and others) were not cogs in any imperial machine, but creatures made in God's image, destined for dignity. Thus the late liturgy responded to a social situation of despair by generating a sacrament of dignity and liberation.

2. *Genesis 17,* in which Abraham circumcises his offspring, is a Priestly document, asserting in the late period that the community must have a visible discipline of identity. Circumcision, albeit sexist, is a visible mark whereby insiders can be distinguished from outsiders, so that members of the community know who was marked by God's promise and who stood under God's commandment. Circumcision emerged in the postexilic period as a decisive mark of Jewishness. Such a text in such a community invites a rethinking of the marking of baptism in a society that is either hostile or neglectful.

3. *Exodus 16,* the story of manna in the wilderness, contains Priestly elements. The wilderness becomes, in such a story, a cipher for exile, so that the exiles, marginated faithful people, live by the gifts of God and not by their managed surplus. It is striking that the text warns against surplus, the kind of surplus that made the temple possible. Moreover, the text relentlessly culminates in Sabbath, the occasion when an abundance of food is given (see Isa. 55:1-3; Daniel 1).

4. *Exodus 26* is a design for the tabernacle in a Priestly tradition. While the model for the tabernacle no doubt reflects the temple, the intent of the text is to permit God mobility, capability of being on the way with God's displaced people. This is a God who has a portable shrine and who will travel.

The point of this linkage of late and early is to suggest that in doing textual work (which became a primary activity of the marginated community), the late community must recast what the early community had done for the sake of its own crisis. This means that after the establishment, as before the establishment, this was essentially a new church start. Postexilic Judaism is a vibrant act of new generativity, not enslaved to its oldest memories and not immobilized by its recent memory of establishment power. Ezra is the great "new church start" leader. A new church start means reformulating the faith in radical ways in the midst of a community that has to begin again. For Ezra as for Moses, new church starts do not aim at strategies for success but at strategies for survival of an alternative community. What must survive is not simply the physical community: what must also survive is an alternative community with an alternative memory and an alternative social perception rooted in a peculiar text, identified by a peculiar genealogy, and signed by peculiar sacraments, a community of peculiar people not excessively beholden to the empire and not lusting after domestication into the empire.

V

Whether this grid is pertinent to our present rethinking partly depends on the cogency of the analysis offered of these traditions. It also depends partly on a judgment about whether we are in a time when our alliance with the dominant culture is being broken, whether the power of the temple is broken, whether the empire is indifferent or hostile, whether the prophets lack a partner in confrontation. This argument receives support from three sources at least:

1. The collapse of modernity is a crucial theme in much contemporary social analysis.[12] We have to face that our dominant models

---

12. I have found most helpful Stephen Toulmin, *Cosmopolis: The Hidden Agenda of Modernity* (New York: Free Press, 1990), but there is a growing literature on the subject.

of church have been fashioned for modernity and depend on its presuppositions, presuppositions that no longer prevail.

2. It is clear that conventional kinds of theological speech are no longer accepted as "public speech." That is, civic leadership is not in any serious way any longer formally committed to established church rhetoric, so that appeals from our tradition are less and less significant politically.

3. Many of our young (particularly the young of good liberals but not only the children of liberals) have only the vaguest idea of what we intend in our faith.

A move *from temple to text,* a move I have stated in the boldest form, requires a reconsideration of our social location, of the resources on which we can and must count and the work we have to do about the infrastructure that has largely collapsed. While we may find wilderness-exile models less congenial, there is no biblical evidence that the God of the Bible cringes at the prospect of this community being one of wilderness and exile. Indeed this God resisted the temple in any case (cf. 2 Sam. 7:4-7). In the end, it is God and not the Babylonians who terminated the temple project. In the face of that possible eventuality in our own time and circumstance, the ways for the survival of an alternative imagination in an alternative community call for new strategies.[13]

---

13. See my suggestions in "Disciplines of Readiness," Occasional Paper no. 1 (Louisville: Theology and Worship Unit, Presbyterian Church [U.S.A.], 1988).

14

Reflections on Biblical Understandings of Property

BIBLICAL FAITH is a peculiar phenomenon in the history of world culture. In every phase of life it seeks to articulate an alternative to commonly accepted presuppositions and widely practiced usages. In every phase of life that alternative is at least strange and perhaps peculiar; sometimes it is scandalous if not absurd. It is the destiny of God's faithful people in each time and place to explore the alternatives and find ways of living them out. On any given topic, the biblical material provides a plurality of alternatives. Among them we may discern some fresh possibilities and resources for our life of faith.

The Bible, of course, is primarily concerned with secular, worldly matters as the place where the purposes and power of God will be discerned. Of these none is more urgent or problematic than the issue of property, how it is secured and legitimated, how it is kept or lost, to what ends it may be used and enjoyed. The prominent model for property in the ancient world and in our own time we may designate as "royal/urban." This view affirmed that "haves" are entitled to have, whether the haves are the king, the nobles, the wealthy landowners, or the managers of legitimated bureaucracy. Possession gives legitimacy, and it is legitimate to so construct social values and social procedures as well as law so that haves may have and legitimately seek more. The right of the have-nots—citizens, peasants, slaves, all the powerless ones—is nil. They are entitled to nothing and must rely upon a generosity and charity upon which they have no claim. So far as the organization of society is concerned, they do not really exist. They lie outside the decision-making process and are, in fact, nonparticipants in the history of the community. There is nothing exceptional about such a view; it occurs both in the world around the Bible and in the narrative of the Bible itself.

The Bible articulates an alternative view of property that is not exclusive to the Bible but receives its most compelling statement there. It may be designated "covenantal/prophetic." It holds that the haves and the have-nots are bound in community to each other, that viable life depends upon the legitimate respect, care, and maintenance of the have-nots and upon restraint of the haves so that the needs and rights of the disadvantaged take priority over the yearnings of the advantaged. Thus the stress is upon *respect* and *restraint* precisely in those areas of public life where the distribution of power makes respect and restraint unenforceable. Such a view of social organization regards property as resource for the common good, as vehicle for the viability of a whole society, as the arena for the development of public responsibility and public compassion. In this view, the rights of the haves are defined in relation to the rights of the have-nots. It is immediately evident that the categories for the discussion have been significantly changed. No longer is there talk about possession and power to control, but now there is talk of respect and restraint, of responsibility and compassion.

The theological legitimation for such an unconventional, even radical view of property is expressed in the commitment of Yahweh, the God of the Bible, as being deeply and primarily directed toward those without property. The exodus provides the central model for a redefinition of property when God intervenes on behalf of the slaves against the establishment of Egypt, on behalf of those without property at the expense of the property owners. Thus the central shaping of the question locates the issue precisely at the meeting place between these two groups. The dynamic of this view of property is that in that meeting there is intervention and inversion. The model of Yahweh on behalf of the powerless against the possessors clearly means to assert that unbridled and oppressive power is not free to assemble for itself all the possessions it is able to amass. This understanding of society and the public handling of property is derived from the biblical view of God. Psalm 82 presents one clear and primitive assessment of the character of Yahweh in contrast to that of the other gods. Yahweh indicts the other gods:

Give justice to the weak and the fatherless;
    maintain the right of the afflicted and the destitute.
Rescue the weak and the needy;
    deliver them from the hand of the wicked.

But they do not do that, and so Yahweh pronounces sentence on the other gods:

You are gods,
    sons of the Most High, all of you;
nevertheless, you shall die like men,
    and fall like any prince. (Ps. 82:3-4, 6-7)

Yahweh is presented precisely as the one engaged for the well-being of those without power to secure their own well-being. And the other gods, who are insensitive and unresponsive to this crunch in social relationships, are denied their claim to be gods.

This view of property already anticipated in the exodus event and rooted in the very character of Yahweh envisions a time when history will be transformed, when ownership will be called into question and redistribution will be based not on power but on the intrusive purpose of Yahweh for justice and equity. Property is subordinated to a holy vision of well-being and freedom. Such a view radically calls into question the present arrangement of property and looks to its yielding to a covenantal alternative. Thus even in the mouth of the Virgin are these statements about property:

He has shown strength with his arm,
    he has scattered the proud in the imagination of their hearts,
he has put down the mighty from their thrones,
    and exalted those of low degree;
he has filled the hungry with good things,
    and the rich he has sent empty away. (Luke 1:51-53)

These two views, royal/urban and covenantal/prophetic, are persistently in conflict. The Bible is never able to resolve them in any enduring way, and the issue must always be faced again. Here we may note several occasions when these alternative understandings stand in sharp tension, even as they do in our time.

In the narrative of 1 Kings 21, King Ahab and his Phoenician queen, Jezebel, embody one view of property. It is their assumption that royal prerogative legitimates their need for, their lust for, and their capacity to take what others have. They act in ways that are perfectly legal and legitimate on the ground of royal legitimacy. This view of property cannot be separated from an ideology about order and governance and the claim of the royal power to be the only barrier against social chaos. It is this pretension to be the guardian of life that legitimates such policy on property.

Naboth, a small landowner, embodies an alternative view of property. While this view of land may be described simply as tribal-peasant, it clearly is also a different understanding of value in community. This, then, is not only a contest between powers and wills, but also a conflict between alternative definitions of social community. Ahab believes that property is to be bought and sold and traded and bargained. The process of transmitting property is one over which powerful human persons and agents have full power and freedom. The royal establishment lives by such procedures, and surely the urban mentality authorizes such a view.[1] In each case a royal figure acts in his or her power and legitimacy and regards property as a commodity that can be transmitted between agents who have power to do it.

Conversely, Naboth uses a quite different term, describing the lands as "inheritance." The land is not a commodity but a birthright. It may not be exchanged because it is irrevocable. It has a history that links it to a person and that person's family. No amount of power or royal authority can negate those historical roots and connections. While Ahab believes that persons, especially royal persons, can own and possess and even seize land, Naboth holds to the notion, primitive by contrast, that persons have rootage in and belong to the land. And those connections cannot be ignored or betrayed for rapacious centers of power. Of course, this encounter may simply be a conflict between royal and tribal orderings of life. But the presence of Elijah, prophet of Yahweh, in the story indicates that fundamental covenantal issues are at stake as well as protection of tribal ways. A view of property that legitimates confiscation and authorizes acts of power against the helpless is not only doubtful politics; it violates Yahweh's purposes for a proper community ordered after the manner of the exodus transaction. And finally it brings death.

---

1. See other royal/urban examples in the purchases by Abraham (Genesis 23), by David (2 Samuel 24), and by Omri, Ahab's father (1 Kings 16); see Siegfried Herrmann, *A History of Israel in Old Testament Times* (Philadelphia: Fortress, 1975), 206, 235, 242.

This narrative is placed in the middle of a long history of kings and prophets. Apparently written out of primitive memory, it was used in the exile to reflect on why land is lost. The placement of the story suggests that land and property are lost and death comes when the covenantal notion of property is violated and royal/urban values are instituted that fail to respect the ways in which people inherit and depend upon inherited land and property. The royal/urban way appears in this narrative to be a threat not just to the rights of a helpless landholder but to the entire community. Thus the very assumption that appears legitimate also appears to be a threat endangering the community over which it means to preside.

A second presentation of the same conflict occurs in the post-exilic community of Jerusalem. Nehemiah sought to reconstruct Jerusalem as a society in which covenantal norms would apply in every phase of life. The demands of torah are regarded as compelling. But even in such an intentional community, destructive models of property do surface. It was within the community, not perverted by any Phoenician princess, but among the members of the covenanting community, that trouble came. Even in that community, inequality happened because of legitimated forms of confiscation. Three accusatory statements of deprivation and destitution are made by Nehemiah's contemporaries against their rapacious fellows:

> Some said, "We are many; let us get grain that we may eat and live."
> [They are in danger of death and look to the bare necessities—cf. Gen. 42:20.]

> Some said, "We are mortgaging our fields, our vineyards, and our houses to get grain because of the famine."
> [There was presumably nothing illegal in such a process; it is simply the doubtful legal right of some to claim the property of others.]

> Some said, "We have borrowed money for the king's task on our fields and our vineyards." (Neh. 5:2-5)

Even in the intentional community of Jerusalem, unjust gain by those who controlled the machinery of government was denying some their personhood, their rightful place in community, and their inheritance. It was a perfectly legal but destructive way to administer property. And the result is that among covenanted people ("our flesh is as the flesh of our covenant fellows"), some are seizing what belongs to others and denying them what is rightly theirs, not because of private acts of greed but because of rapacious organization of social institutions. It is never claimed by Nehemiah that these reprehensible acts are illegal but only that they deny the vision of society to which Judah is committed. The arrangement in Jerusalem leads to one of the harshest and most pointed understatements of the Bible:

> It is not in our power to help it;
> other men have our fields and our vineyards. (Neh. 5:5)

The royal/urban arrangement may be legal but it makes people powerless. It denies them their place in the community and their place in history. Such a view of property reduces some to slavery, and they have no effective means of protest or redress.

Against that stands Nehemiah, bearer of an alternative tradition. He is not exactly a prophet and is often regarded as a rather narrow sectarian. But here he boldly and authoritatively articulates a covenantal notion of property that sees it not as a commodity available to the strong but as an inalienable gift of personhood that must be maintained in the face of exploitative institutions. Property is an extension and embodiment of personal identity and personal power, and it must be protected. He firmly condemns the conventional way of distributing property:

1. He describes the act: "You are exacting interest, each from his brother"—that is, from a fellow member of the covenant community (v. 7).

2. He identifies the wrong: "We, as far as we are able, have bought back our Jewish brethren who have been sold to the nations; but you even sell your brethren that they may be sold to us"—that is, you are acting as though the exodus had never happened among us (v. 8; cf. Deut. 24:7).

3. He asserts a covenantal alternative: "You are doing what is not good"—that is, what is against covenant, which will violate communal solidarity (v. 9).

4. He initiates a program of rehabilitation and restoration of community: "Return to them this very day their fields, their vineyards, their olive orchards, and their houses, and the hundredth of money, grain, wine, and oil which you have been exacting of them" (v. 11).

Nehemiah's intervention transformed a community from a destructive interaction between propertied and propertyless people to a way of solidarity. The narrative does not depict an isolated incident, though presumably it does report an actual event. But it also preserves a model of how society can be ordered and how it may be disordered. Remarkably, the narrative ends with an agreement to covenant and a bold call for the power of God against those who practice an alternative view of property:

> So may God shake out everyone from house and from property who does not perform this promise. Thus may they be shaken out and emptied. And all the assembly said, "Amen," and praised the Lord. (v. 13; NRSV)

The term "shake" is used to describe God's action against the oppressive Egyptians (Exod. 14:27; Ps. 136:15). Yahweh sets them in the sea for their resistance to Yahweh's purposes, which include the well-being of the Lord's people. A biblical view of property cannot disregard this conviction that God shakes up those arrangements that do not honor God's will for community.

Neither in the case of Ahab nor in the case of Nehemiah's contemporaries is there any sign of corruption, illegality, or private scheming. The legitimacy of property as a dimension of personhood is not perverted by personal meanness but by public policy that serves self-interest against the common good and against the well-being of those without power to protect themselves.

The Bible is not ideological about property. It does not affirm or resist capitalist or communist schemes. It rather urges a quite alternative reading of human community that can only be described as covenantal. Property must be managed, valued, and distributed so that every person of the community is honored and so that the well-being of each is intimately tied to that of the others. This view of property is not allied to a primitive tribalism against more sophisticated urban life, but it does observe that the temptations of concentration of urban power when combined with claims of religious sanction can indeed destroy human freedom and equity, and on seemingly legitimate grounds.

In Luke 12:13-21, Jesus is confronted with an urgent question of property division. The very notion of dividing the inheritance smacks of a royal/urban view that regards the inheritance as a negotiable commodity. Jesus refuses to resolve the issue but explores the potential for life and death in the handling of property. He observes that unbounded self-seeking brings death. His teaching radically articulates the hard issue of richness toward self and richness toward God. While the links are not explicit, it may be that the models we have suggested, royal/urban and covenantal/prophetic, find important corollaries in the two forms of richness stated here. In the commentary Luke has placed after the teaching (vv. 22-31; cf. Matt. 6:25-33 on the same teaching in another context), there is a noteworthy juxtaposition of ideas. The narrative has been about *covetousness,* about a way of life that seeks to gain more and more without limit, apparently for the mere accumulation of it all, or at least in the vain hope of securing one's existence against every eventuality. In verses 22 and 25 of the teaching, Jesus places next to covetousness the problem of anxiety, the restless awareness that more and more is not enough, the harsh recognition that such a pursuit of property can never yield either inner security or social security. And the commentary is addressed to those of "little faith" who view life as a problem in self-securing and who are blind to the well-being that is given by the provision of God. It is not clear if the teaching is addressed to those who have or do not have, but it is surely addressed to those who believe that more effort and more energy and more accumulation can somehow do more for our well-being and joy than can the graciousness of God. Such an enterprise seems surer and more controllable and apparently will bring the life-giving resources under our management.

The commentary in verses 22-31 creates an interesting intersection of *coveting, anxiety,* and *little faith.* The Gospel, surely informed by a covenantal/prophetic view of property, has discerned that coveting, driven by a lack of trust, never leads to enough but always to the endless unsatisfied need for more. The Gospel protests against a notion of property that regards it never as a trust or as a gift but as a source of security of which we never have enough. As in other things, Jesus urged in his teaching and in his ministry the power of emptiness, the richness of poverty, the security of living without anxiety. And his faithful community is left to wonder about public policy that yields only anxiety and never security.

We are baptized into another view of property that is surely covenantal. Paul expressed it inescapably:

> Not that I complain of want; for I have learned in whatever state I am to be content. I know how to be abased, and I know how to abound; in any and all circumstances I have learned the secret of facing plenty and hunger, abundance and want. I can do all things in him who strengthens me. (Phil. 4:11-13)

The Bible, of course, does not address problems of modern economic theory. But the models we have located suggest a sharp critique of (1) statism that disregards the precious treasure of personal rootage and (2) untrammeled individualism that secures individuals at the expense of the community. For the Bible the issues concern finally not a view of property but the problem of private and public well-being and the possibilities for securing our existence. Martin Hengel has articulated this in his statement: "The crisis of property also proves to be the crisis of man, his selfish desire to assert himself, his struggle for power and his mercilessness." The invitation of the gospel is to order our common life so that property may be a life-giving resource, when it is purged of its demonic power over us.[2] Isaiah provides a remarkable and strange notion of property and security:

> Those who walk righteously and speak uprightly,
>   who despise the gain of oppression,
> who wave away a bribe instead of accepting it,
>   who stop their ears from hearing of bloodshed,
>   and shut their eyes from looking upon evil, they will dwell on the
>   heights;
>   their refuge will be the fortresses of rocks;
>   their food will be supplied, their water assured.
>
>   (Isa. 33:15-16; NRSV)

That's bread quite in contrast to the leaven of the Pharisees (Mark 8:15)![3]

---

2. Martin Hengel, *Property and Riches in the Early Church* (Philadelphia: Fortress, 1975), 86, 88.

3. For discussion of the topic, see especially Hengel, *Property and Riches*. Herrmann (*A History of Israel*) has identified the purchase of land as a peculiarly Canaanite practice. George Mendenhall has in several places contrasted the property model of Yahwistic tribalism and an urban/monarchal model patterned after the Canaanites. This was first articulated in "The Hebrew Conquest of Palestine," *BA* 25 (1962): 66–87. For a fuller discussion, see George Mendenhall, *The Tenth Generation* (Baltimore: Johns Hopkins Univ. Press, 1973), and even more pointedly, idem, "The Monarchy," *Int* 29 (1975): 155–70. The contrast between these valuing systems is even more fully explicated by Norman Gottwald, *The Tribes of Yahweh* (Maryknoll, N.Y.: Orbis, 1979). On the issue of economic presupposition in Scripture interpretation, see José Miranda, *Marx and the Bible* (Maryknoll, N.Y.: Orbis, 1974).

15

Revelation and Violence:
A Study in Contextualization

THE CONVICTION that Scripture is revelatory literature is constant and abiding among the communities of Jews and Christians that gather around the Book.[1] But that conviction, constant and abiding as it is, is problematic and open to a variety of alternative and often contradictory or ambiguous meanings.[2] Clearly that conviction is appropriated differently in various contexts and various cultural settings.[3] Current attention to hermeneutics convinces many of us that there is no single, sure meaning for any text. The revelatory power of the text is discerned and given precisely through the action of interpretation that is always concrete, never universal, always contextualized, never "above the fray," always filtered through vested interest, never in disinterested purity.[4]

1. David Tracy (*The Analogical Imagination* [New York: Crossword, 1981], chaps. 3–7) has usefully interpreted this conviction in terms of the Bible as a "classic."
2. See David H. Kelsey, *The Uses of Scripture in Recent Theology* (Philadelphia: Fortress, 1975).
3. Jon Sobrino (*The True Church and the Poor* [Maryknoll, N.Y.: Orbis, 1984], 10–21) has shown how "the Enlightenment" as a context of interpretation can be handled in two very different ways, depending on whether one organizes the matter around Kant or Marx. Obviously Kant and Marx were interested in very different notions of what may be enlightened, and the implications for interpretation lead in very different directions. This difference is illustrative of the interpretative options more generally available.
4. Jürgen Habermas (*Knowledge and Human Interests* [Boston: Beacon, 1971]) has shown how all knowledge is related to matters of interest and that any imagined objectivity is likely to be an exercise in self-deception. On such presumed objectivity, see Elisabeth Schüssler Fiorenza, *Bread Not Stone* (Boston: Beacon, 1984).

If that is true for the interpretative end of the process that receives the text, we may entertain the notion that it is also true for the interpretative end of the process that forms, shapes, and offers the text. That is, not only in its hearing, but also in its speaking, the text makes its disclosure in ways that are concrete, contextualized, and filtered through vested interest. While this leaves open the charge of relativism, it is in fact only a candid acknowledgment of the central conviction around which historical-critical studies have revolved for two hundred years. Historical-critical studies have insisted that a text can be understood only in context. Historical-critical study holds that historical context is necessary to hearing the text. But our objectivist ideology has uncritically insisted that knowledge of historical context of a text would let us be objective interpreters without recognizing that from its very inception, the textual process is not and cannot be objective.[5]

Historical-critical study thus gives us access to a certain interpretative act that generates the text, but that original interpretative act is not objective. This acknowledgment of the formation of the text as a constructive event is a recognition of what we know about ourselves, that we are not only meaning receivers but also meaning makers. We not only accept meanings offered but construct meanings we advocate.[6] The receiving, constructing act of interpretation changes both us and the text. This suggests that Scripture as revelation is never simply a final disclosure but is an ongoing act of disclosing that will never let the disclosure be closed. The disclosing process is an open interaction with choices exercised in every step of interpretation from formation to reception.

I

The emergence of two more or less new methods of Scripture interpretation is important for the relation between revelation and interpretation. In this essay I want to consider both of these methods in relation to the revelatory character of the text.

---

5. See the helpful statement by Donal Dorr, *Spirituality and Justice* (Maryknoll, N.Y.: Orbis, 1984), 43–51.

6. On the human person (and derivatively the human community) as a constructor of meanings, see Robert Kegan, *The Evolving Self* (Cambridge, Mass.: Harvard Univ. Press, 1982), and Roy Schafer, *Language and Insight* (New Haven: Yale Univ. Press, 1978).

The first of these methods is sociological.[7] It has become apparent that much historical-critical study has focused on the question of facticity to so large an extent that it has bracketed out questions of social process, social interest, and social possibility. A number of studies have made use of tools of social analysis to ask about the social intention and social function of a text in relation to the community and the situation upon which the text impinges.[8] Among the more important of these studies are Norman Gottwald's on the early period, Robert R. Wilson's on the prophets, and Paul D. Hanson's on the later period.[9] A programmatic formula for such an enterprise is that it is a "materialist" reading,[10] a phrase Gottwald would accept for his work, but perhaps Wilson and Hanson would not. A "materialist reading" suggests that the text cannot be separated from the social processes out of which it emerged. The text also is a product of the community. The community that generates the text is engaged in production of the text, and the community that reads it is engaged in consumption of the text, so that the text needs to be discussed according to processes of production and consumption.[11] In what follows, I will want to consider a materialist reading of a text as an attempt to appropriate its revelatory claim. The text as product for consumption suggests the operation of intentionality and interest in the shaping of the text.

The second method that will be useful for us is literary analysis. Literary analysis seeks to take the text on its own terms as an offer of meaning, as an exercise in creative imagination to construct a world that does not exist apart from the literary act of the text.[12]

---

7. See the summary statement of Robert R. Wilson, *Sociological Approaches to the Old Testament* (Philadelphia: Fortress, 1984).

8. A helpful example of how sociological analysis may shape exegetical interpretation is offered in *God of the Lowly*, ed. Willy Schottroff and Wolfgang Stegemann (Maryknoll, N.Y.: Orbis, 1984).

9. Norman Gottwald, *The Tribes of Yahweh* (Maryknoll, N.Y.: Orbis, 1979); Robert R. Wilson, *Prophecy and Society in Ancient Israel* (Philadelphia: Fortress, 1979); Paul D. Hanson, *The Dawn of Apocalyptic* (Philadelphia: Fortress, 1975).

10. See Kuno Füssel, "The Materialist Reading of the Bible," in *The Bible and Liberation*, ed. Norman Gottwald (Maryknoll, N.Y.: Orbis, 1983), 134–46, and more generally, Michel Clevenot, *Materialist Approaches to the Bible* (Maryknoll, N.Y.: Orbis, 1985).

11. Leonard Boff (*Church: Charisma and Power* [New York: Crossroad, 1985], 110–15) has applied these categories to the sacramental life of the church, even as Füssel has applied them to the character of the text.

12. For a critical assessment of this interpretative view as it pertains to biblical interpretation, see John Barton, *Reading the Old Testament: Method in Biblical Study* (Philadelphia: Westminster, 1984).

The nuances of the text are not simply imaginative literary moves but are acts of world making that create and evoke an alternative world available only through this text. The authoritative voices in such a method are Paul Ricoeur and Amos Wilder.[13] In Old Testament studies, among the more effective efforts at analyses of literature as "making worlds" are those of David Gunn, David Clines, and Phyllis Trible.[14]

This literary approach seeks to receive the world offered in the text, even if that world is distant from and incongruent with our own. Thus the text is not a report on a world "out there" but is an offer of another world that is evoked in and precisely by the text. The text "reveals" a world that would not be disclosed apart from this text. This view suggests that the alternative to the world of this text is not an objective world "out there" but is another "evoked world"[15] from another text, albeit a text that may be invisible and unrecognized by us. We are always choosing between texts, and the interpretative act is to see the ways in which the world disclosed in this text is a compelling, "sense-making" world.[16] Literary analysis assumes that the text is not a one-dimensional statement but is an offer of a world that has an interiority, in which the text is not a monolithic voice but is a conversation out of which comes a new world.

When one puts the sociological and literary methods together in a common interpretative act,[17] it is clear that the voices in the text may speak and be heard and interpreted in various ways. Some

---

13. Paul Ricoeur's work is scattered in many places, but see especially *Interpretation Theory* (Fort Worth: Texas Christian Univ. Press, 1976); idem, *The Conflict of Interpretations* (Evanston, Ill.: Northwestern Univ. Press, 1974); idem, *The Philosophy of Paul Ricoeur*, ed. Charles E. Reagan and David Steward (Boston: Beacon, 1978); and *Semeia* 4 (1975). For a most helpful introduction to Amos Wilder's view of literature as world making, see Wilder, "Story and Story-World," *Int* 37 (1983): 353–64.

14. David M. Gunn, *The Fate of King Saul*, JSOTSup 14 (Sheffield: Univ. of Sheffield Press, 1980); idem, *The Story of King David*, JSOTSup 6 (Sheffield: Univ. of Sheffield Press, 1978). See especially David J. A. Clines, *I, He, We and They*, JSOTSup 1 (Sheffield: Univ. of Sheffield Press, 1978). Phyllis Trible, *God and the Rhetoric of Sexuality* (Philadelphia: Fortress, 1978); idem, *Texts of Terror* (Philadelphia: Fortress, 1984).

15. Milton L. Myers (*The Soul of a Modern Economic Man* [Chicago: Univ. of Chicago Press, 1983]) has shown how the work of Hobbes is "the text" for Adam Smith, which in turn has become the text for the capitalist world, even if unacknowledged.

16. On the active power of "sense making" as the production of sense, see David Jobling, *The Sense of Biblical Narrative*, JSOTSup 7 (Sheffield: Univ. of Sheffield Press, 1978), especially 1–3; and Walter Brueggemann, "As the Text 'Makes Sense,'" *The Christian Ministry* 14 (November 1983): 7–10.

17. See my attempt at such a methodological interface in *David's Truth* (Philadelphia: Fortress, 1985).

voices may be shrill and domineering; some may be willingly quiet; some may be silenced and defeated. It is, nonetheless, the entire conversation in the text that discloses an alternative world for us. This Scripture as revelation is not a flat, obvious offer of a conclusion but is an ongoing conversation that evokes, invites, and offers. It is the process of the text itself, in which each interpretative generation participates, that is the truth of revelation. Such an interaction is not a contextless activity, but the context is kept open and freshly available, depending on the social commitments of the interpreter and the sense-making conversations heard in the act of interpretation. In this strange interpretative process, we dare to claim and confess that God's fresh word and new truth are mediated and made available to us.

II

To pursue this matter of "revelation in context," I will address an exceedingly hard text in the Old Testament, Joshua 11. The reason for taking up this text is to deal with the often asked and troublesome question, What shall we do with all the violence and bloody war that are carried out in the Old Testament in the name of Yahweh?[18] The question reflects a sense that these texts of violence are at least an embarrassment, are morally repulsive, and are theologically problematic in the Bible not because they are violent but because this is violence either in the name of or at the hand of Yahweh.

The question we shall consider is: How are these texts of violence to be understood as revelation? What is it that is disclosed and how shall this disclosure be received as serious, authoritative, and binding as the only rule for life and faith? We shall consider the revelatory question in two dimensions. The first is revelation *within* the text. What has drawn me to Joshua 11 is the awareness that within the text as such very little, surprisingly little, is directly assigned to Yahweh as

18. On the general question, see Patrick D. Miller Jr., "God the Warrior," *Int* 19 (1965): 39–46; Paul D. Hanson, "War and Peace in the Hebrew Bible," *Int* 38 (1984): 341–62; Diane Bergant, "Peace in a Universe of Order," in *Biblical and Theological Reflections on "The Challenge of Peace,"* ed. John T. Pawlikowski and Donald Senior (Wilmington, Del.: Michael Glazier, 1984), 17–30; H. Eberhard von Waldow, "The Concept of War in the Old Testament," *HBT* 6 (1984): 27–48. The journals in which the Hanson and von Waldow articles appear have entire issues devoted to the subject of war and peace in the Bible. See also Robert M. Good, "The Just War in Ancient Israel," *JBL* 104 (1985): 385–400.

revelation. So we ask how the characters in this text discerned God's revelation. Second, we shall go on to ask about how *the whole of the text* is taken as revelation, once the text is stabilized for us. It may well be that this distinction will be useful in understanding how this text should be handled in faith communities that celebrate revelation but flinch from violence linked to God. The warrant for violence within the text may yield a very different disclosure when the text is taken by us as a stable revelatory unit. In our text what Joshua and ancient Israel took as revelation may provide a clue for our hearing the text as revelatory. But the two may not be identified or equated.

III

We may begin with a summary of some standard critical observations.[19] The first half of the book of Joshua, chapters 1–12, concerns the conquest of the land done by God, whereas chapters 13–22 concern the division of the land done by Joshua. The book of Joshua is a theological account in which God acts directly as an agent in the narrative. Within chapters 1–12, the specific narrative accounts concern:

Joshua 2 and 6: the conquest of Jericho;

Joshua 3 and 4: the crossing at Gilgal;

Joshua 5: the institution of circumcision;

Joshua 7 and 8:1-29: the crisis of Achan and Ai;

Joshua 8:30-35: the altar at Shechem;

Joshua 9: the subservience of the Gibeonites;

Joshua 10: the taking of the south.

Albrecht Alt has suggested that these narratives conclude with aetiological formulas that show they were originally teaching tales to justify present phenomena. He has observed that these aetiological narratives tend to be located in a narrow geographical range with particular reference to the tribal area of Benjamin.[20]

---

19. For a summary of the critical discussion, see Brevard S. Childs, *Introduction to the Old Testament as Scripture* (Philadelphia: Fortress, 1979), 241–44.

20. Cf. Albrecht Alt, "Josua," in *Werden und Wesen des Alten Testaments*, ed. F. Stummer and J. Hempel, BZAW 66 (Berlin: Töpelmann, 1936) (reprinted in *Kleine Schriften zur Geschichte des Volkes Israel* [Munich: Beck, 1953], 1:176–92).

Joshua 1, 11:16-23, and 12 are more general statements that make more sweeping claims. It seems apparent that chapters 1 and 12 are placed as a theological envelope for the more specific accounts. Chapter 11 tends to move toward a comprehensive summary (vv. 16-23) but focuses on the specific matter of Hazor, the great city of the north (vv. 1-15).[21] Thus it has affinities with the generalizations of 12 but also balances the southern account of 10 with this northern report on Hazor.[22] To the extent that this chapter generalizes, it may also reflect Deuteronomic stylization.

Within chapter 11, we may present an overview of the following elements:

1. In verses 1-5, the king of Hazor takes the initiative in mobilizing many other kings to resist Israel. It is important that in this case it is not Israel who is the aggressor.[23] The inventory of mobilized kings must be a generalized and stylized list. It includes kings of the north, kings of the south, and nations that characteristically occur in the stereotypical Deuteronomic list of seven nations (Deut. 7:1; 20:17). Thus the list is not to be taken as historically literal. What interests us about the list is that it reflects the power of city-states, armed with "many horses and chariots." Following the general analysis of Gottwald,[24] the city-states are to be understood as monopolies of socioeconomic, political power managed in hierarchal and oppressive ways. "Horses and chariots" reflect the strength and monopoly of arms that are necessary and available for the maintenance of the economic and political monopoly.[25]

---

21. We will consider both parts of the chapter in order to attend to the dynamics of the text. In critical analysis, the first part of the chapter is a specific narrative, whereas the latter part is a general theological summary. Literarily the two parts serve very different functions.

22. See Robert G. Boling and G. Ernest Wright (*Joshua*, AB 6 [Garden City, N.Y.: Doubleday, 1982], 303–14) for the notion of a two-stage presentation of the conquest. See the general discussion of Martin Noth, *The Deuteronomistic History*, JSOTSup 15 (Sheffield: Univ. of Sheffield Press, 1981), 36–41.

23. See Boling and Wright, *Joshua*, 303.

24. Norman Gottwald, *The Tribes of Yahweh* (Maryknoll, N.Y.: Orbis, 1979), 389–419. See also George Mendenhall, "The Hebrew Conquest of Palestine," *BA* 3 (1970): 100–120.

25. See Gottwald, *Tribes of Yahweh*, 542–43. Boling and Wright (*Joshua*, 307) suggest only that chariots are "new-fangled," and therefore Israel did not have them. I suggest that such a chronological explanation misses the point of the theological and sociological practice to which Israel is committed.

2. Verses 16-20[26] are a summary that roughly corresponds to the summary of verses 1-5, where we have the list of enemies of Israel. Here (in vv. 16-20) we are told that Joshua defeated all of them.

3. Verses 21-23 are concerned with a special observation about the Anakim who were defeated, except in cities assigned to Philistia. This section, according to Martin Noth, belongs to the Deuteronomistic Historian. It makes a transition to the distribution of land in what follows, and it ends with the standard formula about rest in the land. Thus in verses 1-5 and 16-23 we have sweeping generalizations that frame the chapter, which is built around an older story. There has been a great effort against Israel, but it, with the intervention of Yahweh, has won, even against enormous odds.

4. In verses 6-9, we have the central narrative element of the text, the command of Yahweh (v. 6), the responsive action of Joshua (vv. 7-8), and the concluding formula that Joshua obeyed the command of Yahweh (v. 9). This unit is of particular interest because verse 6 is the only speech of Yahweh in the entire chapter and indeed the only speech from anyone. All the rest is narrative. For our interest in revelation, we may expect that this speech element will be of particular importance.

5. In verses 10-15, we have a battle report concerning the actual conquest of Hazor, whose king made the initial move toward war in verse 1. These verses are of special interest, as Robert Polzin has seen, because of the settlement made on the traditional command of *ḥerem*.[27]

Thus chapter 11 is framed by a general summary (vv. 1-5, 16-23). The latter part of the envelope may not all be of a piece, but it is all summary. Inside the framework are two much more specific statements that concern us, verses 6-9 on command and obedience, and verses 10-15 on the destruction of Hazor and the problem of *ḥerem*. Even though the chapter tends to be handled as a generalizing conclusion, there is little here that is specifically Deuteronomistic. The parts that concern us stand largely free of that influence, except perhaps the formula of obedience in verse 10.

---

26. Boling and Wright (*Joshua*, 316) consider this as belonging to the Deuteronomistic Historian; Noth (*Deuteronomistic History*, 38) refers to a "compiler" and assigns 20b to the Deuteronomistic Historian. For our purposes, such a refinement of literary analysis is neither necessary nor useful.

27. Robert Polzin, *Moses and the Deuteronomist* (New York: Seabury Books), 123–26.

IV

I hope it will be clear that I wish to deal with the sociology of the monarchal period seriously, even if not directly. I understand monarchy in Israel, or among its neighbors, to be a political concentration of power and an economic monopoly of wealth. When monarchy appears in Israel, it comes along with such concentration and monopoly, though of course there are important models available for royal Israel prior to David and Solomon. Such concentrations and monopolies have to be maintained and therefore defended because such monopoly is not welcomed by everyone, especially those who are disadvantaged by it and exploited for it. Interestingly, Gottwald has suggested that the formation of the monarchy (so disputed in 1 Samuel 7–15) is not simply defense against the Philistines, as is a conventional view, but is the necessary and predictable political counterpart of a growing economic surplus and monopoly.[28] That is, the state did not gather the surplus, but the accumulated, disproportionate surplus necessitated the state in order to legitimate, maintain, and protect a surplus that was already partly in hand.

In Joshua 11, we have no Israelite monarchy. But we do have monarchies that in this narrative are antagonistic to Israel. Following the model of Gottwald, I regard "Israel" as an egalitarian, peasant movement hostile to every concentration, surplus, and monopoly. Conversely it follows then that every such city-state as those listed in verses 1-5 would regard Israel as a threat, for Israel practiced a social alternative that must be destroyed. Thus we can read the mobilization of the Hazor king with sociological realism as a conflict between competing social systems.[29] The initiative of the king of Hazor is preemptive.

We may begin our textual analysis by noting the threefold reference to "horses and chariots" in this narrative. First, in verse 4, the military mobilization of city-states is routinely described as "horses and chariots." Israel has none, for horses and chariots are tools of states and empires, necessary and paid for in order to guard the monopoly. That is a given in this ancient society.

---

28. Norman Gottwald, "Social History of the United Monarchy" (paper read to the SBL seminar on "Sociology of the Monarchy," December 20, 1983).

29. Boling and Wright (*Joshua,* 310) come close to such a conclusion when they speak of "the royal families and ruling aristocracies" and then of the "peasants." They have not, in my judgment, pursued far enough the implications of such a social analysis.

In verse 6, "horses and chariots" are mentioned a second time, this time in a statement by Yahweh:

> Do not be afraid of them, for tomorrow at this time I will give over all of them, slain, to Israel; you shall hamstring their horses, and burn their chariots with fire.

This is a remarkably interesting speech.[30] First it is an assurance, "Do not fear." It is as though Yahweh recognizes how dangerous the situation is for Israel—the military contest is a hopeless mismatch. It is an uneven match because the city-states have advanced military technology, and Israel has no access to such technology. The only counter to military technology, according to the narrative, is the powerful liberating voice of Yahweh. Second, as often following "Do not fear," there is a promise of a quite specific kind, introduced by *ki* (for): "tomorrow I am giving them over to you slain."[31] Third, after the promise and the assurance is the command, with the word order inverted, forming a chiasmus with the promise for accent:

> Their horses you will hamstring,
> their chariots you will burn in fire.

This speech (v. 6) is at the center of our interest in revelation, for it is God's only speech in this chapter. This speech, including assurance, promise, and command, is addressed only to Joshua the leader, not the troops as in Deut. 20:2-4. All of the real action in this unit is to be done by Israelites, who are to sabotage and immobilize the imperial weapons of war. Yahweh undertakes no direct action. We should note that in this direct command, the only object of violence is horses and chariots, that is, weapons. There is nothing here about burning cities, killing kings or people, or seizing war booty. Yahweh's is a very lean mandate that addresses the simple, most important issue, the military threat of monarchal power against this alternative community lacking in military technology.

---

30. Edgar W. Conrad ("The 'Fear Not' Oracles in Second Isaiah," *VT* 34 [1984]: 129–52) has greatly contributed to our understanding of this genre of speech. See, more extensively, Edgar W. Conrad, *Fear Not Warrior*, BJS 75 (Chico, Calif.: Scholars Press, 1985). Conrad has shown how the formula may yield either an assurance or a command. In our text, it yields both. Cf. 8–10.

31. On the function and power of the particle *ki*, see James Muilenburg, "The Linguistic and Rhetorical Usages of the Particle *ki* in the Old Testament," in *Hearing and Speaking the Word*, ed. Thomas F. Best (Chico, Calif.: Scholars Press, 1984), 208–33.

We may wonder most about what exactly Yahweh promises to do. After the assurance and the rather nonspecific participle ("I am giving"), Yahweh does nothing and mandates Israel to do the action. Indeed Yahweh does not even promise to do anything beyond a general commitment of solidarity and legitimation. The action is left to Joshua and to Israel.

The third reference to "horses and chariots" (v. 9) reports that Joshua did as commanded and destroyed the military weapons of the military city-states. Thus there are three references to horses and chariots: (1) The city-kings had them (v. 4); (2) Yahweh mandates their destruction (v. 6); and (3) Joshua destroys them as commanded (v. 9).

The first and third references are factual and descriptive, before and after the war. The second, in the mouth of Yahweh, is wondrously unlike the other two. It is the speech of Yahweh. Here the text is not historically descriptive but theologically evocative. The disclosure is that Yahweh gave permission for Joshua and Israel to act for their justice and liberation against an oppressive adversary. This revelatory word of Yahweh, given directly without conduit or process, is only authorization for a liberating movement that is sure to be violent, but only violent against weapons. We do not know by what means this word has been given and received, and the narrative has no interest in that. The best guess is that it was an oracle to an officer, but that is to speculate outside the narrative presentation. But we do know that the disclosure of permit was taken seriously, not doubted, regarded as valid, and acted upon. What is revealed is that Yahweh is allied with the marginalized, oppressed peasants against the monopoly of the city-state. It is not a summons to violence (though its practice might be construed so) but only a permit[32] that Joshua's community is entitled to dream, hope, and

---

32. On the psychology of granting and receiving permission, see Eric Berne (*What Do You Say after You Say Hello?* [New York: Bantam, 1972], 123–25; and idem, *Beyond Games and Scripts* [New York: Ballentine, 1976], 399) for a definition of the term in the context of one theory of therapy. The "granting of permission" can be done by one in authority to authorize another to act in freedom and courage against old patterns of coercion and repression. John Quigley has helped me find these references and has also helped me see the dangerous distortion of the notion in popular usage with reference to ideological autonomy, which gives "permission" to do what one wants. But free of this distortion, I suggest the notion illuminates our passage and the revelatory speech of Yahweh. The Israelites, on any sociological analysis, were disadvantaged and oppressed. The "permit of Yahweh" authorized this community to act by "hamstringing and burning" for the sake of their own social destiny. Without such "permission," they would have continued in their op-

imagine freedom and is entitled to act upon that dream, hope, and imagination.

Now our focal question is to ask, Would the God of the Bible make such a disclosure as a permit for liberation that entailed violence against oppressive weapons and, by inference, against the systems that sanction such weapons?

1. We are bound to say that such a revelatory word is congruent with the fabric of exodus faith, for Yahweh is there presented as a force for justice and liberation against concentrations of oppressive power. Yahweh's commitment is summarized in the slogan, "Let my people go" (Exod. 5:1; 7:16; 8:1, 20; 9:1, 13; 10:3).

2. The disclosure of Yahweh is not intervention but authorization. The claim of the narrative here is exceedingly modest. How indeed is liberation to happen in such a context? Israel, according to this narrative, is not the recipient of a supernatural intervention. If justice and freedom are to come, Yahweh's way is through actual historical agents who act on their own behalf. That is what the text narrates. This rather obvious fact is of exceeding importance for the general interpretative posture taken here.

3. The authorization is of Joshua, his leadership, and his strategy. No one else has access to the disclosure. No one else heard the disclosure. No one else knows what was said. Revelation is linked to authorized communal authority, or, in other categories, the revelation is the property of the agents who hold a monopoly of interpretation.[33]

4. The authorizing disclosure from God coheres with the dreams and yearning of this oppressed community, has credibility only in that community, and cannot be removed from that community for a more general statement. It was Israel's long-standing and courageous dream of an alternative social organization rooted in the memory of Moses that is the material and mode out of which revelation is articulated. Once this community has glimpsed the imaginative possibility of justice it had glimpsed in the exodus, it could not understand itself unauthorized by God's disclosure. The disclosure that authorizes lives very close to the actual experience of the community. That is,

---

pressed, marginalized condition. Such revelatory permission is a counterpart to the "revolutionary impetus" of these narratives.

33. On the monopoly of interpretation and the power and the problems it yields, see Frank Kermode, *The Art of Telling* (Cambridge, Mass.: Harvard Univ. Press, 1983).

revelation is not an act extrinsic to the social process but is an act precisely embedded in the social community.[34]

Instead of suggesting that revelation comes down to intrude in the community, I submit that this revelation rises up out of the hurt and the hope of this community, so that the dream is understood as certified from heaven; and as that dream is certified from heaven, it has enormous credibility in the life of the community on earth. The dream of liberation and justice has credibility theologically because to deny it is to deny everything Israel knows about Yahweh, the Lord of the exodus. The revelatory word has credibility sociologically because the certitude of disclosure is not simply religious certitude but a much more embedded, visceral, existential certitude that would not be denied. Israel knows deep in its own hurt and hope that this permit is God's truth and God's will.

Revelation for this community in the text is the convergence of the old memory of liberation from the exodus,[35] the peasant yearning for liberation and justice,[36] and the formal speech reported by established leadership. All three elements are indispensable. The disclosure cannot be denied because passion for liberating justice cannot be denied Yahweh, who is known in the exodus tradition. The disclosure cannot be denied because the future social possibility is now unleashed in peasant imagination and will not be nullified. The disclosure cannot be denied because the authorization is reported on the lips of the authorized leader, Joshua, who is understood as fulfilling the function of Moses. The outcome is that no monarchal "horses and chariots" are permitted to stand in the way of such a promise from heaven or such a possibility on earth. All three elements, memory, yearning, and leadership, converge in this permit of Yahweh.

The revelatory speech of Yahweh ends this way: "[Y]ou will hamstring their horses, and burn their chariots with fire." When God

---

34. On the doing of theology that is embedded in local community experience, see Robert J. Schreiter, *Constructing Local Theologies* (Maryknoll, N.Y.: Orbis, 1985).

35. There is of course a methodological problem with making old memory a part of revelation: it leaves open the charge of infinite regress. When one finally reaches the event behind which there is no old memory, that event is no doubt a theophany. On the reality of older memory in the faith of Israel, see the proposal of Gottwald, *Tribes of Yahweh*, 483–97 and passim.

36. Methodologically it is the peasant yearning that is the new and decisive ingredient in our understanding. It is this yearning publicly expressed that evokes the old memory in its powerful authority and mobilizes the present leadership also accepted as authoritative.

speaks, we may expect something more respectable, something like, "This is my beloved son," or "three persons and one substance," or "grace alone, Scripture alone, Christ alone." But here it is "hamstring their horses." In a classic essay, H. Richard Niebuhr has seen that revelation is embedded in community.[37] John McKenzie has argued more specifically the same way.[38] Both Niebuhr and McKenzie have seen that revelation and inspiration arise as a certitude given and received in a community. But it is characteristic of that generation of scholarship represented by Niebuhr and McKenzie that the notion of communities of revelation is understood without adequate reference to specific sociological circumstance.[39] That is, if communities mediate revelation from God, surely different communities in different circumstances will mediate different disclosures. The community of the king of Hazor must have mediated God's intent for greater armed security. But to the community of Israel (understood as a community of marginality), which has given us this text we claim as revelatory, what God discloses is a permit or authorization to demobilize such royal arms that are threats to human welfare and specifically to the welfare of this community of marginality. If revelation is mediated through community, revelation will reflect the truth available to that community in its life, memory, and experience, and will tend therefore to be partisan disclosure. I submit that this community of oppressed peasants through which the winds of liberation blow could not mediate any other revelation from God and could not doubt this disclosure. The high God of eternity dwells with the lowly (Isa. 57:15-16). For that reason, the God of these tribes decrees hamstringing horses as one concrete practice of truth. The truth of the disclosure is that it makes life possible for the community.

---

37. H. Richard Niebuhr, *The Meaning of Revelation* (New York: Macmillan, 1962).

38. John L. McKenzie, "The Social Character of Inspiration," *CBQ* 24 (1962): 115-24.

39. The general notion of Niebuhr and McKenzie is inadequate because they did not reckon with the particularity of the community and therefore the particularity of its revelation. Each community operates through a particular rationality. When the socioeconomic particularity of a community is ignored, communities of marginality are likely to be thought of as irrational, so that their claim to have revelation is discredited. This dismissal of marginality as a habitat for revelation operates both sociologically and psychologically. On the latter, see Brian W. Grant (*Schizophrenia: A Source of Social Insight* [Philadelphia: Westminster, 1975]), who considers that the insights of schizophrenics may be revelational, even if an odd rationality that people with "horses and chariots" are likely to misunderstand and dismiss.

Except for Yahweh's permit and mandate in verse 6, all action in the narrative is left to Joshua and Israel. In their obedience to and trust in Yahweh's permit, Joshua and Israel do everything that is needed, while Yahweh does nothing. It is clear that Yahweh in fact does not "act" in this narrative, except in the important sense that the entire event occurs as Yahweh's act.[40] Yahweh made a promise in verse 6: "I will give over." In verse 8 that promise is kept: "And Yahweh gave them into the hand of Israel." We are not told what Yahweh did or how it was done. Evidently Yahweh has authorized and legitimated, and that was enough. Even in verse 20, where the rhetoric is escalated, Yahweh does not act in a concrete way. Thus I suggest that revelation in this narrative is not self-disclosure of God, for nothing new is shown of God, but revelation is the gift of authorization by which Joshua and Israel are legitimated for their own acts of liberation, which from the side of the king of Hazor are perceived as acts of violence. What is "dis-closed" is that the world of the city-kings is not closed. It is the purpose of "horses and chariots" to close that world and so to render the peasants hopeless and helpless.[41] But the world ostensibly controlled by oppressive city-kings is now dis-closed, shown to be false, and broken open to the joy of Israel. The revelatory decree of Yahweh breaks the fixed world of city-kings. What we label as violence on Yahweh's part is a theological permit that sanctions a new social possibility.

That single, simple act of authorization is, religiously speaking, everything. It permits Israel to act. The main verbs of this chapter, therefore, have Israel, not Yahweh, as subject: they fell upon them (v. 7); they smote (vv. 8, 10, 14, 17); and they utterly destroyed (vv. 11, 12, 20, 21).

The word of Yahweh, given only to Joshua, created new historical and social possibilities for Israel, out of which Israel was able to act. The result is the complete transformation of the power situation of the world of Israel, a transformation wrought by the direct and active intervention of Israel, not of Yahweh.

This is not to make a liberal claim that "God has no hands but ours." Yahweh does the one thing needful. Yahweh legitimates

---

40. On the problematic of "act of God," see Gordon D. Kaufman, "On the Meaning of 'Act of God,'" *HTR* 61 (1968): 175–201.

41. See my chapter, "Blessed Are the History-Makers," in *Hope Within History* (Atlanta: John Knox, 1987), 49–71. I have argued that "history making" depends on vulnerability. Those who move from coercive strength are characteristically "history-stoppers" because they want to stop the ongoing conversation about power.

self-assertion on the part of the powerless. The juxtaposition of God's power and human power needs to be nuanced very differently among those with horses and chariots. But this is not their text.

V

The simple sequence of statements on horses and chariots (vv. 4, 6, 9) is unambiguous. Horses and chariots are a threat to the social experiment that is Israel. Horses and chariots are unqualifiedly bad and unalterably condemned. They symbolize and embody oppression. They function only to impose harsh control on some by others. They must be destroyed. Yahweh authorizes their destruction. Joshua and Israel act in obedience to Yahweh's sovereign command and destroy them. Horses and chariots, according to this narrative, have no positive, useful purpose in the world of ancient Israel, for they serve only to maintain the status quo in which some dominate others. Israel as a liberated community of the exodus has no need for such a mode of social power.[42] Moreover, Yahweh is the sworn enemy of such modes of power.

Israel's sense of cattle, in this narrative and generally, is very different. Cattle are never instruments of war or oppression. They may be a measure of affluence (Gen. 32:15; Jon. 4:11), but they only serve as meat and milk, for domestic and communal well-being. Because they are not symbols of domination and oppression as are horses and chariots, a simple social analysis of cattle is not adequate. In his close reading of Joshua 11, Polzin has discerned a certain playful ambiguity in the narrative concerning cattle and their disposition, an ambiguity that Israel does not have about horses and chariots.[43] Because cattle are not sociologically unambiguous for Israel as are horses and chariots, Israel's sense of Yahweh's will concerning cattle also is not unambiguous. Horses are clearly for domination. But cattle may be either seductive or sustaining, and so Yahweh's will for their treatment requires more careful, nuanced attention.

We have seen that verse 6 gives an unambiguous command on horses and chariots. They are to be destroyed. Concerning cattle and

---

42. It is interesting that horses are never listed in the stylized catalogues of blessings bestowed by God (cf. Job 42:12-16; Deut. 11:15; 28:4; Josh. 1:14; 2 Kings 3:17). Whereas cattle belong in such a list, horses regularly are treated as an imposition upon a community by an occupying force, not as a gift to be treasured in the community. Horses are characteristically threats, not prizes or treasures.

43. Polzin, *Moses*, 113-24.

other spoil, however, the narrative departs from the command of verse 6 in two contrasting directions.

1. A total and massive destruction is commanded, a *harsher* destruction than that authorized in verse 6: (*a*) *Herem*, the ban, is practiced, "as Moses the servant of the Lord had commanded" (v. 12). (*b*) Cattle are taken as spoil, but every man is smote: "[A]s the Lord had commanded Moses his servant, so Moses commanded Joshua, so Joshua did; he left nothing undone of all that the Lord had commanded Moses" (v. 15). (*c*) *Herem* is practiced again: "It was the Lord's doing to harden their hearts that they should come against Israel in battle, in order that they should be utterly destroyed, and should receive no mercy but be exterminated, as the Lord commanded Moses" (v. 20). (*d*) The whole land is seized: "So Joshua took the whole land, according to all that the Lord had spoken to Moses,...and the land had rest" (v. 23).

Two things are striking about these statements. First, they are not the direct speech of Yahweh, in contrast to verse 6, but are attributed to Moses in a former generation. Yahweh speaks directly about horses and chariots but only indirectly through Moses about cattle and spoil. The command (and therefore the revelation) is remembered revelation:

> As Moses had commanded... (v. 12)
> So Moses commanded Joshua... (v. 15)
> Yahweh commanded Moses. (v. 20)
> The Lord had spoken to Moses. (v. 23)

Because the revelation is an unspecified reference to older torah, the community of necessity must interpret. Which older torah teaching is invoked is not self-evident, nor exactly how it applies to this situation. This means that with regard to cattle and spoil, there is room for speculation, maneuverability, and alternative decisions.

Second, these mandates, which are attributed to Yahweh through the memory of Moses, are exceedingly harsh, not as disciplined, specific, and restrained as the command of verse 6:

> to utterly destroy... (v. 12)
> not to leave any that breathed... (v. 14)
> utterly destroyed, no mercy, exterminated... (v. 20)
> take the whole land... (v. 23)

In each case an old textual warrant (presumably Deut. 20:15-18) is claimed as authorization for the present destruction. That old textual warrant is remembered and presented as uncompromisingly harsh.

2. But in Joshua 11, as Polzin has observed, the command regarding other spoil is also *more lenient* than the mandate regarding horses and chariots. The command of verse 6 is harsh. But as the narrative develops and horses and chariots are to be destroyed, cattle may be taken and saved as booty (Josh. 11:14). It is curious that in the very text that urges that "nothing be left breathing," cattle are exempted. The enactment of God's mandate is contextualized by Israel.

The harsh remembered demand of Moses and the permit of Moses to take spoil (cf. Deut. 20:14) both depart from verse 6, the former in a more demanding direction, the latter in a more lenient direction.

Both the harshness and the leniency are based on the old torah memory of Deuteronomy, in 20:10-14 and 20:15-18 respectively. Based on the old torah memory, in the name of Moses our narrative practices both extermination and spoil, both radical rejection of booty and economic prudence, both obedient destruction and self-serving confiscation. Both are warranted by the torah teaching of Deuteronomy 20, a polarity Polzin has not allowed.

I take verse 6, Yahweh's only direct speech in Joshua 11, as the normative revelation within the text. It mandates destruction of a quite specific kind in order to give liberated Israel room to exist. It sanctions neither more nor less than this. In two ways the narrative around verse 6 departs from this normative mandate. On the one hand, in verses 7-8 Israel did *much more* than is authorized: "Israel fell,... smote,... pursued,... smote,... until they left none remaining." They killed people and destroyed cities, surely not decreed by Yahweh in verse 6. On the other hand, one may say they did *less*, for they took cattle as booty, also not authorized by verse 6. One might construe verse 6 as a directive to immobilize anything held by the hostile city-states, but that is not subsequently understood to include cattle.

The narrative of Joshua 11 thus may be sorted out at three levels:

1. Theologically, there is a distinction between what is to be exterminated and what is to be kept as spoil, even though the decree of verse 6 authorizes neither spoil nor extermination. Both extermination and spoil are warranted in the torah tradition of Deuteronomy 20, spoil in verses 10-14 and extermination in verses 15-17.[44]

---

44. On the criticism of this text, see Alexander Rofé, "The Laws of Warfare in the Book of Deuteronomy," *JSOT* 32 (1985): 28–39.

2. Sociologically, there is a distinction between horses (and chariots) and cattle (and other spoil). Horses and cattle symbolize very different things and perform very different social functions. Horses function to dominate because they are a means of military power. Cattle function to sustain by providing meat and milk. Horses can never provide sustenance. Cattle can never aid in oppression.

3. Methodologically, there is a distinction between sociological and literary analysis. On the one hand, I have used only sociological methods to ask what horse and chariot symbolize and what social functions they perform and why Yahweh wills their immobilization. To ask a question of the social symbolization and function of horse and chariot leads to something like a "class reading" of the matter, for clearly horse and chariot are tools of domination.

On the other hand (following Polzin), reference to cattle and spoil has evoked subtle literary questions because we are able to see how the tradition struggles with the tension of spoil and extermination, how cattle require a more subtle sorting out than does the socially unambiguous reality of horses. We are able to see that the revelatory operation within the narrative is indeed subtle and requires careful differentiations. Thus horses as tool and symbol of domination permit a clear, unambiguous announcement of God's will. Cattle, which may be a means of seduction (Deut. 20:15-18) or a means of sustenance (Deut. 20:14-15), require a more delicate articulation of God's will. It will not do simply to ask about "all that violence" because the situation of the text is much more complicated than that. The warrant for violence is grounded in verse 6. One may imagine that Israel took that limited, disciplined warrant of Yahweh and went well beyond its intent or substance in its action, out of rage and oppression.[45] The action against the horses is based on a revelatory permit for liberation. The sanction for keeping cattle looks to the future just community that will replace the oppressive city-states.

What we have, then, is revelation in context. The popular way of putting the question is, Would the God of the Bible mandate such violence? But the question must be posed in context. Of the remembered revelation rooted in the memory of Moses, the answer is yes, in the interest of Israel's survival as a holy people (Deut. 7:6). Of

---

45. On the sociology and power of rage in situations of oppression, see Frank A. Spina, "The Concept of Social Rage in the Old Testament and the Ancient Near East" (Ph.D. diss., University of Michigan, 1977).

the immediate revelation, the answer is yes, as a means of eliminating implements of domination. But I do not want to evade our governing question. Does God mandate violence? Properly contextualized, this narrative answers yes, but of a specific kind, tightly circumscribed, in the interest of a serious social experiment, in the interest of ending domination. The revelation is not really act, but warrant or permit. The narrative requires us to conclude that this community was utterly persuaded that the God of the tradition is passionately against domination and is passionately for an egalitarian community.

It is futile to try to talk such a community of the oppressed out of such a theological conviction. Its certitude does not arise out of religious rumination but out of the visceral sense of pain and oppression that is the stuff of history. This community of Israel, however we articulate its sociology of marginality, knows deep in its bones that God did not intend long-term subservience. Perhaps that conviction came by the bearers of the news of the exodus,[46] but I suggest it came in their particular context of oppression. The conviction of God's disclosure is linked to that context. Its actual implementation of extermination, hamstringing, and taking spoil is also given in the matrix of social practice, not apart from it. Questions about violence authorized by God must be kept very close to the visceral hurt and hope of such communities of marginality. It is remarkable that the judgment and certitude of such a community have been received by us as canonical, but they have indeed been so received.

The matter of revelation inside the narrative finally requires comment on verse 20:

> It was the Lord's doing to harden their hearts that they should come against Israel in battle, in order that they should be utterly destroyed, and should receive no mercy but be exterminated, as the Lord commanded Moses.

The second half of the verse is controlled by two uses of *lema 'an:*

> in order that they should come against Israel . . .
> in order that they should be utterly destroyed . . .

---

46. Gottwald (*Tribes of Yahweh,* 490–96) identifies the Levites as the revolutionary cadre who carry this news of the liberation of Yahweh. Mendenhall, in more "realistic" fashion, urged that the news of exodus was carried specifically by Joshua and Caleb.

But the intriguing statement is, "It was the Lord's doing to harden their hearts."[47] What I find interesting about this statement is the question of knowledge: How did Israel know this? How did Israel decide Yahweh did it? The statement does not claim Yahweh was in the battle but only that Yahweh worked to convene the battle so that there would be a victory. This is a marvelously elusive theological formula to juxtapose to the concreteness of verse 6. God is not immediately involved in any direct way, but Israel knows that governance is finally in Yahweh's hands as was the case in the remembered exodus (Exod. 4:21; 7:3; 9:12; 10:1). The conclusion drawn in verse 20 asserts the majestic, irresistible sovereignty of Yahweh. But that grand claim of sovereignty finally rests on the concreteness of verse 6. Without the concreteness of verse 6, the claim of verse 20 is without substance.

VI

Now we may turn to the second question of revelation, the disclosure given by the narrative as narrative, not to its own participants but to us who now stand outside the narrative, take it as canonical, and heed it as revelatory. A good test is to ask, What would we know of the ways and character of God if we had only this particular rendering, or what would be lost if we did not have this text?

I have proposed that Yahweh's command in verse 6 is theologically normative. It is not as harsh as general extermination. It is not as lenient as taking spoil. This theologically normative disclosure concerns Yahweh's hostility to horses and chariots as monarchal instruments of domination.[48] These instruments of domination (1) require advanced technology, (2) require surplus wealth to finance and maintain, and (3) serve a political, economic monopoly dependent on oppression and subservience. We have ample evidence to suggest the social function of horses and chariots for kings. In the inventory of Solomon's affluence and security, he is said to have

---

47. On the problematic of this theological theme, see Gerhard von Rad, *Old Testament Theology* (New York: Harper and Row, 1965), 2:151–55, and Brevard S. Childs, *The Book of Exodus* (Philadelphia: Westminster, 1974), 170–75.

48. Boling and Wright (*Joshua*, 307) conclude: "Such military efficiency reflects a feudal system in which the charioteers, or *maryanu*, belong to a class enjoying special privileges and performing special services for the king." Gottwald (*Tribes of Yahweh*, 543) writes: "Hamstringing horses and burning chariots were defensive measures against the hated and feared superior weaponry of the enemy."

forty thousands stalls of horses for his chariots and twelve thousand horsemen (1 Kings 4:26). In 10:26, it is reported, "Solomon gathered together chariots and horsemen; he had fourteen hundred chariots and twelve thousand horsemen," partly for trade, but mostly for defense and intimidation.[49] The Bible characteristically associates horses and chariots with royal power, which is regularly seen to be oppressive (cf. Exod. 14:9, 23; Deut. 20:1; 2 Sam. 15:1; 1 Kings 18:5; 22:4; 2 Kings 3:7; 18:23; 23:11).

Yahweh's hostility to horses and chariots bespeaks Yahweh's hostility to the social system that requires, legitimates, and depends upon them. Israel, in its early period of tribal-peasant life, did not have horses and chariots and greatly feared them. The struggle reflected in Joshua 11 is how this community, so vulnerable and helpless, can exist and function against the kings and their powerful tools of domination.

In light of the inventory of the royal use of horses and chariots, we now consider an alternative set of texts—expressed in a very different mode—that present a critical view of horses and chariots. These narrative accounts are in a sense expository comments on the sanction of Josh. 11:6.

The Bible is not content simply to describe the royal status quo that seems beyond challenge. The Bible also offers takes of liberation that show Israel challenging, countering, and overcoming this formidable royal power. The narrative form lends itself to the articulation of another kind of power the royal world neither knows nor credits.[50] The narrative mode challenges royal rationality even as the narrative substance challenges royal policy.

1. In 1 Kings 20, Israel is ranged against Syria in an uneven contest. The Syrians, a prototype of military power, are sure of their strength:

And the servants of the king of Syria said to him, "Their gods are gods of the hills, and so they were stronger than we; but let us

---

49. Clearly Solomon's monarchy embodies much that repelled the Israel of Moses and Joshua. See George Mendenhall, "The Monarchy," *Int* 29 (1975): 155–70.

50. The different sociology of these texts needs to be correlated with the different mode of literary expression in which it is reported. Thus the positive assertion of royal power is characteristically reported in lists, inventories, and memos. By contrast, the alternative power of Yahweh does not come articulated in such controlled modes of expression, but in narratives of a playful kind that allow for surprise and inscrutability. The modes of power are matched to ways of speech and to the different epistemologies and rationalities practiced by the speech forms.

fight against them in the plain, and surely we shall be stronger than they.... [M]uster an army like the army that you have lost, horse for horse, and chariot for chariot; then we will fight against them in the plain, and surely we shall be stronger than they." (20:23-25)

The Israelites, in their own narrative presentation, are helpless by contrast:

> The people of Israel encamped before them like two little flocks of goats, but the Syrians filled the country. (v. 27)

The narrative makes the disproportion of royal power clear. That in turn makes the victory of Yahweh all the more dramatic:

> Because the Syrians have said, "The Lord is a god of the hills but he is not a god of the valleys," therefore I will give all this great multitude into your hand, and you shall know that I am the Lord. (v. 28)

The episode concludes with a great victory. Israel's God and Israel's narrators are undaunted by the odds of royal horses and chariots. They are undaunted because there is another power that overwhelms and overrides the royal establishment and gives victory to these seemingly helpless peasants. Notice that at the crucial point of the narrative where we would want specificity, we are told nothing.[51] At the point where we would like to know how Yahweh defeated the Syrian horses and chariots, the narrative is opaque. We are not told. It is enough to receive the surprising news that is against the data. It is enough to know that Yahweh triumphs over the Syrian gods, and therefore Israel triumphs over Syria, and therefore faith triumphs over horses and chariots.

2. A second narrative that offers a critique of horses and chariots again concerns Syria, Israel, and Elisha (2 Kings 6:15-19). Syria discerns that Elisha is the main threat and sends "horses and chariots and a great army" to seize him (2 Kings 6:14). Israel's prophet is in great danger and seemingly defenseless. But the narrative focuses on the faith of Elisha and the power of Yahweh. First, Elisha issues a formal assurance: "Fear not, for those who are with us are

---

51. The formula "I will give" is characteristically the way of victory, as we have seen it also in Josh. 11:6. On the formula, see the comment of Gerhard von Rad, *Der Heilige Krieg im alten Israel* (Göttingen: Vandenhoeck und Ruprecht, 1958), 7. The phrase promises everything but tells nothing.

more than those who are with them" (v. 16).[52] Second, Elisha prays that frightened Israel, embodied in his servant, may see (v. 17). And third, in answer to the prayer, Yahweh causes the young man to see, "And behold, the mountain was full of horses and chariots of fire round about Elisha" (v. 17). Again the narrative is elliptical just at the place where we would like to know more. It is enough for our purposes, however, to see that through the prophetic person, the power of prayer, and the courage of faith, Yahweh's powerful sovereignty is present in horses and chariots that effectively counter the Syrians (v. 17).

3. In a different episode of this same extended narrative, the motif of Yahweh's defeat of horses and chariots recurs (2 Kings 7:3-8). Four lepers enter the camp of the Syrians, but the Syrians had all fled. Persons as socially irrelevant as lepers can safely enter the Syrian stronghold.

The narrative explanation for the flight of the Syrians is this:

> For the Lord had made the army of the Syrians hear the sound of chariots, and of horses, the sound of a great army, so that they said to one another, "Behold, the king of Israel has hired against us the kings of the Hittites and the kings of Egypt to come upon us." So they fled away in the twilight and forsook their tents, their horses, and their asses, leaving the camp as it was, and fled for their lives. (2 Kings 7:6-7)

The narrative continues, saying that the lepers seized spoil of silver, gold, and clothing (v. 8).[53] Again a victory is inscrutably won by Yahweh against the great odds of the military power of a foreign state. The mode of the victory is comic, whimsical, or hidden. But it is decisive. The Israelites had not hired allies as Syria suspected (v. 6). Israel did not need allies other than Yahweh. The narrator understands this perfectly, but the marching Syrians have no access to the reality evoked by this narrative. The narrative thus delegitimates the rationality of Syrian royal power.

The outcome of all three narratives in 1 Kings 20, 2 Kings 6, and 2 Kings 7 is that Yahweh is shown to be stronger than the military state and is its sworn enemy on behalf of Yahweh's own people.

---

52. The formula is the same as in Josh. 11:6.
53. The seizure of spoil from the strong ones now defeated by Yahweh is parallel to Joshua 11.

Generation after generation, the strange turn of the exodus is reenacted with new characters, but each time on behalf of helpless Israel. The narratives do not tell us all we would like to know about the course of the battles. But they tell us all Israel needs to know about Yahweh, which is that Yahweh is faithful, sovereign, and will not be mocked. The mode of the power of Yahweh is prophetic speech. The prophets mobilize that power against the state. The states may have asked cynically, "How many legions does Elisha have?" But against such cynicism toward Yahweh, the narrative answers, "Enough." It is not royal horses and chariots but the power of Yahweh that ultimately shapes the outcome of the historical process. Clearly we are dealing here with a very different rationality, a rationality that refuses to accommodate royal reason. The narratives have no great attraction to violence, but they also are not embarrassed by what is necessary for survival and well-being.

4. In one other narrative we note the cynicism of the Assyrians who mock Israelite weakness by an offer of two thousand horses if Israel has riders to mount, which obviously Israel does not (2 Kings 18:24). The imperial speaker taunts Israel for depending on Egyptian horses and chariots. But the taunt is defeated, for Yahweh takes the challenge and overcomes the Assyrian threat.

In all these liberation narratives, royal monopoly of power is countered. It is countered by the prophetic oracle that discloses unseen and unrecognized horses and chariots (2 Kings 6:16-17). It is countered in 2 Kings 7:6 by the sound of horses and chariots, created by Yahweh. It is countered in 1 Kings 20:28 when Yahweh hands over the Syrians. It is countered by the powerful angel of Yahweh (2 Kings 19:35). In all these texts, the narrative reveals Yahweh's power that inscrutably and effectively counters hostile, oppressive royal power. The narrative shows Syrian horses and chariots not to be as powerful as was assumed. Israel and the Syrians are permitted to see what they had not seen. And for us, the narrative asserts the reality of Yahweh in modes for which we are not prepared.

In our consideration of revelation and violence, we have juxtaposed two contrasting kinds of material. On the one hand, we have mentioned rather flat, descriptive accounts of royal power (Exod. 14:9, 23; Deut. 20:1; 2 Sam. 15:1; 1 Kings 18:5; 22:4; 2 Kings 3:7; 18:23; 23:11). These texts read like official memos and sound in their rendering like the cool, detached reasoning of technique, as perhaps in the congressional testimony of a secretary of defense in which everything is obvious, acceptable, reasonable, taken for granted and not to be questioned. Such a mode of evidence is hardly revelatory, for it discloses nothing. It only states once again the already known.

By contrast the narratives we have considered disclose what was not known. The narrative of 1 Kings 20:26-30 shows Israel, which seemed to be "like two little flocks of goats," to be powered by Yahweh's response to the mocking and therefore available for a victory. In 2 Kings 6:16-17, reality is evoked by a prophetic oracle of "fear not," which ends in an unexpected vision of horses and chariots of Yahweh, who seemed to have none. In 2 Kings 7:6, it is the very sound of horses and chariots that frightened the Syrians. In 2 Kings 19:35, an angel of Yahweh repels the imperial army. All four stories offer a different mode of presentation, a different epistemology, and a different universe of discourse. This is narrative art that invites to bold, imaginative faith a community that is short on royal technique. But this community is not without its own peculiar rationality that believes that the world is ordered, governed, and powered by an authority to which kings do not have access and over which they cannot prevail.

The narratives reveal that faithful imagination is more powerful than dominating technique. The narratives offer a convergence of: (*a*) narrative primitivism, which is obligated to explain nothing; (*b*) sociological marginality, which cannot rely on human resources; (*c*) epistemological naïveté, which refuses royal modes of certitude; and (*d*) theological amazement, which is innocent and desperate enough to believe, and is not disappointed.

These factors together in the four narratives of 1 Kings 20:26-30; 2 Kings 6:16-17; 2 Kings 7:6; and 2 Kings 18:19—19:37 are indeed revelatory. They disclose what had not been seen. They make known what had not been known. And when this alternative is known and seen, the sure, managed world of royal technique and certitude is stunningly dismantled. The rulers of this age are marvelously put to flight. Israel's life is rendered in these narratives in an alternative rationality that has power, substance, and reality, all rooted in and derived from this subversive disclosure of Yahweh.

Yahweh's inscrutable competence against royal horses and chariots is echoed in the odd prayer and teaching of Jesus:

> "I thank thee, Father, Lord of heaven and earth, that thou hast hidden these things from the wise and understanding and revealed them to babes; yea, Father, for such was thy gracious will...."

> Then turning to the disciples he said privately, "Blessed are the eyes which see what you see! For I tell you that many prophets and kings desired to see what you see, and did not see it, and to hear what you hear, and did not hear it." (Luke 10:21-24)[54]

What is hidden from the kings is disclosed to the prophets in Israel. They see and know another kind of power.

We have, first, observed texts that, in a descriptive way, document the inventory of royal chariots. These texts we take either as actual, factual reports or as polemics against royal power. Second, we have observed texts that tell tales of alternative forms of power that triumph over royal instruments of domination. The contrast between the descriptions of royal domination and narratives of alternative forms of power reflects Israel's alternative reading of the historical process. The mode of expression that contrasts flat description and imaginative narrative corresponds to the modes of power that may be discerned in the historical process. In ancient Israel, the imaginative narrative is characteristically stronger than the descriptive memo. The narrative more nearly articulates the decisive direction of the historical process. That is, the mode of discourse correlates with ways of reality and modes of power. How Israel speaks is related to what Israel trusts in and hopes for.[55]

That contrast between descriptive inventory and imaginative narrative leads to a warning that Israel should not imitate or be seduced by such royal modes of power (cf. Deut. 17:14-20)[56] or royal modes of communication.[57] If Israel imitates the nations or is seduced by their power or their gods, Israel will also become an agent of domination.[58] Israel knows it is not to emulate royal modes of power,

---

54. On the peculiar character of this saying, see M. Jack Suggs, *Wisdom, Christology and Law in St. Matthew's Gospel* (Cambridge, Mass.: Harvard Univ. Press, 1970).

55. Gail O'Day ("Irony and the Johannine Theology of Revelation" [Ph.D. diss., Emory University, 1983]) has shown that the *Wie* (how) of presentation is as important as *Dass* (that) and *Was* (what) for understanding this literature as revelatory.

56. The basis of *ḥerem* is not that Israel should not possess, but that Israel should not be seduced. I am not sure if Polzin has recognized this difference.

57. On the seduction of royal modes of communication, the substantive issues are the loss of narrative, embarrassment over storytelling, and the recasting of reality into technical modes of communication. On this general seduction and its social outcome, see Hans Frei, *The Eclipse of Biblical Narrative* (New Haven: Yale Univ. Press, 1974).

58. The seductive economics of Solomon goes along with the changed modes of communication. It is telling that we have no narratives of Solomon in the sense that we have them about David. One may say that Solomon got horses and chariots and

knowledge, or language. Israel also knows that alternative modes of power, knowledge, and language are available that permit freedom and justice.

VII

Our study has considered in turn, (1) descriptive inventories of royal domination through horses and chariots; (2) imaginative narratives of alternative power concerning Yahweh's power against horses and chariots; and (3) prohibition against imitation and seduction by such horses and chariots.

Israel developed an important and sustained theological tradition that affirmed that the power of Yahweh is stronger than the royal power of horses and chariots. In all parts of the biblical tradition, it is affirmed that the power of Yahweh will defeat oppressive kings who have horses and chariots. The "power of Yahweh" is not exposited in detail. Obviously the power of Yahweh belongs to a very different, nonroyal rationality, but the tradition does not doubt that the power is effective in actual, concrete historical interactions.[59]

The motif of Yahweh's triumph over horses and chariots may be found in three kinds of texts that range over the entire Old Testament literature.

1. Prophetic texts assert the liberating power of God over against royal domination:

(a) I will have pity on the house of Judah, and I will deliver them by the Lord their God; I will not deliver them by bow, nor by sword, nor by war, nor by horses, nor by horsemen. (Hos. 1:7)[60]

(b) Woe to those who go down to Egypt for help,
      who rely on horses,
   who trust in chariots because they are many
      and in horsemen because they are very strong,

---

lost narrative. I suggest we will not understand what is at issue in our present society of militarism until we see the connection between modes of power and modes of speech.

59. On the power of Yahweh articulated as "the hand of Yahweh," see Patrick D. Miller Jr. and J. J. M. Roberts, *The Hand of the Lord* (Baltimore: Johns Hopkins Univ. Press, 1977).

60. On this verse, see Hans Walter Wolff, *Hosea*, Hermeneia (Philadelphia: Fortress, 1974), 20–21.

but do not look to the Holy One of Israel
   or consult the Lord!
   (Isa. 31:1; cf. v. 3 and 30:15-16)[61]

(c) And in that day, says the Lord,
   I will cut off your horses from among you
   and will destroy your chariots.
   (Mic. 5:10)[62]

The text of Micah goes on to speak of destroying cities, sorceries, and images and then states:

And in anger and wrath I will execute vengeance
   upon the nations that did not obey.
   (Mic. 5:15)

(d) Thus says the Lord,
      who makes a way in the sea,
      a path in the mighty waters,
   who brings forth chariot and horse,
      army and warrior;
   they lie down, they cannot rise,
      they are extinguished, quenched like a wick.
   (Isa. 43:16-17)

This reference alludes to the exodus and is followed by the remarkable assertion, "Behold, I am doing a new thing"—that is, Yahweh is crushing the horses and chariots of Babylon and so permitting exiled Israel to go home.

(e) This is the word of the Lord to Zerubbabel: Not by might, nor by power, but by my Spirit, says the Lord of hosts. (Zech. 4:6)

To be sure, in this well-known text, horses and chariots are not mentioned, but I consider this statement to be an extension of the

---

61. On the issue of faith in Isaiah, see von Rad, *Old Testament Theology*, 2:158–69. An investigation of the term *baṭaḥ* (trust) in the tradition of Isaiah would be worth pursuing.

62. One can understand the polemic of the Micah tradition if one accepts the sociological analysis of Wolff that Micah is the voice of the small rural landowner always resistant to imperial impingement. See Hans Walter Wolff, "Micah the More-shite—The Prophet and his Background," in *Israelite Wisdom*, ed. John G. Gammie, (Missoula, Mont.: Scholars Press, 1978), 77–84. Delbert Hillers (*Micah*, Hermeneia [Philadelphia: Fortress, 1984], 72–74) interprets Micah's oracle as a renunciation of all that destroys Israel's true identity.

same trajectory. Yahweh's opposition to royal, military power is in this text couched in apocalyptic language. But the claim of Yahweh's governance is the same. Prophetic faith sets the inscrutable power of Yahweh over against the pretensions of state power. This paradigmatic antithesis is acted out already in the exodus narrative.[63]

2. In the Psalms, the motif of horses and chariots is articulated:

(*a*) Some boast of chariots, some of horses,
       but we boast in the name of the Lord our God.
       (Ps. 20:7)

In this royal psalm, the contrast between conventional royal power and the power of Yahweh is total. The verb "boast" here is a rendering of *zākar*[64] and so should not be overinterpreted. But the conventional rendering "boast" suggests a proximity to Jer. 9:22-23 (which in turn is quoted in 1 Cor. 1:31).[65]

(*b*) A king is not saved by his great army;
       a warrior is not delivered by his great strength.
       The war horse is a vain hope for victory,
       and by its great strength it cannot save. (Ps. 33:16-17)

(*c*) At thy rebuke, O God of Jacob,
       both rider and horse lay stunned.
       But thou, terrible art thou! (Ps. 76:6-7)

(*d*) His delight is not in the strength of the horse,
       nor is his pleasure in the legs of a man;
       but the Lord takes pleasure[66] in those who fear him,
       in those who hope in his steadfast love. (Ps. 147:10-11)

3. The question of what constitutes power also appears in Proverbs:

---

63. The contrast between the power of Yahweh and the pretensions of state power is nicely drawn in 1 Sam. 17:45 and the encompassing narrative. See my discussion in *David's Truth*, in that I have drawn attention to the epistemology of the tribe that is articulated to claim a zone of freedom against a hostile state.

64. The use of the term *zākar* here is peculiar. Its conventional rendering as "boast" is surely correct, but perhaps it also linked the present doxology to concrete memories of the triumphs of Yahweh in the past, which were won against great odds. It is the memory that permits the doxology.

65. The verb in Jer. 9:22-23 is *hithallēl*. On the text from Jeremiah, see Walter Brueggemann, "The Epistemological Crisis of Israel's Two Histories (Jer. 9:22-23)," in *Israelite Wisdom*, 85-105 (reprinted in *Old Testament Theology: Essays in Structure, Theme, and Text* [Minneapolis: Fortress, 1992], 270-95).

66. The verb *ḥāpaṣ* used here is the same as in Jer. 9:23.

> No wisdom, no understanding, no counsel,
>   can avail against the Lord.
> The horse is made ready for the day of battle,
>   but victory belongs to the Lord. (Prov. 21:30-31)

Gerhard von Rad has identified this text along with five others that articulate the hidden, inscrutable ways of Yahweh's governance that challenge all human self-security, whether by way of knowledge, power, planning, or ingenuity.[67]

In all these texts, prophetic assertions (Hos. 1:7; Isa. 31:1; 43:15-17; Mic. 5:10; Zech. 4:6), psalmic doxologies (Pss. 20:7; 33:16-17; 76:6-7; 147:10-11), and sapiential discernment (Prov. 21:30-31), we have eloquent and unproblematic theological statements. In the texts, the difficult issue of Yahweh's involvement in violence is not visible. Yet all these texts are rooted in and derived from the much more primitive statement of Josh. 11:6: "[H]amstring the horses, and burn the chariots." The other, more removed, statements depend on the concreteness of such a warrant. Yahweh's sovereignty over horses and chariots is made visible in that concrete action Yahweh authorizes.

VIII

The theological outcome of Joshua 11 concerns the will and capacity of Yahweh to overturn the present historical arrangements of society that are judged to be inequitable and against the purposes of Yahweh. Yahweh is here revealed as the true governor of the historical-political process, armed alternatives notwithstanding. At the beginning of the narrative, Israel is assaulted by superior force (v. 1). But by word (v. 6) and by inscrutable, hidden intervention (v. 20), Israel receives its inheritance and rest according to God's promise (v. 23). Yahweh is disclosed as a God who keeps promises within the historical arena. The narrative is a tale of a transformation from domination to inheritance wrought by Yahweh's sovereign will through Israel's bold obedience.

Two texts may be cited that marvelously articulate this strange narrative faith that creates social possibility against a new might. First, at the decisive pause in the land narrative, this encounter takes

---

67. Gerhard von Rad, *Old Testament Theology* (New York: Harper and Row, 1962), 1:438-41; idem, *Wisdom in Israel* (Nashville: Abingdon, 1972), 97–110.

316 A Social Reading of the Old Testament

place. The tribes of Ephraim and Manasseh articulate their weakness in the face of Canaanite chariots:

> The hill country is not enough for us; yet all the Canaanites who dwell in the plain have chariots of iron, both those in Bethshean and its villages and those in the Valley of Jezreel. (Josh. 17:16)

Joshua, man of faith, responds with an assurance:

> Then Joshua said to the house of Joseph, to Ephraim and Manasseh, "You are a numerous people, and have great power; you shall not have one lot only, but the hill country shall be yours, for though it is a forest, you shall clear it and possess it to its farthest borders; you shall drive out the Canaanites, though they have chariots of iron, and though they are strong." (vv. 17-18)

It is this summons to faith that makes the difference. The voice of hope is the great equalizer in the historical process.

Second, at the deathbed scene of Elisha (who had considerable experience against horses and chariots), King Joash grieves because he knows that without this prophetic voice of hope he is hopeless and helpless. The king laments:

> My father, my father! The chariots of Israel and its horsemen! (2 Kings 13:14; cf. 2:12)

The king acknowledges that the prophetic figure of Elisha is Israel's mode of power in the world, the only resource this community has in a world of harsh power.

I conclude with four comments:

1. The fundamental claim of Joshua 11 is that Yahweh is disclosed as a God who will invert the historical process and give land to the landless. That claim, so far as the tradition is concerned, is beyond dispute. The command against horses and chariots looks back to the defeat of pharaoh in Exod. 14:6-7, 23 (cf. Exod. 15:1, 21) and of Sisera (Judg. 4:3, 7, 13-16)[68] and forward to the defeat of Babylon (Isa. 43:16-21), all texts concerning horses and chariots and

---

68. Gottwald has established a model of interpretation that takes Moses and Joshua together. He has treated the Egyptian empire and the Canaanite city-state as continuous and as metaphors of oppression. In Josh. 4:23, it is evident that the cultic tradition labored to establish the same equation.

imperial power. The troublesome part is that Yahweh's transforming governance takes place in such concrete, human ways as hamstringing and burning. Everything hinges on this warrant for action; the faithful act of obedience, so featured in Joshua 11, is response to the permit of Yahweh. In Biblical faith the great gift of deliverance comes in historical concreteness.

2. For the people in the text, we ask, Is this really revelation? Does God say such things as in Josh. 11:6? When the permit of Yahweh is embedded in this community of marginality, when revelation is taken as the community's sense of its future with God, this is indeed a disclosure, for it must be so if this community is to have a genuine historical future. None in the community doubted either that God willed such a future or that the future came at great risk.

3. If revelation is to be always embedded in context, then we must see if this narrative of Joshua is disclosure from God for communities of marginality in our own time that face the great odds of horses and chariots. The affirmation of Third World communities of faith is that God's great promise of land and justice is indeed linked to concrete human acts against horses and chariots. As in ancient peasant Israel, none can persuade such communities of faith and hope that the God of justice and freedom withholds such a permit.

4. In our own cultural context, however, we must read the narrative as disclosure "from the other side" within communities of domination. We are more fully embedded in communities of horses and chariots, more fully committed to domination. The narrative and its trajectory, as I have traced it, suggest that such communities of domination have no warrant for arms and control and that this God in inscrutable ways is aligned against the horses and chariots, working through hardness of heart, until the whole enterprise collapses. The powerful lineage of pharaoh, Sisera, and Nebuchadnezzar never learns in time. But the text persists and is always offered again. It is a disclosure of hope to those embedded in reliance on horses and chariots, a warning that all such arms cannot secure against God's force for life. This partisan, contextualized disclosure does not regard hamstringing and burning as unacceptable violence. Rather, the disclosure is aimed against domination by the Canaanites. It is maddening that at the crucial places, the text mumbles about how the power of Yahweh could work against such hardware and such technique. But the text, where it mumbles, mumbles because the power of the Spirit cannot be articulated in the rationality of the kings. Indeed, perhaps what is finally disclosed is that the

power of God, the rush of the Spirit toward liberation, will never be articulated in the rationality of domination.

From that awareness it is not a very large step to claim that

the foolishness of God is wiser than humanity, and the weakness of God is stronger than humanity. (1 Cor. 1:25)

That insight is already celebrated in Joshua 11, where these land-desperate people watched while the powerful city-kings were undone by the command, permit, and warrant of Yahweh. The rhetoric of such a narrative is not congenial to us in our royal rationality. It is precisely emancipation from that royal rationality, however, that lets another mode of speech render another mode of life, wrought by a very different kind of power.

Credits

Permission is gratefully acknowledged for republication of the following chapters of this book:

Chapter 1: *Journal of Biblical Literature* 98 (1979).

Chapter 2: *The Christian Century* 97 (1980). Copyright © 1980 Christian Century Foundation.

Chapter 3: *Covenanting for Peace and Justice.* Geneva: World Alliance of Reformed Churches, 1989.

Chapter 4: *Die Botschaft and die Boten: Festschrift für Hans Walter Wolff zum 70 Geburtstag.* Edited by Jörg Jeremias and Lothar Perlitt. Neukirchen-Vluyn: Neukirchener Verlag, 1981.

Chapter 5: *The Catholic Biblical Quarterly* 43 (1981).

Chapter 6: *Journal of Biblical Literature* 110 (1991).

Chapter 7: *Schöpfung und Befreiung: Für Claus Westermann zum 80 Geburtstag.* Edited by Rainer Albertz, Friedemann W. Golka, and Jürgen Kegler. Stuttgart: Calwer Verlag, 1989.

Chapter 8: *Journal of the American Academy of Religion* 45B (1977 Supplement).

Chapter 9: *Journal for the Study of the Old Testament* 33 (1985).

Chapter 10: *Preaching as a Social Act.* Edited by Art Van Seters. Nashville: Abingdon Press. Copyright © 1988 by Art Van Seters.

Chapter 11: *The Pastor as Prophet.* Edited by Earl E. Shelp and Ronald H. Sunderland. New York: The Pilgrim Press, 1985.

Chapter 12: *The Sage in Israel and the Ancient Near East.* Edited by John G. Gammie and Leo G. Perdue. Winona Lake, Ind.: Eisenbrauns, 1990.

Chapter 13: *Theology Today* 48 (1991): 128-38.

Chapter 14: *International Review of Missions* 64 (1975).

Chapter 15: *Revelation and Violence: A Study in Contextualization* (Pere Marquette Lecture, 1986). Milwaukee: Marquette University Press, 1986.

Index of Scripture References